Beyond Nature Writing

Under the Sign of Nature: Explorations in Ecocriticism

Editors
Michael P. Branch, SueEllen Campbell, John Tallmadge

Series Consultants
Lawrence Buell, John Elder, Scott Slovic

Series Advisory Board
Michael P. Cohen, Richard Kerridge, Gretchen Legler,
Ian Marshall, Dan Peck, Jennifer Price, Kent Ryden,
Rebecca Solnit, Anne Whiston Spirn, Hertha D. Sweet Wong

Beyond Nature Writing

Expanding the Boundaries of Ecocriticism

Edited by Karla Armbruster and Kathleen R. Wallace

University Press of Virginia   *Charlottesville and London*

The University Press of Virginia
© 2001 by the Rector and Visitors of the University of Virginia
Printed in the United States of America
First published 2001

⊗ The paper used in this publication meets the minimum requirements of
the American National Standard for Information Sciences—Permanence of
Paper for Printed Library Materials, ANSI Z39.48-1984.

Library of Congress Cataloging-in-Publication Data is available from
the Library of Congress.

ISBN 0-8139-2013-2 (cloth : alk. paper) — ISBN 0-8139-2014-0 (pbk. : alk. paper)

Contents

Foreword

Edges teem and shift. Ecologists have long been drawn to places where two ecosystems meet because of such zones' special richness, or "edge-effect." Typically, these contain larger numbers of species than are in either adjacent habitat, as well as greater biotic density. These edges, also called ecotones, are often notably dynamic environments—such as a forest's brushy edge advancing into an abandoned New England meadow or a rocky shoreline alternately submerged and exposed to the air. They are places to tell the story of succession and to read the tides. Nature writing, too, represents such a vital edge. On one side is the literary scholarship that has largely confined itself to the genres of poetry, fiction, drama, along with critical theories declaring texts to be no more than self-referential webs of words. On the other side stretches the domain of academic science, where extreme specialization so often muffles the ethical questions and flattens the language. By combining attentiveness to natural phenomena and processes with an eloquent voice and a narrative line, nature writing has not only helped to reinvigorate and reintegrate education but has also inspired environmental activism and confirmed the distinctiveness and value of local landscapes.

Because edges are always on the go, deeper acquaintance with them can teach our minds, too, to move. In Rachel Carson's beloved intertidal zone, for instance, some rocky niches are underwater for all but the lowest of low tides, while certain slippery shelves are exposed to the air for all but the highest highs. Watching them, day after day, one thus begins to register edges within the edge and to perceive a progression of distinct habitats that shine along the gradient. As such edges proliferate, much more encompassing affinities and connections also become discernible. A rocky pool testifies to the vastness of the tides that visit it, but that also sweep away to other shores, other depths. Just so, the kind of personal, reflective essay that we call nature writing points to the power of literature rooted in the earth, but it comes nowhere near to exhausting it. Rather, it invites our attention to literature's much more diverse, and never ending, conversation with the living earth.

Kathleen R. Wallace and Karla Armbruster dramatically expand the circle of our attentiveness in this collection of essays. They lend new resonance to the term "ecocriticism" through the range of authors and traditions explored here, as well as through the variety of methodologies represented. By multiplying the critical habitats, and the edges and connections prevailing between them, they suggest that literature and education may attain their own diverse, balanced, and dynamic ecology. Feminist and multicultural approaches have been especially influential in recent conversations about literature and the natural environment. These approaches are appropriately prominent in the present collection of essays, too, where they are juxtaposed with original and illuminating readings of the Bible, of canonical authors such as Milton and James, and of science fiction and popular films. Such diversity both suggests fresh connections and calls many assumptions into question. Focusing on the role of landscapes in the novels of Hardy and Woolf, for example, helps us rethink the separate, individual status of "character" in such works.

Calling for a new "Land Ethic" in his *Sand County Almanac*, Aldo Leopold described such a development as "an evolutionary possibility and an ecological necessity." Broadening our attention beyond the narrow, if fertile, edge of nature writing is certainly an ecological necessity now. We need to gain a more balanced perspective on both natural phenomena and their potential meanings for human beings—both as individuals and in community. And paying attention to the diverse niches, and the changing seasons, within the literature of earth may bring its own evolutionary possibility, as well. Beyond the basic understanding that literature and nature are richly interwoven, we may come to recognize more clearly that sensitivity to nature grows out of, as well as opposes certain aspects of, the Western tradition; that this sensitivity is renewed and expanded by vivid encounters with non-Western literatures; that for good and bad the beast is always in the drawing room as well as in the jungle; and that horror movies, too, may have something valuable to teach us about this always proliferating, recoalescing world.

John Elder

Acknowledgments

The life of the scholar is too often assumed to be a solitary life, just as the scholar's work is too often assumed to be carried out in isolation. How delightfully wrong these assumptions have been for us and for our collaboration in preparing this collection! Over the two and a half years it took to assemble the contributors and produce the manuscript of *Beyond Nature Writing,* we found to our surprise that our colleagues were as interested in the story of our collaboration as they were in the content of the work. "How do you make it work?" folks would ask. We would usually name some combination of the following—constant communication, similar tastes in writing styles, high expectations, and compatible (or negotiable!) work habits—but the one thing we always mentioned was our friendship. Friends since we first met as graduate students at the Western Literature Association conference in Wichita, Kansas, in 1993, we have supported each other as we finished dissertations, applied for, started, and left jobs, and planned nearly simultaneous weddings in 1998.

Our collaboration aside, *Beyond Nature Writing* would not be the vibrant collection it is without our contributors, who—without exception—have been good-humored, amenable to our suggestions, and willing to make every effort to meet our deadlines. To all of you, we convey our heartfelt thanks. We are grateful for your involvement and friendship.

We would also like to thank our acquisitions editor at University Press of Virginia, Boyd Zenner, whose enthusiasm for this project has consistently matched our own. We are particularly grateful for her masterful job in editing our essay when we were desperate to trim it to the length we had required of everyone else. Holly Carver, of University of Iowa Press, and Patti Hartmann, of University of Arizona Press, also deserve our thanks for their helpful responses to our initial proposal and early manuscript.

We want to acknowledge the support of Karla's colleagues in the English Department at Webster University as well as Bill Eidson, dean of Arts and Sciences at Webster, for supplying funds for Karla's conference travel and for the preparation of the index. In addition, special thanks go to Ellen Satrom, our managing editor, Karen Miller, who provided invaluable assistance with preparing the manuscript, and Kim Kleinman, our indexer. We also want to recognize the members of the Ecocriticism Reading Group at The Ohio State University, who served as a sounding board for many of the ideas that made their way into this book and our other research; in addition, we thank the Department of English at Ohio State for its support of Kathy's research and travel.

On the home front, we salute our canine companions—past and present—who helped inspire our love of the nonhuman and gave us unconditional affection and excuses to go outdoors and neglect other responsibilities: Annie, Cory, Lassie, Caval, Leo, and Zipper. And most important, we want to thank our spouses, Pete Coogan and Tom Dilling, for their boundless support of this project and of us. Their generous spirits, unflagging senses of humor, and peerless editing skills made this book possible in more ways than we can ever express.

Introduction: Why Go Beyond Nature Writing, and Where To?

Kathleen R. Wallace and Karla Armbruster

In the introduction to *The Ecocriticism Reader: Landmarks in Literary Ecology,* Cheryll Glotfelty points to 1993 as the year ecocriticism, which she defines as "the study of the relationship between literature and the physical environment" (xviii), emerged as a recognizable critical school. Eight years later, it is safe to say that ecocriticism is still emerging and will continue to grow and diversify for the foreseeable future. To date, the field has inspired the publication of a successful introductory anthology *(The Ecocriticism Reader);* the establishment of a journal *(Interdisciplinary Studies in Literature and Environment);* the convocation of three meetings of the Association for the Study of Literature and Environment (ASLE); the founding of the Center for Environmental Arts and Humanities at the University of Nevada, Reno; and a National Endowment for the Humanities Summer Institute in 1997. Most recently, ASLE has gained the status of an affiliated organization with the Modern Language Association (MLA), and ecocriticism as a field has given rise not only to a proliferation of environmentally oriented composition and literature courses at colleges and universities but also to a number of anthologies of nature and environmental writing and several excellent critical collections building on the foundations laid by *The Ecocriticism Reader.*[1] These clear indications of the field's vitality and relevance have resulted in attention from general interest publications such as the *New York Times Magazine* and academic journals such as *Lingua Franca, PMLA,* and *New Literary History.*[2] Given the rapid growth and many accomplishments of ecocriticism during its short history, we feel that the time has come for ecocritics to review the field critically and ask what directions it might best take in the future.

Currently, the field—especially when one looks at published works—is domi-

1

nated by critical analyses of nature writing and literature of wilderness.[3] In a presentation at the 1995 ASLE conference, John Elder summed up traditionally defined nature writing as "a form of the personal, reflective essay grounded in attentiveness to the natural world and an appreciation of science but also open to the spiritual meaning and intrinsic value of nature." While a concentration on this form of writing makes perfect sense as a starting point for a critical school that takes the natural environment and human relations to that environment as its special focus, we believe that one of ecocriticism's most important tasks at this time is expanding its boundaries beyond these topics to address a wider spectrum of texts. This sentiment has been expressed within forums such as the three past ASLE conferences, which included sessions on a variety of boundary-stretching topics including ecocritical approaches to multicultural literature; African American fiction; green cultural studies; urban environments and urban nature; environmental justice; the natural world in early America; postmodernism and the environment; and nature and religion. Further pushing and deconstructing ecocriticism's boundaries were individual presentations on a variety of writers not traditionally associated with nature writing, such as Edmund Spenser, Nathaniel Hawthorne, Edith Wharton, Frank Norris, Wilfred Owen, Zora Neale Hurston, Sylvia Plath, Minnie Bruce Pratt, Jane Smiley, Toni Morrison, and Don DeLillo.

These conferences also provided forums for ecocritics to issue direct challenges to the field, including the question of why so few African American voices are recognized as part of nature writing and ecocriticism. This question, raised directly in a presentation at the 1997 ASLE conference, echoed Paul Tidwell's presentation at the 1994 MLA session on nature and environmental writing, "The Blackness of the Whale: Nature in Recent African-American Writing," in which he argued that ecocriticism must strive to become more welcoming and attentive to concerns of African American writers and readers. In his 1995 ASLE conference presentation, John Elder discussed a similar need to go, as he put it, "beyond nature writing." After carefully pointing out the positive ways in which ecocriticism has renewed interest in traditionally defined nature writing, Elder then suggested that it was time to start redefining and broadening our concept of nature writing: "Just as the largely white wilderness movement is called upon today to address the condition of our cities, and to enter into closer collaboration with Americans of color, so too the nature writing so closely associated with it must be defined more inclusively." Individual ecocritics are working to address these very issues in articles and books for publication even now.[4] The third ASLE conference (held in 1999) marked two important shifts in the ways ecocritical theory and practice have responded to these concerns. Its theme—What to Make of a Diminished Thing—directly took on the issue of how to approach and represent nature when it is altered and even degraded by human use, and ASLE members' concern with representing diverse cultural viewpoints on nature and the environment resulted in the formation of a diversity caucus.

Breaking New Trails

Such sentiments and efforts, however, are all but invisible to scholars who have not taken part in these discussions. If ecocriticism is to have a significant impact as a literary methodology beyond the study of nature writing, we believe ecocritics must demonstrate the relevance of our approach to these other scholars. In our experience, the most common question such scholars have about ecocriticism is whether it can usefully be applied to texts outside of nature writing—to the novels of, say, Henry James or other authors who seem less concerned with nature than with culture. This attitude is reflected in Sven Birkerts's review of *The Ecocriticism Reader,* in which he worries "Ecocritics might, one suspects, ignore any uses of language that are not a conduit to the nature they claim such devotion to." He ultimately concludes that "Nature and its preservation is what occupies most of the ecocritics. And this imposes a kind of programmatic simplicity upon the whole movement, gives it a 'crunchiness' that may prove to be a liability. . . . How much more interesting and controversial would be an ecocriticism pledging itself to the more inclusive idea of 'environment'" (6).

The concerns of Birkerts and others like him are serious ones, and if ecocriticism's level of acceptance within the academy is to continue to grow, we believe ecocritics must make a unified and rigorous effort to demonstrate the field's true range and its power to illuminate an almost endless variety of texts. *Beyond Nature Writing* is our attempt to help ensure that ecocriticism does not get sidelined as yet another interesting but ultimately insubstantial subfield within English departments. The contributors to *Beyond Nature Writing* share our belief that ecocriticism offers a critical perspective that can enliven any literary and theoretical field or even an author as ostensibly inimical as the heady Henry James. A "more inclusive idea of 'environment,'" as Birkerts puts it, is at the foundation of this effort. Environment need not only refer to "natural" or "wilderness" areas; as the essays in this collection indicate, environment also includes cultivated and built landscapes, the natural elements and aspects of those landscapes, and cultural interactions with those natural elements. One way ecocriticism can and should widen its range of topics is to pay more consistent attention to texts that revolve around these less obviously "natural" landscapes and human attempts to record, order, and ultimately understand their own relationships to those environments.[5]

In addition to proving ecocriticism's usefulness to scholars outside the field, we believe such an expanded sense of environment and of the potential topics for ecocritical analysis will help ecocriticism grapple with one of its central conceptual challenges—understanding nature and culture as interwoven rather than as separate sides of a dualistic construct. Ecocriticism has built on work in other areas, including ecofeminism, deep ecology, and certain branches of poststructuralism, in developing a critique of the nature-culture dualism.[6] Part of this critique has been to both implicitly and explicitly challenge the prevailing sense that culture is the main purview of literary studies while nature is, if present at all, merely a backdrop for human drama. Founding works of ecocriticism by Scott Slovic and John P. O'Grady, for example, demonstrate that nature—and writing that expressly takes nature as its topic—is as fit a subject for literature and criticism as any other. Yet we believe that a continued focus on nature and wilderness writing within ecocriticism might reinforce this same nature-culture dualism while, this time, privileging nature over culture. A viable ecocriticism must continue to challenge dualistic thinking by exploring the role of nature in texts more concerned with human cultures, by looking at the role of culture in nature, and by attending to the nature-focused text as also a cultural-literary text. Understanding how nature and culture constantly influence and construct each other is essential to an informed ecocriticism, as William Cronon's collection of essays *Uncommon Ground: Toward Reinventing Nature* illustrates for the fields of environmental and cultural history.[7] As a means toward this end, ecocritics should continue to strive for interdisciplinarity and, in particular, continue to turn to existing scholarship in areas such as environmental history, cultural and political geography, American studies, regional and urban studies, and landscape architecture for their insights into the relationship between natural and cultural environments.[8]

We developed *Beyond Nature Writing: Expanding the Boundaries of Ecocriticism* to take on the challenge of applying ecocritical theories and methods to texts that might seem unlikely subjects because they do not foreground the natural world or wilderness. *Beyond Nature Writing* demonstrates ecocritical approaches to literary and cultural texts from a broadly representative range of fields: biblical studies, medieval and Renaissance studies, literature and thought of the Enlightenment era, colonial American studies, nineteenth-century British and American literature, twentieth-century British and American literature, and contemporary texts that push the boundaries of literary study, such as film, science fiction, virtual reality, and theatrical space. While engaging with such a variety of fields, *Beyond Nature Writing* covers not only many well-known literary texts but also texts set in environments where the influence of nature is less than obvious, texts from the point of view of diverse populations with alternative perspectives on nature and human relationships to it, and postmodern texts that might also seem "post-nature."

A Tale of Two Questions

Innumerable conversations, experiences, and interests have contributed to our sense that it is time for ecocriticism to demonstrate its versatility and broad range, but one experience in particular inspired us to think about the issues and interrelated challenges involved in such an effort. During the 1995 Modern Language Association convention in Chicago, we both interviewed for the same assistant professor position in an English Department at a major western state university. We remember those interviews because they helped us clarify the major questions that structure this volume while reaffirming our sense of the need for a book like *Beyond Nature Writing,* which we had been discussing since the inaugural ASLE conference in June 1995.

The job for which we interviewed called for a specialist in western American literature. Although the advertisement did not refer to ecocriticism as a preferred interest, western literature is an area that has historically overlapped with ecocriticism and the study of environmentally oriented literature; reinforcing this connection was the fact that ASLE was formed at a meeting of the Western Literature Association. We also knew that this particular English department was home to several scholars whose work we thought of as ecocritical as well as to a number of creative writers known for their interest in nature and place.

While debriefing after our interviews, we discovered we each had been asked a question that struck at the core of our work, both then and now. Kathy's question grew out of her research emphasis on expanding the nature writing canon and the field of ecocriticism to consider literary works, physical environments, and populations not typically associated with the genre or the field, such as urban-focused literature by African American writers. Taking a devil's advocate position, one of the interviewers had asked Kathy, "Ecocriticism is a new field, just getting established. Why stir things up?" Karla's interview-defining question had followed a discussion of the teaching responsibilities associated with the position. After revealing that one of these responsibilities would be teaching nineteenth-century and early-twentieth-century American literature, the other interviewer had asked how Karla might apply an ecocritical approach to a writer such as Henry James.

These questions struck us because they both speak to the concerns and politics inherent in expanding ecocriticism's boundaries. Our short answer as to why ecocriticism should expand those boundaries is inherently pragmatic: although the difficulties integral to establishing a field justify initially limiting its scope, the shape the field takes in the future will be influenced by the nature and elasticity of the borders established in its early years. In 1995, Kathy answered the question by pointing to the built and natural Chicago landscapes outside the hotel windows, arguing that if ecocriticism is to have any real force as a theoretical and pedagogical approach, ecocritics need to attend to the landscapes in which most people live—cities, suburbs, and rural areas. By reading texts set in environments profoundly and clearly altered by humans and calling attention to the interactions of culture and nature represented in those texts, we might help students understand how their home places resonate with issues similar to those found in texts describing more exotic or wild landscapes. As Gary Snyder points out so beautifully in *The Practice of the Wild,* nature—even in its wildest forms—is everywhere, and it is almost always intermingled with the forms of culture:

> [W]ildness is not limited to the 2 percent formal wilderness areas. Shifting scales, it is everywhere: ineradicable populations of fungi, moss, mold, yeasts, and such that surround and inhabit us. Deer mice on the back porch, deer bounding across the freeway, pigeons in the park, spiders in the corners. . . . Exquisite complex beings in their energy webs inhabiting the fertile corners of the urban world in accord with the rules of wild systems, the visible hardy stalks and stems of vacant lots and railroads, the persistent raccoon squads, bacterias in the loam and in our yogurt. (14–15)

In addition to these pedagogical concerns, we believe if ecocriticism limits itself to the study of one genre—the personal narratives of the Anglo-American nature writing tradition—or to one physical landscape—the ostensibly untrammeled American wilderness—it risks seriously misrepresenting the significance of multiple natural and built environments to writers with other ethnic, national, or racial affiliations. If such limits are accepted, ecocritics risk ghettoizing ecocriticism within literary and cultural studies generally.

The second question brings up a different although related issue: how productive can an ecocritical approach be when used with texts as far "beyond nature writing" as the works of Henry James would seem? While it is true that James's fiction devotes little space to descriptions of the physical aspects of place, concentrating instead on human interiority and culture, we believe that issues of human relationships to nature and environment are still quite relevant to James's fiction. As William Howarth writes in "Some Principles of Ecocriticism," "although we cast nature and culture as opposites, in fact they constantly mingle, like water and soil in a flowing stream" (69); teasing out the meaning of James's focus on culture and the human psyche in seeming isolation from nature is the kind of task that best demonstrates ecocriticism's range and power. If we were to pursue this task, we might start with the ecocritical premise that the natural environment is always a shaping force of individual and group psychology and identity—and that this force can only be ignored or suppressed at a price. We find it striking how often James's characters are represented as fundamentally cut off from relationships with the physical and cultural places they might call home. Think, for instance, of some of his more well-known works, such as "Daisy Miller" and *The Portrait of a Lady*, that focus on young, female American expatriates who find themselves in environments where they are distinctly out of place. In our ecocritical analysis, we would trace the connections between this lack of grounding in physical and cultural place and the misunderstanding, objectification, and alienation these young women experience.[9]

Another potential ecocritical approach to James is already beginning to take shape as ecocritical scholars look more extensively at his life, travels, and non-fiction writing, including his travel writing.[10] This scholarship might lead to a better sense of what, if any, views on the natural environment James possessed and how his views related to the dominant attitudes of his time and culture. Additional scholarly work might consider why Henry James has been so valorized by the literary establishment, while most nature and environmentally focused writing has been more or less marginalized. Are the standards for "great literature" biased toward representations of the disembodied mind and of various cultural and aesthetic issues and away from representations that clearly speak to human relationships with nature? If so, how is our profession contributing to our culture's perceptions of the relative importance of nature and environment to our lives?

Expanding the Boundaries: Essays in this Collection

We have spent the better part of our graduate and professional lives thinking about and answering the two important questions we encountered in that interview, and now we and our contributors take up this challenge explicitly in *Beyond Nature Writing*. The essays included in this book chart some of the exciting directions that ecocriticism is currently taking and could take in the future. By demonstrating how elastic and permeable the boundaries of this field can be, as a group these essays make a powerful argument for the depth, breadth, and rigor of an ecocritical approach for literary and cultural studies in general.

The contributors to the first section of *Beyond Nature Writing*, "Reevaluating the Roots of Western Attitudes toward Nature," all address dominant religious, philosophical, and literary traditions within Western culture through the Enlightenment. Perhaps because environmentalism as we know it today is so much a product of twentieth-century experiences, discoveries, and thinking and because nature appreciation in literature is often traced to the British romantics and Thoreau, most environmental history, philosophy, and criticism tends to characterize Western thought through the Enlightenment as profoundly antienvironmental and deeply invested in the notion of human beings as separate from and superior to nonhuman nature. Lynn White Jr.'s classic essay "The Historical Roots of Our Ecologic Crisis" is a prime example; White traces antienvironmental attitudes to the biblical account of creation and medieval Christian thought and flatly asserts that "We shall continue to have a worsening ecologic crisis until we reject the Christians' axiom that nature has no reason for existence save to serve man" (1207). As Kate Soper and Carolyn Merchant point out, medieval and Renaissance thought was dominated by the concept of the Great Chain of Being, which placed humans midway between nature and the divine in a hierarchical order. While this concept did position humans as part of a greater whole that included the natural world, its hierarchical nature often justified and encouraged human domination of nature.

For many philosophical and literary chroniclers of Western attitudes toward nature, though, the shift in thinking most destructive toward nature began in the Renaissance and then flowered during the seventeenth and eighteenth centuries, the periods associated with the Scientific Revolution, the Enlightenment, and the rise of a money-based economic system.[11] The rationalism of René Descartes and the empiricism of Francis Bacon are most often singled out as representing this shift; by denying mind or spirit to any beings other than humans, Descartes gave philosophical support to Bacon's project of gaining mastery over nature through scientific experimentation. In addition, other scholars point out that the European colonization of the New World occurring at this time was characterized not only by greed and racism but also by shameless plundering of natural resources.[12]

Despite the bleak record that we often find when looking back at the history of Western attitudes toward nature, these attitudes were far from monolithic. This is the crucial premise of the essays in this first section of *Beyond Nature Writing*, which all persuasively point us toward alternative threads in the history of literary and philosophical attitudes toward nature in the West. As many religious groups and organizations are beginning to assert, some of the most important of these threads can be found in the Bible—a text all too frequently used to justify antiecological attitudes and practices. In the essay that opens this section, "Beyond 'Thou Shalt Not': An Ecocritic Reads Deuteronomy," Betsy S. Hilbert provides a compelling rereading of Deuteronomy, which she identifies as the most challenging of the five books of the Pentateuch for an ecocritical interpretation. By skillfully contextualizing its seeming intolerance and preoccupation with war, Hilbert shows that its central message is one of social and environmental responsibility: a vision of human beings as intricately connected not just to each other but to the earth, and of the just and ethical relationships humans must establish and maintain "as a condition of their continued survival in the places that gave them nurture." In doing so, Hilbert demonstrates that the complexity of ecocritically "difficult" texts such as Deuteronomy may yield some of the most interesting and important illuminations of human history with landscape and place.

Medieval and Renaissance thought also encompassed traditions that lent the natural world great importance and even agency, as Lisa J. Kiser and Diane Kelsey McColley argue in their essays in this section.[13] In "Chaucer and the Politics of Nature," Kiser analyzes Chaucer's complex representation of Lady Nature in the *Parliament of Fowls,* arguing that this poem reveals an explicit awareness of the social construction of the natural world and of the ways that this construction serves gender and class interests. However, she emphasizes that Chaucer does not deny the existence of a natural world outside of cultural constructions; in fact, she finds that Chaucer's self-conscious use of animals to make points about human conduct reminds his readers of "the natural world outside the parameters of his artistic colonization." By establishing Chaucer's engagement with the relationship between nature and culture, an issue of great concern within current environmental thought, Kiser astutely demonstrates that medieval thinking about the environment was more varied and sophisticated that many critics suppose.

In "Milton's Environmental Epic: Creature Kinship and the Language of *Paradise Lost,*" McColley also broadens the discussion of pre-nineteenth-century conceptions of nature by showing that Milton's "pervasive ecological consciousness" encompassed a number of important issues still with us in today's environmental discourse. Through a careful examination of Milton's use of language in

Paradise Lost, she illuminates the "heterodox anti-dualistic theology of nature" at the heart of this epic so crucial to the Western cultural legacy. Ultimately, by establishing that Milton took the "human dominion over all the earth" as mandated by Genesis to mean beneficent care, McColley places Milton in a minority tradition going against the intellectual tide in a time when a managerial and exploitative attitude toward nature was gaining ascendancy over a theology of stewardship.

Despite its association with the views of Descartes and Bacon, even the Enlightenment period gave rise to thinkers and writers with a variety of attitudes toward the natural world and the ways humans should relate to that world. As William C. Horne illustrates in his essay "Samuel Johnson Discovers the Arctic: A Reading of a 'Greenland Tale' as Arctic Literature," Johnson was one major Enlightenment figure who possessed a deep interest in both the natural environment and human inhabitants of the Arctic. By positioning Johnson's 1751 "Greenland Tale" in terms of a larger tradition of arctic literature, Horne argues that this narrative of people indigenous to the Arctic not only participated in ideological debates of its time about the "noble savage" but also offered implicit critiques of materialism and imperialism. In doing so, Horne demonstrates that Johnson's tale anticipates modern discussions about whether it is realistic or romantic to view indigenous cultures as possessing harmonious relationships with nature.

Finally, in "Before Nature Writing: Discourses of Colonial American Natural History," Michael P. Branch challenges the common ecocritical tendency to assume that the literary discovery of American nature occurred in 1854, with the publication of Henry David Thoreau's *Walden.* As Branch points out, Thoreau recognized his predecessors in the natural historians and other writers of the seventeenth and eighteenth centuries who documented the aesthetic, ecological, and spiritual value of the New World landscape. In addition to providing an astute analysis of why ecocritics have hesitated to explore the works of such writers, Branch takes an important step toward tracing this all-but-invisible tradition by discussing the work of William Wood and Cotton Mather and their impact on the ways that later literary writers would express their encounters with the American land.

The essays in the second section of *Beyond Nature Writing,* "Uncovering New

Ecocritical Perspectives on Nineteenth- and Twentieth- Century Authors," explore the intersections of nature and culture in the works of eight well-known nineteenth- and twentieth-century American and British authors—Harriet Beecher Stowe, Thomas Hardy, Virginia Woolf, Mary Wilkins Freeman, Frederick Douglass, Michael S. Harper, and Toni Morrison—to ask what new light we can shed on their work by attending to their representations of human relationships with nature. These essays also ask what these authors, who are not nature writers in the traditional sense, can contribute to ecocriticism's ongoing attempt to theorize literary representations of the human-nature relationship.

As we have emphasized elsewhere in this introduction, ecocritical attention thus far has primarily focused on nineteenth- and twentieth-century British and American texts, predominantly nonfiction nature writing by authors such as Henry David Thoreau, John Muir, Mary Austin, Aldo Leopold, Rachel Carson, Edward Abbey, Annie Dillard, Barry Lopez, and Terry Tempest Williams, and also nature-conscious fiction and poetry by authors and poets such as James Fenimore Cooper, Willa Cather, Robinson Jeffers, Wallace Stegner, and Mary Oliver. While some of ecocriticism's most important accomplishments thus far include bringing rich, complex critical perspectives and increased attention to bear on the works of such writers, we believe every literary and cultural text holds implications for human relationships with nonhuman nature. Certainly, nature and the nonhuman environment have been a prominent part of works by many nineteenth- and twentieth-century British and American writers who are widely taught in American high schools and universities, such as Herman Melville, Walt Whitman, Emily Dickinson, Charlotte Perkins Gilman, William Faulkner, Wallace Stevens, Gerard Manley Hopkins, D. H. Lawrence, and Ted Hughes. However, with the possible exception of the British romantics and the American transcendentalists, critical treatments of the role of nature in these writers' works have largely settled for examining its function as setting or its symbolic significance. But as Cheryll Glotfelty suggests in the introduction to *The Ecocriticism Reader* when she asks, "How has literary discourse defined the human?" (xxiv), an ecocriticism that sees humans as fundamentally part of nature will attend to representations of human cultures in all their diverse interactions with nature rather than focusing only on texts that show humans observing or experiencing nature in wild or rural settings.

This section opens with three essays that examine such intersections and interactions of nature and culture as manifested in the works of writers seldom associated with an interest in the natural world. In "Cultivating Desire, Tending Piety: Botanical Discourse in Harriet Beecher Stowe's *The Minister's Wooing*," Mark T. Hoyer provides a fascinating account of how Stowe drew on her extensive knowledge of natural history and gardening in order to use the sexualized language of mid-nineteenth-century botany to make a culturally radical point about the role of sexual passion in selecting one's mate. Hoyer highlights the social norms and conventions embedded in gardening and other horticultural activities of Stowe's era by contextualizing Stowe's employment of botanical discourse within the debates of her time about the tradition of sexualizing plants, a tradition that extends back to Linnaeus. In establishing the important role that such discourse plays in this novel, he broadens our estimation of Stowe from a figure who played a major role in the cultural debates of her time over slavery and women's rights to one who also wrote tellingly about the cultural currency of human interactions with nature.

Richard Kerridge also advocates for examining nature and culture, place and person, in relationship to each other in his essay "Ecological Hardy." Kerridge establishes that Hardy used his personal knowledge of the rural English landscape in a highly political way, employing narrative strategies that construct readers as "situated observers" complicit in—and potentially responsible for—the lives of his characters. Ultimately, Kerridge persuasively argues that Hardy conceptualized place as a set of relations, both among characters and their natural environments and between readers and characters. In doing so, Kerridge makes an eloquent case against the assumption that withdrawal from society is an essential characteristic of nature writing.

In "The Book 'Laid Upon the Landscape': Virginia Woolf and Nature," Charlotte Zoë Walker explores what she calls "the intertextuality of nature and literature" in Woolf's fiction and in her reviews of prominent naturalists (including the eighteenth-century English naturalist Gilbert White of Selborne) and cultural events, such as the British Empire Exhibition of 1924. In particular, Walker elaborates on the parallels Woolf often drew between the positions of women and nature within patriarchal society. She also traces Woolf's use of the concept of the book "laid upon the landscape," a type of metawriting that investigates the connections among language, silence, and human experience of the natural world. Ultimately, Walker's illuminating analysis of Woolf's deep engagement with the natural world broadens our sense of Woolf's feminism and political engagement.

The next grouping of essays in the second section offers new, ecocritically informed readings of writers whose reception has to date been filtered through critical perspectives focusing on region, gender, or race. Terrell F. Dixon's essay "Nature, Gender, and Community: Mary Wilkins Freeman's Ecofiction" significantly repositions Freeman's critical reception by examining how her deep interest in the natural world of New England goes beyond the label "regional writer" and its pejorative gender associations that so much previous scholarship has emphasized. Specifically, Dixon makes the case that many of Freeman's short stories can be read as works of ecofiction that present a vision of "green women and green men" who love and defend nature while engaged in ordinary life. Overall, Dixon's essay illustrates that Freeman's sense of community was not limited to human beings, extending to embrace the natural environment as well.

Elizabeth Dodd provides a different perspective on this idea of an expanded environmental community in her analysis of what she calls "the absence of black writers from existing ecocritical discussion" in her essay "The Great Rainbowed Swamp: History as Moral Ecology in the Poetry of Michael S. Harper." For Harper, Dodd argues, human actions become embodied in the landscape, and so his poetry articulates a kind of ethical ecology that infuses the material world with the ethical consequences of historical events. In particular, she points out, Harper links the historical commodification of human beings with the cultural commodification of nature in a way that echoes Aldo Leopold's "The Land Ethic." By emphasizing how Harper's poetry weaves together both natural and cultural history, Dodd shows how African American literature might be productively approached using an ecocritical methodology.

Such interconnections between history and place are also central to Michael Bennett's essay "Anti-Pastoralism, Frederick Douglass, and the Nature of Slavery," in which he asks the fundamental question, "What use is ecocriticism if the culture under consideration has a different relationship with pastoral space and wilderness than the ideal kinship that most nature writers and ecocritics assume or seek?" In order to answer this question, Bennett reads *The Narrative of the Life of Frederick Douglass* as an inversion of the pastoral mode in which Douglass leaves behind the landscape of rural plantations and wilderness—which he experiences as places of enslavement and danger—for the city, which promises more freedom and the possibility of escape. In the end, Bennett establishes Douglass's *Narrative* as central to the development of an anti-pastoral tradition in African American literature and culture.

Like Dodd's and Bennett's contributions, our essay "The Novels of Toni Morrison: 'Wild Wilderness Where There Was None'" contributes to the growing critical assessment of an African American tradition of engagement with the natural world. In a discussion of all of Morrison's novels, but especially *Song of Solomon, Tar Baby, Beloved,* and *Paradise,* we explore Morrison's extensive representations of the varied relationships that human individuals and communities—and especially African Americans—develop with plants, animals, and landscapes. We argue that Morrison's work illuminates how cultural and racial history inevitably inflects human understanding of the natural world; thus, she provides a significant challenge to mainstream environmental discourse and the practice of ecocriticism. Our analysis of Morrison's complex approach to the concept of wildness is but one example of how she productively complicates concepts fundamental to dominant environmental discourse. Through this exploration, we demonstrate that her novels can diversify contemporary environmentalist attitudes toward nature as well as the ways critics typically read African American literature.

In the third section of *Beyond Nature Writing,* "Expanding Ecocriticsm across Genres and Disciplines," we include a group of essays that move beyond two kinds of boundaries within current ecocritical practice: the generic boundaries established by a focus on nonfiction nature writing and the disciplinary boundaries left unchallenged when ecocritics unnecessarily limit their senses of what other fields might enrich their analyses of literary and cultural texts.[14] By examining genres that may reach a wider audience than traditional nature writing, the first three essays in this section do the important work of asking what kinds of textual messages are reaching the majority of people in our culture and what new issues these texts can raise for the practice of ecocriticism. By self-consciously reaching out to other genres and disciplines, the authors of the last five essays also expand the range and power of ecocriticism.

The opening grouping of essays within the third section begins with Cheryll Glotfelty's "Literary Place Bashing, Test Site Nevada," in which she raises important questions about the real-life consequences of literary representations of place by examining a genre she calls the "place basher." Using her own state of Nevada as a case study, Glotfelty points out that much of Nevada's finest writing pillories the state, reviews the tradition of the Nevada "place basher," and reflects on the extent to which such devaluing representations may have paved the way for cultural and political realities such as the nuclear testing at the Nevada Test Site. In an interesting twist, Glotfelty also identifies the emergence of a more positive Nevada nature writing tradition and speculates about the environmental consequences it may engender.

In "Heading Off the Trail: Language, Literature, and Nature's Resistance to Narrative," Rebecca Raglon and Marian Scholtmeijer challenge contemporary notions that language inevitably constructs oppressive attitudes, including those toward nature. They argue that the "best" literature can help undermine such attitudes by evoking a powerful, mysterious natural world, one that resists literary representation. Raglon and Scholtmeijer draw from works by Nadine Gordimer, Russell Hoban, and Franz Kafka to make the case that fiction, rather than nonfiction (the traditional ecocritical focus), is the genre that most effectively conveys nature's resistance to narrative. In doing so, they demonstrate that literature can undermine the human conceit that nature can be controlled, even in our writing.

In "The Non-Alibi of Alien Scapes: SF and Ecocriticism," Patrick D. Murphy calls attention to the growing tendency of science fiction, or SF, to take the form of "nature-oriented literature." Murphy's analysis of a range of science fiction highlights how some writers provide loopholes, or what Murphy calls "alibis," to sidestep or justify ethical dilemmas, while other writers, such as Kim Stanley Robinson, foreground these questions and push readers to confront major socioenvironmental concerns. Murphy's cogent analysis demonstrates the relevance of science fiction to contemporary environmental concerns because, as a popular genre, science fiction can both reveal and influence environmental thought in our culture at large.

In an essay that likewise bridges the boundary between ecocriticism and popular culture, Stacy Alaimo argues that ecocriticism's tendency to promote literature that conveys an explicitly environmental message has led it to neglect texts, such as popular films, that portray nature negatively. In "Discomforting Creatures: Monstrous Natures in Recent Films," Alaimo makes the insightful point that contemporary monster films such as *The Beast, Congo,* and *The Island of Dr. Moreau* enact some of the most vaunted ideals of environmental philosophy and ecocriticism: the collapse of boundaries between humans and nature and the agency of the nonhuman. However, she establishes that these films represent such developments as horrifying and transgressive rather than positive. Alaimo speculates as to what this might mean for public discourse about the environment, ultimately directing our attention to films such as *Habitat* and *Safe* that productively complicate the idea of monstrous nature.

Public culture is likewise a focus for Kent C. Ryden's reexamination of several of Frost's best-known New England poems in "Robert Frost, the New England Environment, and the Discourse of Objects." Using the lens of material culture studies, Ryden chronicles Frost's regular inclusion of traditional, handmade artifacts such as tools and stone walls in his poems to represent local communities' economic, imaginative, and experiential relationships to the landscapes they inhabit. Ryden makes an eloquent argument for incorporating material culture studies into ecocritical analysis, demonstrating that we need not automatically react to a Frostian stone wall as yet another example of human incursion into nature. Ryden helps us see that such a "vernacular artifact . . . does not erase nature"; rather, it "helps us understand nature" as perceived by people who create and use such objects.

In "The Poetry of Experience," John Elder also attends to how the material reality of the New England landscape infuses Frost's poetry, making a significant argument for "the role of natural experience in the study of literature." This argument grows out of Elder's evocative description of a day spent with his students learning how to scythe. Elder explains that because Frost's poetry displays such an intimate, detailed knowledge of the natural and working environment of New England, the experience of this kind of work opened up Elder's interpretation of Frost's poem "Mowing." In his call for scholars, teachers, and students of nature-oriented literature to participate in an embodied, experiential pedagogy that sends us outside to encounter the activities, plants, and wildlife we are reading about, Elder offers us a way to significantly expand our understanding of and appreciation for the literature of nature.

In "Performing the Wild: Rethinking Wilderness and Theater Spaces," Adam Sweeting and Thomas C. Crochunis put the disciplines of ecocriticism and theater studies into productive conversation by comparing the space we call wilderness with the space of realist theater. They convincingly demonstrate that both types of space are produced through social relations and depend on strict dichotomies between wilderness and society and between stage and audience. By learning to see past the ways these spaces work to naturalize such dichotomies, Sweeting and Crochunis assert, we can come to understand our own roles, or "performances," in constructing them. In particular, they argue that we need to choose "alternative performances," or different ways of seeing and relating to natural spaces, which acknowledge that we are never really apart from wildness. Through this innovative interdisciplinary discussion, Sweeting and Crochunis bring a new perspective to current debates about the idea of wilderness.[15]

Finally, in "Beyond Nature/Writing: Virtual Landscapes Online, in Print, and in 'Real Life,'" H. Lewis Ulman offers an important contribution to contemporary discussions of what the ascendancy of computer simulated virtual reality might mean for human relationships to nature. Taking the provocative position that virtual reality is nothing new, Ulman persuasively argues that computer simulations, textual representations, and even managed landscapes are all examples of virtual worlds. Through discussions of the computer game *Riven*, contemporary American nature writing, and his own experiences in "real" nature, Ulman considers how our experiences of material landscapes inform our experience of virtual landscapes, and vice versa. Finally, Ulman directs our attention to the crucial issue of the degree to which the "virtual" and the "real" can provide the "imaginative and conceptual resources we need to construct ethical and healthy relationships" among virtual and material worlds.

In bringing these essays together in this volume, we hope to begin to fill the need expressed by a growing number of ecocritics and other interested scholars and teachers for a collection of essays that demonstrates ecocriticism's range of potential topics. We believe that *Beyond Nature Writing* can enrich classes on ecocriticism, introduction to graduate studies courses, and introduction to theory and criticism courses that cover a variety of critical approaches. But *Beyond Na-*

ture Writing is more than a classroom text; we selected the essays included here because of their appeal and accessibility to literary and cultural scholars who have an interest in ecocriticism but are looking for examples of how this approach might intersect with their primary fields of study. Finally, we and the other contributors have put a priority on making *Beyond Nature Writing* accessible to an educated, nonacademic audience interested in the cultural aspects of environmental issues. By constructing this volume with such an audience in mind, we hope to help nurture an ever-growing, interconnected community of people committed to fostering a profound sense of engagement with and responsibility toward our surroundings, along with all its human and nonhuman inhabitants.

Notes

1. See the syllabus archive on the ASLE Internet site for a sampling of courses. For recent anthologies of nature writing and environmental literature, see Elder *(American);* and Torrance. For recent edited collections of ecocriticism, see Branch, Johnson, Patterson and Slovic; Kerridge and Sammels; and Murphy *(Literature).*

2. See McGurl; McNamee; Parini; and Winkler.

3. See, for example, critical works by Bate; Brooks; Buell; Elder *(Imagining);* Kroeber; McClintock; O'Grady; and Slovic. By citing these founding works of ecocriticism, we do not mean to suggest that they take a simplistic or limited approach to their topics; we merely intend to point out that the authors they discuss—such as the British romantics, Henry David Thoreau, John Muir, Aldo Leopold, Rachel Carson, Edward Abbey, and Annie Dillard—fit into traditional categories of nature and wilderness writing. One book that seems to be an exception to this trend is Louise H. Westling's *Green Breast of the New World,* in which she discusses Thoreau and Emerson but moves on to authors who are deeply concerned with the natural world but are not known as nature writers: Willa Cather, Ernest Hemingway, William Faulkner, and Eudora Welty.

4. Multiculturalism and nature writing have been the focus of at least one conference, Sharp Eyes II: Multicultural Perspectives on Environmental Writing (Oneonta, New York, 22–24 June 1996), organized by Charlotte Zoë Walker, a contributor to this collection. Several essays from that conference were collected in a special issue of *Phoebe: Journal of Feminist Scholarship, Theory, and Aesthetics.* See Cheng-Levine;

Hegarty; Platt; Murphy ("Commodification"); and Wallace. Other works that have been helpful in laying a foundation for ecocritical attention to African American literary treatments of nature include Norwood; and Dixon.

5. Attention to nature in the built environment is receiving increased attention, both in literary studies in general (see Scruggs; Bremer) and within ecocriticism in particular (see Bennett and Teague).

6. For important works in ecofeminism, see Diamond and Orenstein; Gaard; Mellor; Plant; Plumwood; Sturgeon; and Warren *(Hypatia, Ecological,* and *Ecofeminism)*. For a sense of the deep ecology approach to dualism, see Devall and Sessions; Fox; and Naess, as well as essays published in *Environmental Ethics.* For works using poststructuralist theory to approach questions of environment, see Soja; Dipose and Ferrell; Campbell; and Cheney ("Postmodern," "Ecofeminism").

7. Recently published works of ecocriticism that address these issues include Bennett and Teague; Hochman; and Stein.

8. The selected citations here are those we have found most helpful. In environmental history, in addition to Cronon, see Worster *(Nature's Economy, Wealth)*; and Limerick. In cultural and political geography, see Jackson; Gould and White; and Meinig. In American studies, see Franklin and Steiner. In urban studies, see Hayden *(Power)*. In landscape architecture, see Spirn.

9. An earlier version of this introduction included an extended if preliminary ecocritical analysis of *The Portrait of a Lady*. We solicited ideas and advice for that brief analysis from our colleagues on the ASLE listserv; see the ASLE Internet site. Cheryll Glotfelty contributed a particularly helpful response in a private e-mail.

10. In the course of preparing this introduction, we became aware of several scholars—Bonney MacDonald, Adam Sweeting, and Helena Feder—who have begun to consider Henry James's travel writing in relation to his representations of nature.

11. For a variety of perspectives on this shift in thinking, see Berman; Evernden; Glacken; Leiss; Merchant; Soper; and Worster *(Nature's Economy)*.

12. For discussions of this issue, see Lopez; Marx; Nash *(Wilderness);* and Kolodny *(Land, Lay)*.

13. For other discussions of such traditions, see Berman; and Merchant.

14. To most ecocritics, interdisciplinarity is one of the most important defining features of the field; for example, it is mentioned by virtually all of the sixteen participants in the roundtable session "Defining Ecocritical Theory and Practice" at the 1994 Western Literature Association Meeting.

15. See Callicott and Nelson.

Works Cited

Abbey, Edward. *Desert Solitaire: A Season in the Wilderness.* 1968. New York: Ballantine, 1971.

Association for the Study of Literature and Environment. ⟨http://www.asle.umn.edu/⟩.

Bate, Jonathon. *Romantic Ecology: Wordsworth and the Environmental Tradition.* London: Routledge, 1991.

Bennett, Michael, and David Teague, eds. *The Nature of Cities: Ecocriticism and Urban Environments.* Tucson: U of Arizona P, 1999.

Berman, Morris. *The Reenchantment of the World.* Ithaca: Cornell UP, 1981.

Birkerts, Sven. "Only God Can Make a Tree: The Joys and Sorrows of Ecocriticism." Rev. of *The Ecocriticism Reader: Landmarks in Literary Ecology,* ed. Cheryll Glotfelty and Harold Fromm. *The Boston Book Review* 3.1 (Nov./Dec. 1996): 6+.

Branch, Michael P., Rochelle Johnson, Daniel Patterson, and Scott Slovic, eds. *Reading the Earth: New Directions in the Study of Literature and the Environment.* Moscow: U of Idaho P, 1998.

Bremer, Sidney H. *Urban Intersections: Meetings of Life and Literature in United States Cities.* Urbana: U of Illinois P, 1992.

Brooks, Paul. *Speaking for Nature: How Literary Naturalists from Henry Thoreau to Rachel Carson Have Shaped America.* San Francisco: Sierra Club, 1980.

Buell, Lawrence. *The Environmental Imagination: Thoreau, Nature Writing, and the Formation of American Culture.* Cambridge: Belknap-Harvard UP, 1995.

Callicott, J. Baird, and Michael P. Nelson. *The Great New Wilderness Debate.* Athens: U of Georgia P, 1998.

Campbell, SueEllen. "The Land and Language of Desire: Where Deep Ecology and Post-Structuralism Meet." *Western American Literature* 24 (1989): 199–211.

Cheney, Jim. "Postmodern Environmental Ethics: Ethics as Bioregional Narrative." *Environmental Ethics* 11 (1989): 117–34.

———. "Ecofeminism and Deep Ecology." *Environmental Ethics* 9 (1987): 115–45.

Cheng-Levine, Jia-Yi. "Mahasweta Devi's *Imaginary Maps:* Colonial Legacy and Post-Colonial Ecology in India." *Phoebe: Journal of Feminist Scholarship, Theory, and Aesthetics* 9.1 (1997): 11–20.

Cronon, William, ed. *Uncommon Ground: Toward Reinventing Nature.* New York: Norton, 1995/1996.

"Defining Ecocritical Theory and Practice." Roundtable. 1994 Western Literature Association Meeting. Salt Lake City, Utah. 6 Oct. 1994. ⟨http://www.asle.umn.edu/conf/other_conf/wla/1994.html⟩.

Devall, Bill, and George Sessions. *Deep Ecology: Living as if Nature Mattered.* Salt Lake City: Peregrine Smith, 1984.

Diamond, Irene, and Gloria Feman Orenstein. *Reweaving the World: The Emergence of Ecofeminism.* San Francisco: Sierra Club, 1990.

Dipose, Rosalyn, and Robyn Ferrell, eds. *Cartographies: Poststructuralism and the Mapping of Bodies and Spaces.* North Sydney, Austral.: Allen and Unwin, 1991.

Dixon, Melvin. *Ride Out the Wilderness: Geography and Identity in Afro-American Literature.* Urbana: U of Illinois P, 1987.

Ecocriticism. Spec. issue of *New Literary History* 30.3 (1999).

Elder, John C., ed. *American Nature Writers.* 2 vols. New York: Scribner's, 1996.

———. *Imagining the Earth: Poetry and the Vision of Nature.* Urbana: U of Illinois P, 1985.

Evernden, Neil. *The Social Creation of Nature.* Baltimore: Johns Hopkins UP, 1992.

Forum on Literatures of the Environment. *PMLA* 114 (1999): 1089–1101.

Fox, Warwick. *Toward a Transpersonal Ecology.* Boston: Shambhala, 1990.

Franklin, Wayne, and Michael Steiner, eds. *Mapping American Culture.* Iowa City: U of Iowa P, 1992.

Gaard, Greta, ed. *Ecofeminism: Women, Animals, Nature,* Philadelphia: Temple UP, 1993.

Glacken, Clarence J. *Traces on the Rhodian Shore: Nature and Culture in Western Thought from Ancient Times to the End of the Eighteenth Century.* Berkeley: U of California P, 1967.

Glotfelty, Cheryll, and Harold Fromm, eds. *The Ecocriticism Reader: Landmarks in Literary Ecology.* Athens: U of Georgia P, 1996.

Gould, Peter, and Rodney White. *Mental Maps.* 1974. Boston: Allen and Unwin, 1986.

Hayden, Delores. *The Power of Place: Urban Landscapes as Public History.* Cambridge: MIT P, 1996.

Hegarty, Emily. "Linda Hogan: Genocide and Environmentalism." *Phoebe: Journal of Feminist Scholarship, Theory, and Aesthetics* 9.1 (1997): 41–50.

Hochman, Jhan. *Green Cultural Studies: Nature in Film, Novel, and Theory.* Moscow: U of Idaho P, 1998.

Howarth, William. "Some Principles of Ecocriticism." Glotfelty and Fromm 69–91.

Jackson, J. B. *Discovering the Vernacular Landscape.* New Haven: Yale UP, 1984.

Kerridge, Richard, and Neil Sammels, eds. *Writing the Environment: Ecocriticism and Literature.* New York: St. Martin's, 1998.

Kolodny, Annette. *The Land before Her: Fantasy and Experience of the American Frontiers, 1630–1860*. Chapel Hill: U of North Carolina P, 1984.

———. *The Lay of the Land: Metaphor as Experience and History in American Life and Letters*. Chapel Hill: U of North Carolina P, 1975.

Kroeber, Karl. *Ecological Literary Criticism: Romantic Imagining and the Biology of Mind*. New York: Columbia UP, 1994.

Leiss, William. *The Domination of Nature*. New York: Braziller, 1972.

Limerick, Patricia Nelson. "Disorientation and Reorientation: The American Landscape Discovered from the West." *Journal of American History* 79 (1992): 1021–49.

Lopez, Barry. *The Rediscovery of North America*. New York: Vintage-Random House, 1990.

Lovejoy, Arthur O. *The Great Chain of Being*. Cambridge: Harvard UP, 1974.

Marx, Leo. *The Machine in the Garden: Technology and the Pastoral Ideal in America*. New York: Oxford UP, 1964.

McClintock, James. *Nature's Kindred Spirits: Aldo Leopold, Joseph Wood Krutch, Edward Abbey, Annie Dillard, and Gary Snyder*. Madison: U of Wisconsin P, 1994.

McGurl, Mark. "Green Ideas Sleep Furiously: Andrew Ross on Ecocriticism." *Lingua Franca* (Nov.–Dec. 1994): 57–65.

McNamee, Gregory. "Wild Things: Forget Deconstruction—Today's Hippest Literary Critics Have Gone Green." *Utne Reader* (Nov.–Dec. 1997): 14–15.

Meinig, Donald. *The Interpretation of Ordinary Landscapes*. New York: Oxford UP, 1979.

Mellor, Mary. *Feminism and Ecology*. New York: New York UP, 1997.

Merchant, Carolyn. *The Death of Nature: Women, Ecology, and the Scientific Revolution*. New York: Harper and Row, 1980.

Murphy, Patrick D. "Commodification, Resistance, Inhabitation, and Identity in the Novels of Linda Hogan, Edna Escamill, and Karen Tei Yamashita." *Phoebe: Journal of Feminist Scholarship, Theory, and Aesthetics* 9.1 (1997): 1–10.

———, ed. *Literature of Nature: An International Sourcebook*. Chicago: Fitzroy Dearborn, 1998.

Naess, Arne. "The Deep Ecological Movement, Some Philosophical Aspects." *Philosophical Inquiry* 8 (1986): 10–13.

Nash, Roderick. *Wilderness and the American Mind*. 1967. 3rd ed. New Haven: Yale UP, 1982.

Norwood, Vera. *Made from this Earth: American Women and Nature*. Chapel Hill: U of North Carolina P, 1993.

O'Grady, John P. *Pilgrims to the Wild: Everett Ruess, Henry David Thoreau, John Muir, Clarence King, Mary Austin.* Salt Lake City: U of Utah P, 1993.

Parini, Jay. "The Greening of the Humanities." *New York Times Magazine* 29 Oct. 1995: 52–53.

Plant, Judith, ed. *Healing the Wounds: The Promise of Ecofeminism.* Philadelphia: New Society, 1989.

Platt, Kamala. "Environmental Justice in Chicana and South Asian Poetics." *Phoebe: Journal of Feminist Scholarship, Theory, and Aesthetics* 9.1 (1997): 21–29.

Plumwood, Val. *Feminism and the Mastery of Nature.* New York: Routledge, 1993.

Scruggs, Charles. *Sweet Home: Invisible Cities in the Afro-American Novel.* Baltimore: Johns Hopkins UP, 1993.

Slovic, Scott. *Seeking Awareness in American Nature Writing: Henry Thoreau, Annie Dillard, Edward Abbey, Wendell Berry, Barry Lopez.* Salt Lake City: U of Utah P, 1992.

Snyder, Gary. *The Practice of the Wild.* San Francisco: North Point, 1990.

Soja, Edward. *Postmodern Geographies: The Reassertion of Space in Critical Social Theory.* London: Verso, 1989.

Soper, Kate. *What Is Nature?* Cambridge: Blackwell, 1995.

Spirn, Anne Whiston. "The Poetics of City and Nature: Toward a New Aesthetic for Urban Design." *Landscape Journal* 7 (fall 1988): 108–27.

Stein, Rachel. *Shifting the Ground: American Women Writers' Revisions of Nature, Gender, and Race.* Charlottesville: UP of Virginia, 1997.

Sturgeon, Noël. *Ecofeminist Natures: Race, Gender, Feminist Theory, and Political Action.* New York: Routledge, 1997.

Torrance, Robert M. *Encompassing Nature: A Sourcebook.* Washington, DC: Counterpoint, 1998.

Wallace, Kathleen R. "Audre Lorde and Ecocriticism: Notes toward Urban Nature Writing." *Phoebe: Journal of Feminist Scholarship, Theory, and Aesthetics.* 9.1 (1997): 31–40.

Warren, Karen J., ed. *Ecofeminism: Women, Culture, Nature.* Bloomington: Indiana UP, 1997.

———, ed. *Ecological Feminism.* New York: Routledge, 1994.

———, ed. *Ecological Feminism.* Spec. issue of *Hypatia.* 6.1 (1991).

Westling, Louise H. *The Green Breast of the New World: Landscape, Gender, and American Fiction.* Athens: U of Georgia P, 1996.

White, Lynn, Jr. "The Historical Roots of Our Ecologic Crisis." *Science* 155 (1967): 1203–7.

Winkler, Karen J. "Scholars Embark on Study of Literature about the Environment." *The Chronicle of Higher Education* 9 Aug. 1996: A8+.

Worster, Donald. *Nature's Economy: A History of Ecological Ideas.* 2nd ed. New York: Cambridge UP, 1994.

———. *The Wealth of Nature: Environmental History and the Ecological Imagination.* New York: Oxford UP, 1993.

Part I

*Reevaluating the Roots
of Western Attitudes toward Nature*

Beyond "Thou Shalt Not":
An Ecocritic Reads Deuteronomy

Betsy S. Hilbert

> These are the words which Moses spoke to all Israel on the far
> side of the Jordan, in the desert in the Aravah, near Suf.
> —Deuteronomy 1:1

Of the five books of the Hebrew Bible, Deuteronomy—the last—immediately centers on a sense of place. A people who have wandered for forty years since the exodus from Egypt, led by the prophet Moses and seeking their singular space in the universe, are now poised to cross the Jordan River and enter the land that they have been promised they will occupy. In the ensuing narrative, Moses will remind his people over and over that the price of their continuance in the Promised Land is social justice—justice not only among themselves but for every other occupant: human, animal, and the land. From its first words, spoken in and from the wilderness, Deuteronomy is suffused with the theme of connection to the landscape; it consistently expounds the idea that human beings, in their intricate connections to the earth and to one another, bear the responsibility of justice and righteousness as a condition of their continued survival in the places that give them nurture.

> Through the wilderness, in the Arabah near Suph, between Paran and
> Tophel, Laban, Hazeroth, and Di-zahab, it is eleven days from Horeb to
> Kadesh-barnea by the Mount Seir route.[1] (1:1–2)

Nature writing has its roots in travel writing, but this is a guidebook of a different sort. The names of places here not only reconstruct tribal memory but locate the narrative from its opening verses. The framing narrative of Deuteronomy is Moses' last speech to his people, for they are making a crossing he will not live to join. He reminds them of the places they have been and the history they have endured, and he instructs them again in the laws that must be applied if they are to succeed and survive. The book of Deuteronomy speaks of ethics and ecology, warfare and social justice, and of the treatment of skin eruptions and the rules for returning lost property, as well as the Ten Commandments and a list of predatory birds that may not be eaten. All of life is holy, the Pentateuch insists, and life should be lived every day as a manifestation of that holiness; thus the seemingly smallest rules of daily life are offered contiguous in this text with matters that touch the most sacred. The life that Deuteronomy demands is a life lived in daily mindfulness of the gifts of creation.

How many environmentally oriented critics read the Bible these days? More than one might imagine. Fewer, probably, than ought to. In the community of ecological awareness, one often comes across a sense that traditional Western religions have historically been at fault in rationalizing and supporting traditional Western environmental destruction. Religion is blamed for the idea that human beings are separate and above the rest of creation, leading to the "go forth and rape" mentality that has regarded nature as either a useful but disposable commodity or a hostile antagonist. In the late 1960s, with the environmental movement in the United States gathering new steam, the historian Lynn White Jr.'s essay "The Historical Roots of Our Ecologic Crisis" struck nerves among environmentalists in blaming the ecological crisis on a Judeo-Christian value system that from the Middle Ages has emphasized technological control over nature.

A closer reading of White's essay, however, reveals that the self-identified "churchman" was far from rejecting Western religion. In an issue of *Sierra* on the theme Religion and the Environment, Carl Pope, executive director of the Sierra Club, confesses that he too had originally misconstrued White and now had discovered "to my chagrin that I and many others had badly misread him. . . . This lesson of open-mindedness and democracy is only part of what environmentalists can learn from religion. . . . [T]he recognition that we are not the only ones with a commitment to the preservation of Creation is gaining ground" (16–17). Pope believes that many environmentalists had missed White's point that "since the roots of our trouble are so largely religious, the remedy must also be essentially religious, whether we call it that or not. We must rethink and refeel our nature and destiny" (16–17). White's proposal of St. Francis of Assisi as "a patron saint for ecologists" was hardly a repudiation of traditional Christianity. Instead, White pointed the way for contemporary rethinking about religious attitudes toward the environment, seeking the strands within traditional religions that have persistently avowed human responsibility for the care of creation.[2] In the present essay, I will show that a close reading of biblical texts from an environmental perspective illuminates not only the scripture but also our understandings of human relations to the environment. Such discussions add immensely to what the editors of this collection have identified as a central conceptual challenge: "understanding nature and culture as interwoven rather than as separate sides of a dualistic construct."

To assume we know exactly what the Bible says on any given subject is to impose the simplicity of fundamentalist readings on a complex text that has occupied interpreters for millennia. A major distinction of the Bible is its subtlety and openness to rereading and reinterpretation, and one of the crucial discoveries when one engages in biblical studies is how much there is yet to be discovered. Even those who would challenge the Bible may tend to oversimplify it. Ruth Adler, for example, describes her initial difficulties in teaching biblical literature to a women's studies course. "Both the religiously oriented students who read the Bible frequently and heard it cited from the pulpit and the nonreligious ones, who knew it from hearsay or feminist readings, were convinced that they knew about the Bible's portrayal of women. In the beginning, some of them even resisted doing the assigned readings because they felt they knew the subject so well" (92). Adler's students learned, of course, that the Bible's portrayals of women are far less stereotypical and far more complex than prejudgments could allow. By the same token, reading the Bible from an ecological point of view is a challenge to critical discovery.

The contemporary scholar Regina M. Schwartz points out the complexity of alternate voices in biblical texts as well as the need to come to terms with the scriptures' influence.

> We may know, vaguely, that it was quoted extensively during the revolutions in France and the New World, during the civil wars in Great Britain and

America, that the Bible was invoked both to justify slavery and to abolish it, invoked for missionary imperialism and revolutionary response, that its cadences were intoned at the birth of various nationalisms and its verses infused not only the rhetoric of Zionism and liberation theologies of Latin America and South Africa, but also considerably less overt biblical polities. But what these superficial allusions belie is the much deeper influence the Bible has had on the way we think. . . . All this is to warn that, if we do not think about the Bible, it will think (for) us. (8)

In thinking about Deuteronomy, I speak from the stance of a late-twentieth-century academic of liberal, feminist, environmental bent and as a practicing Jew. I return to biblical scripture over and over (weekly, in the great round of readings that constitute the Jewish calendar), precisely because it is such a challenge and there is so much with which to wrestle. The Bible is fascinating, frustrating, infuriating, and comforting by turns. Deuteronomy, like the rest of the Pentateuch, is demanding, recursive, and deeply invested in both tribal memory and universal law. Studying it is an endless adventure.

Deuteronomy is a feast for linguistic and textual analysis. It is the only book of the Pentateuch unified by a framing narrative, in the voice of Moses. Its Greek name "Deuteronomy," or "second law," characterizes the way this book repeats—and, in subtle ways, redacts and shifts—historical and legal passages from the previous four books. Jewish tradition does not consider the material in this book as superseding or voiding the earlier books, for precisely the same reason that Jews do not refer to the "Old" Testament as such. The Hebrew term for this fifth book derives from its first significant word: *d'varim*—words, things, statements, teachings. The story told in 2 Kings is that this scroll was found by the High Priest Hilkiah during a reconstruction of the Temple in 622 B.C.E., during the reign of King Josiah. Its authenticity verified by the prophetess Hulda, this culminating book of the law, according to legend, ushered in to the kingdom of Judah a renaissance of renewed optimism, faith, and national strength. The discovered scroll was called "Book of Teaching" (*Sefer ha-Torah,* which can also be translated as "Book of the Law" or "Book of the Way"). Scholarship is reasonably certain that this was the text we presently have, although there still remain questions of when it was first inscribed and by whom it was initially hidden.

For an ecocritical reading, Deuteronomy is probably the most challenging of the five books. What, for example, is a contemporary environmentalist, respectful of the cultures of indigenous people, to do with 7:3, which details the actions the Israelites are to take against the Canaanite religions, "lest they become a snare to you"? "[Y]ou shall tear down their altars, smash their pillars, cut down their sacred posts [early translations read this as 'sacred groves'], and consign their images to the fire."

It is a shock to the contemporary sensibility, not the least from awareness that passages such as this were historically misused by colonial European nations against indigenous populations all over the globe. For all our understanding that the Bible limits this intolerance to the specific practice of human sacrifice (demanding the destruction of the places where children were "put to the fire") and even knowing that the injunctions to suppress indigenous religious practices were never actually accomplished (why else the ongoing opposition to those practices of which the later prophets preached?), it would be easier to simply declare the entire message outdated and meaningless, if not actively repellent. One could choose for a spiritual text something a lot less complicated and less questionable, a text that does not confront us so blatantly with militaristic patriarchy rolling down like thunder.

There is certainly for the contemporary sensibility plenty to which one may object. Deuteronomy specifies that specific cities (those and no others), once given the opportunity to surrender and if they refuse, must be destroyed completely. It rumbles threats of the manifold evils awaiting those who turn from the direction of the One God, proscribes the children of certain unions from entering the congregations of the faithful, and exacts obedience in precise matters of religious ritual. Moreover, not only does the text appear on the surface to support warmongering and religious intolerance, it has been notably misused for millennia as a rationale for a variety of oppressions.

We must also recognize, however, that the Hebrew Bible, and especially the work of the prophets, specifically inveighs against the kind of murderous landgrabbing practiced historically by gangs of self-supremacists. Deuteronomy expressly limits violence, even the violence of warfare (21:10–14), and unequivocally demands justice under laws administered equitably for all. "Cursed be he who misdirects a blind person on his way. . . . Cursed be he who subverts the rights of the stranger, the fatherless, and the widow" [the unprotected] (27:18–19). The text enjoins the people to follow the example of God, who "shows no favor and takes no bribe, but upholds the cause of the fatherless and the widow, and befriends the stranger, providing him with food and clothing.—You too must befriend the stranger, for you were strangers in the land of Egypt" (10:17–19).

For all of the text's apparent dwelling on battlefield victory, the point of view of the book's narrative must be remembered: Moses the prophet-leader is speaking to a tiny group of people who will soon have to fight an entrenched assortment of powerful empires for possession of a place to live. As the Israelites cross the Jordan in search of a homeland, under the direction of Joshua (not Moses, who is permitted to see the Promised Land but not to enter it), they will be almost hopelessly outnumbered. And Moses, in his last speech, must give them whatever courage he can convey that they can carry with them. Thus the arrow rattling of Deuteronomy, coupled with the insistence on Law (armies in conflict are notoriously badly behaved), is a necessary component of the story. Unfortunately, however, the text can easily lend itself to the kind of misuse it emphatically rejects and that, as White pointed out, has often occurred.

Schwartz confronts the issue of biblical violence in *The Curse of Cain: The Violent Legacy of Monotheism*. Detailing some of the ways that the identity formation described in the Bible has since been used to foster antagonism and even genocide directed at a variety of Other People (with all sides often quoting the same text), Schwartz links the problem of misuse to a "principle of scarcity." Where the assumption exists that there is not enough of anything to go around, she points out, exclusive and defining boundaries must be established between "us" and "them."

> However much biblical narratives themselves may caution against such authorization, offering critique after critique to unseat each of its own authorized institutions (judgeship, priesthood, monarchy, prophecy) and revising each of its covenant codes (Noachic, Mosaic, Davidic, prophetic), nevertheless, its interpreters have insisted upon canonizing, codifying, and authorizing, in short, in turning the text, despite itself, into a weapon. And in the violent tactics of identity formation, that weapon is most often wielded against the Other. (9)

A biblical text can thereby become an easy excuse for whatever its interpreters want it to justify, a call to action for whatever action is currently contemplated. Everyone gets to quote scripture. Why, then, are we (am I) still struggling with this text?

Precisely because of its openness and its complex subtleties, the biblical text that can be so misused also illuminates issues of human activity in a way that less complex or less open literature cannot approach. Deuteronomy, like the previous four books of the Pentateuch, provides its readers with an interactive, recursive set of questions, embodying layers behind layers of meanings. The Bible endures not as Truth Writ Firm (as narrow-minded readings would imprison it) but as a constant challenge to revisioning and reinterpretation.

The biblical text of Deuteronomy, those teachings that Moses speaks to "all Israel"—those who stood on the banks of the Jordan and generations yet unborn, including the present—refuses to leave us in our comfortable generalizations and placid assumptions. For the voice of Deuteronomy gives the utmost respect to its opponents. The Deuteronomist would never countenance, for example, an easy participation in New Age rituals as ersatz Native American religious ceremonies, co-opting the ceremony without the commitment. Biblical opposition to idol worshipping is there specifically because it knows how superstitious human beings can become. It understands fully the human conviction that the universe can be controlled if only we can find the right scientific formula, or maybe chant a little louder.

If we are uncomfortable with parts of Deuteronomy, the Word is uncomfortable with us: our failures at social justice, our greed, our wastefulness, and our destructive capabilities. The Hebrew Bible is a long record of humans falling progressively into distance from God; it is also an account of human attempts, with varying success, to reconnect with our own nature. As biblical texts invoke and record death, doom, and destruction, they also point to an alternate course of redemption. If cities may be destroyed for the inhabitants' behavior to one another, as families are torn apart by anger, and dynasties fail through overreaching ambition, the Law establishes boundaries of conduct. Specified cities, and only those, may be assaulted; other places and people must be left untouched— and thus the text specifically prohibits empire building. Live on your own land, Deuteronomy enjoins, in your own space, and do not practice the murderous acquisition of your neighbors. Viewing the successive militarism of Israel's ancient neighbors, such as the Syrians, Assyrians, Babylonians, and Egyptians, and the grief that imperialism has brought to the region from biblical times to the present, Deuteronomy was, in retrospect, the voice of reason.

Do not cut down useful trees, it insists, even in the extremities of warfare— "for the tree of the field is human life" (20:19). Do not destroy in expedience what you may need later (20:20). Practice humility, for you have received much more than you have earned, and love is an open gift (8:12–18). Do not show prejudice toward the "stranger," the minority Other, who lives among you, for you have known what it is like to be alien in another country (24:17–22). Safeguard the rights of the oppressed, of the helpless (23:16–17; 24:19; 24:20–22)— especially of the women who are most severely vulnerable, such as widows and war captives (19:14). Beware of scams and self-proclaimed preachers (18:9–22). Watch what you eat (14:3–21). Do not take what is not yours (21:1–3). Be honest in business (25:13–16), and treat fairly the people who work for you (24:14–15). Keep the politicians from getting above themselves, and hold the monarch in check (17:14–20). Ensure that domestic animals are treated kindly and sympathetically (5:14; 22:1–4; 22:6–7; 22:10; 25:4). (Note the number of separate laws demanding kindness to animals, in what is probably the first code in human history requiring humane treatment of animals.) Do not bring down on yourselves the inexorable consequences of power hunger, greed, ambition, denial of another's suffering, or wanton destruction of natural resources. The Law of Deuteronomy protects even as it forbids. It requires justice for the environment, for all creation, as it does for the human beings who live within that environment.

Beyond the declarative imperatives of this text lie complex patterns of meaning, which yield a rich harvest of questions and implications when approached from an ecocritical perspective. Consider the requirements that are suggested by the commandment "If you see your fellow's ass or ox fallen on the road, do not ignore it; you must help him raise it" (22:4). Why not yoke a donkey and an ox together (22:10)? Why the injunction "If, along the road, you chance upon a bird's nest, in any tree or on the ground, with fledglings or eggs and the mother sitting over the fledglings or on the eggs, do not take the mother together with her young" (22:6)? There are rabbinic interpretations that suggest the injunction against taking mother and young together is actually a prohibition against extinguishing any entire species. What other qualities may be called forth by that same interdiction: compassion? conservation? humility? simplicity of spirit? The verse that follows 22:6 extends the ambiguities: "Let the mother go, and take only the young, in order that you may fare well and have a long life" (22:7). In what sense is this action conducive to long life—especially when "long life" in biblical terms typically refers to generations succeeding generations?

Environmental readings of passages in Deuteronomy can also clarify the "curses and blessings" dichotomies in the text that often trouble contemporary readers. Modern prayer books for Jewish services have tended to downplay the passage that was traditionally recited following the She'ma, or central statement of faith, because it seems to imply a theologically simplistic, one-to-one relationship between sin and punishment.

> If, then, you obey the commandments that I enjoin upon you this day, loving the Lord your God and serving Him with all your heart and soul, I will grant the rain for your land in season, the early rain and the late. You shall gather in your new grain and wine and oil—I will also provide grass in the fields for your cattle—and thus you shall eat your fill. Take care not to be lured away to serve other gods and bow to them. For the Lord's anger will flare up against you, and He will shut up the skies so that there will be no rain and the ground will not yield its produce; and you will soon perish from the good land that the Lord is assigning to you. (11:13–17)

Consider the preceding passage from an environmental perspective, however, and it makes perfect sense. Deuteronomy insists that the God[3] referred to here is one of active and loving kindness, mercy, and justice—the "other gods" mentioned, therefore, must be identified with the principles of avarice, self-centeredness, and failure of caring. In an environmental sense, the passage is completely accurate. Follow the gods of greed, and destructiveness will inevitably rebound against the whole community. Follow a god of warfare, for example, and the skies will fill with burning oil. Wipe out rain forests in the name of a god called International Economics, and changes in weather patterns will have worldwide effects. Wreak havoc on the vegetation of environments such as those in the Middle East, and desertification follows. Degrade productive agriculture, and we will certainly perish from the good land we were given. Natural law is quite prepared to carry out Deuteronomic warnings.

Environmental readings also come into play in Deuteronomic attitudes toward the land. Moses' teaching begins at a specific place by the river in the Land of Moab; it ends with a vision of the landscape of the future: "Gilead as far as Dan; all Naphtali; the land of Ephraim and Manasseh; the whole land of Judah as far as the Western Sea" (34:1–2). The book is wrapped in landscape, from beginning to end, at once the description of a physical and spiritual journey and a book about human relationships to the earth.

For the land, as Deuteronomy makes clear, is never owned by human beings. It is a temporary gift, earned by righteousness, including righteous behavior to the land. Those to whom it is given, who now possess it, have only specific rights and responsibilities of stewardship to the earth's gifts, and, like the Canaanites before them, the Israelites may (and will) be dispossessed of this land for their failures of justice. The biblical scholar Moshe Weinfeld points out that "possession" has historically been interpreted as conquest—the narrative, after all, is set at the moment of crossing the Jordan into increasingly hostile territory and going into battle for the right to settle. Yet the force of meaning of the term "occupy" actually refers to the rights of poor farmers to inherit and work their lands in peace, safe from the predations of taxation and seizure by the wealthy and more powerful (313–16). As Deuteronomy expands on the principles of the preceding four books, and as it subtly redacts and redirects the law, Weinfeld notes, it moves to an increased religious liberalism, toward greater protections for the poor and oppressed, and toward the partnership of men and women in the religious life of the community.

Can texts such as Deuteronomy speak to contemporary concerns for the earth and aspirations for human equality? Among those who recognize that the heart of our environmental crisis is a spiritual crisis is Rabbi Ismar Schorsch, who finds in Judaism—based on its teaching texts—"a sacred canopy of legal regulations, theological notions, and intellectual values [constructed] on a bedrock of a transcendent God concept, the outcome of which is a decidedly modest sense of man's place and purpose in the universe" (30). The theologian Sallie McFague, speaking of a similarly broad view of creation, points out that "One clear directive that this gives theology is to understand human beings as earthlings (not aliens or tourists on the planet) and God as immanently present in the processes of the universe" (87).

A vision of peace in the land and peace with the land is the longing that suffuses Deuteronomy. Life, love, and the landscape are inextricably interconnected. Wherever in this text there is the voice of imperative, there is also the voice of compassion: justice for the earth and its inhabitants, including trees and animals. It is the quiet voice of conscience and nurturing, of protection from oppression and from the iron hand of force. If humans are to live, the Deuteronomist insists, if their children and the following generations survive, it will only be in righteous connection to one another and to the earth.

> See, I set before you this day life and prosperity, death and adversity. . . . I call heaven and earth to witness against you this day: I have put before you life and death, blessing and curse. Choose life—if you and your offspring would live. (30:15, 19)

Notes

1. All quotations are from the *Tanakh: The Holy Scriptures* translation.

2. One case in point was Wendell Berry's beautifully argued response to White, which offered an environmental reading of the Bible that insisted on the principles of stewardship and "right occupation."

3. Note that "Lord" is actually a misnomer, an English translation of only one of the manifold names of God; and the masculine designations of "Lord" and "He/Him" are in English translations because the original Hebrew has no other way to express the generic singular.

Works Cited

Adler, Ruth. "Rereading Eve and Other Women: The Bible in a Women's Studies Course." *Approaches to Teaching the Hebrew Bible as Literature in Translation.* Ed. Barry N. Olshen and Yael S. Feldman. New York: Modern Language Association, 1989. 93–97.

Berry, Wendell. "The Gift of Good Land." *The Gift of Good Land: Further Essays Cultural and Agricultural.* San Francisco: North Point Press, 1981. 267–81.

McFague, Sallie. "An Earthly Theological Agenda." *Ecofeminism and the Sacred.* Ed. Carol J. Adams. New York: Continuum, 1994. 84–98.

Pope, Carl. "Reaching beyond Ourselves." *Sierra* (Nov./Dec. 1998): 16–17.

Schorsch, Ismar. "Learning to Live with Less: A Jewish Perspective." *Spirit and Nature: Why the Environment Is a Religious Issue.* Ed. Steven C. Rockefeller and John C. Elder. Boston: Beacon Press, 1992. 27–38.

Schwartz, Regina M. *The Curse of Cain: The Violent Legacy of Monotheism.* Chicago: U of Chicago P, 1997.

Tanakh: The Holy Scriptures. New York: Jewish Publication Society, 1988.

Weinfeld, Moshe. *Deuteronomy and the Deuteronomic School.* Oxford: Oxford UP, 1972.

White, Lynn, Jr. "The Historical Roots of Our Ecologic Crisis." *Science* 155 (1967): 1203–7.

Chaucer and the Politics of Nature

Lisa J. Kiser

Identifying and analyzing environmental perspectives in medieval texts can contribute both to the projects of medievalists, who seek to understand medieval cultures as thoroughly as possible in their full historical contexts, and to those of ecocritics, who hope to comprehend how modern cultural assumptions about the environment have developed from their originary Western roots. Yet both medievalists and ecocritics have largely ignored the subject of environmental perspectives in medieval texts, and when not ignoring it, they have generalized broadly, and therefore not always usefully, about medieval approaches to the environment. Literary historians of the Middle Ages, for example, have tended to restrict their analyses to commentary on medieval theological and philosophical conceptions of nature and to the role of animal symbolism in allegorical Christian conceptual schemes. Although sound in every scholarly way, studies with these foci—most of them reflecting the views of the clerical classes alone—result in projects that cannot account for the variousness of medieval perspectives on the environment.[1] Likewise, environmental ethicists, historians of the environment, and ecological critics have also relied on restricted data to generalize about the medieval world, often summing up the entire period in a few bold strokes preparatory to advancing theses about the Renaissance or the Enlightenment as watershed periods in the history of environmental thought.[2] Clearly, both the fields of medieval studies and ecological criticism can be enriched by attention to what each can offer the other, whether that be expanded databases for analysis coupled with more nuanced and discriminating historical assessments such as medievalists are able to provide or the benefits made possible by the interdisciplinary methodologies modern ecological critics employ, approaches that unite history, philosophy, anthropology, geography, political science, ecology, and sociology.

One structure visible in medieval texts and worth exploring from a modern ecocritical perspective is that of the nature-culture dualism, along with the other binaries that arise from it. Many writing today in the fields of environmental ethics and ecological criticism are preoccupied with the fact that Western thinking about the natural world has been dominated by dualisms and oppositions; indeed, the analysis—and critique—of common conceptual binaries and the related interlocking analogies they spawn (that is, for example, nature is to culture as female is to male or male is to culture as female is to nature) figures importantly in much of the cultural criticism that is attempting to turn our attention to the theoretical underpinnings of common binarized conceptualizations of the environment. When nature is opposed to culture, for example, nature takes a subordinate position, just as female becomes the less valued of the two categories in a male-female split, as ecofeminists have been quick to argue, pointing out that women and nature both suffer when they are linked together as subordinates in these two-term interlocking oppositions.[3]

It is usually assumed that such dichotomous categories derive from Cartesian assumptions, claims not in full operation until Cartesian rationalism came to dominate the structure of Western thought beginning in the seventeenth century (see, for example, Plumwood 104–19). That a medieval author might recognize such categories, much less be able to critique them, has not before been argued, perhaps because a culture's beliefs about nature (as about so much else) are often obscure, demonstrated especially in early texts only as part of an invisible ideology, a dominant mode of thinking neither overt in a work nor consciously registered by its author. And certainly in texts from earlier periods during which nothing like a modern environmental consciousness existed, one would expect to find only in oblique forms—if at all—the concepts and distinctions that today we regard as central to environmental thought, including an awareness of the role of social constructivism in interpreting the environment.

This is not so, however, with Chaucer's *Parliament of Fowls*. Written, most likely, in the early 1380s, the *Parliament of Fowls* depicts, in dream-vision form, Lady Nature's supervision of the mating habits of a group of birds. It is a poem that thus foregrounds its concern with nature (it personifies—and genders—

its central character, Lady Nature), and it pointedly raises for its audience the question of the relationship between nature and culture (a dichotomy that the poem sets up but does not always confirm). It is also a poem that forces on our attention the question of how the construction of nature "is itself an exercise of cultural power" (Mazel 142). In this essay, I will show, through an examination of the *Parliament of Fowls,* that in medieval culture we can find environmental thinking of a more sophisticated sort than has been claimed in existing scholarship.

The structure of the *Parliament of Fowls* is complex. It is framed by the voice of its first-person narrator, who expresses frustration at the task of writing about love. Seeking inspiration through reading, the narrator falls asleep over his book, dreaming about a literary garden of love featuring Venus's temple and an array of allegorical personifications relating to courtly amatory experience (Plesaunce, Curteysie, Delyt, Gentilesse, Flaterye, Desir, and so on). The narrator then witnesses, in a space annexed to the garden, Lady Nature's springtime "parliament," at which the bird participants are assigned (or given permission to choose) their mates. Although many kinds of birds are involved in these parliamentary proceedings, the major focus is on the selection of a mate for the royal female eagle. Her three suitors (all eagles and all figured as aristocratic) are given time to woo her with idealized courtly speeches, while the other birds (figured as belonging to a lower class) interject, in comic fashion, their impatience with the lengthy aristocratic mating rituals. The female eagle finally postpones her decision to marry, and the other birds noisily disperse with their mates, waking up the dreaming narrator, who concludes his poem by promising to read more in order (presumably) to write better in the future.

Chaucer's immediate purpose in the *Parliament of Fowls* and the circumstances in which it was written have remained obscure to scholars. However, there is general agreement that the poem shares some of the concerns visible in the poet's other works: an emphasis on the limitations of human knowledge; an interest in the uncertain relationship between textual representations and the events or objects they purport to describe; a celebration of the diversity of human perspectives on the world; and—most important for the purposes of this essay—an understanding of how nature had been theorized in a variety of medieval traditions.[4]

Indeed, in its approach to nature, the *Parliament of Fowls* participates in virtually all of the medieval paradigms available to Chaucer; that is, it betrays clear influences from the ancient bestiaries; the folkloric tradition; medieval encyclopedic sources (including what were judged to be natural histories); academic and theological conceptualizations of nature; and the medieval European beast fable and beast epic genres. The latter traditions were primary enabling forces behind Chaucer's configuration of the social classes through his birds, for in the late medieval period, beast fables were generally acknowledged to be vehicles of social satire, often casting the weak and the powerful in scenes of social struggle (Löfgren; Henderson "'Of Heigh,'" "Animal," "Medieval"; Ziolkowski 6–9). Although the *Parliament of Fowls* is not technically a beast fable (as is Chaucer's *Nun's Priest's Tale),* its talking birds, which represent the classes in conflict, participate unmistakably in the comic and socially divisive atmosphere of the medieval beast fable tradition.

Yet one of the major differences between this poem and its medieval ancestors is that the *Parliament of Fowls* is continually aware of its own tendencies to construct nature socially, that is, to identify its birds and its symbolic Lady Nature as classist, sexist, and, most interesting, as species-ist constructions. And although no other work by Chaucer takes up the subject of nature in this particular way, readers accustomed to his poetry will recognize in the *Parliament of Fowls*'s handling of nature a typical Chaucerian strategy. After setting up some putatively authoritative construction of the world, the same work proceeds to critique it, often from "below," that is, from the perspective of an oppressed or dominated group that finds itself excluded from (or irrelevant to) the work's original conception. This strategy, visible in all of Chaucer's major works, usually employs human subjects in principal roles—but with the *Parliament*'s birds-as-humans, Chaucer provides himself with the chance to include the subject of nature in his poem, especially the ways in which nature is constructed and controlled by human intellectual schemes. That is, although the birds in the *Parliament* are always personified and anthropomorphized as humans acting out certain class-based roles, Chaucer never loses sight of how his poem has implications for our thinking about nonhuman nature. Indeed, the poem raises the seemingly modern idea that the act of representing nature is determined by social codes involving concepts of gender and class.

Chaucer's poem most overtly recognizes the social construction of nature in the figure of Lady Nature herself, who is cast in the image of a human, an aristocratic female, implicitly with royal standing. Epithets used to describe Lady Nature emphasize her royal identity; she is a "queene" and a "noble empresse" (298, 319).[5] Unlike Alain de Lille and Jean de Meun, Chaucer's immediate medieval predecessors in the creation of female nature figures,[6] Chaucer has no qualms about assigning to this female the task of overseeing sexual behavior in the sphere she governs. Yet Lady Nature's governance of sexual practices demonstrates a strong element of social control that is visible in her use of parliamentary procedure and legal decree to determine mating patterns. Her court configures mating among all classes (although especially the nobility) as a form of public rule-bound behavior, a spectator sport open to social scrutiny; her tightly controlled procedures would never permit the kind of furtive, unbridled, or socially unacceptable forms of mating to which Alain de Lille's Lady Nature in *De planctu Naturae* (one of Chaucer's sources) alludes. Even the lower birds, who are not particularly relevant to the aristocratic experience that this poem privileges, are there to accept Lady Nature's "dom and yeve hire audience" (308), to follow her "statut" and accept her "governaunce" (387).[7] Moreover, Chaucer's Lady Nature imposes other forms of social control on the wildfowl around her. She orders each bird to "take his owene place" (320) in her parliament in a fashion strictly consonant with the bird's social standing: noble birds of prey are highest (and get to choose their mates first), then come the worm-fowl, water-fowl, and seed-fowl in a descending order of social status, an arrangement that—in keeping with aristocratic will—discourages the idea of social mobility or intermarriage across social classes. This method of classifying wild creatures by means of human social categories is concocted by Chaucer with the help of medieval scientific lore about birds combined with stereotypical caricatures of the interests and social behavior of members of different social classes, and—of course—it is a classification heavily biased in favor of aristocratic interests.[8]

For all her wisdom and laudable skills in mediation and governance, Chaucer's Lady Nature is clearly serving dominant social ideologies. She bolsters and confirms a set of aristocratic beliefs about the innate superiority of the upper class, beliefs not necessarily held by Chaucer himself but certainly welcomed by the noble audience he is trying to please. Her function is to preserve social hierarchies and reinforce dismissive stereotypes of those classes beneath the aristocratic ones; only the aristocrats are given full space to display their courtly mating rituals, whereas the classes below them are given short shrift (and are even implied to be unable to comprehend noble behavior).[9] Tellingly, Lady Nature is not shy about informing us who her favorite birds are—they are the royal female eagle ("of shap the gentilleste / That evere she among hire werkes fond / The moste benygne and the goodlieste" [373–75]) and the royal tercelet "the gentilleste and most worthi / Which I have wrought" [635–36]).

Also, Lady Nature's law, as expressed in this poem, contains many gender-specific doctrines that bear on the social codes of Chaucer's day. She calls for males to choose their mates first, but females must be given a chance to agree to the match (407–11), a condition that appears to be binding for birds of all classes. Thus, Chaucer's Lady Nature is working against the medieval practice of forced marriages (a point that J. A. W. Bennett made long ago) and for a woman's right to have a say in the choice of her marriage partner, a right not always happily recognized among the fourteenth-century noble classes.[10] And for the noble bird in question here, Lady Nature is willing to alter her decrees to empower this female even more, for she gives the usually male prerogative of initial choice to her ("Thanne wol I don hire this favour" [626–30]), also allowing for a delay to suit the woman's desire to remain temporarily unmarried. Here, then, the aristocratic female is seemingly permitted special powers above and beyond those normally accorded her in late medieval society, a move that Chaucer makes in order to suggest that his Lady Nature is enlisted in the service of aristocratic— especially female—interests, the concerns of a large portion of his intended audience.[11]

Yet Lady Nature's advocacy of female interests is only a mirage. The fact that the delay of the marriage is temporary and that the female eagle's choice is largely illusory (feudal interests will ultimately force her to pick one of her three suitors, whether or not she wants him),[12] raises questions about just how empowered Chaucer's female eagle—and his Lady Nature—really are. As with the female eagle, Chaucer's Lady Nature seems to exhibit substantial control and power over her sphere of existence, but on closer analysis that sphere reveals itself to be organized around class- and gender-based ideologies much larger than can be affected by her individual will. Both Lady Nature and the female eagle can only delay the inevitable, not prevent it; and the parliamentary rules, although bendable, are not breakable, persisting, as they do, "alwey, fro yer to yeere" (411). Chaucer's female nature figure thus encodes his culture's dominant conceptions of the distribution of power in the social order, and that power is not vested in women or in the natural world, which is represented as feminized and therefore subordinated to the cultural dominance of males. Here, indeed, male is to culture as female is to nature.

Clearly, then, Chaucer's personification of Lady Nature is constructed along the lines of prevailing social ideologies; she is a social construction of the natural world, a point that may not seem a surprising one in today's academic culture, where to argue that texts contain social constructs is to engage in a frequently practiced exercise. What is remarkable about Chaucer's poem, however, is that its author seems to know all about his complicity in the practice of social construction and to want to signal this knowledge to his wisest readers—and he does so in several extraordinary ways. First of all, before Lady Nature appears in the garden, at the moment the narrator initially enters it, Chaucer describes its trees in a catalogue that signals to his readers that all representations of nature in the vision that follows will be carried out with human needs and projects in mind:

> The byldere ok, and ek the hardy ashe;
> The piler elm, the cofre unto carayne;
> The boxtre pipere, holm to whippes lashe;
> The saylynge fyr; the cipresse, deth to playne;
> The shetere ew; the asp for shaftes pleyne;
> The olyve of pes, and eke the dronke vyne;
> The victor palm, the laurer to devyne.
>
> (176–82)

[The oak for building, and also the hardy ash; the elm both for pillar-support and for coffins for corpses; the boxwood tree for making pipes; the holm-tree for whips; the fir for ship's masts; the cypress as a symbol of mourning; the yew for arrows; the aspen for bow-shafts; the olive as a symbol of peace; the vine as a symbol of drunkenness; the palm as a symbol of victory, and the laurel for divination.]

In these lines, we are told that nature, for the purposes of this poem, should be viewed as the raw material for human symbolic systems and, even more practically, as the source of technology—not as an entity existing in and of itself, with its own laws, purposes, or essence. A little later in the poem, there appears a similarly constructed bird catalogue, wherein birds are given symbolic attributes based on comparisons between their observed natural behavior and the social behavior of humans. This catalogue, in fact, begins to provide the basis for the social divisions among the *Parliament*'s birds. For example, since the worm-fowls eat disgusting food (from a human perspective), they are implicitly of a lower order (326); the turtle-dove is a good bird because it chooses to marry (a human social practice) and is always true to its mate (355), truth in love being a human virtue; the cormorant is a glutton (362) and the stork an adulterer (361), both being analyzed as showing vice, a moral and sociolegal category of human invention but certainly not one suitable to nonhuman communities; the raven is said to be wise (363), the crow sad (363), and the jay scornful (346), each bird assigned an adjective whose meaning falls within the register of human interests or values but that seems inappropriate, on reflection, to the avian community. In both these catalogues, then, of trees and of birds, the reader is overtly coerced into interpreting nonhuman nature in terms of distinctly human categories; that is, Chaucer has taken pains to tell us just how we are supposed to proceed as decoders of the natural world portrayed in his poem. And such an overt program of reader coercion suggests that Chaucer knows that the natural world may well be understood to have mysterious, indeed inscrutable, meanings of its own— but that for the purposes of his poem we must abandon this view and accept his crafty anthropomorphizing for what it is, namely, an interested human act of turning the world to one's own species-specific purposes.

Moreover, Chaucer denies to his Lady Nature any of the godlike attributes visible in her earlier appearances in other medieval poems about nature's dominion and power. Here, she is humanized so thoroughly that even her dwelling in the forest is based on human-made architectural patterns; although it is constructed out of branches, her house has "halles" and "boures" (304) as do houses of other humans of her class. She is not a dweller in Heaven, as are Alain de Lille's and Jeun de Meun's female nature figures—and thus Chaucer is careful to make no claims about her theological significance or her Christian authority.

Chaucer's Lady Nature has been so thoroughly co-opted by aristocratic human social codes that she (as well as the narrator) seems alienated from the lower orders of birds that she herself has presumably created—a source of much of the poem's humor. Their speech to her is but "noyse" (523)—and the narrator is complicit in this social judgment; to him, too, the speech of the lower birds is "noyse" (312, 491, 500), "kakelynge" (562), and "lewednesse" (silliness)(520). These judgments are a form of othering all those creatures who are not members of the noble class whose ideology is championed in this courtly poem—and such a suggestion is clearly advanced by this work, which corroborates the inarticulateness that privileged members of society believed to be endemic to low social station.[13] But there are other things to say about the divisions between Lady Nature and her lower birds. Although these birds are humanized along with Lady Nature (thus participating in the poem's larger species-ist project of co-opting the natural world for human interests), at one point Chaucer reminds us forcefully that there is indeed a nonhuman world, one that lies unrepresented in his poem, for readers to contemplate. In one of the oddest but most memorable passages in English literature, Chaucer lets us hear three of the lower birds, a goose, a cuckoo, and a duck, speak in a remarkably unmediated fashion, each uttering a phrase in its own untranslatable tongue: "The goos, the cokkow, and the doke also / So cryede, "Kek kek! kokkow! quek quek" (498–99). These syllables, although designated, of course, in a written phonetic system of representation devised by human users of language, are not human language at all, suggesting that there is a nonhuman world outside of this poem's artistic rendering of the natural and that this world may well be inaccessible to our understanding. What, Chaucer asks us to ponder, could those birds possibly be saying with such inexplicable sounds? [14]

All literary works that present us with animals in the guise of humans or humans in the guise of animals (whichever way one wishes to analyze it) are playing fast and loose with category distinctions, largely by blending the human and the nonhuman into hybrids that bring pleasure to those who perceive the continually shifting boundaries between the animal and the human.[15] We need only to remember that Chaucer's own *Nun's Priest's Tale* takes this premise to an astonishingly comic level. And, certainly, much of the *Parliament of Fowls* works in the same way; we read the birds as human citizens, as part of the social community in which we ourselves play roles, yet we are also distanced from them by reminders of their nonhuman identities. But this poem is trying to say something more, something not only about Chaucer's awareness of the process of anthropomorphizing that makes beast fables tick but also about the kinds of arrogant assumptions we humans make every time we attempt to make claims about the nonhuman world around us. Aggressively appropriating the nonhuman world in his representation of it, and ensuring that his readers notice this act of appropriation, Chaucer suggests that there is a natural world outside the parameters of his artistic colonization, one that has been silenced and suppressed and one about which he has no authority to write. With his human Lady Nature and his anthropomorphized catalogues of trees and birds, Chaucer calls attention to the human domination of nature, and, although he does not exactly "let the subaltern speak" (Spivak "Subaltern"), he makes his readers aware that it has a voice to be heard.

Chaucer, in other words, is advancing an issue that has preoccupied modern ecological critics, the issue of the extent to which it is philosophically sound (and politically justifiable) to insist on extreme social constructivism as the basis on which to ground one's view of the environment. Chaucer's poem elevates (although rather coyly and in the course of a decidedly comic vision) the same question one of our contemporaries, the anthropologist Kay Milton, poses when she echoes the recent concerns of other environmentalists: "In both the extreme and the moderate versions of the constructivist model, culture is seen as determining the environment by defining it, by imbuing it with truth or meaning. This raises the question of what constitutes the raw material for the cognitive construction. If the environment in the absence of human thought is devoid of truth or meaning, can there be anything of substance out of which to construct the cultural image?" (51).[16] And although Chaucer does not answer this question, he is ready to see its relevance to any project that attempts to represent the nonhuman world. If his poem confesses to its socially constructed view of the environment, it also admits to a realm outside of itself, one signaled by the firm restrictions of the tree catalogue and the unassimilated voices of the lower birds.

The nature-culture distinction and the human-nonhuman one, then, are strongly visible in the *Parliament of Fowls*. But to Chaucer, such distinctions are themselves human categories, not necessarily right and true ones and not inexorably stable as philosophical categories worthy of belief. Distinctions between nature and culture and between the nonhuman and the human are present in Chaucer's poem, but they are simultaneously elided and destabilized even as they form part of the poem's essential framework. To Chaucer, such distinctions, however slippery, are always going to be part and parcel of the species-ist representational projects of self-interested human perceivers, who perforce have little other way in which to comprehend a universe fairly incomprehensible. For a medieval poet to have such an awareness is remarkable, and it should give pause to those historiographers of nature who say that only the environmental ethicists and ecological critics of today could possibly understand the politics of nature, the strengths and limitations of the social constructivism model, or the vexed philosophical dimensions inherent in binarized and oppositional categories of thought.

Notes

1. See especially Chenu, Economou, Roberts, and Salisbury *(The Medieval World)* for the theological and philosophical backgrounds. For analyses of medieval views of the nonhuman natural world that focus especially on animals in Christian symbolic schemes, see Baxter, Clark and McMunn, Hassig, Payne, and Rowland. Salisbury *(The Beast Within)*, although not argued with an ecocritical emphasis, is a good survey of some of the ways in which animals figured in medieval life and thought.

2. There are many examples of this argumentative strategy in the literature, but see especially Collingwood 3–13; D. White 42–49; Merchant 6–41; Evernden 41–46; and Macnaughten and Urry 8–10. For a recent, more nuanced survey of nature in the medieval period, see Coates 40–66, although the brevity of his treatment precludes depth. Glacken remains useful in spite of dated generalizations (171–351).

3. The investigation of dichotomous categories with respect to a culture's beliefs about the environment began in earnest among social anthropologists earlier in the century, and it has taken a central role in the current scholarly writings of ecological theorists, especially the work of ecofeminists and environmental ethicists. See especially MacCormack and Strathern 1–24, 42–69, 174–222; Robertson, Mash, Tickner, Bird, Curtis, and Putnam, passim; Warren, "Power" 125–46, *Ecological* 19–41; Dunayer 11–31; Plumwood 41–68; Salleh 225; Harlow 27–42; Roach 52–65; Lahar 91–117. See also Turner, where he writes, "Indeed, one might almost categorize societies . . . solely by the content of their nature/culture distinction. . . . Do not the factional, ideo-

logical, and political conflicts within all cultures consist to a large extent in a struggle over the strategic definition of these words and their exclusive possession?" (41).

4. For a recent survey of the major scholarly and critical work on the *Parliament of Fowls*, see Minnis 252–321.

5. All references to the *Parliament of Fowls* are to the *Riverside Chaucer*, gen. ed., Benson.

6. On the other major medieval female nature figures that were created before Chaucer's, especially Alain de Lille's in *De planctu Naturae* and Jean de Meun's in *Roman de la Rose*, see Kiser.

7. On the legal atmosphere of this scene, and on how its vocabulary recalls fourteenth-century parliamentary discourse, see Bennett 140 and Brewer 37–38.

8. Chaucer has carefully selected his bird lore from Vincent of Beauvais's *Speculum naturale*, Bartholomaeus Anglicus's *De proprietatibus rerum*, Isidore's *Etymologies*, Pliny's *Natural History*, and a variety of popular sources, some of them distilled in bestiaries of the period. For identification of some of the sources behind specific lines, see the notes to the *Parliament* in Benson.

9. On courtship practices as markers of social class in this poem, see Emslie 1–17. Also relevant is Patterson's discussion of the self-legitimization of the aristocratic classes through social display in his chapter on the *Knight's Tale*, esp. 168–74, 181–94.

10. Bennett 143–44. For a recent discussion of the degree of female consent in marriage practices among the English nobility of the late medieval period, see Ward 12–33.

11. We should remember also that this poem may well be alluding to the actual marriage negotiations between Richard II and Anne of Bohemia. See Benson 994.

12. For a gender-based reading of the *Parliament of Fowls* that addresses in greater detail the poem's submerged conflict between feudal interests and courtly codes, see Hansen 117–28.

13. See Ganim 108–20 for other applications of this social attitude. See also Crane 210–21 and Justice.

14. Relevant to the issue of a dominant culture allowing—but not understanding—voices from an oppressed culture is the postcolonial framework of Spivak in "The Politics of Translation" and "Can the Subaltern Speak?" For a medieval example of a Latin poem that catalogues the verbs used to represent animal noises, see Ziolkowski 37–38. Chaucer's line, however, is more daring in its appropriation of avian phonetics because it actually quotes the birds.

15. On the human-animal categories and the blurring of distinctions between them, see the work of Ritvo, which is relevant to the issues raised here, even though

it focuses mainly on the eighteenth and nineteenth centuries. See also Shepard 90–114.

16. Kay Milton's response to the radical constructivist position is only one of the recent critiques of poststructuralism by ecological critics. See also Soulé and Lease, especially the essay by Hayles.

Works Cited

Baxter, Ron. *Bestiaries and Their Use in the Middle Ages.* Phoenix Mill: Sutton, 1998.

Benson, Larry D., gen. ed. *The Riverside Chaucer.* Boston: Houghton Mifflin, 1987.

Bennett, J. A. W. *The Parlement of Fowles: An Interpretation.* Oxford: Clarendon P, 1957.

Brewer, D. S., ed. *The Parlement of Foulys.* London: Thomas Nelson and Sons, 1960.

Chenu, M. D. "Nature and Man: The Renaissance of the Twelfth Century." *Nature, Man, and Society in the Twelfth Century.* Ed. and trans. Jerome Taylor and Lester K. Little. Chicago: U of Chicago P, 1968. 18–32.

Clark, Willene B., and Meredith T. McMunn. *Beasts and Birds of the Middle Ages: The Bestiary and Its Legacy.* Philadelphia: U of Pennsylvania P, 1989.

Coates, Peter. *Nature: Western Attitudes since Ancient Times.* Berkeley: U of California P, 1998.

Collingwood, R. G. *The Idea of Nature.* Oxford: Oxford UP, 1960.

Crane, Susan. "The Writing Lesson of 1381." *Chaucer's England: Literature in Historical Context.* Ed. Barbara Hanawalt. Minneapolis: U of Minnesota P, 1992. 210–21.

Dunayer, Joan. "Sexist Words, Speciesist Roots." *Animals and Women: Feminist Theoretical Explorations.* Ed. Carol J. Adams and Josephine Donovan. Durham, NC: Duke UP, 1995. 11–31.

Economou, George. *The Goddess Natura in Medieval Literature.* Cambridge: Harvard UP, 1972.

Emslie, Macdonald. "Codes of Love and Class Distinctions." *Essays in Criticism* 5 (1955): 1–17.

Evernden, Neil. *The Social Construction of Nature.* Baltimore: Johns Hopkins UP, 1992.

Ganim, John M. *Chaucerian Theatricality.* Princeton: Princeton UP, 1990.

Glacken, Clarence J. *Traces on the Rhodian Shore: Nature and Culture in Western Thought from Ancient Times to the End of the Eighteenth Century.* Berkeley: U of California P, 1967.

Glotfelty, Cheryll, and Harold Fromm, eds. *The Ecocriticism Reader: Landmarks in Literary History.* Athens: U of Georgia P, 1996.

Hansen, Elaine Tuttle. *Chaucer and the Fictions of Gender.* Berkeley: U of California P, 1992.

Harlow, Elizabeth M. "The Human Face of Nature: Environmental Values and the Limits of Nonanthopocentrism." *Environmental Ethics* 14 (1992): 27–42.

Hassig, Debra. *Medieval Bestiaries: Text, Image, Ideology.* Cambridge: Cambridge UP, 1995.

Hayles, N. Katherine. "Searching for Common Ground." Soulé and Lease 47–63.

Henderson, Arnold Clayton. "Animal Fables as Vehicles of Social Protest and Satire: Twelfth Century to Henryson." *Third International Beast Epic, Fable and Fabliau Colloquium, Munich, 1979: Proceedings.* Ed. Jan Goossens and Timothy Sodmann. Cologne: Böhlau, 1981. 160–73.

———. "Medieval Beasts and Modern Cages: The Making of Meaning in Fables and Bestiaries." *PMLA* 97 (1982): 40–49.

———. "'Of Heigh or Lough Estat': Medieval Fabulists as Social Critics." *Viator* 9 (1978): 265–90.

Justice, Steven. *Writing and Rebellion: England in 1381.* Berkeley: U of California P, 1994.

Kiser, Lisa J. "Alain de Lille, Jean de Meun, and Chaucer: Ecofeminism and Some Medieval Lady Natures." *Mediaevalitas: Reading the Middle Ages.* Ed. Piero Boitani and Anna Torti. The J. A. W. Bennett Memorial Lectures. Ninth Ser. Cambridge: D. S. Brewer, 1996. 1–14.

Lahar, Stephanie. "Roots: Rejoining Natural and Social History." *Ecofeminism: Women, Animals, Nature.* Ed. Greta Gaard. Philadelphia: Temple UP, 1993. 91–117.

Löfgren, Orvar. "Our Friends in Nature: Class and Animal Symbolism." *Ethnos* 3–4 (1985): 184–213.

MacCormack, Carol P., and Marilyn Strathern, eds. *Nature, Culture and Gender.* Cambridge: Cambridge UP, 1980.

Macnaughten, Phil, and John Urry. *Contested Natures.* Theory, Culture and Society Ser. London: Sage, 1998.

Mazel, David. "American Literary Environmentalism as Domestic Orientalism." Glotfelty and Fromm 137–46.

Merchant, Carolyn. *The Death of Nature: Women, Ecology and the Scientific Revolution.* New York: Harper, 1980.

Milton, Kay. *Environmentalism and Cultural Theory: Exploring the Role of Anthropology in Environmental Discourse.* New York: Routledge, 1996.

Minnis, A. J. *Oxford Guides to Chaucer: The Shorter Poems.* Oxford: Clarendon, 1995.

Patterson, Lee. *Chaucer and the Subject of History.* Madison: U of Wisconsin P, 1991.

Payne, Ann. *Medieval Beasts.* New York: New Amsterdam Books, 1990.

Plumwood, Val. *Feminism and the Mastery of Nature.* New York: Routledge, 1993.

Ritvo, Harriet. "Border Trouble: Shifting the Line between People and Other Animals." *In the Company of Animals.* Spec. issue of *Social Research: An International Quarterly of the Social Sciences* 62.3 (1995): 481–500.

————. *The Platypus and the Mermaid and Other Figments of the Classifying Imagination.* Cambridge: Harvard UP, 1997.

Roach, Catherine. "Loving Your Mother: On the Woman-Nature Relation." *Ecological Feminist Philosophies.* Ed. Karen J. Warren. Bloomington: Indiana UP, 1996. 52–65.

Roberts, Lawrence D., ed. *Approaches to Nature in the Middle Ages.* Medieval and Renaissance Texts and Studies 16. Binghamton: Center for Medieval and Renaissance Studies, 1982.

Robertson, George, Melinda Mash, Lisa Tickner, Jon Bird, Barry Curtis, and Tim Putnam. *FutureNatural: Nature, Science, Culture.* New York: Routledge, 1996.

Rowland, Beryl. *Animals with Human Faces: A Guide to Animal Symbolism.* Knoxville: U of Tennessee P, 1973.

————. *Birds with Human Souls: A Guide to Bird Symbolism.* Knoxville: U of Tennessee P, 1978.

Salisbury, Joyce. *The Beast Within: Animals in the Middle Ages.* New York: Routledge, 1994.

————, ed. *The Medieval World of Nature: A Book of Essays.* Garland Medieval Casebooks 5. New York: Garland, 1993.

Salleh, Ariel. "Class, Race, and Gender Discourse in the Ecofeminism/Deep Ecology Debate." *Environmental Ethics* 15 (1993): 225–44.

Shepard, Paul. *The Others: How Animals Made Us Human.* Washington, DC: Island P, 1996.

Soulé, Michael E., and Gary Lease, eds. *Reinventing Nature? Responses to Postmodern Deconstruction.* Washington, DC: Island P, 1995.

Spivak, Gayatri Chakravorty. "Can the Subaltern Speak?" *Marxism and the Interpretation of Culture.* Ed. C. Nelson and L. Grossberg. Basingstoke: Macmillan, 1988. 271–313.

————. "The Politics of Translation." *Outside in the Teaching Machine.* New York: Routledge, 1993. 179–99.

Turner, Frederick. "Cultivating the American Garden." Glotfelty and Fromm 40–51.

Ward, Jennifer C. *English Noblewomen in the Later Middle Ages.* London: Longman, 1992.

Warren, Karen J., ed. *Ecological Feminist Philosophies.* Bloomington: Indiana UP, 1996.

———. "The Power and the Promise of Ecological Feminism." *Environmental Ethics* 12 (1990): 125–46.

White, Daniel R. *Postmodern Ecology: Communication, Evolution, and Play.* Albany: SUNY P, 1998.

White, Lynn, Jr. "The Historical Roots of Our Ecological Crisis." *Science* 155 (1967): 1203–7.

Ziolkowski, Jan M. *Talking Animals: Medieval Latin Beast Poetry, 750-1150.* Philadelphia: U of Pennsylvania P, 1993.

Milton's Environmental Epic: Creature Kinship and the Language of *Paradise Lost*

Diane Kelsey McColley

Shortly after the Restoration, John Evelyn visited the king's palace at Whitehall, found it filled with smog, and announced that "[I]t will become our Senators . . . that they will consult as well the State of the Natural, as the Politick Body of this Great Nation . . . since, without their mutual harmony, and well-being, there can nothing prosper, or arrive at its desired perfection" (23). This proposition might have had more effect and received a less managerial formulation if the body politic had been less preoccupied with the commodification of nature and more attuned to those unacknowledged legislators, poets.

Seventeenth-century poets went beyond traditional pastoral and georgic genres to encompass ethical consideration of the natural world itself. They questioned the dominion of human beings over other beings at a time when mechanistic and imperialistic attitudes toward nature were just getting started; when agricultural experiment, colonization, and global commerce were subduing the earth; and when theologians and philosophers were disputing whether the natural world was made only for temporal use or would participate in a material eternity.

John Milton brought the relation of the body politic and the body of the land into comprehensive epic form. For Milton the health of both the natural and the politic bodies are affected by the health of language, which depends on both poetics and debate. *Paradise Lost* debates issues still present in environmental discourse: the nature of the dominion granted in Genesis; the implications of monotheism for human attitudes toward nature; conceptions of human language as managerial and alienating or as nature's voice; the abuses of those who "with impious hands / Rifl'd the bowels of their mother Earth / For treasures better hid" (1.686–87); the sentience and intelligence of animals and the possibilities of an empathetic but not anthropocentric relation of human to other-than-human beings; relations between tyranny over other creatures and tyranny over human lives; and the prospects of reparation by those who hope, in Adam's now ironic words, that "Man shall live / With all the Creatures, and thir seed preserve" (11.872–73).[1] The epic presents these issues in the dramatic voices of characters with a range of attitudes, but it does so with a pervasive ecological consciousness in its ethics, theology, and language.

Ecology is a scientific discipline, but the word also means thinking about nature as connected in an evolving and interactive way. Although the term was not coined until the nineteenth century, and many ecological critics deny that such a consciousness was possible in pre-Darwinian literature, *Paradise Lost* encompasses its etymological meaning of knowledge of the household, or shared habitat, of Earth in language ethically responsive to the diversity, connectedness, and well-being of Earth's offspring. "Ecology" better expresses Milton's habits of mind than the nearest contemporary equivalent, "economy"; both come from the Greek *oikos* (household), but economy's other root is *nomos* (law), while ecology comes from *logos* (word, the expression of thought). Economy meant estate management, and advises on prudent and profitable use of land, the *locus classicus* being the *Economics* of Xenophon, while ecology, etymologically speaking, means expressed thought about the household: in the case of Adam and Eve, the Garden of Eden with all its inhabitants and the earth it epitomizes.

Milton admired Xenophon, but his depiction of human care of prelapsarian Eden, the lost best place, represents both the primary calling and the renewed vocation of lapsed humanity: to restore in body and spirit and in the rest of the natural world the relatedness broken by an intemperate act of consumption, through which Adam and Eve attempted to transcend their responsibilities toward all creation. The epic is anti-Baconian and anti-Cartesian in its representation of the noncommodified community of species, in which every animal from whale to earthworm has beauty and interest and a right to its life and nurturing habitat, and where the gentle sustaining of plants and an amical relation to animals is a source of spiritual and intellectual growth. Adam and Eve do not yet know, for example, the value of earthworms for aerating the soil, but they are learning through observation, without the traps and vivisections of the Baconian science that intended to restore Edenic dominion in the un-Edenic way of making all of nature serve human beings, rather than the other way around.

Thinking connectedly is the method of Milton's poetics. His heterodox, anti-dualistic theology of nature claims that all creatures are made of "one first matter" and evolving toward more "spiritous" states (5.469–79), which however have nothing to do with transcendence: body and spirit in his monistic materialism are forever one and inseparable. The ethical implications of this monism are similar to Darwin's but without the threat of eugenics; all creatures are kindred, and human beings are responsible to use reason and language in ways that are morally responsible toward the whole household of beings.

As a lifelong champion of liberty from tyrannous rule, Milton incorporates into the work of Adam and Eve a nontyrannous dominion deriving from delighted observation of the governed. They are called to dress and keep a garden that is the epitome of global nature, "planted with the Trees of God" (7.738)—clear-cutters take note—and Milton, unlike most Western poets and artists, shows Adam and Eve doing so. They care for a "fruitful Earth" (8.96) prolific of other species that are not for profit but are a community of kindred creatures derived from "one first matter all" (5.472). In their calling "To prune these growing Plants, and tend these Flow'rs" (4.438), Adam and Eve learn about the nature of other beings for whom they are benignly responsible, all in some degree sentient and responsive to human care: animals, plants, and Earth. Their prelapsarian management of nature is minimal, however, and draws forth its native capacities. They prune trees whose "wanton growth" (4.629) interferes with fruitfulness, pick up debris—yes, blossoms fall in Milton's organic Eden—to smooth paths for their bare feet, wind vines around elms, and engage in limited planting for creative pleasure. Eve waters and props her fruits and flowers, going forth

> To visit how they prosper'd, bud and bloom,
> Her Nursery; they at her coming sprung
> And toucht by her fair tendance gladlier grew.
>
> (8.45–47)

These ministrations are opposed to the attitudes of those explorers and scientists who hoped to turn the natural world into a factory of profitable commodities.

The Edenic model of government that Adam and Eve are learning by encouraging each species and assuring growing room by mild restraint can apply also to the body politic.

The animals are naturally obedient to Adam and Eve but are not subservient to them. Because of Eve's innocence—a harmlessness based on intimate knowledge—"[E]very Beast" is "duteous at her call" (9.521). In their first scene, Adam explains to Eve that God has

> Conferr'd upon us . . . Dominion giv'n
> Over all other Creatures that possess
> Earth, Air, and Sea.
>
> (4.429–32)

By acknowledging that their governing is a responsibility conferred by the creator of all creatures, Adam accepts his vocation to serve them; by acknowledging that creatures possess their habitats, he might be called the first ecologist.

Ecocriticism is rightly concerned with the problem of naming as appropriation: catagorical taxonomies can abet a utilitarian or objectifying way of speaking. When the Creator presents the animals to Adam "to receive / From thee thir Names, and pay thee fealty / With low subjection" (8.343–45), hierarchical dominion is disturbingly (for us) and evocatively (for Adam) introduced; but what this test evokes from him is not the language of appropriation and command. "I nam'd them, as they pass'd, and understood / Thir Nature," Adam says, "with such knowledge God endu'd / My sudden apprehension" (8.352–54). At a time when animals were beginning to be thought of as robots, Milton through Adam granted them feelings: "they rejoice / Each with thir kind, Lion with Lioness" (8.392–93). From this observation Adam learns that he, too, needs a mate of his own "kind" or species and requests one. The Creator playfully replies,

> What call'st thou solitude? is not the Earth
> With various living creatures, and the Air
> Replenisht, and all these at thy command
> To come and play before thee; know'st thou not
> Thir language and thir ways? They also know,
> And reason not contemptibly.
>
> (8.369–74)

But the Creator approves Adam's request on the grounds that the divine image in which Adam was created is "not imparted to the Brute" (8.441) and creates Eve, in whom, as in Adam, "the image of thir glorious Maker shone" of "Truth, Wisdom, Sanctitude" (4.292–93). It is this likeness to the Creator that gives Adam and Eve their authority, and they are to be "Magnanimous to correspond with Heav'n" (7.511). This is a hierarchical opinion, yet it opposes the Cartesian attitude that denies animals reason and feeling and modifies the Baconian principle that the human race has "a right over nature which belongs to it by divine bequest" (118–19).

The animals' "play" implies free movement as well as performance and pleasurable exercise, and the word itself plays fitfully against "command." All kinds of animals play before Adam and Eve:

> Bears, Tigers, Ounces, Pards
> Gamboll'd before them, th'unwieldy Elephant
> To make them mirth us'd all his might, and wreath'd
> His Lithe Proboscis.
>
> (4.344–47)

And as with other descriptions of animals, this one creates a kinetic empathy with them: the bouncing line gambols, and we must use our lingual might and wreathe our tongues lithely to pronounce the unwieldy line.

Adam and Eve do not use animals for the usual fallen purposes of food, clothing, labor, and war. What animals supply them is delight in otherness. They are not servants to human beings; human beings serve them by preserving their shared environment in pristine biodiversity. Had there been no Fall, their future offspring would have spread this primal human vocation through a world of which the Garden of Eden would have been the "Capital Seat" (11.343).

One sacred taboo, one fruit tree withheld amid plenty, exercises human wills in self-restraint and might have deterred the first man and first woman from exercising dominion as domination by reminding them to respect their maker and not become exploiters and rampant consumers of what he has made. When first Eve and then Adam devour the sacred reminder of that responsibility,

> Earth felt the wound, and Nature from her seat
> Sighing through all her Works gave signs of woe . . . .

Earth trembl'd in her entrails, as again
In pangs, and Nature gave a second groan.

$$(9.782-83, 1000-1001)$$

The environmental ethic depicted in the vocation of Adam and Eve and their defection from it is the more striking if we add to our late-twentieth-century understanding of its urgency a comparison with the intellectual tide against which Milton strove. He was up against Baconian and Cartesian science, which made nature the insensate storehouse of human commodities to be extracted by technology and which included vivisection; an expanding idea of the dominion over nature given in Genesis that set out to shape all habitats for human use; a conception of the New World as an inexhaustible wilderness in need of being subdued; and a theological conception among Calvinist writers that the natural world was made exclusively for the sustenance of the human soul, the only part of this world deemed immortal, in its earthly pilgrimage.[2]

One First Matter and the Kinship of Creatures

Milton's theology of nature is based on the kinship of creatures and represented in the ways diverse characters speak about them. This diversity allows debate; yet there is a clear connection between the origins of evil and the attitudes of fallen and unfallen beings toward other creatures and toward creaturehood itself.

When God sends the archangel Raphael to tell unfallen Adam and Eve that the rebellious archangel Satan has become their adversary, he also teaches them that all beings come from "one first matter," derived not *ex nihilo* but *ex Deo*:

> O Adam, one Almighty is, from whom
> All things proceed, and up to him return,
> If not depraved from good, created all
> To such perfection, one first matter all,
> Indu'd with various forms, various degrees
> Of substance, and in things that live, of life;
> But more refin'd, more spiritous, and pure,
> As nearer to him plac't or nearer tending

Each in thir several active Spheres assign'd,
Till body up to spirit work, in bounds
Proportioned to each kind.

(5.469–79)

Raphael speaks traditionally of a scale of nature rising from plant to animal to man to angel, and of spirit as a superior state toward which bodies work by a process of refinement; but body and spirit are not separate. The "first matter" of which human and angelic beings are made is the same matter of which the elements of water, air, earth, and fire, the stars and planets, the plants, fish, birds, insects, and all other animals are made; and all these "proceed" from "one." Milton's monism was considered heretical by dualists because it imbues all matter with spirit. Instead of a material, instrumental, and perishable earth and a spiritual heaven, Milton presents all matter as emerging from God, who diversifies it into beings that share both substance and soul. If, as Milton says in *Areopagitica,* "a good Booke is the pretious life-blood of a master spirit" (2:493), the good creation might be considered to contain, not only in its sacral revelation but in its sacred sentience, the communicated lifeblood of God.

When fallen Adam laments the loss of Paradise, Michael assures him of two other things many readers would have considered heretical: that God's "Omnipresence fills / Land, Sea, and Air, and every kind that lives," and that after the Last Judgment the faithful will be received "into bliss, / Whether in Heav'n or Earth, for then the Earth / Shall be all Paradise" (12.462–64)—suggesting that for Milton, who read Genesis literally, bliss includes all the inhabitants of Eden, fish, fowl, beast, and plant. God's presence in each "kind" or species is not polytheistic, however; God is both transcendent and immanent. His transcendent otherness assures his creative and redemptive freedom, while his immanence gives sacred significance to each creature, so that nature is not be feared and propitiated but honored and preserved.

Each rational species on the scale of nature is responsible for the well-being of those "below": angels for humankind, the human family for animals and plants. The varied responses of the epic's characters to this creation spring from the scene, chronologically the first in the epic, of the annointment of the Son of God as vicegerent of the angels in Book 5. This act provokes Satan's rebellion:

"New Laws from him who reigns, new minds may raise / In us who serve"
(5.680). His subordinate Abdiel argues that, on the contrary, the Son's headship
exalts their state; after all, it is the Son

> by whom
> As by his Word the mighty Father made
> All things, ev'n thee, and all the Spirits of Heav'n
> By him created in thir bright degrees.
>
> (5.835)

Satan, seized with ambition, denies his creaturehood and so renounces his kinship to other inhabitants of Milton's monistic heaven and earth:

> We know no time when we were not as now;
> Know none before us, self-begot, self-rais'd
> By our own quick'ning power.
>
> (5.799–801)

By renouncing creaturehood, Satan sets himself above other species and spends
the rest of his epic career exploiting them.

According to Beelzebub, the creation of the new world did not, as Satan alleges
later, take place as a result of Heaven's depopulation; it had been foretold

> by ancient and prophetic fame in Heav'n [to be] the happy seat
> Of some new Race call'd Man, about this time
> To be created like to us.
>
> (2.345–51)

The Son's appointment as leader of the angels is logically connected to his forthcoming role as agent of the new creation, which the angels, to Satan's disgust, will
serve: "Man he made," Satan complains later,

> and, O indignity!
> Subjected to his service Angel wings,
> And flaming Ministers to watch and tend
> Thir earthy Charge.
>
> (9.152–57)

His refusal to serve the Son includes a repudiation of service to his fellow creatures in an order where the higher serves the lower. The identity that he sees as threatened, although Abdiel does not, becomes a self devoid of awe and thus an abuser of other creatures in the service of a trifling yet monstrously cruel goal, initiating the individual and collective pain that not only the human race but all species on Earth must suffer.

To the fallen angels nature is entirely instrumental. The Stygian Council plans either to "waste" the "whole creation" or enslave its "puny habitants" (3.365–67). The chief advocate for the exploitation of nature is Mammon, the personification of wealth, who advises Hell's new tenants to "Live to ourselves . . . to none accountable" and "raise / Magnificence" (2.254–55, 272–73); it is by his suggestion that, later, fallen men

> Ransack'd the Center, and with impious hands
> Rifl'd the bowels of thir mother Earth
> For treasures better hid.
>
> (2.686–87)

Satan plots with his colleagues to enslave humankind, masquerades as cormorant, lion, tiger, and toad, and having "with inspection deep / Consider'd every Creature" to find "which of all / Most opportune might serve his Wiles" (9.83–85), exploits the Serpent's body but hates being incarnated as "Bestial slime" (9.165). Nature is merely the tool of his revenge, by which the whole creation is "made subject to vanity" and "groaneth and travaileth in pain together" awaiting deliverance from "the bond of corruption" (Rom. 8.20–22).

Natural Language

Like the web of being, the web of language in *Paradise Lost* absorbs the effects of each action throughout its structure: the invocation to light, the eating of a single fruit, the mention of a single place or historical fact, each image or phrase reverberates through the epic, affecting our responses to each passage. Similarly, the speeches of each character acknowledge (or, in the case of "fallen" and arrogant beings, fail to acknowledge) the other inhabitants of the world fabric. Characters possessing what Rudolph Otto calls "the consciousness of creaturehood" (11–12)[3] speak a language both numinous and creature-filled. This kind of conscience and consciousness—they are in unfallen beings the same thing—permeates their speech. To speak about a fellow creature is imaginatively to enter its life without anthropomorphizing it and to acknowledge that life in the sounds of words.

Ecological consciousness, a connected way of thinking about the diverse world, is represented in the language of the narrator, Adam and Eve, Raphael and Michael, and the creating Son. They are mindful of multiple presences and incorporate this awareness into their speeches. In conversations and prayers, Adam and Eve link together God, angels, planets, stars, elements, animals, plants, work, their future children, and the arts of poetry and song in numerically apt meter, visual imagery, and onomatopoetic sound (4.634–735, 5.153–208). Raphael, describing the creation of the animals, represents the life of each within its habitat not only in observant imagery but in kinetically and sensuously empathetic prosody and perspective (7.387–504). The archangel does not humanize, angelify, or demonize the animals he describes. Rather, he observes their habits, delineates the particularities of their otherness, situates their perspectives from within their habitats of water, sky, and land, and imitates their motions by the rhythms, syntactical arrangements, and onomatopoeia of his prosody. Our tongues and lips experience their motions and textures; we see their views and share their observable sensuous experience as we read; we know them, not as having our thoughts and emotions, although the possibility is not denied, but as flesh like us, with senses and awarenesses of their own. Raphael does not say that the flight of birds is an emblem of the soul, but that "the Air / Floats, as they pass, fann'd with unnumber'd plumes" (7.431–32) and the fricatives recreate with the reader's breath an experience that he, an angel, has shared. He does not say that oysters are good to eat, but that they "in their Pearly shells at ease, attend / Moist nutriment" (7.407–8), noting in flowing syntax their nurturing element. The animals live for their own sake, pronounced good and blessed and told to increase and multiply by their creator (Gen. 1), and our enjoyment of their beauty and interest can move us to love them for their own sake while appreciating the benefits of their otherness to our knowledge and delight.

Satan and his followers, in contrast, speak a language of instrumentality and appropriation with no concern for the nature of the being spoken of, rifling mother earth and mother tongue alike. Having given numerous examples of animal poetics elsewhere,[4] I shall mention three characters' talk about beings of special significance in the epic, both symbolic and botanical: trees.

When Raphael teaches Adam and Eve that diverse beings come from "one first matter," he shows how matter is refined to spirit by the natural analogy of a fruit-bearing plant, which is not only metaphorical but also an actual part of the process he is describing; and his sounds and syntax imitate the manner of its growth:

> So from the root
> Springs lighter the green stalk, from thence the leaves
> More aery, last the bright consummate flow'r
> Spirits odorous breathes: flow'rs and thir fruit
> Man's nourishment, by gradual scale sublim'd
> To vital spirits aspire, to animal,
> To intellectual, give both life and sense,
> Fancy and Understanding, whence the Soul
> Reason receives, and reason is her being,
> Discursive, or Intuitive; discourse
> Is oftest yours, the latter most is ours,
> Differing but in degree, of kind the same.
>
> (5.479–490)

He begins at the root, grounded at the end of a line by the entangling consonants of "root / Springs," so that "Springs lighter" does what it says: the quicker syllables of "lighter" spring from the groundedness of "root" and the energy wound into the double consonants and framing sibilants of "springs." "Green stalk," another spondee, is lightened by its longer vowels but retains the solidity of clustered consonants. "From thence the leaves / More aery" has airier, soft consonants, while "last the bright consummate flow'r / Spirits odorous breathes" rises like fragrance in rounded vowels and aspirates that themselves "breathe." The whole sentence does something syntactically tree-like as well; it begins with long phrases and branches into shorter ones, each growing out of the one before, then further divides into compounds to show the difference and yet relatedness of human discourse and angelic intuition, to which the matter of the plant has been refined. Raphael notices how trees grow and how that growth corresponds with the growth of mind and soul he is describing, and his sentence grows to match.

When Eve proposes to Adam that they might work separately for a morning to prevent their vocation of earth keeping from being hampered by too much "Casual discourse" (9.223), she says,

> Let us divide our labors, thou where choice
> Leads thee, or where most needs, whether to wind
> The Woodbine round this Arbor, or direct
> The clasping Ivy where to climb, while I
> In yonder Spring of Roses intermixt
> With Myrtle, find what to redress till Noon.
>
> (9.214–19)

Her proposal is a serious one. The work of Adam and Eve is the unfallen model of the work of regeneration, both personal and public, and Eve's program of redressing the Garden of Eden corresponds with that of the georgic revival. Recent scholarship that Michael Leslie and Timothy Raylor have collected on the Hartlib circle and the Georgical Committee of the Royal Society discloses a horticultural program for restoring the land after the civil wars that its promoters hoped would also restore health of body and soul and the moral integrity of England, and for many constituted a preparation for the new heaven and earth prophesied in Revelation. John Evelyn wrote to Sir Thomas Browne in 1660, Graham Parry points out, that gardens "do influence the soule and spirits of man, and prepare them for converse with good Angells." In 1659 John Beale proposed to Evelyn "the idea of perfuming the whole region around his great garden by plantations of eglantine, lilac and woodbine, so that the air may be purified and restored, adding that London might benefit from such a 'sweet and easy remedy' of its pollution" (Parry 135, 141);[5] and Evelyn's *Fumifugium* of 1661 suggests "all the woodbinds" among the cures of London's noxious fumes. Eve's choice of woodbine and ivy is horticulturally and politically apt for keeping the world in reparation.

Like Raphael's, but with the purpose of actual care, Eve's language shows her consciousness of the forms and needs of created things. Syntactically, the thought winds from enjambed verse to verse around the pole formed by the beginnings of the lines, as Eve suggests winding the woodbine and the ivy around the trunks of trees in their arbor.[6] She is not obsessed with domestic tidiness; growing in shade, vines need to climb for light and are constructed to clasp. But, if allowed, they can also choke the trees. The image is an emblem of marriage, and it illustrates Eve's concern that erotic and discursive pleasure should not so completely obsess the lovers that they confine each other or forget their responsibilities to other beings. Her syntax recognizes the habits of these plants and their need for tending. It also puts "choice," "wind," and "direct" at the ends of enjambed lines, giving impulsion to these energetic ideas. "Where choice / Leads thee, or where most needs" leads the thought from line to line: specifically to a line that contains a choice and imitates choosing by its alternatives. This syntax mimes not only the action of guiding the plant to the form it was formed for but also the thought at the heart of Eve's suggestion to Adam of dividing their morning's work: the pattern of "choice" that she wants to preserve. The debate that follows (9.226–375) is a political one; Adam and Eve are working out a form of government that will preserve their liberty even in the face of the predatory invasion of Satan of which Raphael has warned them. Eve wants neither pleasure nor fear to reduce their creative freedom or their attention to the other lives in their care. Like the horticulturalists who linked gardens with restorative virtues, but in language more responsive to the plants themselves, Eve combines horticulture with ethical choice.

Satan, in contrast, has no interest in trees except for the harm he can do with them. Having purloined the body of a snake he lies to Eve about an experience he has not had, claiming that eating the forbidden fruit gave him speech and reason.

> About the mossy Trunk I wound me soon,
> For high from ground the branches would require
> Thy utmost reach or Adam's; Round the Tree
> All other Beasts that saw, with like desire
> Longing and envying stood, but could not reach.
>
> (9.589–93)

Milton avoids winding the line to say "About the mossy Trunk / I wound me soon"; the Serpent, who makes "intricate seem straight" (9.32), speaks in one straight line and adds flatly, "Round the Tree / All other Beasts . . . stood, but could not reach." His lines do not imitate his action: "Stood" is not end-stopped, and "reach" is not enjambed. His language is disconnected from experience. One can also lie convolutedly and tell the truth in plain speech, but the connectedness of truth speaking to natural experience, not only one's own but that of numerous others, is the weft on which Milton's paradisal language weaves.

In the mouths of the narrator and the unfallen or repentent characters, Milton's language displays an awareness of the reality and value of the features of the land, the presence of other creatures, and the capacity of sentient ones—which include mountains and flowers in the presence of the Son (6.780–84) and trees and flowers in the presence of Eve—for suffering and joy. At the Fall, human language becomes impoverished as Adam and Eve temporarily lose interest in otherness, both God and other creatures, and become wholly self-absorbed.

Tyranny

Francis Bacon distinguished three "grades of ambition in mankind": to extend personal power, national power, and "the power and dominion of the human race itself over the universe," which is "a more wholesome thing and a more noble than the other two" and which he calls "the empire of man over things" (118)—"things" being whatever is not man. Milton brings these kinds of ambition together in the story of Nimrod, the "mighty Hunter" and the type of all tyrants (12.33; Gen. 10.9), which follows Adam's vision of Noah's Ark and his expression of joy that, in spite of the depredations and purgations issuing from the Fall, "Man shall live with all the creatures, and their seed preserve." Michael foresees that

>   one shall rise
> Of proud ambitious heart, who not content
> With fair equality, fraternal state,
> Will arrogate Dominion undeserv'd
> Over his brethren, and quite dispossess
> Concord and law of Nature from the Earth;
> Hunting (and Men not Beasts shall be his game)

With War and hostile snare, such as refuse
Subjection to his Empire tyrannous.

(12.24–32)

Adam's response to the story of Nimrod is politically, but not ecologically, satisfactory.

O execrable Son so to aspire
Above his Brethren, to himself assuming
Authority usurpt, from God not giv'n:
He gave us only over Beast, Fish, Fowl
Dominion absolute; that right we hold
By his donation; but Man over men
He made not Lord: such title to himself
Reserving, human left from human free

(12.64–71.)

What does Adam, still fallen but beginning the process of regeneration, mean by "Dominion absolute"? His provocative words express an attitude that needed much scrutiny as science sought to subdue nature systematically and Europe set out to conquer the American wilderness. They should be weighed in the context of the kind of dominion Adam has been exercising until the Fall and in the context of the human servitude to passions and hence to tyrants that Michael's ensuing reply foretells.

Many of Milton's readers would have been aware of two philosophical traditions that link tyranny over animals to tyranny over human beings: on the one side Aristotle and the Peripatetics, who thought it natural and right that animals, women, and slaves should devote their lives to the sustainance of others capable of the philosophical life, and on the other the Pythagoreans, who, as represented in Renaissance translations of Ovid (Metamorphoses 15) and Plutarch (572–73), opposed flesh eating and every other kind of violence to sentient beings and suggested that the slaughter of animals for sacrifice and food inured men to bloodshed and made them capable of war. Michael does not imply, as Ovid had done for Renaissance readers through Arthyr Golding's passionate and gory translation, that sacrificing and eating animals were precursors of war and tyranny. But Adam's idea of dominion has nothing to do with eating or enslaving; he recognizes that it is only by God's "donation" that his species holds power over other species, and, the reader may infer, human government of them now must be concerned with preserving their seed. Can human beings practice a benevolent custody of nature without tyranny? Can they avoid becoming inwardly tyrannical and imposing willful power on nations a well as nature?

Milton leaves this discussion open: readers may decide for themselves, since that is the basis of liberty of conscience, without which, for Milton, tyranny holds sway. But he has shown that human beings have a choice between tyranny and depredation, represented by Mammon and Nimrod, and replenished biotic communities, represented by Noah's Ark. And for Milton the relationships between human beings and other beings are connected to their relationship to the divine, both transcendent and immanent. By representing human dominion as beneficent care, Milton challenges the Nimrods and Mammons of colonization and commodification. By making all creatures citizens of the house of poetry, he shows how the plenitude of speech and the plenitude of the natural world can interact to each other's benefit. The scientist John Ray thought it "highly improbable that any Species should be lost" (350). The kinds of human activity that accelerate such losses had already begun; and Milton promoted an ethic and provided a language with which to cultivate a conscience that might have forefended them, that still might reduce tyrannical abuse of other species and the habitats we share with "every kind that lives."

Notes

1. All references to *Paradise Lost* are by book and line number.

2. Rudrum and Fitter both have shown that the biblical mandate of dominion over all the earth that patristic writers had interpreted as stewardship was swayed to instrumentalism by Calvinism, the growth of global commerce, and a new managerial attitude toward property as profit. On the earlier history of interpretation, see Cohen.

3. Milton's creature consciousness does not entail Otto's sense of self-annihilation.

4. McColley, *A Gust for Paradise* 140–44, "All in All."

5. See also DuRocher for a discussion of Milton's antecedents among the classical writers of agriculture and his polysemous emphasis on seeds, fruit, and growth,

implying "that the natural process of growth underlies the argument of *Paradise Lost*" (92).

6. "Arbour: 3. A bower or shady retreat, with sides and roof formed mainly by trees and climbing plants" *(New Shorter Oxford English Dictionary).*

Works Cited

"Arbour." *The New Shorter Oxford English Dictionary on Historical Principles.* Ed. Lesley Brown. 2 vols. Oxford: Clarendon, 1993.

Aristotle. *Aristotles Politiques, or Discourses of Government. Translated out of Greek into French, with Exposition taken out of the best Authours . . . By Loy Le Roy, called Regivs.* English trans. J. Dickenson. London, 1598.

Bacon, Francis. *The New Organon and Related Writings.* Ed. Fulton H. Anderson. Trans. James Spedding, Robert Leslie Ellis, and Douglas Denon Heath. Indianapolis: Bobbs Merrill, 1960.

Cohen, Jeremy. *"Be fertile and increase, fill the earth and master it": The Ancient and Medieval Career of a Biblical Text.* Ithaca: Cornell UP, 1989.

DuRocher, Richard J. "Careful Plowing: Culture and Agriculture in *Paradise Lost.*" *Milton Studies* 31 (1994): 91–107.

Evelyn, John. *Fumifugium: or, The Inconveniency of the Smoak of London dissipated.* London, 1661.

Fitter, Chris. *Poetry, Space, and Landscape: Toward a New Theory.* Cambridge, 1995.

Leslie, Michael, and Timothy Raylor, eds. *Culture and Cultivation in Early Modern England: Writing and the Land.* Leicester: Leicester UP, 1992.

McColley, Diane Kelsey. "All in All: The Individuality of Creatures in Paradise Lost." *"All in All": Unity, Diversity, and the Miltonic Perspective.* Ed. Charles W. Durham and Kristin P. McColgan. Selinsgrove, PA: Susquehanna UP, 1999. 21–38.

———. "Ecology and Empire." *Milton and the Imperial Vision.* Ed. Balachandra Rajan and Elizabeth Sauer. Pittsburgh: Duquesne UP, 1999. 112–29.

———. *A Gust for Paradise: Milton's Eden and the Visual Arts.* Urbana: U of Illinois P, 1993.

Milton, John. *Areopagitica*, in vol. 2 of *The Complete Prose Works of John Milton.* Don M. Wolfe, gen. ed. 8 vols. New Haven: Yale UP, 1953–1983.

———. *Paradise Lost: A Poem in Twelve Books.* Ed. Merritt Y. Hughes. New York: Odyssey Press, 1962.

Otto, Rudolph. *The Idea of the Holy.* Trans. John W. Harvey. London: Oxford UP, 1958.

Ovid, *The xv. Bookes of P. Ouidius Naso, entytuled Metamorphosis, translated . . . by Arthyr Golding*. London, 1567.

Parry, Graham. "John Evelyn as Hortulan Saint." Leslie and Raylor 130–50.

Plutarch. *The Philosophie, commonlie called, The Morals*. Trans. Philémon Holland. London, 1603.

Ray, John. *Philosophical Letters*. London, 1718.

Rudrum, Alan. "Henry Vaughan, The Liberation of the Creatures, and Seventeenth-Century English Calvinism." *The Seventeenth Century* 4 (1989): 33–54.

Samuel Johnson Discovers the Arctic: A Reading of a "Greenland Tale" as Arctic Literature

William C. Horne

Johnson and the Arctic

In his introduction to an anthology of nature poems, Robert Bly generalizes: "I decided to begin at the eighteenth century, when the poets were least interested in nature. It was the peak of human arrogance. Bushes were clipped to resemble carriages, poets dismissed the intensity and detail of nature and talked instead of idealizations or 'goddesses,' empires were breeding, the pride in human reason deformed all poetry and culture" (3).

We should be suspicious of sweeping generalizations such as Bly's that tar an entire literary era. However, setting aside his overstatement for rhetorical effect, Bly's assertions may have some truth to them. Take, for example, the writings of Samuel Johnson, that preponderant literary figure of the mid-eighteenth century. Johnson's favorite theme, the vanity of human wishes, is hammered home in his poems, his prose narrative *The History of Rasselas,* his literary criticism, and his periodical essays in *The Rambler, The Adventurer,* and *The Idler.* Showing us repeatedly that, as the saying goes, "you can't always get what you want," Johnson excoriates intellectual pride and literary vanity. Yet he relies egoistically on his reason in passing judgment on all he observes. And what he observes, almost exclusively, is the behavior of humans—the manners, literary fashions, and aspirations of "mankind":

> Let observation with extensive view,
> Survey mankind, from China to Peru;

Remark each anxious toil, each eager strife,
And watch the busy scenes of crowded life;
"The Vanity of Human Wishes"
1–4 in *Poems* 91–92)

Bly is right when he says the "intensity and detail of nature" is not Johnson's focus. In *Rasselas*, the teacher Imlac says to his student Rasselas: "The business of a poet . . . is to examine, not the individual, but the species; to remark general properties and large appearances. He does not number the streaks of the tulip, or describe the different shades in the verdure of the forest" (Johnson 527).

Even so, in defense of the eighteenth century's empirical curiosity about the natural world, it must be said it was a great age of travel writing. As Thomas M. Curley points outs, "Between 1660 and 1800 eight encyclopedic collections and forty-five smaller compilations appeared in England. Beside the major works, there were thousands of individual accounts and miscellanies of local tours, distant expeditions, and Continental travels" (53). And the authors of these voyages and journeys were careful to study, as Imlac notes, "all the appearances of nature" and "every country" (Johnson, *Rasselas* 527).

If many of the best writers of the eighteenth century such as Daniel Defoe, Jonathan Swift, James Thomson, Oliver Goldsmith, and Tobias Smollett show the influence of travel writing, Samuel Johnson's life and work set a standard: "Few authors read more widely in travel books, wrote more wisely about them, or made them serve more ends in morality and fiction than he. The incredible range and amount of his reading take in virtually the entire history of travel literature up to his own time" (Curley 51). Johnson's first major prose publication was a translation in 1735 of *Father Lobo's Voyage to Abyssinia*. His philosophical fable *The History of Rasselas* (1759) takes the form of an oriental tale and draws on Father Lobo's *Voyage*. Johnson traveled to Wales in 1774, to France with his close friends the Thrales in 1775, and to the highlands of Scotland with James Boswell in 1773. Johnson's observations of Scotland he recorded in *A Journey to the Western Islands of Scotland* (1775).

Bly might dismiss Johnson's interest in travel as civilization-centered, as a manifestation of the age's voracious appetite for new experiences just as its empire builders were acquiring land and riches in their pursuit of material happiness. But Johnson's curiosity about exotic locations is not only an expression of his age's acquisitive appetites; at times it carries as a sub-current a romantic sense of wonder, a respect for the other. Johnson approved the extension of what he and his contemporaries regarded as the benefits of civilization to so-called primitive societies, but he attacked throughout his life the abuses of European imperialism.

Arctic exploration and Johnson's fascination with it is an interesting case in point. Initiated by Martin Frobisher at the end of Elizabeth's reign, arctic exploration and the search for the Northwest Passage developed throughout the seventeenth century and increased somewhat in intensity during Johnson's lifetime. Arctic activity that interested Johnson included the missionary efforts of the Moravian Hans Egede in Greenland in the 1720s and 1730s, the naturalist Joseph Banks's expedition to Iceland in 1768, and the aborted polar voyage of Constantine Phipps in 1773 (Curley 18). In his thirties and forties, Johnson developed a romantic curiosity about the Arctic. Indications include his recommendation of the study of polar geography in his preface to the *Preceptor* (1748) and his short account of Greenland in his review of Thomas Birch's *History of the Royal Society of London* for *Literary Magazine* (May 1756). In *Boswell's Life of Johnson,* for March 1752, Boswell mentions in passing talk of Johnson's traveling to Iceland with his close friend Dr. Richard Bathurst. Boswell says the trip would probably have happened had the intended traveling companion lived (171).[1]

As Arthur Sherbo shows, Johnson read Egede's *A Description of Greenland* (1745) assiduously, and he drew from it heavily in preparing the "Greenland Tale" for *The Rambler* (no. 186, 28 December 1751, 210–15; no. 187, 31 December 1751, 215–20). Johnson's handling of the Arctic and its "noble savages" in his "Greenland Tale" is much more than another treatment of the vanity-of-human-wishes theme. From an ecocritical perspective, we can read Johnson's narrative in terms of a two-part tradition of nineteenth- and twentieth-century exploratory and metaexploratory works, which I call arctic literature. From this perspective, not only does Johnson anticipate the curiosity of the great arctic explorers but his handling of the noble savage motif offers a critique of materialism and also imperialistic exploitation of the environment.

The Two Traditions of Arctic Literature

I propose we consider Johnson's "Greenland Tale" a work of arctic literature, a genre whose most notable texts embody a conflict between the actualities of the arctic environment and human dreams, between the harsh compulsions of nature and the escapist fantasies or artistic visions that the exotic, mysterious, and primitive in the Arctic evoke from visitors who write about it. Drawing on this definition, arctic literature can be divided into two main traditions. First, the exploratory tradition encompasses the great exploration accounts of the late eighteenth through the early twentieth centuries, those, for example, of Samuel Hearne, Sir John Franklin, Elisha Kent Kane, Robert Scott, and Ernest Shackleton. In these accounts the conflict between the actualities of arctic nature and the vision or codes of the encounterers usually occurs in the perception of the leader or narrator. Exploratory tradition accounts are full of situations in which visitors from the south are baffled or deluded by physical features of the Arctic or by the behavior and culture of indigenous people. Second, the metaexploratory tradition, in contrast, is composed of ideologically focused nature descriptions, narratives, and quasi-fictions, usually of the twentieth century. The latter may treat the Arctic firsthand but use it as a forum for social, environmental, or philosophical commentary. In these works the dream-actuality conflict can be a premise of the narrative or fiction, or it may be the announced theme.

Since Johnson's "Greenland Tale" is not an exploration narrative or even a firsthand account of the Arctic, it cannot, technically, be placed in the exploratory tradition. Even so, we can read it as a preface to the tradition, as Johnson's personal (imaginary) discovery of the Arctic. Johnson's tale does exhibit an empirical curiosity and an exotic, romantic flavoring that carries the imagination of its readers toward arctic actuality, almost in spite of Johnson's vanity-of-human-wishes moralizing. Using Egede's account as a map, Johnson the explorer guides readers through his arctic dreamscape.

Intriguingly, the "Greenland Tale" is more closely linked with the metaexploratory tradition. Its focus is ideological and reminiscent of the texts in this tradition. Johnson's use of the "Greenland Tale" as a forum for his responses to the primitive gives him a place in the long-standing debate on whether the Arctic and its indigenous inhabitants should be seen in their idealized or actual roles.

Johnson's tale is thus linked thematically with such metaexploratory texts as Robert Marshall's utopian *Arctic Village* (1940); Barry Lopez's epistemological *Arctic Dreams* (1986); William T. Vollman's *The Rifles* (1994, the sixth of his *Seven Dreams: A Book of North American Landscapes)*; and *The Last Light Breaking* (1993), a critical utopia by the Alaskan writer Nick Jans.

No doubt the most significant question in this modern tradition concerns the status of people indigenous to the Arctic, the Inuits and the northern Indians. Today, most arctic people no longer live directly off the land; they have moved into villages where they have adopted many of the material benefits and cultural attitudes of civilization as well its many-headed problems. The modern tradition of arctic literature is an inheritor of the tendency, given impetus largely by Jean-Jacques Rousseau, to romanticize the indigenous as noble savages or primitives living in harmony with their environment. Running counter to this is the inclination, also exhibited in the modern tradition, to describe indigenous people more naturalistically—naifs who have bought into or have been corrupted by the problematic or ugly manifestations of the American dream, such as Pampers and prepared food, television and VCRs, alcohol and drugs, and oil drilling and massive mining operations on the North Slope.

Closest to Johnson in his conflicted handling of the noble savage motif are the contradictory portrayals of modern Inupiat village life in *The Last Light Breaking* by Nick Jans, a white outsider who became a schoolteacher and long-term resident of Ambler, Alaska. On the one hand, Jans pays loving tribute to the positive forces of community that bind together an Inuit village. In several sections, Jans idealizes Inuit elders who preserve the quasi-traditional ways of fishing and hunting, even if they use outboard motors or snowmobiles. But, on the other hand, Jans can also be direct, even satiric at times, in describing the social, cultural, and environmental problems that consumerism and exploitation of the environment have brought to Alaska's northwestern Arctic.

Although grounded in eighteenth-century moralization and essentially civilization-centered in its valuation of nature, Johnson's critical handling of the idea of the primitive in his tale raises some of the same questions that the metaexploratory tradition does in trying to decide whether people indigenous to the Arctic are to be romanticized for their harmonious or respectful connection with the arctic environment or criticized for their corruption by civilization, specifically by consumerism that encourages exploitation of the environment for profit. Let us look more specifically at how the dream-actuality conflict in Johnson's "Greenland Tale" serves as a preface to the exploratory tradition and places it in the metaexploratory, or second, tradition.

A "Greenland Tale" as Arctic Literature

Ostensibly just another expression of the vanity-of-human-wishes theme, the "Greenland Tale," as critics have suggested, uses the primitive setting as a vehicle for direct moralizing about the human condition and the possibility of achieving happiness. As with other exotic settings in Johnson's work (Abyssinia in *Rasselas*, for example), the Greenland setting appears less than naturalistic. It is not mainly intended to give the reader the actualities of surviving in the Arctic as does, for example, Robert Flaherty's classic film *Nanook of the North* (1922). Johnson wanted to communicate a lesson to those who lived in the comparative luxury of English society of the late eighteenth century, a society in which the average person's expectations of material happiness were escalating. The "Greenland Tale" therefore shows us through the "dilatory coyness" of the charming Ajut toward her "fond lover," Anningait, that the failure to embrace a present good for some imagined better future can easily result in total unhappiness.

In the tale, Ajut delays accepting the hand in marriage of Anningait, proposing as "a trail of his constancy" that he renew his request at the end of the summer. Warning Ajut that because of fish migrations he must temporarily move away and that his return might be prevented by forces of nature in their harsh environment, Anningait is unable to persuade her to marry and accompany him. He thus departs sorrowfully from her on his expedition, bravely harpooning whales to increase his store. In the meantime, Ajut's beauty catches the eye of Norngsuk, a bachelor of wealth greater than Anningait's. When Ajut refuses Norngsuk's gifts, he has "recourse to stratagem" and persuades Ajut's parents to promise her to him in marriage. Ajut runs to meet the large boat laden with its catch on which Anningait should have returned, but she is informed that Anningait, impatient to be rejoined with his love, had paddled ahead in a smaller boat. Desperate and distracted that Anningait has not yet returned, Ajut tells onlookers she is going in search of him; she rows out alone and is seen no more. The tragic fate of both lovers "gave occasion to various fictions and conjectures," but, says Johnson, most are of the opinion that they are "in that part of the land of souls where the sun never sets, where oil is always fresh, and provisions always warm" (220).

By his "Greenland Tale," Johnson wanted to show his readers that even a primitive of Greenland such as Ajut, who might be expected to be inured to the harshness of present necessity and not to be a dreamer, can allow material expectation motivated by pride to poison her and Anningait's lives. In civilized society as well as in arctic society, Johnson would illustrate for us, human nature can be deluded by vain wishes.

Yet is the moral the only reason for paying attention to Johnson's "Greenland Tale"? In *The Rambler* Johnson observes: "Yet learned curiosity is known to have found its way into these abodes of poverty and gloom: Lapland and Iceland have their historians, their criticks, and their poets; and love, that extends its dominion wherever humanity can be found, perhaps exerts the same power in the Greenlander's hut as in the palaces of eastern monarchs" (no. 186, 212). Johnson's "Greenland Tale" may be more than his moralizations on the dominion of love in primitive as well as civilized lands. We can tell from the voraciousness with which he devoured Egede and appropriated its details that Johnson was fascinated with the arctic landscape and its indigenous Greenlanders. As Curtis B. Bradford tells us, Johnson's use of Egede's *Description of Greenland* in his "Greenland Tale" is the only instance in *The Rambler* in which Johnson borrows so extensively and openly from a single source. As Johnson discovers the Arctic via Egede's account, the "learned curiosity" may well be Johnson's own (see 212). It is this that makes Johnson's "Greenland Tale" a preface to the exploratory tradition.

Most revealing of Johnson's imaginary journeying is the comparative specificity of reference to the Arctic: to the sometimes foggy Greenland weather and to its icy and mountainous topography; to Arctic flora such as willows and thyme and to fauna such as swans, foxes, hares, deer, bear, roefish, porpoises, seals, whales, morses (or walruses), and sea unicorns (or narwhals); to details of Inuit living conditions such as using animal skins for clothing or tents and gathering moss for the winter lamps and dried grass to line the boots; to techniques of hunting and fishing; and to Inuit cultural institutions such as the Angekkok, or diviner (216, 218, passim). Even the names have an authentic Inuit sound because Johnson did not coin them but borrowed them directly from Egede.[2]

In Johnson's use of Egede, we see that although he occasionally simplified or poetically heightened Egede's language, he almost always took great care to be authentic. This, I argue, cannot be accounted for simply by Johnson's depending on Egede to achieve fictional verisimilitude. Johnson's fascination with specific detail from Egede, the "streaks" of the Arctic "tulip," as it were, goes well beyond what he would have needed to give his eighteenth-century English readers a sense of arctic actuality. The "Greenland Tale" clearly has a subtext vis-à-vis Johnson's imaginative exploration of the Arctic using Egede's work as a map (see Curley 19).

If Johnson's imaginative appropriation of the details of Egede's Greenland makes a "Greenland Tale" into a preface to the exploratory tradition as Johnson in effect discovers the Arctic, his striking contradiction of Egede's conclusion leads us to view the "Greenland Tale" as participating in the metaexploratory tradition.

After more than two hundred pages of empirically based observations of Greenland flora and fauna and the physical appearance, customs, and culture of its indigenous inhabitants, Hans Egede concludes his *Description of Greenland* with an unexpectedly romantic-sounding assertion:

> Their desires do not extend further than to necessary things . . . . Is not this the greatest happiness of this life? O happy people! What better things can one wish you, than what you already possess? Have you no riches? Yet poverty does not trouble you. Have you no superfluity? Yet you suffer no want. Is there no pomp and pride to be seen among you? Neither is there any slight or scorn to be met with. . . . And what is happier than contentedness? But one thing is yet wanting: I mean, the saving knowledge of God and his dear son Christ Jesus, in which alone consists eternal life and happiness. (224–25)

Egede's concluding points could not be stated more prominently. Yet in *The Rambler* Johnson's central theme, even more unmistakable than Egede's, is that vain dreaming and other "unnecessary" passions flourish in the Arctic just as they do everywhere else (no. 186, 212; no. 187). Indeed, says Johnson, one might expect that the residents of the Arctic are controlled by the requirements of their environment to such an extent that they have no time for futile dreaming and the passions that, "in lands of plenty, influence conduct and diversify characters" (212). Not so, says Johnson: "Learned curiosity is known to have found its way into these abodes of poverty and gloom: Lapland and Iceland have their historians, and their criticks, and their poets; and love, that extends its dominion wherever humanity can be found, perhaps exerts the same power in the Greenlander's hut as in the palaces of eastern monarchs" (212).

Why does Johnson, who took many specific hints and details from Egede, sometimes verbatim, explicitly contradict his most prominent point? Most obvious, Johnson may have contradicted Egede in order to promulgate his favorite theme: the vanity of human wishes. Johnson's desire to use Greenland as a vehicle for this theme is revealed in the third paragraph of *The Rambler,* where he says that thinking on the unpleasantness of the Arctic will help the inhabitant of England "recover his tranquillity" and "reflect how much he owes to providence that he is not placed in Greenland or Siberia" (no. 186, 212). In 1751, as Walter Jackson Bate notes, Johnson had many personal problems from which he might have dreamed of escaping. These include a gravely ill, alcoholic wife, progress on his dictionary so slow that his publishers were disturbed, and consequent indebtedness (254). Thinking of how unpleasant it would be to live in Greenland may have been Johnson's way of reconciling himself to the difficulties of his life in England, and he recommends this method to his readers.

Another reason Johnson may have contradicted Egede was because he believed his theme paved the way for Christian apologetics more solidly than Egede's question and reply. If, Johnson may have reasoned, he showed his readers that vain desires and passions are a human universal, then they may be more open to the argument that their only lasting happiness is in Christian belief. Suggesting, as Egede does, that there is a land where the indigenous are basically content can encourage English readers to be unhappy with their present situation. This is the problem, Johnson implies, with stories of tropical paradises (no. 186). Johnson seems intent on not allowing his "Greenland Tale" to become similarly a vehicle for romantic escapism.

We can grant that Johnson contradicted Egede because he wished to promulgate his vanity-of-human-wishes theme and also because as a Christian Johnson believed that all humans, even those he regarded as primitives, live in a fallen state. A more pertinent explanation is that Johnson was taking a position in Europe's long-standing noble savage debate, a debate in which he would participate in his conversations and writings for much of his life. As the "Greenland Tale" of 1751 takes a position, albeit a conflicted one, in the noble savage debate, it also takes a place in the metaexploratory tradition.

Johnson tended to be distrustful of those who idealized the happiness of life in primitive societies, yet he allowed himself to admire at times the comparative nobility and simplicity of such societies. Throughout his life, Johnson's attitude toward the noble savage was dichotomous, although he seems to have suppressed his romantic views more strenuously as he got older. In Johnson's *Life of Drake* (1740), for example, he praises Drake for "treating the inhabitants" of the countries he visited "with kindness and generosity . . . to the neglect of which may be attributed many of the errors suffered by our sailors in distant countries, which are generally ascribed, rather to the effects of wickedness of our commanders than the barbarity of the natives who seldom fall upon any unless they have first been plundered or insulted" (*Reviews* 340). On Johnson's observations in his *Life of Drake*, Curley tells us, Johnson's "abhorrence of primitive ignorance and squalor is qualified by generous praise of primitive simplicity, strength, native intelligence, and benevolence far surpassing the depravity of European oppressors" (63).

In contrast, in July 1763, in an interchange Boswell recorded, Johnson, as was his wont, picks a side in the noble savage debate and argues to win.[3] Taking on what he describes as Rousseau's paradox in his 1755 "A Dissertation on the Origin and Foundation of the Inequality of Mankind," Johnson sets out to demolish it. He may have done so for political and philosophical as well as, perhaps, for more personal reasons. Whereas Rousseau (as had Egede earlier) espoused the position that primitive societies are freer and happier in what he saw as their lack of social structure and possessions, Johnson in 1763 characterizes such a position as threatening to the existing socioeconomic order. He sees Rousseau's stance as incipiently revolutionary.

Responding to George Dempster's observation that "the advantages of fortune and rank were nothing to a wise man, who ought to value only merit," Johnson says:

> If a man were a savage, living in the woods by himself, this might be true; but in civilized society we all depend upon each other, and our happiness is very much owing to the good opinion of mankind. Now, Sir, in civilized society, external advantages make us more respected. A man with a good coat upon his back meets with a better reception than he who has a bad one. . . . Pound St. Paul's Church into atoms, and consider any single atom; it is, to be sure, good for nothing: but, put all these atoms together, and you have St. Paul's Church. So it is with human felicity, which is made up of many ingredients. . . . And, Sir, if six hundred pounds a year procure a man more consequence, and, of course, more happiness than six pounds a year, the same proportion will hold as to six thousand, and so on as far as opulence can be carried. Perhaps he who has a large fortune may not be so happy as he who has a small one; but that must proceed from other cause than his having the large fortune: for, *caeteris paribus,* he who is rich in a civilized society, must be happier than he who is poor. (Boswell 311)

As Johnson counters Rousseau's paradox, he is willing to grant the happiness of the primitive in a hypothetical natural state: "If a man were a savage, living in the woods by himself, this might be true." However, Johnson opposes the imperative to reform the corruptions and tyrannies of civilization that is implicit in the contrast of the natural and civilized orders central to Rousseau's 1755 essay. Johnson in 1763, the year Boswell first met him, was fifty-four, had achieved a measure of literary fame, and had recently been granted a pension of £300 a year by the government. Although the pension was not large, Johnson saw himself as affluent (see Bate 356). In 1763, property and riches were for Johnson a source of happiness, not the chief cause of inequality and misery as Rousseau would have them.

In 1751, at the time he wrote the "Greenland Tale," Johnson's position on the noble savage was similarly conflicted. But perhaps Johnson had not then moved as far as he would in 1763 to suppress his earlier tendency to romanticize the nobility of primitives and to deplore the imperialistic abuses of civilization. Are Anningait and Ajut heroic primitives to be romanticized or are they people who have the same vain, materialistic desires as those in England? If an English person visited such a society for a time, would he or she find the indigenous to be happy, or would the person discover that even in the Arctic "you can't always get what you want." In the "Greenland Tale" Johnson indulges his "learned curiosity" about Greenlanders, romanticizing them in the process. Imaginary journeying leads to actual plans for travel. And then at some point Johnson must have realized that such a trip would be physically demanding as well as expensive. With all the problems he faced in 1751, he even then may have been trying to steel himself to the realization that arctic travel would not be possible. Johnson was pushing aside his dream of the heroic primitive at the same time he was nurturing it.[4]

In his "Greenland Tale," Johnson does allow himself some latitude to romanticize the heroic primitive. The important point, however, is that he does so but then chooses to undercut it by presenting Greenland society as essentially a civilized order. Anningait and Ajut are not Rousseauian savages surviving as individuals in the wild but rather are complicated people living in a society made up of numerous interdependent elements, just as St. Paul's Church is composed of many atoms.

In the "Greenland Tale," the reader can discover numerous manifestations of the heroic primitive, although not always unqualified ones. Anningait places before Ajut the tail of a whale, a Greenland delicacy as Egede explains. He also sends her his heroic ode that concludes with an epic boast threatening anyone who would hinder his "union with Ajut" (213). While Ajut awaits the return of Anningait, she busies herself with the feminine employments of an Inuit woman and sings a romantic song praying for superhuman powers for her lover. This sort of material anticipates the celebration of the heroic primitive in poems such as MacPherson's *Fingal* (1762) and *Ossian* (1765); yet we know how suspicious Johnson was later of MacPherson's effort to lend historical authority to his fictions (see Boswell 588). This was not just because MacPherson was a literary forger but because he set up the heroic primitive as superior to the civilized, a position that, as we saw in the case of Rousseau, Johnson came to hold as pernicious.

It must be granted that in the deaths of Anningait and then Ajut, there is a haunting romantic-tragic mood that draws on both primitive and civilized arctic mythology. In his last paragraph treating the fate of the lovers, Johnson initially entertains but rejects the pantheistic fictions that they are transmogrified into stars or that they become part of arctic flora and fauna, he as a genius of the rocks and she as a mermaid. Yet the final image places the departed lovers in an arctic paradise: "that part of the land of souls where the sun never sets, where oil is always fresh, and provisions always warm" (220). Arctic mythology, even as late as the nineteenth century, imagined that if one penetrates deeply enough into the Arctic, one will discover at its center an oasis of warm water and semitropical vegetation. Curiously, the romantic myth on which Johnson may be drawing in his portrayal of an arctic paradise could be based on the existence of polynyas, or large areas of persistent open water in sea ice where wildlife flourish. Even so, Johnson unmistakably presents the myth as a fiction.

In spite of muted and deflected romantic elements in a "Greenland Tale," the gist of it is cautionary and decidedly unromantic. Its thrust is at base satiric: in her coquetry induced by vanity or affectation, Ajut is a descendant of the foolishly romantic women characters treated as a moral warning in a satiric subgenre I have called elsewhere the woman's progress poem.[5]

In Johnson's "Greenland Tale" the romantic and satiric elements stand beside one another and in the final analysis may not quite gel. The dream-actuality conflict of arctic literature operates ambiguously, even paradoxically, both in the tale's theme and ideology and also in its autobiographical subtext. The tale's ostensible moral is that humans everywhere, even in the Arctic, tend to delude themselves by vain dreams. Johnson is deeply suspicious of the philosophical glorification of the primitive that suggests that the so-called uncivilized is somehow exempt from the socioeconomic compulsions of human society and the delusions of human imagination. Reading the subtext of the tale, we can see that Johnson must have had his romantic dreams of the heroic primitive, dreams that he evidently struggled to bring within the compass of his conservative ideology and what was physically and financially practical for him.

Conclusions

Reacting to the image of Greenlanders as noble savages, Johnson, in keeping with the writers of the modern metaexploratory tradition, has a conflicted response, and in his "Greenland Tale," similar to Nick Jans in *The Last Light Breaking,* he has something to say to us about the impact of consumerism and the pressures for environmental degradation in present-day arctic society. It may be objected that since Johnson had no firsthand experience of indigenous arctic people, not to speak of the Inuits and the northern Indians of today, his portrayal of them has no validity. However, it may be seen to have truth by deduction if not by induction.

If, as Johnson would have it, a defining desire of all who are civilized is for material happiness and since present-day arctic people must be acknowledged to be civilized, then they must be seen to share this desire. As such, they should not be held to a higher standard than the rest of us. As participants in the civilized order, we must therefore criticize ourselves as much as we do them for consumerism and willingness to allow environmental exploitation. From Johnson's Christian point of view, since all humans on this earth have fallen from innocence, all must share in the guilt for greed and materialism. But since imperialism is greed on a grand scale, it must have been for Johnson all the more culpable. And if indigenous people have been corrupted by imperialism, it is civilization that bears the greater guilt (see Curley 36). As Johnson in *The Idler* has an Indian chief say as he watches the British army move up the St. Lawrence toward Quebec: "'Their arts they have studiously concealed from us. Their treaties are only to deceive, and their traffick only to defraud us'" (no. 81, 3 November 1759, qtd. in Greene 59).

As a Gwich'n native living in Kaktovic on the North Slope said to me when I questioned him about the majority of the Kaktovic Inupiats' support for Congress's opening the 1002 area of the Arctic National Wildlife Refuge to oil drilling: "First of all, let me ask you if you drive a car, if you consume petroleum products." Johnson would have approved of such a question if only because of its fairness. As Johnson said concerning slavery in America, "How is it that we hear the loudest *yelps* for liberty among the drivers of negroes?" (qtd. in Boswell 876; appeared originally in *Taxation No Tyranny* [1775]). If we romanticize indigenous people as heroic primitives, then we create an idealized valuation by which to criticize our consumerism and greed. However, we may have a difficult time reconciling this dream with the materialistic desires of many arctic people, passions Johnson would not have been surprised to discover are remarkably similar to the corrupted materialistic desires of many North Americans living below the Arctic Circle.

Notes

1. For another instance of such talk, see Curley 228. Richard Bathurst had taken a medical degree at Cambridge, but his practice did not flourish. "Bathurst . . . became a physician in the navy and died of fever, like hundreds of others, in the expedition against Havana, in Cuba (October 1762)" (Bate 269). Johnson was deeply saddened by the sacrifice of his friend to this imperialistic venture.

March 1752, the date when Boswell mentions Johnson's talk with Bathurst of traveling to Iceland, was the month when Tetty, Johnson's wife, died. Tetty at this time was distancing her herself from Johnson. She was often away at Hampstead and frequently was confined to bed due to alcoholism and illness. At this time Johnson depended heavily on his friendship with Bathurst to alleviate his loneliness; even during visits to Hampstead he talked late into night with Bathurst, who for a while lived nearby (Bate 263). His dependence must have increased after Tetty's death.

2. Arthur Sherbo does this with minute care for almost all of Johnson's borrowings from Egede (577–79). For the composition of odes, see Egede 157 (Sherbo 577).

3. Even as late as 1773, Johnson exhibits some diffidence on this issue and seems willing to argue on either side. In his letter to Hester Thrale of 25 August 1773, Johnson reports on a discussion he had had four days earlier with Lord Monbodo: "the Scotch Judge who has lately written a strange book about the origin of Language, in which he traces Monkeys up to Men, . . . says that in some countries the human Species have tails like other beasts." Johnson continues his anecdote: "I hope, we parted friends, for we agreed pretty well only we differed in adjusting the claims of merit between a Shopkeeper of London, and a Savage of the American wilderness. Our opinions were, I think, maintained on both sides without full conviction; Monbodo declared boldly for the Savage, and I *perhaps for that reason* sided with the Citizen" (*The Letters of Samuel Johnson* 2.57; emphasis added).

4. Johnson's journey to the Hebrides of Scotland in 1773 with Boswell might be seen as his substitute for arctic travel.

5. Examples of such a character are Jonathan Swift's Phillis (in "Phillis, or, The Progress of Love" [1727]) and Henry Fielding's Leonora, the heroine of "The Unfortunate Jilt" in *Joseph Andrews* (1742). See Horne 119–28.

Works Cited

Bate, W[alter] Jackson. *Samuel Johnson*. New York: Harcourt Brace, 1975.

Bly, Robert. Introduction. *News of the Universe: poems of twofold consciousness*. San Francisco: Sierra Club, 1980.

Boswell, James. *Boswell's Life of Johnson*. New Ed. London: Oxford UP, 1953.

Bradford, Curtis B. "Samuel Johnson's *Rambler*." Diss. Yale U, 1937.

Curley, Thomas M. *Samuel Johnson and the Age of Travel*. Athens: U of Georgia P, 1976.

Egede, Hans. *A Description of Greenland*. 1818. 2nd ed. Millwood, NY: Kraus, 1973.

Horne, William C. *Making a Heaven of Hell: The Problem of the Companionate Ideal in English Marriage Poetry, 1650–1800*. Athens: U of Georgia P, 1993.

Greene, Donald J. "Samuel Johnson and the Great War for Empire." *English Writers of the Eighteenth Century*. Ed. John H. Middendorf. New York: Columbia UP, 1971. 37–68.

Jans, Nick. *The Last Light Breaking: Living among Alaska's Inupiat Eskimos*. Seattle: Alaska Northwest, 1993.

Johnson, Samuel. *Poems*. Ed. E. L. McAdam Jr. and George Milne. New Haven: Yale UP, 1964. Vol. 6 of *The Yale Edition of the Works of Samuel Johnson*.

———. *The Letters of Samuel Johnson*. Ed. Bruce Redford. Vol. 2 (1773–1776). Princeton: Princeton UP, 1992.

———. *The Rambler*. Ed. W. J. Bate and Albrecht B. Strauss. New Haven: Yale UP, 1969. Vol. 5 of *The Yale Edition of the Works of Samuel Johnson*.

———. *Rasselas, Poems, and Selected Prose*. Ed. Bertrand H. Bronson. New York: Holt, 1952.

———. *Reviews, Political Tracts, and Lives of Eminent Persons*. Vol. 6 of *The Works of Samuel Johnson*. Oxford: W. Pickering, 1825. 11 vols.

Rousseau, Jean-Jacques. "A Dissertation on the Origin and Foundation of the Inequality of Mankind." 1755. *Great Books of the Western World*. Ed. Robert Maynard Hutchins. Vol. 38. Chicago: Encyclopedia Britannica, 1952. 333–66.

Sherbo, Arthur. "The Making of *Ramblers* 186 and 187." *PMLA* 67 (1952): 575–80.

Before Nature Writing: Discourses of Colonial American Natural History

Michael P. Branch

> Sometimes a lost man will be so beside himself that he will not
> have sense enough to trace back his own tracks in the snow.
> —Henry David Thoreau, *The Journal of Henry D. Thoreau*

Tracing Back Tracks

Because humans have always used art to comprehend, mediate, and express their relationship to the nonhuman world, it may be said that some form of nature writing has long been a significant artifact of human culture. In critical practice, however, the term "nature writing" has usually been reserved for a brand of nature representation that is deemed literary, written in the speculative personal voice, and presented in the form of the nonfiction essay. Such nature writing is frequently pastoral or romantic in its philosophical assumptions, tends to be modern or even ecological in its sensibility, and is often in service to an explicit or implicit preservationist agenda.

Limited by this circumscribed generic definition of nature writing, most critical studies of American environmental literature examine works written since the mid-nineteenth century, often citing Henry David Thoreau as the progenitor of the American nature writing tradition. Thoreau, however, was explicit in his discussion of the many earlier American literary natural historians on whose work he built. Unlike Thoreau, who deeply appreciated the scientific and literary value of colonial natural history, many ecocritics would find it difficult to name even a few of the important writers on nature who worked in the nearly two centuries between the settlement of the colonies and the establishment of American political sovereignty.

This state of ecocritical affairs may simply be a consequence of the fact that the current renaissance in nature writing studies has been inspired by a particularly modern, ecological sensibility—one shaped in response to the accelerated degradation of American environments during the twentieth century. But it is profitable to consider other reasons why we have hesitated to critically examine earlier American writing about nature. First, our restricted generic definition of nature writing as the nonfiction personal essay has discouraged us from considering colonial writing about nature, which usually takes less familiar rhetorical forms such as the relation, report, sermon, tract, letter, providential history, spiritual autobiography, or personal diary. Second, we may also fear to engage writers whose ideology threatens or offends our sensibilities; yet colonial writers are typically so orthodox in their Christianity or so anthropocentric in their natural philosophy that we may be discomforted by their approach to nature. Third, we may be uncertain about how to discuss nature writing from the period before it became identifiably "American"; yet colonial natural history is not only written before America gained political sovereignty and, subsequently, national identity, it is also frequently written by Europeans who are only temporary residents of or travelers in the colonies. Fourth, it may embarrass some ecocritics to take seriously representations of the natural world that are often flawed in matters of scientific accuracy, despite our knowing that even the giants of early natural history believed that snakes paralyzed their prey with a gaze, or that swallows hibernated underwater, or that insects spontaneously generated in the carcasses of animals. Finally, would-be students of early American nature writing have also been discouraged by the unfortunate dearth of scholarly editions in this field.

Recognizing these temporary limitations on the bailiwick of ecocriticism, it is time for scholars to examine environmental writing in different genres, from earlier periods, and organized according to various ideological assumptions. One of the richest areas of study in this second generation of ecocritical scholarship will be representations of nature in the diverse and challenging writing of the American colonial period—a body of work that rewards ecocritical attention in a number of ways. First, early American natural history writing gives us a window onto the American environment in its earliest stages of European occupation; it shows us "The vanished world of the unravaged American wilderness can be seen by us most clearly now through the eyes of pioneer naturalists" (Savage 23). Second, we need to rediscover and describe a minority tradition of American concern for the aesthetic, ecological, and spiritual value of the natural world; in recovering the "lost paradigm" of natural history (Regis xi), we find that many colonial writers anticipate modern environmental sensitivity in surprising and valuable ways. Third, we also need to study earlier American conceptions of nature in order to better understand how certain misguided and destructive ideas gained prominence in our culture; environmental degradation during the past half century has often been the consequence of earlier American environmental attitudes such as fear of wilderness; narrow adherence to theological imperatives of predestination and conversion; ignorance of functional interrelationships in ecological systems; and the sanctioned exploitation of women, indentured servants, Native Americans, and African Americans. Finally, we must explore the roots of contemporary American nature writing if we wish to gain a deeper and more enriching sense of our environmental literary history.

In order to give a sense of the generic and ideological range of colonial American natural history writing, I have chosen two major, representative works for closer examination: William Wood's *New England's Prospect* (1634) and Cotton Mather's *The Christian Philosopher* (1721). Wood's relation, written in the initial years of New England settlement, is a classic work of nature reportage distinguished for its ambitious, secular approach to cataloging and describing the wonders of the New World. Mather's tract, written nearly a century later at the dawn of the Linnaean age of Enlightenment science, is a monumental work of natural philosophy distinguished for its sustained, theological argument that close study of nature will demonstrate the existence and wisdom of God. These two important books—virtually unknown to ecocritics—antedate nearly all of the historical, scientific, and literary ideas that made possible the cultural accomplishments we usually refer to as "nature writing."

In order to appreciate the circumstances under which Wood, Mather, and other early American literary naturalists wrote, one must trace the tracks back to before the current heyday of nature writing as it is suggested by the cultural status of Barry Lopez, Wendell Berry, Gary Snyder, Terry Tempest Williams, and Rick Bass; to before the popular environmentalism that enabled the writing of Edward

Abbey; to before the advent of the scientific ecology that informed the work of Rachel Carson; and to before the literary environmental ethics introduced by Aldo Leopold. And then one must go back further, to before the wilderness preservation movement as personified by John Muir; to before the establishment of the national parks and forests associated with Theodore Roosevelt or the urban parks inspired by William Cullen Bryant and Andrew Jackson Downing; and to before the popular vogue for natural history so expertly tapped by John Burroughs. Now imagine attempting a comprehensive description of nature absent the benefit of Charles Darwin's insights into the origin of species and without the pioneering literary ecology of Henry Thoreau to suggest a rhetorical and epistemological model for one's work. Go back still further, before the romanticism and transcendentalism of Rousseau, Goethe, Coleridge, Wordsworth, Carlyle, and Emerson had placed its blessing on the literary celebration of nature; to before Herman Melville had described the wilderness of the sea and James Fenimore Cooper had depicted the wilderness of the forest; and to before the writing of John Wesley Powell and, even earlier, Lewis and Clark revealed something of the other side of the continent. Go back still further, to before the flowering of the literary natural history essay in the work of William Bartram; to before the pastoral agrarian philosophy of Thomas Jefferson and Hector St. John de Crevecoeur; and to before Enlightenment and Deist ideas of natural philosophy and their elaboration in the scientific accomplishments of Benjamin Franklin. Now go back to a time when natural history was not taught in American colleges or schools; when there were no American museums of natural history; when paper, books, and scientific instruments sufficient for the study of natural history were beyond the means of most colonists; and when few in the New World even imagined the idea of professional natural history. Keep going back to before the formation of the American Philosophical Society provided naturalists a sense of community and to before the British colonies of North America declared their independence from England. Now take a large step back to before the more than fifty editions and three hundred abridgments of Buffon's monumental, fifteen-volume *Histoire naturelle* (1749–1767) and, finally, one giant leap back to a time before Linnaeus's revolutionary *Species Plantarum* (1753) and tenth edition of the *Systema Naturae* (1758) provided naturalists a systematic means by which to observe, classify, and describe every living thing on Earth. Now imagine that, without the benefit of any of the achievements, institutions, and ideas mentioned above, one was to attempt to write natural history. In that imagination our story begins.

William Wood

Little is known about William Wood, including his birth and death dates. Wood's 1634 *New England's Prospect* is the earliest attempt at a comprehensive record of the manifold natural wonders of New England. His relation indicates that he arrived in Massachusetts in 1629 and returned to England in 1633, but remaining biographical information is speculative. Circumstantial evidence suggests that Wood was a member of John Endecott's scouting party, which arrived in Salem a year before John Winthrop disembarked with over a thousand settlers and a royal charter establishing the Massachusetts Bay Colony. Although it is unlikely that Wood was trained in what would then have been called "natural philosophy," his reference to the works of that "thrice memorable discoverer" Captain John Smith demonstrates his familiarity with other early accounts of North American landscape (25). Wood's secular approach to nature description and the notable infrequency of his references and allusions to Christian doctrine strongly suggest that he, although probably a scout for the colony, was not a Puritan. Wood is a particularly fine example of the subspecies of nature writer that David Scofield Wilson identifies as the "nature reporter" (1): neither scientist nor theologian, he is a gifted amateur—-a traveler, observer, scribe, and celebrant of the wonders of nature in the New World.

The full title of Wood's book is *New England's Prospect: A true, lively, and experimentall description of that part of America, commonly called New England: discovering the state of that countrie, both as it stands to our new-come English planters; and to the old Native Inhabitants: Laying downe that which may both enrich the knowledge of the mind-travelling Reader, or benefit the future Voyager.* The book, which appears to have been substantially composed after Wood's return to England, was first published in 1634; a second edition (with minor corrections by the author) followed in 1635, and a third appeared in 1639. The publication of three London editions in the 1630s suggests how interested early-seventeenth-century European readers were in news from the New World, and it attests to the literary and natural historical value of Wood's tract. American editions were published in 1764, 1865, and 1898, but the book remained out of print and obscure until the completion of Alden T. Vaughn's University of Massachusetts Press edition in 1977.

Although Wood was not alone in attempting to document the natural wonders of North America, several important qualities distinguish his book from other early accounts of New World landscape. Most significant to ecocritical studies is Wood's unusually explicit emphasis on the landscape, flora, and fauna of New England. Part 1 of *New England's Prospect* is divided into chapters we would now identify under the disciplinary headings of geography ("Of the Situation, Bays, Havens, and Inlets"); climatology ("Of the Seasons . . ."); geology ("Of the Nature of the Soil"), botany ("Of the Herbs . . ."); zoology ("Of the Beasts that Live on the Land"); ornithology ("Of the Birds and Fowls . . ."); and ichthyology ("Of Fish"). Only when this ambitious natural historical survey is complete does Wood turn his attention to three chapters describing the New England plantations and how best to prepare to settle them. Part 2 of the book focuses on Native American tribes and cultural practices, but even here natural history is prominent in many chapters (such as "Of Their Huntings" and "Of Their Fishings"). By comparison, many precolonial and colonial relations of North America were either narrow promotional tracts calculated to attract settlers or dense providential histories designed as evidence of God's favor upon the Chosen. Although Wood's relation includes elements recognizable from each of these cognate rhetorical forms, *New England's Prospect* is unprecedented in its deliberate, organized, and surprisingly thorough attempt to account for the natural productions of the New World. Indeed, it was not until the publication of *New England's Rarities Discovered* (1672) by John Josselyn that a more complete description of American landscape and creatures became available.

Like all pre-Linnaean natural histories, however, Wood's book contains its share of troubling scientific errors. Wood agreed with most early writers that the porcupine defends itself by darting its quills (44), and he repeated the common belief that the root of the snakeweed was effective as an antidote for rattlesnake venom (65); less forgivable is his unaccountable claim that wolves "have no joints from their head to the tail" (46). Despite these errors, so egregious by modern standards, Wood is considerably less credulous than most nature reporters of his day. Recall that he wrote during a period in which scientific rationalism had not yet banished folk legend from the realm of nature study, and that it was not until the later seventeenth century that unicorns, phoenixes, griffins, and other monsters of the medieval bestiary were routinely omitted from natural histories (Thomas 79–80). Indeed, it is Wood's concern with descriptive accuracy—a concern never to be taken for granted in writers of his day—that he claims inspired him to write *New England's Prospect*. "I have undertaken this work," he explains in his preface to the reader, "because there hath been many scandalous and false reports past upon the country. . . . But my conscience is to me a thousand witnesses that what I speak is the very truth, and this [book] will inform thee almost as fully concerning [the New World] as if thou wentest over to see it" (20). Considering the fabulous description so common in natural histories of his day, Wood does an admirable job of restricting himself, as the subtitle of his book promises, to "experimentall description"—reportage that is the product of his own experience and observation (15). He not only resists repeating many of the errors then common in natural history but also offers unusually perceptive speculations about bird migration, reptile hibernation, and the balance maintained by the predator-prey relationship between wolves and deer.

Because Wood is usually a reliable nature reporter, *New England's Prospect* gives a rare glimpse into the fecund wilderness of the New World, and, therefore, it provides a natural historical baseline against which later changes in New England ecology may be measured. We learn from Wood that wolves were so common as to be a genuine threat to settlers, that spring alewife runs in rivers were so large that two men could in two hours capture ten thousand fish with the use of a simple rock weir, that oysters were often a foot in length and clams were so plentiful that they were used to feed hogs, that lobsters grew to twenty pounds and that "their plenty makes them little esteemed and seldom eaten" (56). In one of the earliest accounts of the migration of the now-extinct passenger pigeon, Wood writes that "I have seen them fly as if the airy regiment had been pigeons, seeing neither beginning nor ending, length or breadth of these millions of millions" (50). *New England's Prospect* also teaches us important things about nature-culture interactions: the forest was kept clear of underbrush through regular burning by Native Americans of the region; beavers, thought to be extremely cunning, were seldom hunted successfully by settlers; colonial farmers often fertilized their fields with fish harvested by the thousands in setnets placed in tidal creeks.

Thoreau certainly appreciated the environmental historical value of Wood's book when, on 3 January 1855, he devoted a lengthy journal entry to comparing plant and animal populations of his day to the prevalence of the same flora and fauna as described in *New England's Prospect,* which he was then reading in the American edition of 1764. "The wild meadow-grasses appear to have grown more rankly in those days," writes Thoreau, noting that Wood "describes them as thick and long, as high as a man's middle; some as high as the shoulders" (7:132). Reading Wood's account of the strawberry, Thoreau observes that "Strawberries too were more abundant and large before they were so cornered up by cultivation" (7:136). And one can sense Thoreau's excitement as he reads in *New England's Prospect* of the commonness of various birds that had become rare or extinct in Massachusetts by the mid-nineteenth century: "Think of that! They had not only brant and common gray wild geese, but 'a white goose,' probably the snow goose" (7:136). Thus, the detail of Wood's natural historical report allows readers—whether Thoreau or ourselves—a valuable window onto the lost wildness of the New England coast.

As a literary natural historian, Wood is unusual for the lucidity, energy, and precision of his writing; in an age of terse and tortuous prose, *New England's Prospect* is remarkable for its readability. Self-conscious as a stylist and sensitive to readers' tastes, Wood explains that he has attempted to "spice" his "serious discourse" in order to make it "more pleasant" (20). Indeed, his descriptions are not simply detailed and visually rich but they are also dramatic, narrative, and even humorous. It is telling that Wood has added the descriptor "lively" to the subtitle of *New England's Prospect.* Unlike early New England literary luminaries such as William Bradford and John Winthrop, whose writing literally preached to the converted, Wood addresses himself to a larger audience of readers who craved both information and stories from the New World and who wished to go there as "mind-travelling Reader[s]" if not as "future Voyager[s]." Wood's unusual sensitivity to his audience is further suggested by a chapter that begins as follows: "To satisfy the curious eye of women readers, who otherwise might think their sex forgotten or not worthy a record, let them peruse these few lines" (112). In order to entertain as well as instruct his readers, Wood even relates important natural historical information through the rhetorical vehicle of lyric poetry. He composes and interpolates four catalog-poems, one each on trees (39), mammals (41–42), birds (48–49), and fish (with which he includes marine mammals) and shellfish (54). The lines opening the poem on trees give a sense of how Wood uses the entertainment of rhyme to combine a natural historical catalog with pertinent information about the distinctive qualities or human use of the species being described:

> Trees both in hills and plains in plenty be,
> The long-lived oak and mournful cypress tree,
> Sky-towering pines, and chestnuts coated rough,
> The lasting cedar, with the walnut tough;
> The rosin-dropping fir for masts in use,
> The boatmen seek for oars light, neat-grown spruce. (39)

Although he was never so bold a recruiter as was John Smith, it is true that Wood was to some degree a publicist for the New England plantations and that his descriptions of the plenitude of New World nature were partly intended to encourage settlement by the "future Voyager" mentioned in the subtitle of his book. Nevertheless, Wood's enthusiasm for the diversity and beauty of nature is sincere, and his customary focus on species useful to the "future Voyager" neither compromises the genuine pleasure he takes in describing nature nor reduces his admiration for the marvelous creatures he encounters in the New World. Wood writes that the "wisdom and understanding" of the beaver "almost conclude him a reasonable creature," and he notes approvingly that the beavers' industry results in "a firm and curious damhead which may draw admiration from wise, understanding men" (48). "The humbird is one of the wonders of the country," he marvels, "being no bigger than a hornet, yet hath all the dimensions of a bird, as bill and wings, with quills, spider-like legs, small claws. For color, she is as glorious as the rainbow" (50). Wood declares the flying squirrel—which he cannot resist describing although it is of no apparent human use—"a creature more for sight and wonderment than either pleasure and profit" (45). His admiration for the wisdom and wonder of the creatures is mirrored in his general enthusiasm for the wildness and fecundity of the New World landscape. He finds the climate of New England healthful, its soil rich, and its water so fine as to almost be preferable to beer. And Wood's relation maintains an authoritative and engaging first-person narration that combines observation, participation, and appreciation—three qualities vital to the tradition of American nature writing that evolved in the quarter millennium following the publication of *New England's Prospect.*

"What a strong and hearty but reckless, hit-or-miss style had some of the early writers of New England, like Josselyn and William Wood," writes Thoreau in his journal. "They are not to be caught napping by the wonders of Nature in a new country. . . . The strong new soil speaks through them. I have just been reading some in Wood's 'New England's Prospect.' . . . Certainly that generation stood nearer to nature, nearer to the facts, than this, and hence their books have more life in them." Using Wood as an occasion to remark on the historical and literary value of studying earlier American naturalists despite their scientific shortcomings, Thoreau further observes, "Sometimes a lost man will be so beside himself that he will not have sense enough to trace back his own tracks in the snow" (7:108–9).

Cotton Mather

Unlike William Wood, an obscure figure known only by a single book, Cotton Mather (1663–1728) was among the most recognized, influential, and prolific figures in colonial America. Widely read in all fields then engaged in by the intelligentsia on either side of the Atlantic, he published at least 450 works on every subject imaginable: from theology, history, and biography; to education, ethnography, and agriculture; to medicine, natural science, and even witchcraft. At the time of his death, Cotton Mather was plausibly the leading intellectual in the British colonies of America.

It is unfortunate that a figure of such intellectual range and accomplishments has often been dismissed on the grounds that he believed in witches and other occult forces. Ecocritics can scarcely afford such a critical stance, by which most precolonial and colonial writers on nature would be banished for their failure to conform to the standards of modern, rationalist science. We should remember that the separation of the now distinct epistemological paradigms we call "religion" and "science" is a relatively recent event in intellectual history and that crucial advances in human knowledge have frequently been offered by people whose understanding of the world encompassed both the things they could see and those they could not.

Although Mather was born in an era when nature study was still dominated by scholasticism and Peripatetic physics, he lived to see the dawn of the Enlightenment in the form of Newtonian science. As a transitional figure between the old ecclesiastical order and the new scientific worldview, he attempted to synthesize the insights of natural history with the Christian doctrine he had been ordained to preach. Mather enthusiastically proclaimed the study of nature a means of worship, and he was optimistic that advances in scientific knowledge would provide evidence of the divinity of the Creation, thus checking and perhaps reversing the troubling declension of orthodox religious faith so prevalent in early-eighteenth-century New England.

Believing in the power of science to purify his understanding of the Deity, Mather studied nature with religious enthusiasm and, as a result, was among the most accomplished natural philosophers of his day. As early as 1682 he published a paper describing his observations of a comet; in 1683 he helped form the Boston Philosophical Society, one of the earliest scientific societies in the New World; and in the early 1690s he preached several sermons on his understanding of nature as evidence of divinity (Solberg xxxv–xxxvi). Beginning in 1693 he worked tirelessly on his *"Biblia Americana"*—a still unpublished work that eventually ran to six thousand manuscript pages—in which he "sought to reconcile revelation with the new science and suggest 'scientific' explanations of biblical accounts" (Stearns 412). Cotton Mather's ambitious studies of both biblical and natural history clearly placed him among the elite virtuosi to whom his father had referred as the "Learned Men, of these later times, wherein light in things natural as well as divine hath been admirably discovered" (Miller 438).

Among Mather's most substantial contributions to natural science is his *"Curiosa Americana,"* a series of at least eighty-two letters he sent to the Royal Society of London between 1712 and 1724. These letters address a range of subjects related to North American climate, landscape, flora, fauna, and indigenous inhabitants. While many letters describe the geography and wildlife of New England, some also speculate on poorly understood natural phenomena such as fossils, hurricanes, lightning, and earthquakes. Although several of Mather's letters met with skepticism among the Fellows, others were admired and subsequently published or extracted in the Society's *Philosophical Transactions*. For his contributions to natural philosophy Mather was honored, in 1713, to be among the first and few colonials elected to membership in the Royal Society during the early years of the eighteenth century.

Mather's magnum opus in the field of natural philosophy, however, is *The Christian Philosopher: A Collection of the Best Discoveries in Nature, with Religious Improvements,* completed by 1715 and published in London in 1720 (but bearing a 1721 imprint). This recondite treatise on natural philosophy often quotes Latin, Greek, and scriptural texts, and it contains references to some 415 pagan, Hebrew, Islamic, Greek, Roman, and modern authors from antiquity, the Middle Ages, the Renaissance, and the early Enlightenment. *The Christian Philosopher* is a work of metaphysics, theology, and science so ambitious and accomplished that many eighteenth-century intellectuals regarded it as "New England's major contribution to modern thought" (Miller 437). A highly derivative work, it is nevertheless the "first comprehensive treatise on all the sciences known at the time to be written by an American" (Solberg xi). Perhaps because of Mather's remarkable erudition, *The Christian Philosopher* has remained obscure, and since its publication it has been republished only twice—in a bowdlerized American edition in 1815 and in a difficult-to-use facsimile edition in 1968—before Winton U. Solberg's superb 1994 edition made Mather's monumental work of natural philosophy accessible to intrepid students of American cultural, literary, and environmental history.

In order to understand the place of *The Christian Philosopher* in the intellectual history of American writing about the natural world, it is necessary to understand the argument of the book in the cultural context of natural theology and its correlative, the argument from design. In Mather's day, those who inquired into the nature of nature were called not scientists but "natural philosophers." The term "natural historian" came into wide use only in the mid- to late eighteenth century; the word "scientist" was not coined until 1840; "ecologist" was not defined until 1866; and the embattled term "nature writer" was a cultural product of the late nineteenth and early twentieth centuries ("ecocritic" entered the language in 1978) (Worster 130; Egerton 342; Scheese 28). Chief among the natural philosophers of Mather's day were those interested in "natural theology," a branch of natural philosophy inspired by the fundamental belief that nature study could provide religious insight. The argument from design—strong in Western culture since pagan antiquity and eloquently expressed by Cicero in his *De natura deorum*—might be termed the "thesis" of most treatises of natural theology, for it held that the study of nature offered a revelation of God's certain existence, infinite wisdom, and (often qualified) benevolence. During the late seventeenth and early eighteenth centuries, works of natural theology were popular and were often referred to as "physico-theology"—studies that pursue the physical world as a means to religious ends.

Inspired by the argument from design, Mather's *Christian Philosopher* was the first American treatise to make the sustained claim that rational study of the physical world would reveal the glory of God as the author of *liber natura,* the Book of Nature. Later secularized and transformed by romanticism, this idea of nature study as a conduit to divinity engendered the sensibility we now associate with William Bartram, Henry Thoreau, John Muir, and their literary descendants. Mather makes his thesis clear in the opening sentence: "The Essays now before us will demonstrate, that *Philosophy* [natural science] is no *Enemy,* but a mighty and wondrous *Incentive* to *Religion."* The naturalist is a *"Priest* for the *Creation"* (7), he explains, a servant of "a Philosophical Religion: And yet how *Evangelical!"* (9). In his preface, Mather describes his project, thus:

> *Chrysostom,* I remember, mentions a *Twofold Book* of GOD; the Book of the *Creatures,* and the Book of the *Scriptures."* . . . We will now for a while read the *Former* of these *Books,* 'twill help us in reading the *Latter:* They will admirably assist one another. The Philosopher being asked, What his *Books* were; answered, *Totius Entis Naturalis Universitas* [the whole universe of natural things]. All Men are accommodated with that *Publick Library. Reader,* walk with me into it, and see what we shall find so legible there. (17–18)

Mather preached that, rather than rejecting science as threatening, Puritans should use the new investigative methods to "fetch *Lessons of Piety* from the whole Creation of GOD" (22). Consider Mather's prayer of thanks for new scientific technologies: *"Glorious* GOD, I give Thanks unto thee, for the Benefits and Improvements of the *Sciences,* granted by thee unto these our latter Ages," he writes. "The *Glasses* [the microscope and telescope], which our GOD has given us the *Discretion* to invent, and apply for the most noble Purposes, are favours of Heaven most thankfully to be acknowledged" (28).

The structure of *The Christian Philosopher* was roughly dictated by the natural theological tradition of which it is a part. Mather first describes astronomical phenomena and objects in a series of chapters that includes studies such as "Of the Stars," "Of Venus," and "Of Comets." These chapters demonstrate Mather's often advanced understanding of planetary motion and prove him a convert to the new physics of that *"Perpetual Dictator* of the learned World, in the *Principles of Natural Philosophy,"* Sir Isaac Newton (65); even going so far as to dismiss astrology as "foolish" (34), Mather organizes his astronomical analyses according to the insights of Newton's widely influential *Principia* (1687) and *Optics* (1704). Mather next turns his attention to Earth and earthly phenomena in chapters such as "Of Thunder and Lightning," "Of the Wind," and "Of Gravity." In these chapters Mather's theological imperatives appear more clearly. For example, although he describes current scientific theories concerning gravity, he ultimately attributes the force to "our most wise Creator, who, by appointing this *Law,* throughout the material World, keeps all Bodies in their proper Places and Stations, which without it would soon fall to pieces, and be utterly destroy'd" (90). The final part of *The Christian Philosopher* addresses classes of organisms in chapters such as "Of the Vegetables," "Of the Feathered," and "Of the Four-Footed." Here Mather's religious enthusiasm for the wonders of the Creation is energetically expressed in his descriptions of animals. For although he often admonishes against the pagan heresy of *"ador[ing] the Creatures more than the Creator"* (129), Mather's admiration for the creatures is patent throughout. "The *Sagacity* of some *Quadrupeds,"* he writes, "is a matter of Astonishment to *Man"* (225). He explicitly repudiates what he considered the soullessness of Cartesian mechanism, observing of the care of adult birds for their hatchlings: *"'Tis beyond the possibility of a meer Machine to perform such a thing as this!"* (208). Even the lowly gnat prompts an exclamation that "the Story of his Proceedings would give you a thousand astonishments!" (169).

Mather was of course unable to wholly avoid what he called *"vulgar Error"* (156): he believed that dancing was a cure for a tarantula bite (182) and that painting the shell of an egg would influence the color of the bird contained within (203); and his catalog of reptiles includes inevitable speculation concerning sea monsters and dragons (179). If these errors seem ludicrous, we should remember that *The Christian Philosopher* also contains some of the earliest correct descriptions of the hybridization of plants (131) and the nest building of birds (201–2) and that Mather's book is ahead of its time in explicitly dismissing common beliefs concerning astrology (34), the fabulous bird of paradise (198), and the spontaneous generation of animals (154–55).

Although unrecognized, Cotton Mather's legacies to American nature writing are numerous and important. He parts from earlier Puritans and anticipates the ethics and aesthetics of the romantics when he emphasizes the divine beauty, rather than the demonic bestiality, of nature. Arguing against those who believe mountains to be "Warts deforming the Face of the Earth," for example, Mather instead considers mountains "admirable *Tools of Nature*" that ensure life-giving rainfall. Concerning the vegetable creation, he writes that a wise man cannot observe the wonders of a plant "without some wishing, that if a *Metamorphosis* were to befal him, it might be into one of these" (140). Moved to admiration by the intelligence of elephants, he declares that the creatures "almost have *Religion* in them" (228). Even the humble fishes inspire Mather: "The *Papists* have a silly and foolish Legend of their St. *Anthony* preaching to the *Fishes;* it will be a Discretion in me to make the reverse of the *Fable,* and hear the *Fishes* preaching to me, which they do many Truths of no small importance. As *mute* as they are, they are *plain* and *loud* Preachers; I want nothing but an *Ear* to make me a profitable Hearer of them" (191). Although Mather subscribed to the dominant cosmological paradigm of the *scala natura*—that hierarchical chain of being that placed God above humankind and humankind above the beasts of the field— his passion to understand the workings of nature and his admiration for the beauty of the Creation help establish a tradition of curiosity and respect that is vital to environmental literature.

Mather made a pioneering attempt to reconcile the methods of modern science with the imperatives of spiritual value. As both preacher and natural philosopher, he had in common with many contemporary nature writers a primary goal of demonstrating and celebrating the sacredness of the natural world. When the title page of *The Christian Philosopher* identified Mather as both "D.D. [Doctor of Divinity]" and "Fellow of the Royal Society," it certified that he was a virtuoso in both theology and science. And although Mather would not have understood the severity of our culture's distinction between theological and scientific understandings of the wonders of the natural world, he would have appreciated the modern nature writer's celebration of the spiritual value of the Creation.

As an appreciative student of literary natural history, Henry Thoreau was familiar with Cotton Mather's natural philosophy. After an 1855 visit to Mather's personal library, then housed in Worcester, Massachusetts, Thoreau reflected in his journal on the boldness and vigor of colonial natural history writing, jotting in particular that "Cotton Mather, too, has a rich phrase" (7:109). And the following year Thoreau's journal contained a lengthy quotation from Mather's 1717 letter describing in detail the record snowfall of that year. Mather's letter ends apologetically, noting that he would forbear any further stories of the snow, "there not being any relation to philosophy in them." Thoreau, who deeply valued Mather's meticulous meteorological observations, closed the entry appreciatively: "[Mather] little thought that his simple testimony to such facts as the above would be worth all the philosophy he might dream of" (8:165).

Henry Thoreau once alluded to the study of early American natural history writing as an intellectually orienting activity by which a sensible person might "trace back his own tracks in the snow" (7:108–9). It would seem, perhaps ironically, that Thoreau knew something that ecocritics have so far failed to adequately recognize: American nature writing did not begin with Thoreau, or even with Bartram; rather, it began with those "hearty but reckless, hit-or-miss" colonial American natural history writers whose work Thoreau so much appreciated (7:108).

Works Cited

Egerton, Frank N. "Ecological Studies and Observations before 1900." *Issues and Ideas in America.* Ed. Benjamin J. Taylor and Thurman J. White. Norman: U of Oklahoma P, 1976. 311–51.

Mather, Cotton. *The Christian Philosopher*. 1721. Ed. Winton U. Solberg. Urbana: U of Illinois P, 1994.

Miller, Perry. *The New England Mind: From Colony to Province*. Cambridge: Harvard UP, 1953.

Regis, Pamela. *Describing Early America: Bartram, Jefferson, Crevecoeur, and the Rhetoric of Natural History*. DeKalb: Northern Illinois UP, 1992.

Savage, Henry, Jr. *Lost Heritage: Wilderness America through the Eyes of Seven Pre-Audubon Naturalists*. New York: William Morrow, 1970.

Scheese, Don. *Nature Writing: The Pastoral Impulse in America*. New York: Twayne, 1996.

Solberg, Winton U. Introduction. *The Christian Philosopher*. By Cotton Mather. Urbana: U of Illinois P, 1994. xix–cxxxiv.

Stearns, Raymond Phineas. *Science in the British Colonies of America*. Urbana: U of Illinois P, 1970.

Thomas, Keith. *Man and the Natural World: A History of the Modern Sensibility*. New York: Pantheon, 1983.

Thoreau, Henry David. *The Journal of Henry D. Thoreau*. 14 vols. Ed. Bradford Torrey and Francis H. Allen. Boston: Houghton Mifflin, 1906.

Wilson, David Scofield. *In the Presence of Nature*. Amherst: U of Massachusetts P, 1978.

Wood, William. *New England's Prospect*. 1634. Ed. Alden T. Vaughn. Amherst: U of Massachusetts P, 1977.

Worster, Donald. *Nature's Economy: A History of Ecological Ideas*. Cambridge: Cambridge UP, 1977.

Part II

Uncovering New Ecocritical Perspectives on
Nineteenth- and Twentieth-Century Authors

Cultivating Desire, Tending Piety: Botanical Discourse in Harriet Beecher Stowe's *The Minister's Wooing*

Mark T. Hoyer

In 1858 the preeminent American botanist Asa Gray opened his book *Botany for Young People and Common Schools* by quoting Matthew 6:28: "Consider the lilies of the field, how they grow" (1). Gray explains this verse as Christ's mandate to study the plants and, in so doing, to examine God's plan for humans. Later in the same volume, in describing flowers, Gray elucidates part of that plan: "The object of the flower is the production of seed. The flower consists of those parts, or *organs,* which are subservient to this end" (84). Those flowers that have "no proper covering or floral envelope" are "naked" (90).

Ten years later, in the first issue of the popular journal *American Naturalist,* another author began his article "The Fertilization of Flowering Plants" by declaring, "It is now universally accepted by botanists that there exist distinct sexes in the vegetable kingdom, and that nature's method of maintaining the existence of a specific form, is to bring the male and female elements in contact." He went on to use the terms "nuptials" for fertilization, and "marriage priests" for the insects and winds that "carry the pollen from one flower to another" (Rothrock 64–65).

The year after Gray's *Botany* appeared, in 1859, Harriet Beecher Stowe published her third novel, *The Minister's Wooing.* In it, Miss Prissy, the spinster dressmaker who, according to one critic, is the novel's "moral center" (Shea 293), utilizes language and imagery in ways remarkably similar to those found in the pages of Gray's *Botany* and of the *American Naturalist.* As Miss Prissy is preparing to make a wedding dress, she muses aloud to the gathered women: "I was saying to Miss General Wilcox, the other day, *I* don't see how we [women] could 'consider the lilies of the field,' without seeing the importance of looking pretty. I've got a flower-de-luce in my garden now . . . which is just the most beautiful thing you ever did see; and I was thinking, as I looked at it to-day, that, if women's dresses only grew on 'em as handsome and well-fitting as that, why, there wouldn't be any need of me" (195).

Miss Prissy's likening of women's clothes to flowers echoes the narrator's language when Miss Prissy is introduced several pages earlier, where we read that the dressmaker engages "in that important art on which depends the right of presentation of the floral part of Nature's great horticultural show" (188). Stowe's equation of women with flowers highlights the novel's double-consciousness. When we consider that Miss Prissy is called on to sew a wedding dress, the wedding representing the ritualized public event that officially legitimates the woman's transformation from a pre-sexual into a post-sexual state, we see the novel's sexualized dimension. As we see in Gray's *Botany,* and as is common in much botanical literature of the day, however, the sexual dimension in the novel is pushed into shadow by the bright sun of divine intent, which in the story takes the form of an easily recognized theological debate between the systematists, or abstract theologians, on the one hand, and those of a more antinomian cast on the other.[1]

Several critics have traced the ways in which Stowe manages in the novel "to package radical materials in a conservative frame" (Hedrick 287).[2] Susan K. Harris, in particular, has focused on the gendering of spaces and objects and the multiple ways in which such objects "open us to an arena of [sexual] pleasure which the text cannot openly admit" (185). Ironically, however, Harris misses the language of flowers, a characteristic she notes is common in other women's writing of the period (Susan Warner's *Queechy,* for example); thus, Harris emphasizes what she believes is a subconscious or unconscious autoerotic and, perhaps, homoerotic dimension to the novel. By paying attention, though, to the language of flowers, a language that would have been particularly accessible to Stowe's (primarily female) readership, and to the double-consciousness that such language carries with it, we can see a message that is radical for its time. The message is radical not because, as Harris proposes, it involves a rejection of men, marriage, and heterosexuality but rather because it advocates the notion that sexual passion is a legitimate and necessary criterion in a woman's choice of a mate and that, indeed, it was morally incumbent on young women to choose mates using the entirety of their beings—their physical as well as their spiritual beings—in gauging the rightness of their choices.[3]

To deliver this message in *The Minister's Wooing,* as we will shortly see, Stowe engages and intertwines the discourses of several debates going on during two historical periods: the eighteenth-century debates in botany over the nature of reproduction and in theology over the nature of faith with the nineteenth-century debates over slavery and over the rights of women. Examined in this light, Stowe's novel becomes a prime example of how women writers and artists have adapted male-dominated discourses of nature and of science to their own purposes and to the needs of their female audience.

Sexualizing plants had been standard practice in both scientific and popular accounts since the Swedish botanist Linnaeus had introduced his taxonomic system, also called the sexual system, over one hundred years previously. As François Delaporte points out in *Nature's Second Kingdom: Explorations of Vegetality in the Eighteenth Century,* in sexualizing plant reproduction Linnaeus and his popularizers had identified the flower with woman, an equation that often moved Jean-Jacques Rousseau to states of near rapture: "The sweet fragrances, the lively colors, the most elegant shapes seem to vie with one another for our attention. One need only love pleasure to abandon oneself to such sweet sensations" (qtd. in Delaporte 139). According to some sexualists, such as Charles Bonnet, women were not excluded from such pleasures, and, by paying attention to the analogy of flower-as-woman, they could "find in plant love pure and delicious enjoyment." Even when the botanist deflected the explicit identification between the woman's and the flower's sexual organs—by transforming the flower into mere clothing, or even the plant's wedding gown—the implication was clear: "woman is flower—that is, sex: she dresses and ornaments herself the better to unveil her essence" (Delaporte 139–40).

In the late eighteenth and early nineteenth centuries, when a series of religious revivals swept western Europe and the United States, this kind of overt sexualization of plants did not long remain unchallenged. Among those who objected to the sexual system were the so-called agamists, those who believed that plants reproduced asexually and who therefore considered any analogy to human reproduction to be spurious. Among the agamists and those who disliked the sexual orientation of botany for other reasons, though, a desexualized taxonomy still met a fundamental need—in Delaporte's words, "the need for severe repression: name and classify rather than dream" (138).

However practiced, then, botany, according to Delaporte, becomes "an activity that is both innocent and guilty. It is guilty because the botanist rediscovers what he is pretending to flee. Nature must therefore reflect the image of a sublimated beauty." Yet simultaneously, it is innocent "because it gives its sanction to imaginary gratifications." By "contemplating the loves of plants," one "bring[s] into being an economy of desire" (138–39).

The Linnaean system continued to provide rich verbal coin within that economy well into the nineteenth century. Despite—or perhaps because of—the fact that the debate between sexualists and agamists continued to rage, botanical language never lost its sexualized connotation. This sexual dimension was reinforced in popular and scientific literature either by the ubiquity of Linnaean analogies or by their conspicuous absence, which made the language and imagery used in proxy seem sterile by contrast.

How, then, did botany, foremost among all the natural sciences, become such a popular pastime in the late eighteenth and early nineteenth centuries? And how did it become so popular among women in particular in an age when, as Nancy Cott points out, women's "passionlessness" was the "central tenet of Victorian sexual ideology" (220)?[4] The explanation for the paradox lies in natural theology. As Gray's quoting of the biblical passage reminds us, it was not just Linnaeus's sexual system that people thought they were internalizing in studying botany but (they believed) God's system for ensuring that humans, no less so than plants, would reproduce. Thus, those who botanized and discoursed in the language of plants always carried a kind of double-consciousness: sex and piety were the two sides of the verbal coin circulating within the economy of desire.

Such coin circulated widely. Popular botany texts sold over a quarter of a million copies; botany was a standard part of the school curriculum; the top botanical writers were stars on the lyceum circuit; journals such as *Godey's Lady's Book, Youth's Companion, North American Review,* and *Atlantic Monthly* carried major articles on botany and offered reviews of the latest botanical literature; and literary and parlor clubs were as apt to discuss the latest botanies of Asa Gray and

Almira H. Lincoln Phelps as the novels of Charles Dickens and Samuel Richardson. In short, botany and botanical discussion were so much a part of middle-class Protestant culture that it was impossible to avoid at least some familiarity with the subject.

Harriet Beecher Stowe had more than a passing acquaintance with these notions. Not only did she grow up in a family that encouraged intellectual pursuits through a wide range of reading, not only was she trained at female seminaries where natural history and natural theology were fundamental parts of the curriculum, not only was she a member of literary clubs that would have discussed the latest botanical literature, not only did she publish in magazines that regularly ran articles on botany, not only did she have friends and relatives who were knowledgeable about the subject, and not only was she an enthusiastic painter of flowers but more than all of these Stowe was an avid gardener who could at times, as the biographer Joan Hedrick puts it, garden with "manic fury" (125). Even Harriet's husband, Calvin, complained in letters of her devoted attention to raising flowers, sometimes to the neglect of her wifely and motherly duties. So passionate was she about her gardening that when she and Calvin were building a new home in 1838, Harriet "planned and executed grand gardens involving tons of manure and eight kinds of geraniums" (125). Her brother, George, was something of a plant expert, and Harriet was knowledgeable enough to have written for a local horticultural and agricultural newspaper while living in Walnut Hills, a suburb of Cincinnati.

The language of flowers in *The Minister's Wooing* is woven into a more conventional surface plot. The story, set in Newport, Rhode Island, in the late 1700s, involves two kinds of conflicts—one religious, the other romantic—that both require mediation in the person of Mary Scudder. The religious conflict centers on finding a middle ground between the abstract and depersonalized theological system of the minister, Dr. Samuel Hopkins, and a more personally experienced state of grace—a contrast between abstract intellect and intuitive emotion, between system and experience. The romantic conflict is presented through a love triangle. Mary's cousin James, with whom she has always shared an attraction, is (presumably) lost at sea—and no one can be certain about the state of his soul at the time of his death, leaving everyone wondering whether he is spiritually saved. Some time after James is reported lost, Dr. Hopkins, unaware of Mary's feelings toward James (and, indeed, Mary is loathe to admit her feelings, as James has not publicly declared his Christian faith), asks Katy Scudder, Mary's mother, for her daughter's hand in marriage. Mrs. Scudder joyfully accepts; and Mary assents but struggles with the fact that, although she admires the Doctor, she feels toward him only the love of Christian duty, a love of the head rather than of the heart. Practically on the eve of the Doctor and Mary's wedding day, James returns, but Mary refuses to break her bond to the Doctor. When Miss Prissy takes it upon herself to inform the Doctor of Mary's true feelings, which are obvious to most of the women, the Doctor subdues his feelings and bends his will to what he perceives as Divine Will, releasing Mary from her obligation and giving his blessing to the young couple.

Reader sympathies are with James and Mary all along, for the narrative has made it clear that Mary feels for him a passion that she lacks toward the Doctor. From the beginning of the novel, Stowe so consistently discourses on gender relations using the language of botany that readers of her day could not have missed its implications. People are said to be of a particular "*genus*" (3), the belles of Newport are labeled "specimens" (19), and several narrative reflections are prefaced with the words, "Naturalists say" (10, 45). Even more explicit, however, the women in the story are consistently likened to individual flowers, and almost every significant interaction between men and women occurs against a backdrop that includes flowers or other vegetation.

By using the language of flowers to develop gender relationships in general and the entanglements surrounding Mary's two romantic relationships in particular, Stowe's narrator guides readers toward an understanding that it is this quality of passion that Mary feels for James but not for the Doctor that validates their ultimate union. When we first see Mary, she is coaxing a dove out of the apple blossoms of the tree just outside her bedroom window; these are the same blossoms through which James makes his first appearance, stepping forward and warmly embracing Mary (19, 32). According to the language of flowers, apple blossoms are associated with preference and with a measure of fame that, in the words of one book of the time, "speaks him great and good" (*Language of Flowers* 1).[5] Mary's later assessment of James, "I think him so noble and grand" (79), clearly reflects the association the flower imagery already established. Our introduction to the Doctor is likewise guided by flower imagery. Writing that he boards in a room in the Scudder household that is "dark and fragrant with the shade and perfume of blossoming lilacs" (59)—flowers that are associated with first emotions of love—Stowe, in describing the setting, forecasts the romantic attraction on the Doctor's part that will later become manifest.

The contrast between the flower imagery Stowe uses to introduce the two characters might be sharpened even further by noting that apple blossoms represent an earlier stage of the fruit of sexual knowledge that is bound to fall. Stowe soon makes clear that sexuality is a subtext by presenting a subplot that engages the issue both explicitly, at the level of plot, and implicitly, through imagery that reinforces the association between women and flowers. The subplot involves Madame Frontignac, a married French woman who is visiting Providence with her soldier husband, an older man whom she sees as more of a father than a lover; Colonel Burr, who is attempting to seduce Madame Frontignac; and Mary, whom Burr also wishes to seduce. When Colonel Burr first sights Mary, he sees her framed against the backdrop of a garden, and later he introduces her to Madame Frontignac as "a charming specimen of our New England flowers" (210, 221). In contrast to Mary, whose beauty is characterized by freshness and youth, Madame Frontignac possesses a beauty of refinement, or mature elegance, a quality that the narrator both overtly evokes by comparison of her to a Rembrandt painting and tacitly announces by the language of flowers employed to describe Madame's "pomegranate cheeks" (297).[6]

Through Burr's response to women's beauty as well as through his lascivious designs, Stowe presents him as a counterpoint to the Doctor. Whereas Burr is the serpent of Christian allegory (304), the Doctor, as the narrative repeatedly indicates, is a rock, seemingly (although not actually) so unmoved and stunned into silence by Mary's beauty that all he can manage to mutter at times are the biblical quotations he knows so well. Burr is one who practices the deceptive art of eliciting and then preying on passion; the Doctor, one who cannot give it voice in anything but religious language, thus translates passion out of conscious existence.

This contrast, too, is developed partially through references to botanical science. Burr is implicitly likened to the kind of scientist who has no social conscience and analyzes situations and people only for what he can gain from them. He studies Mary and Madame Frontignac with cold calculation; in both cases,

Burr is compelled "to experiment" on them—in Mary's case because her "calm dignity . . . piqued and stimulated his curiosity" and in Madame Frontignac's case "because he felt an artistic pleasure in the beautiful light and heat" that he enkindled in her (264, 230). The Doctor, by comparison, is one whose conscience and self-analyzing tendencies are so overdeveloped that he demonstrates no awareness of his needs as a human and little awareness of others' perceptions and needs (as he repeatedly demonstrates in his sermons). "The Doctor had practised his subtle mental analysis till his instruments were so fine-pointed and keen-edged that he scarce ever allowed a flower of sacred emotion to spring in his soul without picking it to pieces to see if its genera and species were correct" (289).[7]

While the two men differ in their motivations, they share in common a view that places them, as men, in a "natural" position of superiority over women— just as, in the Doctor's view, God holds ascendancy over Man. Burr, for instance, is described as being motivated by his desire to "subdue" women, or to "gain and hold ascendancy" over them, and he dreams of an Arcadian existence where the "animal wants" of men are attended to not by the labors of servants but rather "by the ministrations of the most delicate and exalted portion of the creation" (264, 219, 267)—that is, by women. The Doctor, for his part, first recognizes his attraction to Mary in terms that highlight his assumed air of "natural" superiority. With "unconscious majesty," the "strong, heroic man" sees, in the person of Mary, an "answer to his higher soul in the sweet, tremulous mirror of womanhood" (148–49). Furthermore, the narrator goes to some lengths to point out that the Doctor, like all men, remains blissfully unaware of the labor (performed by women) that purchases his leisure time; it is a situation for which, as the narrator puts it, "most of our magnanimous masters" would express gratitude if only they were aware of it (168–69).

As with the novel's botanical discourse, its treatment of the relative power between the sexes points simultaneously in another direction. The passage just cited, for example, appears during a scene in which a group is debating the issue of slavery, the issue over which the Doctor, in the preceding chapter, has confronted one of the most influential members of his congregation. When the Marvyns' African American servant, Candace, is asked for her opinion on the slavery issue, she declares that it is not right, and she cites the Declaration of Independence and the Bill of Rights as proof. "It stands to reason," she posits, because "I a'n't a critter. . . . I's a reasonable bein',—a woman,—as much a woman as anybody" (176). Thus, she claims her equality and freedom on the basis of her status not merely as a human being, the contrasting category she logically suggests by "critter," but specifically as a woman. The implication of this move is reinforced two pages later when, in describing Candace's relationship with her husband, the narrator tells of a time that a deacon admonished her, "You ought to give honor to your husband; the wife is the weaker vessel." To this, Candace, who was physically far larger and more imposing than her husband, could only reply, "*I* de weaker vessel. Umph!" The narrator then editorializes: "A whole woman's-rights' convention could not have expressed more in a day than was given in that single look and word" (178–79). This entire passage, in the context of the narrator's earlier comment on the "magnanimous masters," shows the issues of slavery and of gender inequality to be mirrors of each other.

The gender inflections of this discourse highlight the reason James is the only suitable mate for one such as Mary. Both the Doctor and Burr are guided almost wholly by what many considered to be the preeminent male (and deific) characteristic—Reason—although their reason is directed toward achieving different ends. James is guided by emotion and intuition as well as reason, and he approaches life as a series of experiences from which one must learn and to which one must accommodate oneself rather than as a system to be mastered and then systematically applied to reach a predetermined end. Like Stowe's women in general, and Mary in particular, James displays "a subtile keenness of perception outrunning slow-footed reason" (131). In contrast to the Doctor's "subtile mental analysis," which impels him to dissect and classify the "flower[s] of sacred emotion" rather than to act on them, and also in contrast to Burr, who performs and acts on his mental calculations but only in the service of preying on others' emotions, James exhibits qualities akin to Mary's "blessed gift of womanhood,—that vivid life in the soul and sentiment which resists the chills of analysis, as a healthful human heart resists cold" (289). James's balanced embodiment of emotive-intuitive and logical temperaments suits him, since he, like Mary, had "always craved . . . outward demonstrations" of sincere affection (427).

Because James possesses both feminine and masculine qualities, it is no surprise to find descriptions of him such as the following: "He was tender as a woman to his mother, and followed her with his eyes, like a lover, wherever she went; he made due and manly acknowledgments to his father, but declared his fixed and settled intention to abide by the profession he had chosen; and he brought home all sorts of strange foreign gifts for every member of the household" (116). James's habit of generosity to all within the household shows him to be a mediating figure, as well, in terms of race. He and Candace evidence a special relationship with and understanding of each other, and, like her, he stands in the place of one who is, according to his society, both "savage" and "civilized." The narrative makes this point clear in at least two ways: first, by having Katy Scudder, here voicing the estimation of polite society, call him "an infidel," in reference to the fact that he has not publicly declared his conversion to Christianity (81); and second, by visually casting him as a savage when describing him, as a child, emerging from his mother's cosmetic bag "showing a face ghastly with blue streaks" — clearly a heathen in sheep's clothing (106). James's position as mediator between genders, between races, and between theological temperaments, makes him the ideal companion for Mary.

What the narrative traces, however, is not the logical reasoning behind Mary's preference for James — indeed, in the reasoning of her society, all logic points to the Doctor — but rather a feeling toward him that is palpable yet for which she has no name. That this indefinable feeling is attributable to passion is most clearly revealed in the narrative's reliance on the language of botany.

After James's apparent death, Mary rationalizes giving herself to the Doctor to be his wife with the observation that "the flower must fall before fruit can perfect itself" (411). In *Nature's Second Kingdom*, Delaporte makes clear that this "floral chronology," paralleled in the minds of the sexualists by a "sexual topography," was a truism of botanical study even for those who wished to desexualize reproduction (both plant and human) by focusing on the outcome rather than the process, on plant design rather than anatomy (95). Mary's response to the Doctor partakes of this kind of thinking. Clearly devoid of any anticipation of the process — sex — that would be an inevitable part of her union with the Doctor, Mary instead concentrates on the grand design, the end for which (according to the

Doctor's system of belief) she was created: physically, to bear children; and spiritually, if we repress the physical dimension entirely, to bear fruit in the dissemination of the gospel message.

In contrast is the obvious passion Mary feels toward James (before he goes to sea) and toward his memory (after he is presumed dead). In their last visit together before James heads off to sea, a scene that, significantly, takes place in the apple orchard, Mary is shown "shiver[ing] and trembl[ing], as she heard his retreating footsteps, and saw the orchard-grass fly back from under his feet. It was as if each step trod on a nerve,—as if the very sound of the rustling grass was stirring something living and sensitive in her soul. And, strangest of all, a vague impression of guilt hovered over her." Within the apple orchard, Mary, as a kind of Eve figure, experiences guilt, as if she has had a foretaste of that sexual union with James that she, an unmarried woman, could not yet either experience or even, in light of the uncertain state of his faith, anticipate. Upon Mary's return from the orchard, her guilt is so apparent that her mother is shocked at her appearance, and she comments, "your cheeks are as red as peonies" (41–42). Regardless of the extent to which Mary is conscious of her budding sexuality, however, Stowe's reliance on the language of flowers and of botany brings it before the reader's consciousness and makes clear that one purpose of the rest of the story must be to transform the guilt of passion into the pleasure of passion, to bring it into the economy of desire, by proving its legitimacy through the office of marriage.

Later in the story—immediately after Mary offers her rationalization ("the flower must fall before fruit can perfect itself") for marrying the Doctor—we again see her passionate, clearly physical feelings of longing for James:

> [S]he had a kind of shadowy sense of a throbbing and yearning nature that seemed to call on her,—that seemed surging towards her with an imperative, protesting force that shook her heart to its depths.
>
> Perhaps it is so, that souls, once intimately related, have ever after this a strange power of affecting each other,—a power that neither absence nor death can annul. How else can we interpret those mysterious hours in which the power of departed love seems to overshadow us, making our souls vital

with such longings, with such wild throbbings, with such unutterable sigh-ings, that a little more might burst the mortal bond? (411)

Not only do the "throbbings" and "yearnings" and "surgings" articulate Mary's far more active feeling of passion toward James but, likewise, her soul being made "vital with such longings" and the near "bursting" of the "mortal bond" evoke the essential processes of reproduction, the sexual act itself. And Mary reveals her feelings in language that parallels discourse used in botany—words to describe, for instance, on the one hand, pollen rising to the tip of the an-ther, ready to fertilize the ovules, and, on the other, the bud bursting into full flower.

Lest this example suggest that I go too far in ascribing such bald physicality to words that instead concern metaphysical longings, let me emphasize again the reciprocity, in Stowe's world and in the language of natural theology that helped make sense of that world, between sex and piety. Mary must come to realize within her person the same kind of double-consciousness that already exists within the novel's botanical language, with its sense that God has given us sexual passion as a gift that helps guide our selection of a mate. Ironically, Mary gives voice to this idea when she wonders aloud to her mother about what role she might play in bringing James to declare his Christian faith: "[D]oes not God use the love we have to each other as a means of doing us good?" (82). The discourse on Christian belief as a species of passion that partakes of both earthly and heav-enly pleasures takes on an added dimension when Stowe, in explaining the tribu-lations Mary undergoes on hearing of James's death, likens God to a gardener and Mary to a flower that needs tending:

It is said that gardeners, sometimes, when they would bring a rose to richer flowering, deprive it for a season, of light and moisture. Silent and dark it stands, dropping one fading leaf after another, and seeming to go down patiently to death. But when every leaf is dropped, and the plant stands stripped to the uttermost, a new life is even then working in the buds, from which shall spring a tender foliage and a brighter wealth of flowers. So, often in celestial gardening, every leaf of earthly joy must drop, before a new and divine bloom visits the soul. (361–62)

While this passage on one level allows the narrator and thus the reader to see Mary through her grief, on another it serves to document a season of dryness, winter, and dormancy in her passionate life, and thereby it helps us anticipate the rebirth that will soon be accomplished through James's timely reappearance. That Mary, after James's return, makes a conscious decision to give up passion for duty is Stowe's representation of how thoroughly conventional mores—a collective consciousness—tended to govern individual behavior and thwart individuality, especially for women. Mary's decision signals her obedience to the system, one which, as pointed out earlier, is in Stowe's view patriarchal, sustained by male privilege and power. Mary must (she believes) subordinate her will to God's will, and her feelings to the Doctor's feelings. That other women such as Miss Prissy are the ones who are truly in touch with God's will, with a higher wisdom that impels them to acquaint the Doctor with Mary's true feelings and thereby set in motion the chain of events that frees Mary to act on her passionate feelings for James, signals Stowe's validation of an alternate (female) sensibility.

In *The Minister's Wooing*, then, Stowe's intertwining of the discourses of eighteenth-century debates in botany over the nature of reproduction and in theology over the nature of faith with the nineteenth-century debates over slavery and over the rights of women reveals a pattern of rich complexity that blurs the boundaries between nature and culture. Her layering of histories in language brings to mind a point that Gary Snyder makes in *The Practice of the Wild*, in a section called "Nature's Writing": "The layers of history in language become a text of language itself" (66). In this light, even if we never choose to call Stowe a nature writer, we can credit her as being one of those writers whose experiments record nature's writing. By attending to such a distinction, we gain an image of Harriet Beecher Stowe that highlights both similarities and differences to heralded nature writers such as Henry David Thoreau. Specifically, we attain an image of a woman of genteel culture rather than of the adventuring class, one who could garden—and write—with manic fury. But this is also a woman who, rather than wandering far afield from where most of her contemporaries lived in order to glean the wild, took them into their own backyards, choosing to plant herself squarely within the garden of her culture and time and, from there, gently broadcasting the seeds and nurturing the seedlings of a more humane society.

Notes

I presented a shorter version of this essay at the session "Women Imagining Science," chaired by Professor Karen Waldron of the College of the Atlantic, at the MLA Northeast Conference in April 1997. Thanks also to Mary Ellen Bellanca at the University of Delaware for many useful references and for interest in the topic.

1. In discussing the intermingling between earthly and heavenly realms, the narrator raises the issue of double-consciousness when, addressing the reader, she writes that, as long as we have both body and soul, "Two worlds must mingle . . . wreathing in and out" (205).

2. See also Romines.

3. For insightful analyses of women's interest in botany and their use of the language of flowers, see Keeney; Seaton; Shteir; and Bewell.

4. Between 1850 and 1890, botany became so associated with women that some writers felt the need to advocate why it made a "proper" study for males.

5. Numerous books of the period, published in both the United States and England, contain poems about and provide the vocabulary for the language of flowers. One of the most widely reprinted, *The Language and Poetry of Flowers,* compiled by S. C. (Sarah Carter) Edgarton, was first published in London in 1849. Derby and Jackson, the publisher of Stowe's novel, brought out a reprint from an 1853 volume entitled *The Language and Poetry of Flowers,* by H. G. Adams, in 1858, the year before *The Minister's Wooing* was published. While the associations I reference appear in an undated and anonymous book, *The Language of Flowers,* published in London by Frederick Warne, they accord with those I have found in other books with similar titles.

Further examples of Stowe's use of botanical imagery in the novel are too numerous to list, but two more should suffice to show the pattern. The Doctor is elsewhere likened to a great elm, a tree that, according to the language of flowers, connotes dignity, the quality that Mary and others recognize in him. Later in the story, as Mary struggles emotionally to deal with the news that James is lost at sea, she is likened to "a bruised flax-flower," flax being associated with fate (320).

6. The pomegranate flower is also associated with foolishness, a characteristic that, in light of Madame's infatuation with Burr, is in implicit accord with the narrator's estimation of her.

7. The contrast between the two men is also dramatized in a theological debate that centers on the question of whether one should focus, as the Doctor does, on the Christian millennium, or, as Burr does, on the present moment (261).

Works Cited

Bewell, Alan. "'Jacobin Plants': Botany as Social Theory in the 1790s." *Wordsworth Circle* 20.3 (1989): 132–39.

Cott, Nancy F. "Passionlessness: An Interpretation of Victorian Sexual Ideology, 1790–1850." *Signs: Journal of Women in Culture and Society* 4.2 (1978): 219–36.

Delaporte, François. *Nature's Second Kingdom: Explorations of Vegetality in the Eighteenth Century.* Trans. Arthur Goldhammer. Cambridge: MIT P, 1982.

Edgarton, S. C. (Sarah Carter). *Language and Poetry of Flowers.* London: Thomas Nelson, 1849.

Gray, Asa. *Botany for Young People and Common Schools.* New York: Ivison, Blakeman, Taylor & Co., 1858.

Harris, Susan K. "The Female Imaginary in Harriet Beecher Stowe's *The Minister's Wooing.*" *New England Quarterly* 66.2 (1993): 179–97.

Hedrick, Joan. *Harriet Beecher Stowe: A Life.* New York: Oxford UP, 1994.

Keeney, Elizabeth. *The Botanizers: Amateur Scientists in Nineteenth-Century America.* Chapel Hill: U of North Carolina P, 1992.

The Language and Poetry of Flowers. London: Milner and Sowerby, 1867.

The Language of Flowers: Including Floral Poetry. London: Frederick Warne, n.d.

Romines, Ann. *The Home Plot: Women, Writing, and Domestic Ritual.* Amherst: U of Massachusetts P, 1992.

Rothrock, J. T. "The Fertilization of Flowering Plants." *American Naturalist* 1 (1868): 64–72.

Seaton, Beverly. *The Language of Flowers: A History.* Charlottesville: UP of Virginia, 1995.

Shea, Maura E. "Spinning toward Salvation: The Ministry of Spinsters in Harriet Beecher Stowe." *ATQ: American Transcendental Quarterly* 10.4 (1996): 293–310.

Shteir, Ann B. *Cultivating Women, Cultivating Science: Flora's Daughters and Botany in England, 1760–1860.* Baltimore: Johns Hopkins UP, 1996.

Snyder, Gary. *The Practice of the Wild.* San Francisco: North Point, 1990.

Stowe, Harriet Beecher. *The Minister's Wooing.* 1859. New York: Derby and Jackson; Hartford: The Stowe-Day Foundation, 1978.

❧ Ecological Hardy

Richard Kerridge

Thomas Hardy is an obvious candidate for the ecocritical canon. The best known of English rural novelists, he is intensely responsive to the natural world and human relations with that world. Some of the most exciting passages of English nature writing are in his novels, integrated with a complexity of cultural, political, economic, and emotional life. I suggest that the ecocritical canonization of Hardy would help to produce an ecocriticism (and a nature writing) less preoccupied with deep withdrawal from society. Hardy is concerned with the multiplicity of uses—material, cultural, and emotional—that human beings have for the natural environment. He writes of nature as seen, variously, by the agricultural laborer, urban visitor, Romantic poet, lover, naturalist, young country-dweller longing for city glamour, ambitious entrepreneur, prosperous or struggling farmer, and many others. If we are searching for narrative procedures that correspond to ecological principles, Hardy's novels are a good place to start.

The natural world does not appear in these novels as wilderness to be reached only by crossing a difficult threshold. Since long before Hardy's time England has not possessed any remote wilderness. The area he named Egdon Heath in *The Return of the Native* (1878) was the nearest thing southern England could offer even then. Today the heath survives only in patches among roads, quarries, and suburbs. An ecocriticism that canonizes Hardy will be one concerned with crowded environments.

Maps for Tourists

Most editions of the novels have at the beginning a map of southern England entitled "Thomas Hardy's Wessex" or "The Wessex of the Novels." Real place

126

names such as Portsmouth and Stonehenge appear alongside fictional names (in different typeface) such as Casterbridge and Egdon Heath. Many of the fictional names clearly designate real towns. According to Michael Millgate, the first of these maps was "specifically authorized by Hardy" (*Biography* 250–51, 361) for the 1895–1897 edition of the novels, while the map used in the Wessex edition of 1912 was adapted from Hardy's own drawing (*Career* 397).

Some editions add a glossary identifying Hardy's fictional places. Hardy sometimes teased his readers about the real identities of these places. His 1912 preface to *The Woodlanders* (1887) declines to name a real village as the model for Little Hintock, but in it he identifies the locality by naming several real landmarks. Hardy tells us that he "once spent several hours on a bicycle with a friend in a serious attempt to discover the real spot" (*Woodlanders* 36). While preserving the idea that readers might actually visit the ground of the novel, he mocks the pedantry of a searcher more interested in finding the real place than in accepting the characters' experiences as realistic.

That idea has been the basis of the Hardy tourist industry in Dorset ever since. Perhaps Hardy would have viewed it with distaste, but the tourism is consistent with his practice of commodifying the scenes of his rural childhood for a mainly urban and middle-class readership. After his first manuscript, "The Poor Man and the Lady," had been rejected in 1868 because of its inflammatory politics (Millgate, *Biography* 110; F. E. Hardy 58–59), Hardy turned to more conciliatory modes of fiction. His first published novel, the melodramatic *Desperate Remedies* (1871), had a mixed reception but was praised for its rural scenes. Then came his first commercial and critical success, *Under the Greenwood Tree* (1872), a novel set in a Dorset village and likely (despite its subtle complications) to be received as elegiac pastoral. Yet as Hardy became more successful, he grew increasingly determined to confront his readers with their complicity in the sufferings of his characters.

Hardy started from a class position immediately above that of the rural laboring classes. Peter Widdowson has traced in Hardy's work a complicated alternation between anger on behalf of the rural poor and disavowal of personal identity with them. Roger Ebbatson finds the same ambivalence in "The Dorsetshire Labourer," Hardy's essay of 1883 (129–53). These critics discern a pattern in which Hardy's intimate knowledge of rural working-class life becomes at once extremely valuable and profoundly shameful to him. The effect was to equip Hardy superbly as a commentator on the intricacy and eroticism of class relations and relations between city and country and to make him subject to severely conflicting desires and loyalties.

Sometimes Hardy demands that his readers should feel trapped by these pressures in an almost bodily way. "Where are you, in relation to these people?" is often an implied question. The idea of chance intervention, of a random passerby arriving to offer help at crucial moments, frequently is flung almost accusingly at the reader. In *Tess of the d'Urbervilles* (1891), a gossipy remark by one of the villagers, months after Tess's rape, suggests that passersby might easily have happened on her in time to save her. "There were they that heard sobbing one night last year in The Chase; and it mid ha' gone hard wi' a certain party if folks had come along" (119). At the moment of the rape, when Tess is most in need of intervention, Hardy forecloses the narrative. As our sense of her danger intensifies, the narrator seems mockingly to cast his gaze around for someone who might come upon the scene as rescuer. The only witnesses present are "primeval yews and oaks," "gentle roosting birds," and "hopping rabbits and hares" (101): ironic, useless mock witnesses. A human witness, present in body, would have to intervene or be guilty of intolerable complicity. The reader is not permitted to become a ghostly voyeur, free from this responsibility. Without bodily presence, it seems, we have no right to look. As Alec d'Urberville materializes above Tess's sleeping body, the narrative leaves her to his mercies, abandoning description (relinquishing narrative, in effect) and ascending into a series of rhetorical questions and generalizations in the present tense. A break follows. When we next encounter Tess, several weeks have passed.

Early in *Jude the Obscure* (1896), the working-class boy Jude lies weeping by the roadside, having looked for the first time into a Latin grammar. "Somebody might have come along that way who would have asked him his trouble, and might have cheered him by saying that his notions were further advanced than those of his grammarian. But nobody did come, because nobody does" (55). This switch from past to present generalizes Jude's plight, undermining the sense of distance that absolves the reader of responsibility. Despite its fatalism, the present tense insists on a present need for remedy and on the reader's membership of the social system that has no use for Jude's desire to read. Readers, in the act of reading, are made to see that activity in the context of an economy in which Jude's reading is superfluous waste.

The idea of crossing the space that divides us from Jude is held out too late. Only in seeing that nobody did come do we recognize the possibility that somebody might have. And, of course, none of us could have come upon Jude, because Jude is a fiction. The principal function of Jude's fictitiousness at this point is that it means we can do nothing to help him. He is in the novel and we are outside it. Hardy often forecloses abruptly in this way, as if readers, because they are unable or unwilling to intervene, should forfeit the right to watch.

At the end of *The Mayor of Casterbridge* (1886), Michael Henchard walks out of the town to die. One of his laborers, Abel Whittle, follows him. This is Whittle's report: "And I followed en over Grey's Bridge, and he turned and zeed me, and said, 'You go back!' But I followed, and he turned again, and said, 'Do you hear, sir? Go back!' But I zeed that he was low, and I followed on still" (330–31). "You go back!" might be a command to the readers also. Henchard turns his back on the world. In his humiliation, he does not wish to be an object of scrutiny, whether the eyes belong to Whittle or anyone else. Whittle persists, however, and if the narrative had taken up Whittle's viewpoint here, the reader might have had access to the scene of Henchard's death. Whittle would have become the reader's proxy. But Whittle, as his dialect shows, is socially too far beneath the implied reader for such a merging of identity. His speech could not be integrated acceptably with the vocabulary of the narrative voice. He is excluded from the consensual viewpoint the narrative implies, and we are shown that exclusion unsparingly. Whittle follows Henchard, but the reader may not, and Henchard is permitted to walk out of the novel, away from our consuming gaze.

Henchard's request in his last note, his will, is "that no man remember me" (331), a wish that the whole narrative has flouted, as we now realize. The novel ends. Too late, we see our readership as a scrutiny that Henchard seems to have felt and flinched under. Henchard's note momentarily transfers some of the shame to the reader, who has been watching the scene without accepting the responsibilities of bodily presence.

Hardy demands that readers should take seriously the way their presence is implied by the narrative. They should acknowledge that a visitor is not a ghostly, free-moving figure who watches and leaves no imprint but a bodily presence engaged in an act of consumption that will have material consequences. Tourists are not external to the economy or ecosystem they visit; they are part of it, engaged in an activity likely to transform it.

An ecologist studies forms of life not in isolation but as parts of a system, an economy that sustains them and that they constitute. Hardy's narrative forms bring interdependency to the fore. He has a distinctive way of introducing characters that shows how they ceaselessly make and remake each other's identity. Gabriel Oak at the beginning of *Far from the Madding Crowd* is a floating signifier whose perceived "character" varies not so much because of his actions as according to the mood of the perceiver. "Or, to state his character as it stood in the scale of public opinion, when his friends and critics were in tantrums, he was considered rather a bad man; when they were pleased, he was rather a good man; when they were neither, he was a man whose moral colour was a kind of pepper-and-salt mixture" (41). The same formula introduces William Dewy in *Under the Greenwood Tree.* "Character," here, means not the person occupying his physical space but the various impressions people have of that person. Oak's "character" has no hard boundaries but is always in flux, always a product of relations with whatever surrounds him.

This remarkable manner of introduction allows the characters to be at once elusively singular and the product of shifting popular opinion. A contrast is drawn between the physical, vulnerable body that must always be somewhere and the "character" as perceived by others, an endlessly changing procession of ideas. To other people, the narrative reminds us at one point, "Tess was only a passing thought. Even to friends she was no more than a frequently passing thought" (*Tess* 119). The character is clearly located in time and space but open to unlimited interpretation. Description is denied the power to stabilize character. The meanings people have, that constitute their "character," are shown to be the product of an environment, a field of meaning in which both readers and characters move.

A similar emphasis is given to the material interdependencies between places: the flow of goods, information, and travelers. A moorland in *Far from the Madding Crowd* is marked by "forms without features; suggestive of anything, proclaiming nothing, and without more character than that of being the limit of something else" (113), rather like Oak's "pepper-and-salt mixture." And in *Tess of the d'Urbervilles,* Tess and Angel Clare deliver milk one morning to a train: "'Londoners will drink it at their breakfasts tomorrow, won't they!' she asked. 'Strange people that we have never seen. . . . Who don't know anything of us, and where it comes from; or think how we drove two miles across the moor to-night in the rain that it might reach 'em in time?'" (*Tess* 215). Tess experiences a Wordsworthian pleasure at this glimpse of the profusion of interconnected life, but Angel mildly patronizes her and the moment passes. The reader may be more responsive to Tess's vision, for this is tantalizingly close to a moment of reciprocity: she might almost be imagining the life of her reader. These narrative forms are especially right for novelists responsive to ecological concerns, since ecology is the study of relationships and interdependencies within shared local environments and of the relation of such environments to larger ecosystems.

Situated Observers

A pointer to an ecocritical theory of narrative is provided by Donna J. Haraway's influential essay "Situated Knowledges," in which she criticizes the stance of objectivity that scientific writers assume. Hardy's narrative does more than most to meet her requirement that every viewpoint should be "embodied" and "situated": "I would like to insist on the embodied nature of all vision, and so reclaim the sensory system that has been used to signify a leap out of the marked body and into a conquering gaze from nowhere" (188). The marked body is "situated"; it always occupies a particular place and time and is identified in its gendered, racial, and cultural particularity. The unmarked body is ghostly and irresponsible, claiming "the power to see and not be seen, to represent while escaping representation" (188). Haraway argues that in Western scientific traditions the white male body has normally been endowed with this unmarked status. White masculine subjectivity has been able to disembody itself and masquerade as a viewpoint of scientific objectivity. Haraway calls this the "god-trick" (189, 193): a rhetorical assumption of godlike externality, objectivity, and freedom of movement. She proposes that scientists who are responsive to feminism and ecology should renounce the god-trick, and instead place themselves, as embodied observers, marked bodies, into the descriptions and narratives they produce.

Haraway is asking writers of science to adopt narrative strategies similar to those of novelists who abandon omniscient narrative for a "situated" narrator who is both storyteller and character. Hardy shows that this need not be a restrictive movement from the social and consensual to the inward and individual. Narrative in his novels is not yielded up to unreliable character-narrators, whose viewpoint is closed and clearly differentiated from that of the implied reader. Hardy retains an impersonal narrative voice, but one that is constantly changing position, moving from one proxy observer to another and drawing on various genres of public address: sermon, newspaper editorial, academic lecture, scientific article, literary essay, and topographical guidebook.

He uses this public domain to construct the readership as an implied moral community. The phantom interventions that, had they happened, might have rescued characters from distress are presented as random interventions ("somebody might have come along that way") and therefore as potential communal interventions. There is a community of villagers and a much wider community of readers, any of whom might have happened along that way. The narrative commentary on Tess's rape breaks off after these words, "As Tess's own people down in those retreats are never tired of saying among each other in their fatalistic way: 'It was to be.' There lay the pity of it. An immeasurable social chasm was to divide our heroine's personality thereafter from that previous self of hers who stepped from her mother's door to try her fortune at Trantridge poultry-farm" (*Tess* 101–2). "Tess's own people," of her locality and class, are differentiated from the wider community of readers proposed in that possessive pronoun "our." It is "our heroine" but "their fatalistic way." The "we" precariously constituted is middle class, cosmopolitan, and mobile (at least, it does not live down in those retreats). "We," it seems, are expected to respond to Tess's story with feelings other than the fatalism attributed to her own people. Yet the image that follows, of "an immeasurable social chasm," deters us from seeing ourselves as more enlightened than her immediate community. We have no right to claim possession of Tess ("our heroine") in the name of a generalized community while we remain physically distant from her—and while we preserve that social chasm.

Soon, Angel Clare will chance upon Tess and become her middle-class lover, embodying (and eroticizing) the readerly fantasy of rescuing Tess. In this role he will fail her catastrophically. His failure might be called a tourist's failure. Drawn to her because of a cultural fantasy he projects onto her, he recoils when she reveals her difference from that fantasy. "I thought I should secure rustic innocence as surely as I should secure pink cheeks" (*Tess* 263–64).

Communities may be sheltering or punitive. Refuge from them may be sought either by appeal to a still wider circle or by retreat into privacy. Tess, Jude, Henchard, and others are exposed, throughout the novels, to a rich mixture of local commentary that is gossipy, joky, sympathetic, and scornful. Many of these comments are clearly distanced from those of the narrator and from the viewpoint of the implied reader, but some comments are indeterminately placed, possibly both "ours" and "theirs," so that the distance between the village community and the community of implied readers alternately widens and shrinks.

Henchard's feeling that he is under scrutiny apparently persists even when he is alone. About to throw himself into a river, he sees floating beneath him his own effigy, discarded by the crowd that has mocked him (*Madding Crowd* 300). He encounters his own gaze, as if he has himself joined the circle of his accusers. Eventually he is permitted to walk away from our scrutiny, but he seems unable to escape the shaming narrative he has internalized, the public crowd inside his head, until he dies. Insistently, these novels remind us that the most private stories inside people's heads are of external origin, that each anecdote told in public has private repercussions, and that public and personal narratives are as interdependent as country and city.

Haraway asks for a "commitment to mobile positioning": a practice of science and writing in which "one cannot relocate in any possible vantage point without being accountable for that movement. Vision is always a question of the power to see—and perhaps of the violence implicit in our visualizing practices" (192). Hardy's narrative begins to answer these requirements, repeatedly pressing us to account for the multiple and shifting positions in which it places us. Haraway asserts, "Positioning is, therefore, the key practice grounding knowledge organized around the imagery of vision, as so much Western scientific and philosophic discourse is organized. Positioning implies responsibility for our enabling practices" (193).

In Hardy's narrative it is the frequent shifting, in spatial and social terms, of the reader's perspective that brings to life such a sense of responsibility. The reader may be positioned close to a character and then made to retreat to the perspective of a passing tourist. Suddenly, after long, intimate knowledge of them, we are shown how Tess and the other milkmaids might have seemed at first glance. "Differing one from another in natures and moods so greatly as they did, they yet formed, bending, a curiously uniform row—automatic, noiseless; and an alien observer passing down the neighbouring lane might well have been excused for massing them as 'Hodge'" (*Tess* 167). This move places the reader in an intermediate position, distanced both from the dairymaids and from this insensitive observer. Yet at times Tess might have found sanctuary precisely by losing herself in the identity of a group. Conspicuousness is often her undoing. Twice, Angel picks her out from among her peers. Camouflage might have protected her. Each shift of the narrator's position asks us to reassess our own.

Two Ways of Loving Nature

Two forms of pleasure in the natural world appear in Hardy's novels. The unalienated lover of nature inhabits; the alienated lover of nature gazes. The first is a native, deeply embedded in a stable ecosystem; the second is a Romantic, a tourist, a newcomer, and a reader. The conventional assumption is that the transition from preindustrial to industrial society abolishes the first and engenders the second. Many of Hardy's characters are enmeshed in the technological and social changes that produce this transition. His novels are appreciative of both ways of loving nature and intent on exploring the relationship between them. Environmentalists hope it may be possible to break the sequence in which estrangement from nature is followed by Romantic regret and desire. They believe in the possibility of sustainable forms of development that will not estrange communities from their natural environments. Environmentalists seek to build alliances between tourist and native, hoping for an eventual society in which everyone will move between these positions.

The alienated observer tends to see unreflective happiness in the lives of the unalienated. In a journal entry dated 1889, Hardy takes this to a point of splendidly gloomy absurdity: "A woeful fact—that the human race is too extremely developed for its corporeal conditions, the nerves being evolved to an activity abnormal in such an environment. Even the higher animals are in excess in this respect. It may be questioned if Nature, or what we call Nature, so far back as when she crossed the line from invertebrates to vertebrates, did not exceed her mission. This planet does not supply the materials for happiness to higher existences" (qtd. in F. E. Hardy 218). Happiness is attributed sardonically to "lower" animals, such as the maggots Mrs. Yeobright watches "heaving and wallowing with enjoyment" in a heathland pool (*Return* 285). Deep in their immediate ecosystem, they have no horizon beyond it.

The Romantic subjectivity of the lover of natural history is here taken to an uncomfortable extreme. More usually, the turn of attention to nature in the form of small-scale life at the margins of human affairs brings relief from the pressure of events. This is the naturalist's pastoral: a diversion from the unhappiness that burdens "higher existences." Concentrated in a moment, the effect can be obliquely erotic, suggestive of intense focus on small areas of a person's body. Hardy sometimes places these moments of diversion at points of extreme pressure. Grace, in *The Woodlanders,* sheltering in Giles Winterborne's cottage, is becoming uneasy about Giles's failure to reappear. She hears a rustling outside the window, the sound of a newt moving in the fallen leaves (322). Her heightened, expectant senses catch a sound she would normally miss—an example that is almost hallucinatory in its extension of normal perception. The moment registers a peculiar mixture of ennui and apprehension, as Grace holds off her growing anxiety. The emotional function of such a glimpse is foregrounded, not concealed.

Lawrence Buell asks why nature writers so often "create landscapes in which obscure or overlooked objects become magnified or more densely rendered than they would be in the ordinary experience of them?" (103). He argues that the purpose of this "deliberate dislocation of ordinary perception" is to remind us of neglected nonhuman perspectives and move us toward "environmental literacy" (104, 107). An ecocentric vision seeks not only to assert the value of these perspectives but also somehow to accommodate them in the human sphere, in "plot," since they are constitutive of human life. It is not fanciful to credit Hardy with similar aims.

Jude is the character with the most highly developed sympathy for nonhuman creatures. He is punished for allowing hungry birds to feed (*Jude* 39). He tiptoes to avoid crushing earthworms (41). He pities his pig and sacrifices some of its economic value by killing it swiftly (86–89). In all this he is an ironically ineffectual version of an omniscient God who sees even the woe of a sparrow. Jude attempts a godlike compassion without the advantages of God's position. Jude's determination to take account of the feelings of small creatures—interests for which the normal human economy has no room—is a benign, quixotic version of Haraway's god-trick. Jude's human attempt at godly omniscience is a reproof to a supposedly loving God who has not provided an economy merciful to all forms of life. Unlike Christ's intercession, Jude's is ineffectual: he takes the punishment onto himself without saving others.

Jude's concern for all creatures is scorned, like his aspiration to study at Christminster, as foolishness or vanity. At the pig killing, Arabella tells him with moral force, "Poor folks must live" (88). Jude may be one of those "higher existences" whose nerves have evolved to a degree that unfits them for life on this planet, but he does not himself draw this conclusion, despair of the planet, and retreat into private concerns. Even at his most weary, Jude rejects the flattering charge that he is unworldly, preferring the idea of incremental progress. "It takes two or three generations to do what I tried to do in one," he says (336). "Our ideas were fifty years too soon to be any good to us" (405).

Jude's concern for the natural world is ineffectual because it is not a shared, communal concern. His gaze is anguished while the tourist's is delighted, but both gaze from outside. Unalienated pleasure in nature occurs, by contrast, neither in distress nor leisure; it happens in the course of daily work. "Winterborne's fingers were endowed with a gentle conjuror's touch in spreading the roots of each little tree, resulting in a sort of caress under which the delicate fibres all laid themselves out in their proper directions for growth" (*Woodlanders* 93). To outsiders such as Grace and the reader, Giles's unalienated labor seems a kind of magic or lovemaking. His is the communal knowledge that comes from growing up, living, and working in a stable ecosystem. It is lost when social mobility carries a person away from their community and work, as Grace is sent from Little Hintock to learn the manners of a higher social position. On her return, she has forgotten the names of the apples grown around her home (72). After Giles's death, Grace feels wistful amazement when she discovers how Giles and Marty used to work together in the woods. Theirs was a knowledge of minutiae that was neither eccentric nor self-conscious. "From the light lashing of the twigs upon their faces when brushing through them in the dark either could pronounce upon the species of the tree whence they stretched; from the quality of the wind's murmur through a bough either could in like manner name its sort afar off. They knew by a glance at a trunk if its heart were sound, or tainted with incipient decay; and by the state of its upper twigs the stratum that had been reached by its roots" (340–41). To this narrator, their work, hard as it is, possesses the undividedness of mind and body, self and environment, that is the object of so much Romantic longing. The reader stands outside the book, but Giles and Marty inhabit the woods. The novel's very tribute to their culture is an act of commodification.

Giles and Marty have a practical knowledge of the woodlands of the type that Ray Dasmann attributes to the communities he calls "ecosystem people." These are communities "totally dependent, or largely so, on the animals and plants of a particular area" (21), deeply accustomed to that area and in stable, sustainable relation to the local ecosystem. Gary Paul Nabhan explores the interdependency of work, play, and story that enables such communities to live in practical intimacy with their environment. Nabhan's examples are the O'odham people of Arizona and the Australian Aboriginals of Alice Springs. Hardy's Wessex villages are not exactly indigenous preindustrial communities, but they are the nearest thing to what Nabhan identifies as a "culture of habitat" still to be found in late-nineteenth-century England. Little Hintock, in its wooded enclave, is the most secluded and unadulterated of Hardy's communities: the most deeply engrossed in its immediate environment. The plots often turn on the disruptive arrival in such places of forces from outside. Characters arrive or return; new technologies are introduced. Giles and Marty's close association with trees signifies deep-rootedness but also vulnerability. Like trees they are unable to flee.

Yet each newcomer is only relatively new. Grace returns to Little Hintock as an alienated outsider, but to Fitzpiers she seems indigenous to that community while he stands outside it. The continual shifts of perspective make it difficult for the reader to see intervention merely as destructive. Each change of perspective itself marks an intervention: a moment of arrival. Such narrative mobility is incompatible with a simply conservative attitude to change. True, the ambiguity of Grace's social position causes disastrous confusion. True, Tess's calamities follow from the indeterminate position that makes her both aristocrat and laborer, while Jude's misfortune comes of his unrealistic aspirations. But in Hardy's novels the message that social mobility brings disaster is as bitterly ironic as the suggestion that nature would have done better not to progress from invertebrates to vertebrates. To read Hardy as conservative and hostile to social mobility is to misrepresent him brutally. His novels are profoundly—one might say dangerously— unreconciled to inequalities of wealth and power. Restless desire for advancement and novelty is the source of vitality and pleasure as well as tragedy. The novels show the havoc wrought by such desires but also the mortifying effect when they are thwarted.

The conservatism that depicts an idealized preindustrial past as a natural way of life is still strong. Environmentalism is often confused with this nostalgia, sometimes by environmentalists. Ecocriticism may have been slow to gain recognition in England because of a prevalent assumption that nature writing cannot escape this conservatism. The ruralists of the interwar period, most of them admirers of Hardy, brought nature writing in England into grave disrepute. Writers such as H. V. Morton, H. J. Massingham, and Henry Williamson sought in villages and farming communities the ideal England for which British soldiers had fought. Authentic rural life, free from encroachment, was the antidote to the modernity that had produced the war. In Williamson's case, the conservatism became fascism. After 1945, public enthusiasm for "nature" was evident in the popularity of natural history books and the emergence of television wildlife documentaries, but literary nature writing remained heavily tainted.

Environmentalism calls for a new nature writing, clearly differentiated from the conservative tradition and aware of its appeals and dangers. To ecocritics, Hardy's great value is that he shows the possibility of a nature writing not always in search of stability, not simply hostile to change and incursion. His abundant relativity shows nature writers an alternative to the genre's most menacing traditions: Nietzschean admiration of nature's amoral power and conservative nostalgia for mythical feudal harmonies. Against these, Hardy offers the endless generation of meaning as the vivid life of a place, produced by its human, animal, and plant life: a creative life that newcomers enhance if they come with an awareness of relative positions. Hence the suggestion that we might visit his places now.

A vision Nabhan expresses with eloquence is that a creative relationship may be possible between indigenous cultures of habitat and postmodern cultures of technology. Such a relationship would bypass the familiar sequence in which industrialization destroys the culture of habitat that then becomes an object of nostalgic desire: the perversity that catches so many characters in Hardy and compromises so much nature writing. In this utopia (to sketch it a little flippantly), a postmodern Giles Winterborne would not die of exposure, nor would he lose his dwelling because of a feudal property law. He would retain his native understanding of the woods and continue his sustainable forestry, protected by a modern health service and enjoying access to the wider world through television and the Internet. Indigenous culture would no longer stand as the binary opposite of modernity and would no longer be the lost golden age, the innocent primitive, or (the flip side of that) the narrow, ignorant, and brutal primitive. Frail as this hope seems, it does attempt the difficult task of properly valuing three things often seen as incompatible: natural environments as loved by tourists and other alienated romantics, indigenous cultures of habitat, and the material benefits of modernity.

This utopia would require of its inhabitants a high degree of self-consciousness about their own continually shifting positions. Such self-consciousness is required of environmentalists who wish to avoid simple nostalgia for an idealized preindustrial culture. Nabhan duly situates himself, in *Cultures of Habitat*, telling a story of himself as an Arab American adolescent lover occupying a complex cross-cultural position (89–96). He suggests that we might value our own shifts from position to position as a sort of rich diversity, as necessary as biodiversity. A famous passage from *The Return of the Native* shows us some ways of doing this.

Clym Yeobright is working as a furze-cutter on Egdon Heath:

> This man from Paris was now so disguised by his leather accoutrements, and by the goggles he was obliged to wear over his eyes, that his closest friend might have passed by without recognising him. He was a brown spot in the midst of an expanse of olive-green gorse and nothing more. Though frequently depressed in spirit, when not actually at work, owing to thoughts of Eustacia's position and his mother's estrangement, when in the full swing of labour he was cheerfully disposed and calm.
>
> His daily life was of a curious microscopic sort, his whole world being limited to a circuit of a few feet from his person. His familiars were creep-

ing and winged things, and they seemed to enroll him in their band. Bees hummed around his ears with an intimate air, and tugged at the heath and furze-flowers . . . . The strange amber-coloured butterflies which Egdon produced, and which were never seen elsewhere, quivered in the breath of his lips . . . . Litters of young rabbits came out from their forms to sun themselves upon hillocks, the hot beams blazing through the delicate tissue of each thin-fleshed ear, and firing it to a blood-red transparency in which the veins could be seen. None of them feared him. (*Return* 262)

This is nature as paradise temporarily and inadvertently regained. Yeobright's damaged eyesight has forced him to give up his studies. In training to be a schoolteacher he has already taken a step of deliberate, downward social mobility. Now he descends even further and finds an unexpected happiness. Reading represents his aspiration to see beyond his immediate surroundings; deprived of this, Yeobright discovers, in work rather than contemplation, a release from self-consciousness and alienation. He has literally come closer to nature. The move is symbolized by his absorption into the landscape. Simultaneously, Yeobright is the man from Paris and a brown spot in an expanse of gorse. This juxtaposition does not merely show us the distance he has come; it positions us where we can see both Yeobrights. Neither perception is to be abandoned.

The capacity Yeobright has lost is tacitly compared to the knowledge Adam and Eve gained from the forbidden fruit, which caused them to feel shame and to be expelled from Paradise. Renouncing it, Yeobright is able to return to the Egdon of his childhood and to Paradise. In an unfallen world, the animals no longer fear him. Briefly he returns with a completeness never accomplished by others who return, such as Grace and Angel. But Hardy is insistent about the cost of return. This closeness to nature means loss of vision—loss, for example, of the longer scientific perspectives that may now enable us to foresee ecological disaster. Yeobright becomes as vulnerable as the animals and insects with whom he shares the heath.

That amber-colored butterfly poses the problem in miniature. It is almost certainly the Lulworth Skipper, *Thymelicus aeteon*. Tom Tolman's *Field Guide to the Butterflies of Britain and Europe* lists this butterfly as first recorded in Britain in 1832, giving its range as "in Britain restricted to the Dorset coast" (275).

Hardy's narrator does not give the scientific name, nor even the English name, although elsewhere, as the narrative shifts in register, we have, with *Ulex europaeus*, just the scientific name (*Return* 89), and with the Cream-Coloured Courser, just the English name (109). If we know the scientific name, we may also know that the butterfly's whole range includes much of southern Europe and northern West Africa. Its rarity is relative. The withholding of these names presents the butterfly as it is known locally, intimately. The narrative keeps both perspectives in play.

Buell identifies Richard Jefferies rather than Hardy as "Thoreau's English counterpart" (105). Hardy he finds problematical as an ecocentric writer because, despite the depth of his portrayal of such environments as Egdon Heath, "the heath is in the long run ancillary to Clym's story," and the novel "is about people in place, not about place itself" (255). I have attempted to show that the special value of Hardy to ecocritics is precisely in the way he does not separate place and person. He will not allow anything, place or person, to stabilize in meaning; its meaning is always the product of a shifting set of relations and always seen in the act of generation by those relations. Paradoxically, this is to create a stronger sense of the elusive, excessive presence of places, since the descriptions and narratives they generate never cohere for long and are quickly exposed as relative.

Works Cited

Buell, Lawrence. *The Environmental Imagination.* Cambridge: Belknap-Harvard UP, 1995.

Dasmann, Ray. *Wildlife Biology.* New York: John Wiley, 1964.

Ebbatson, Roger. *Hardy: The Margin of the Unexpressed.* Sheffield: Sheffield Academic, 1993.

Haraway, Donna J. *Simians, Cyborgs, and Women: The Reinvention of Nature.* London: Free Association, 1991.

Hardy, Florence Emily. *The Life of Thomas Hardy, 1840–1928.* London: Macmillan, 1972.

Hardy, Thomas. *Desperate Remedies.* 1871. London: Macmillan, 1975.

———. *Far from the Madding Crowd.* 1874. London: Macmillan, 1975.

———. *Jude the Obscure.* 1896. London: Macmillan, 1975.

———. *The Mayor of Casterbridge.* 1886. London: Macmillan, 1975.

———. *The Return of the Native.* 1878. London: Macmillan, 1975.

————. *Tess of the d'Urbervilles.* 1891. London: Macmillan, 1975.

————. *Under the Greenwood Tree.* 1872. London: Macmillan, 1975.

————. *The Woodlanders.* 1887. London: Macmillan, 1975.

Millgate, Michael. *Thomas Hardy: His Career as a Novelist.* London: The Bodley Head, 1971.

————. *Thomas Hardy: A Biography.* Oxford: Oxford UP, 1982.

Nabhan, Gary Paul. *Cultures of Habitat: On Nature, Culture, and Story.* Washington, DC: Counterpoint, 1997.

Tolman, Tom. *Field Guide to the Butterflies of Britain and Europe.* London: HarperCollins, 1997.

Widdowson, Peter. *Hardy in History: A Study in Literary Sociology.* London: Routledge, 1989.

The Book "Laid Upon the Landscape": Virginia Woolf and Nature

Charlotte Zoë Walker

Prologue: An Urban Nature Experience

My lifelong passion for Virginia Woolf's writing began with a mud puddle—one of those puddles that Rhoda in *The Waves* found it so difficult to step across. A friend and fellow graduate student at the University of Chicago had lent me her copy of *To the Lighthouse,* telling me I would love it. But before I could read it, it fell from my arms into a rain puddle and was completely soaked. That small, gray, cloth-bound book was in a terrible state, and it could not honorably be returned as it was. I had to buy my friend a new copy from my meager graduate student income, over my then-husband's objections. The lovely, rain-soaked, baptized copy of *To the Lighthouse* became a permanent part of my life, giving me years later the topic for my doctoral dissertation and supplying throughout my life an impossible ideal for my fiction writing. I have always treasured, and have taught many times from, that little book with its water stains, its molded, gray fabric shredded at the corners, and its marks of a very wet voyage to the lighthouse.

Reading Nature, Silence, and Time

In an essay entitled "Reading," Virginia Woolf revives in a modernist context an old trope, that of the natural world as a text to be read; from a postmodern perspective, we might say that she expresses the intertextuality of nature and literature. "Instead of being a book it seemed as if what I read was laid upon the landscape, not printed, bound, or sewn up, but somehow the product of trees and fields and the hot summer sky, like the air which swam, on fine mornings, round the outlines of things" (*Essays* 142). Woolf would, of course, no more accept the conventionally religious interpretation of "The Book of Nature" than she would any form of institutionalized religion.[1] And yet, her reading of nature is often imbued with a sense of illumination, while at other times it is tinged with a critique of patriarchal society. That is, her reading of the book "laid upon the landscape" is both revelatory and revolutionary. This essay proposes to explore both these aspects of Woolf's explorations of nature from an ecofeminist point of view. With *A Room of One's Own* and *Three Guineas* as classic early feminist texts, Virginia Woolf is widely acknowledged as one of our feminist foremothers. Although she wrote decades before ecofeminism emerged as a useful theoretical and critical concept, it is not inappropriate to consider her an ecofeminist foremother as well.

With the emergence of ecocritical approaches to literature, readers of Woolf are becoming increasingly conscious of the remarkable and varied representations of nature in many of her novels.[2] The Virginia Woolf we have read for so many other reasons—her modernism, her feminism, the beauty of her language, her brilliant experiments with narrative form, and her subtle explorations of consciousness, culture, and relationships—that Virginia Woolf now appears to us in a new way. We have always known that the waves pounded on the shore in Woolf's writing, that the tree was pelted with starlings, that flowers blazed their colors and presence throughout her work; but suddenly we see them foregrounded. Bringing Woolf's nature writing to the fore changes our reading of her work and gives it even greater texture, depth, and dimensionality than it had before.

Often Woolf's writing about nature is a conversation with it. Nature was for her an intense and crucial interlocutor in the questionings about life and death, patriarchy and gender, and spirituality and the rejection of traditional religion that are at the heart of her literary achievement. The conversation ranges from what some might dismiss as an essentialist identification of woman and nature (I would argue a greater complexity, however) to a sophisticated and ironic political critique, to a kind of metawriting—the book laid upon the landscape—

that explores the links among language, silence, and our experience of the natural world.

One of the most compelling aspects of this dialogue is that Woolf often conveys it through silence: images of silence woven into nature and actual silences woven into her text. A quarter of a century ago, I completed a doctoral dissertation on Woolf that was influenced by phenomenological criticism; two chapters concerned with Woolf's treatment of silence were later published, and as I look back on that work, I find it interesting to discover how much Woolf's exploration of silence is interwoven with her representation of nature—and how little I realized that connection at the time. As a reader, I needed the emergence of ecofeminist and ecocritical thought to make me more conscious of these elements in Woolf's work. As a writer, Woolf had been exploring them all along. She is like the woman in the yellow gown in the painting in *Between the Acts* (1941): "She led them down green glades, into the heart of silence" (49).

In *Between the Acts* silence and nature are juxtaposed against civilization and culture, with the specter of war in the background. There is not space here for a thorough exploration of all these elements. However, the interminglings of silence, nature, and words are especially represented by certain moments in the village pageant created by Miss LaTrobe. Several times when the characters in the pageant speak, we are told that the wind has blown their words away (78, 80, 124, 125). And when Miss LaTrobe experiments by giving her audience "ten mins. of present time. Swallows, cows, etc." (179), the audience is uncomfortable with both the silence and the sounds of nature.

A variation on Woolf's treatment of the connections between silence and nature is her presentation of nature as mediator of those great concepts that haunted her, time and death. Her narratives explore time in numberless ways, most extensively, perhaps, in the "Time Passes" interlude of *To the Lighthouse* (1927), and in *The Waves* (1931) and *The Years* (1938). In each of these novels, Woolf interpolates lyrical suggestions of the cyclical life of nature into the sequence of her narrative. Often these are expressed through imagery of silence, where silence mediates between the self and nature.

The entire "Time Passes" section of *To the Lighthouse* is a symbolic silence made of words, placed "between the acts" of the two longer sections in which the drama of the characters is acted out, and depicting both the passage of time and the impersonal power of nature to absorb human tragedies of loss and death. It is a major literary experiment, an attempt to create through words an interlude that is like Keats's urn, "a foster child of silence and slow time."

> Nothing, it seemed, could disturb that image, corrupt that innocence, or disturb the swaying mantle of silence which, week after week, in the empty room, wove into itself the falling cries of birds, ships hooting, the drone and hum of the fields, a dog's bark, a man's shout, and folded them round the house in silence. (129–30)

Silence in "Time Passes" is far more than the absence of sound. And although it is related to death, it also speaks of life in the hands of nature as unseen power. Through the many voices of silence in "Time Passes," Woolf continually suggests nonhuman forms of consciousness that she locates in nature. "Did Nature supplement what man advanced? Did she complete what he began? With equal complacence she saw his misery, his meanness, and his torture" (134). A less devastating, yet still intrusive, kind of nature is depicted as time continues its work on the deserted house: "Toads had nosed their way in. Idly, aimlessly, the swaying shawl swung to and fro. A thistle thrust itself between the tiles in the larder. The swallows nested in the drawing-room" (137–38).

"Time Passes" concludes with something like a lullaby: "Through the open window the voice of the beauty of the world came murmuring, too softly to hear exactly what it said . . . entreating the sleepers . . . if they would not actually come down to the beach itself at least to lift the blind and look out. They would see then night flowing down in purple" (142). Lily Briscoe, the artist friend of the Ramsays, a guest in the newly opened house (whose artist's vision will create the triumphant ending of the novel) receives this blessing, this nature lullaby: "The sigh of all the seas breaking in measure round the isles soothed them; the night wrapped them" (142). As Lily Briscoe opens her eyes in the morning, it is clear that the "voice of the beauty of the world" had done away with the imperceptiveness, the dullness of habit in ordinary life. The last sentence of "Time Passes" is a single word, "Awake" (143).

The question of consciousness, and the individual's possible transcendence through a Wordsworthian apprehension of nature, is explored throughout Virginia Woolf's work. Those moments of transcendence in her fiction, and in her personal writings—as when she wrote in her diary that she could "pass from outer to inner and inhabit eternity" (27 November 1935; *Diary* 355)—are characteristically expressive of an expansive view of nature. In another passage in "Time Passes," for instance, the merging of inner and outer is demonstrated as the self (in the person of "the wakeful, the hopeful, walking the beach") disperses outward in "flesh turned to atoms" and inward, with "stars flashing in their hearts" (132). For Woolf, nature encompasses infinity and the infinitely small, inhabits both science and poetry.[3] In the final chapter of *The Years*, moments of revelation are conveyed through images of nature interwoven with silence. The party that closes the novel has lasted all night, and North Pargiter is musing sleepily on "silence and solitude . . . the only element in which the mind is free now," and he imagines "that he was lying in a great space on a blue plain with hills on the rim of the horizon. He stretched out his feet" (424). In this strange moment, which is one of life's "spaces between," North Pargiter is carried briefly into a different level of reality in which he has expanded to become part of a landscape.

Shocks of Perception and the Book Laid Upon the Landscape

Woolf's explorations of nature are intricately intertwined with consciousness; the "shock" of certain moments of perception are for her crucial to being fully alive. She describes this sense of ecstatic wakefulness in her brief autobiography, "A Sketch of the Past," through early impressions of light, air, and sounds from her nursery at St. Ives: "The quality of the air above Talland House seemed to suspend sound, to let it sink down slowly, as if it were caught in a gummy blue veil. The rooks cawing is part of the waves breaking—one, two, one, two—and the splash as the wave drew back and then it gathered again, and I lay there half awake, half asleep, drawing in such ecstasy as I cannot describe" (66).

Later in "A Sketch of the Past," Woolf proposes her idea of sudden shocks that penetrate what she called the "cotton wool" of nonbeing that makes up much of our lives. She describes both the shock of human disaster—a death, a suicide—and the shock of beauty in nature. "'That is the whole,' I said. I was looking at a plant with a spread of leaves; and it seemed suddenly plain that the flower itself was a part of the earth; that a ring enclosed what was the flower; and that was the real flower; part earth; part flower" (71). Woolf goes on to say, "I suppose that the shock-receiving capacity is what makes me a writer" (72). Woolf's childhood memory of the wonder of beholding a flower is expressed fictionally in *Between the Acts* when the narrative suddenly and briefly enters the consciousness of Isa Oliver's little boy, conveying his experience of going deeply into the yellow chamber of a flower—"it blazed a soft yellow, a lambent light . . . it filled the caverns behind the eyes with light" (11)—when he is suddenly interrupted by a rough joke from his grandfather.

Again and again, Woolf's fiction demonstrates in moments of intense sensuous particularity how consciousness is fed by such perceptions. Indeed, she often suggests a consciousness in what is perceived as well as in the perceiver. In another essay I discuss Woolf's exploration of the forces that enable us to break through the sequences of everyday life, to position ourselves differently by means of such moments ("Creative"). At the time of writing it, I was interested in Woolf's ideas about the creative process, about the relationship between language and silence and what she called the "blade of consciousness." What did not strike me so clearly then was how deeply Woolf associates this process with her perceptions of the natural world.

The "blade of consciousness" in the intervals in *The Waves,* the beam of sunlight that enters through the window of a house, slices through the ordinariness of daily life. "The sun laid broader blades upon the house," Woolf writes in one interval (194), and in another: "Now, too, the rising sun came in at the window. . . . Now in the growing light its whiteness settled in the plate; the blade condensed its gleam" (226). In these intervals the progress of the sunlight's entering a room through a window can be interpreted as representing an individual mind being illuminated by consciousness. This symbolic use of light as consciousness in Woolf's writing often connects to specific images of nature.

In 1954, long before we had thought of reading Woolf through an ecocritical or ecofeminist lens, Woolf's friend and sometime lover Vita Sackville-West, in "The Landscape of a Mind," relates a conversation in which she asked Virginia Woolf about the particularities of nature in her work:

I remember the startled look Virginia Woolf once gave me when I asked why she was always dragging in sea-buckets and spades, and sending little crabs scuttling through rock-pools. She had not realized it, but supposed ("Now that you say so") a hark-back to her childhood at St. Ives. And moths, why was she so haunted by moths? They were always flying in, the moment anyone opened a window. She had written about the death of a moth; she had intended to call one book *The Moths* instead of *The Waves*. Ah, that she could easily explain: in her youth she used to put grease-bands round the apple trees and go out with a torch and a jam-pot after dark. And leaves—why this preoccupation with leaves? Leaves seen against the sky; leaves green; leaves browning; leaves fluttering down, blown about a London street; leaves decaying; leaves everywhere. But I forgot to ask her that. (267–68)

Vita Sackville-West was right about the leaves. Perhaps for Woolf they have a punning connection to reading—to pages in the book laid upon the landscape. In any case, leaves are everywhere in her work—blown by the wind, as in *The Years,* or creating a hiding place for children, as in *The Waves,* where the evocation of children hiding together among leaves conveys the sensory intensity of childhood and is also associated with storytelling:

> "Let us now crawl," said Bernard, "under the canopy of currant leaves, and tell stories." Let us inhabit the underworld. Let us take possession of our secret territory. . . . This is our world, lit with crescents and stars of light; and great petals half transparent block the openings like purple windows. Everything is strange. Things are huge and very small. The stalks of flowers are thick as oak trees. Leaves are high as the domes of vast cathedrals. We are giants, lying here, who can make forests quiver. (23)

Just as Woolf's characters, and through them her readers, relate sensuously to nature, often receiving through it the shocks that bring them out of the "cotton wool," to use Woolf's phrase again, of daily life and into the state of creativity that leads to transformation and to art, Woolf also hints from time to time at a merging of writing, reading, and nature. The characters in *The Waves* are haunted by their memory of a woman writing in a garden, who seems to have written their whole world. At the end of *Between the Acts,* Miss LaTrobe's inspiration for her next play comes first in simple words, mingled with the earth: "Words of one syllable sank down into the mud. She drowsed; she nodded. The mud became fertile. Words rose above the intolerably laden dumb oxen plodding through the mud. Words without meaning—wonderful words" (212). As her inspiration grows, the imagery takes flight, becomes more exalted. "Suddenly the tree was pelted with starlings. She set down her glass. She heard the first words" (212).

Such rootedness of reading and writing in nature occurs in other novels as well. In *Orlando* (1928), the poem that Orlando carries throughout his/her long life is entitled "The Oak Tree" and is rooted in an oak tree from Orlando's earliest days. In *To the Lighthouse* the act of reading transforms Mrs. Ramsay into a sort of tree climber or feathered flyer through the words: "she read and turned the page, swinging herself, zigzagging this way and that, from one line to another as from one branch to another, from one red and white flower to another" (119). On the voyage to the lighthouse at the end of the book, Cam observes her father reading in terms that suggest a kind of trail breaking: "He read, she thought, as if he were . . . wheedling a large flock of sheep, or pushing his way up and up a single narrow path . . . and sometimes it seemed a branch struck at him, a bramble blinded him, but he was not going to let himself be beaten by that; on he went, tossing over page after page" (190).

In *The Waves* the reader is given instructions on how to read a poem that is encrusted with bits of nature:

> Certainly, one cannot read this poem without effort. The page is often corrupt and mud-stained, and torn and stuck together with faded leaves, with scraps of verbena or geranium. To read this poem one must have myriad eyes. . . . One must have patience and infinite care and let the light sound, whether of spiders' delicate feet on a leaf or the chuckle of water in some irrelevant drainpipe, unfold too. (198–99)

And so we return to "Reading," that essay we began with, where Woolf imagines herself reading a book "laid upon the landscape, not printed, bound, or sewn up, but somehow the product of trees and fields and the hot summer sky, like the air which swam, on fine mornings, round the outlines of things." (*Essays* 142) Perhaps one of the authors whose work is read in the course of this essay is an influence on that trope. Woolf enters into a dialogue with the work of Thomas Browne, who in *Religio Medici* refers to nature as a religous text.[4] Woolf does not quote this assertion, however, but rather his statement that "The world that I regard is myself, it is the microcosm of my own frame that I cast mine eyes on" (*Essays* 155). And she asks, "What . . . is ever to stop the course of such a mind, unroofed and open to the sky?" (155).

Throughout "Reading" Woolf speaks not only of the sensuous pleasure of reading in a natural setting and the pleasures of the mind in ranging between book and landscape; as the essay continues, she also links reading to childhood adventures in nature, recalling not only the moths ("the moths came out, the swift grey moths of the dusk, that only visit flowers for a second . . . vibrating to a blur" [*Essays* 150]) but also the childhood "scientific" expeditions she had mentioned to Vita Sackville-West:

> The business of dinner now engrossing the grown-up people, we made ready our lantern, our poison jar, and took our butterfly nets in our hands. The road that skirted the wood was so pale that its hardness grated upon our boots unexpectedly. It was the last strip of reality, however, off which we stepped into the gloom of the unknown. The lantern shoved its wedge of light through the dark, as though the air were a fine black snow piling itself up in banks on either side of the yellow beam. (150)

Here in her account of a childhood "expedition," the naturalist in Woolf once again emerges. "[T]he little circle of forest where we stood became as if we saw it though the lens of a very powerful magnifying glass. . . . Then there emerged here a grasshopper, there a beetle, and here again a daddy longlegs, awkwardly making his way from blade to blade" (*Essays* 150). As the children of Woolf's memory are first awed by the beauty of a moth and then driven to pursue and collect it, they are shocked by the sound of a falling tree in the forest, "a hollow rattle of sound in the deep silence of the wood. . . . It waned and spread through the forest: it died away, then another of those deep sighs arose. An enormous silence succeeded. 'A tree,' we said at last. A tree had fallen" (152).

From the shock of this remembered sound deep in a wood penetrated by children on a stealthy journey in the night, Woolf is moved to consider the same shocks of perception that she explores in "A Sketch of the Past." Despite the image of disintegration in the falling tree, she says, "the process I have in mind is just the opposite" and is rather "of a creative character" (*Essays* 152). "Through the tremor and vibration of daily custom one discerns bone and form, endurance and permanence. Sorrow will have the power to effect this sudden arrest of the fluidity of life, and joy will have the same power. Or it may come without apparent cause, imperceptibly, much as some bud feels a sudden release in the night and is found in the morning with all its petals shaken free" (153).

The Naturalist Essays and the Short Stories: Clues to an Ecofeminist Perspective

Virginia Woolf wrote several review essays on literary naturalists or nature writers: Dorothy Wordsworth, Henry David Thoreau, W. H. Hudson, Gilbert White, and others. These long-forgotten essays throw additional light on Woolf's perspective on nature in her fiction. In an essay on Dorothy Wordsworth, Woolf revisits the time in which Wordsworth was walking and enjoying nature with her brother and with Samuel Taylor Coleridge:

> Now after the hardships and separations of youth they were together under their own roof; now they could address themselves undisturbed to the absorbing occupation of living in the heart of Nature and trying, day by day, to read her meaning. . . . Dorothy could ramble all day on the hills and sit up talking to Coleridge all night without being scolded by her aunt for unwomanly behaviour. The hours were theirs from sunrise to sunset. . . . Custom, convention, everything was subordinated to the absorbing, exacting, exhausting task of living in the heart of Nature and writing poetry. (*Collected Essays* 1967, 201)

There is a feminist ring to Woolf's account here, a pleasure in Dorothy Wordsworth's liberation from custom, that calls to mind how much Woolf herself chafed under convention. It is also reminiscent of her more urban time of freedom in a household of siblings, when she and her sister and brothers set up housekeeping together, free of parental authority.

The essay goes on to explore the unique effect of Dorothy Wordsworth's writing. "It is strange how vividly all this is brought before us, considering that the diary is made up of brief notes such as any quiet woman might make of her garden's changes and her brother's moods and the progress of the seasons. . . . She met a cow in a field. 'The cow looked at me, and I looked at the cow, and whenever I stirred the cow gave over eating'" (*Collected Essays* 1967, 201). Woolf notes that in Dorothy Wordsworth's brief journal entries, "one feels the suggestive power which is the gift of the poet rather than of the naturalist, the power which, taking only the simplest facts, so orders them that the whole scene comes before us, heightened and composed, the lake in its quiet, the hills in their splendour" (202).

Reading further in her description of Dorothy Wordsworth leads to a new apprehension of Woolf's quest for catching some kind of truth in her own work, a quest she frequently described in images of nature: "the fin in the waste water" that haunts *The Waves,* or the wild goose of *Orlando,* for instance. We see through Woolf's description of Dorothy Wordsworth's work how closely that search may be linked to observation. "Her first concern was to be truthful—grace and symmetry must be made subordinate to truth. . . . But then truth is sought because to falsify the look of the stir of the breeze on the lake is to tamper with the spirit which inspires appearances. . . . A sight or sound would not let her be till she had traced her perception along its course and fixed it in words" (202). Although Woolf may not have seen herself as the same kind of careful recorder of natural phenomena that she characterizes in Dorothy Wordsworth, Woolf's passionate search for truth in language and the sense of seeking "some secret of the utmost importance" (*Collected Essays* 1967, 203) are recorded often in her diaries and are closely related to the passion she attributes to Wordsworth.

Virginia Woolf's appreciation of the naturalist's eye is also apparent in her essay on the eighteenth-century English naturalist Gilbert White of Selborne. She describes *The Natural History of Selborne* as "one of those ambiguous books that seem to tell a plain story . . . and yet by some apparently unconscious device of the author's has a door left open, through which we hear distant sounds" (*Collected Essays* 1967, 122). Woolf sees "the story of Selborne [as] a vegetable, an animal story. The gossip is about the habits of vipers and the love interest is supplied chiefly by frogs. . . . The crop of the cuckoo is examined; the viper is dissected; the grasshopper is sought with a pliant grass blade in its hole; the mouse is measured and found to weigh one copper halfpenny" (123).

Woolf then plays the pleasant trick of assuming the role of the naturalist herself, with White as the object of her study. "This is the moment, then, when his eyes are fixed upon the swallow, to watch Gilbert White himself. We observe in the first place the creature's charming simplicity. He is quite indifferent to public opinion. He will transplant a colony of crickets to his lawn; imprison one in a paper cage on his table; bawl through a speaking trumpet at his bees" (123). After more description of White and his work, Woolf comments, "So we observe, through our field-glasses, this very fine specimen of the 18th century clerical naturalist" (125). This whimsical exercise conveys not only Woolf's humor but also her sense of the intertextuality of literature and nature; the act of reading transforms the naturalist to a creature of nature and gives him the power of flight, not only through space but through time. "In that moment of abstraction he hears sounds that make him uneasy in the early morning; he escapes from Selborne, from his own age, and comes winging his way to us in the dusk along the hedgerows. A clerical owl? A parson with the wings of a bird? A hybrid? But his own description fits him best. 'The kestrel or wind-hover,' he says, 'has a peculiar mode of hanging in the air in one place, his wings all the time being briskly agitated'" (125–26).

Woolf's essays on Thoreau and W. H. Hudson further indicate that she was conversant with and appreciative of the work of the literary naturalist. Also, notable among her essays that indicate Woolf's pre-ecofeminist bent is "The Plumage Bill," which caused her so much trouble at the time of its publication. In this essay Woolf emphatically defends women against being blamed for the predation and near extinction of some bird species for millinery purposes. Reginald Abbott interprets the essay as a defining feminist text for Woolf, saying that it "stands as the first feminist statement of the early twentieth century's most eloquent and influential 'champion of women'" (*Collected Essays* 1988, 278). What Abbott does not elucidate, and what is significant to our discussion here, is that Woolf's position is a distinctly ecofeminist one, pointing the blame for environmental destruction on the male-dominated institutions behind an industry aimed at exploiting women's socially induced desire to be attractive to men. Those who criticized Woolf at the time completely missed the point she was making, because her irony was either too fine or too blunt an instrument for the issue and audience at hand.

Woolf's environmental awareness is also apparent in "Thunder at Wembley," an essay on the British Empire Exhibition of 1924. Just as she was to do later in certain passages of *To the Lighthouse, The Waves,* and *Between the Acts,* Woolf juxtaposes a somewhat stately, civilized country event with the nature that surrounds it. "It is nature that is the ruin of Wembley," the essay begins wickedly, "yet it is difficult to see what steps Lord Stevenson, Lieutenant-General Sir Travers Clarke, and the Duke of Devonshire could have taken to keep her out. They might have eradicated the grass and felled the chestnut trees; even so the thrushes would have got in, and there would always have been the sky" (*Collected Essays* 1988, 410–11). Woolf juxtaposes against nature the management, architecture, and economics of this exhibit honoring British imperialism. Then she notes that "just as one is beginning a little wearily to fumble with those two fine words—democracy, mediocrity—Nature asserts herself where one would least look to find her" (411). Not only does one not expect nature in a space cleared for imperialism but one does not always think to look for it in people, as Woolf does. Describing the people attending the exhibit, Woolf sees them not as separate from nature but as part of it, even pausing "now and again to remove some paper bag or banana skin and place it in the receptacles provided for that purpose" (411). She marvels that they can have an interest in the empire—"How, with all this dignity of their own, can they bring themselves to believe in that?" (412)—but she quickly attributes this question to a nonhuman source. That is, Woolf places her questioning of patriarchal imperialism in an alliance with nature. "But this cynical reflection, at once so chill and so superior, was made, of course, by the thrush. Down in the Amusement Compound, by some grave oversight on the part of the Committee, several trees and rhododendron bushes have been allowed to remain; and these, as anybody could have foretold, attract the birds. As you wait your turn to be hoisted into mid-air, it is impossible not to hear the thrush singing" (412). Despite all efforts to distract the visitors with man-made amusements, the thrush's critique is not drowned out.

The essay's thundering conclusion is clearly a send-up of all that patriarchy and imperialism can assemble and put on display:

The wind is rushing and shuffling along the avenues; the Massed Bands of Empire are assembling. . . . Men like pin-cushions, men like pouter pigeons, men like pillar-boxes, pass in procession. . . . But let them hasten! . . . The sky is . . . in violent commotion. . . . Colonies are perishing and dispersing in spray of inconceivable beauty and terror which some malignant power illuminates. . . . Cracks like the white roots of trees spread themselves across the firmament. The Empire is perishing; the bands are playing; the Exhibition is in ruins. For that is what comes of letting in the sky. (413)

Several of Woolf's short stories also may be viewed from this double perspective of feminism and ecocriticism, although space permits us to consider only two stories here.

"Lappin and Lapinova," one of Woolf's better known stories, takes a fiercely satirical look at feminist issues, with a twist that is of interest today from an ecofeminist point of view. The honeymoon fantasy of a young married couple, in which they create alter egos as rabbits named King Lappin and Queen Lapinova, becomes symbolic of a rather crippled attempt to find something deep and natural in their relationship. When the husband, Ernest, moves on to a more practical view of life, the wife, Rosalind, is left behind in her fantasy-natural world. Because Rosalind is presented as rather pathetic in this story, it is easy to miss that what she finds in her Lapinova identity is more genuine than the false conventions of her everyday life, which are made more monstrous to her through the characters of her in-laws. A key point in the story involves Lapinova's narration of crossing an imaginary stream, for it becomes the locus of a new border, a new distance, between husband and wife. Her husband interrupts her narrative with annoyed questions, and as she tries to explain, he shuts her off: "What the deuce are you talking about?" (*Shorter Fiction* 260) At the end of the story, the broken Rosalind laments to her husband that she cannot find Lapinova, that she has "lost her." His reply is cruelly deliberate: "'Yes,' he said at length. 'Poor Lapinova . . . . Caught in a trap,' he said, 'killed,' and sat down and read the newspaper. So that was the end of that marriage" (262).

There is a greater harshness in this ending than is usually found in Woolf's novels. The husband's ruthless "killing off" of Lapinova, the fantasy rabbit, clearly kills something in his wife as well. Yet the ironic and angry narrative voice seems to be directed nearly as much at Lapinova for her feeble attempts to find something life affirming in such a marriage as it is at the entire social structure that surrounds and subsumes the marriage and at the husband who gives his allegiance to that deadly structure. Lapinova is ridiculous—but within her is a wild creature longing for the forest and hunted by a patriarchal system.

Woolf's short story "The Mark on the Wall" contains several of the approaches to nature we have seen in her work: a bit of the naturalist observer, a spiritual exploration of life and death through nature, and an ecofeminist critique of patriarchy and war. "The Mark on the Wall" opens with an analogy that reminds us of the naturalist: "How readily our thoughts swarm upon a new object, lifting it a little way, as ants carry a blade of straw so feverishly, and then leave it" (*Shorter Fiction* 77). Later, as she speculates on life and death, the narrator offers an imaginative description of an afterlife, made vivid by its use of images of nature from an insect-like perspective:

> But after life. The slow pulling down of thick green stalks so that the cup of the flower, as it turns over, deluges one with purple and red light. Why, after all, should one not be born there as one is born here, helpless, speechless, unable to focus one's eyesight, groping at the roots of the grass, at the toes of the Giants? As for saying which are trees and which are men and women, or whether there are such things, that one won't be in a condition to do for fifty years or so. There will be nothing but spaces of light and dark, intersected by thick stalks, and rather higher up perhaps, rose-shaped dots of an indistinct colour—dim pinks and blues—which will, as time goes on, become more definite, become—I don't know what. (78)

As Woolf imagines here the impressions one might have in an afterlife, she echoes her language of infant and early childhood impressions in "A Sketch of the Past" and the intimate child's eye view from *The Waves*. One might link this as well to her memories of childhood observations of nature and to the sense that there is something luminous and spiritual about such moments of pure observation.

"The Mark on the Wall" presents other natural images and topics, a tree tapping on a window and a memory of people in a room discussing botany, but it proceeds from this to speculations on loss of self in a hollow society. Unexpectedly, the story moves to "an airless, shallow, bald, prominent world . . . a world not to be lived in" (79), and it progresses to what becomes a distinctly ecofeminist perspective.

Although she wrote long before such a perspective was theorized, Woolf's feminist theorizing is well established; and here, as in other places, she places nature in opposition to patriarchal forms of order and hierarchy, using "Whitaker's Table of Precedency," a standard guide to protocol and the order of precendency of dignitaries, as synecdoche for the whole system. "What now takes the place of those things I wonder, those real standard things? Men perhaps, should you be a woman; the masculine point of view which governs our lives, which sets the standard, which establishes Whitaker's Table of Precedency . . . which soon, one may hope, will be laughed into the dustbin" (80).

Yet Woolf continues to use Whitaker's Table of Precedency as a symbol for patriarchal domination and places it in opposition to a natural world, including an underwater world of silence and beauty. "Yes, one could imagine a very pleasant world. . . . [A] world which one could slice with one's thought as a fish slices the water with his fin. . . . How peaceful it is down here, rooted in the centre of the world and gazing up through the grey waters, with their sudden gleams of light, and their reflections—if it were not for Whitaker's Almanack—if it were not for the Table of Precedency!" (81–82).

In that distinctive, satirizing voice—the voice one hears in *A Room of One's Own* and *Three Guineas* exposing and ridiculing the absurdities of patriarchy—Woolf allows the archbishops and high chancellors to parade their assumed precedence over nature. But she hints at nature's actual precedence over them, suggesting a complicity between nature and a woman with no investment in Whitaker's Table of Precedency:

> Here is Nature once more at her old game of self-preservation. This train of thought, she perceives, is threatening mere waste of energy, even some collision with reality, for who will ever be able to lift a finger against Whitaker's Table of Precedency? The Archbishop of Canterbury is followed by the

Lord High Chancellor; the Lord High Chancellor is followed by the Arch-bishop of York. . . . Everybody follows somebody, such is the philosophy of Whitaker . . . and let that, so Nature counsels, comfort you, instead of en-raging you; and if you can't be comforted, if you must shatter this hour of peace, think of the mark on the wall. (82)

And so, following nature's counsel, Woolf's narrator in this story turns back to the landscape, immerses herself in nature rather than the parade of dominance and precedency, and plunges so deeply that she enters into the feeling of being a tree—an extraordinary passage of considerable complexity:

I like to think of the tree itself: first the close dry sensation of being wood; then the grinding of the storm; then the slow, delicious ooze of sap. I like to think of it, too, on winter's nights standing in the empty field with all leaves close-furled, nothing tender exposed to the iron bullets of the moon, a naked mast upon an earth that goes tumbling, tumbling all night long. The song of birds must sound very loud and strange in June; and how cold the feet of insects must feel upon it, as they make laborious progresses up the creases of the bark or sun themselves upon the thin green awning of the leaves, and look straight in front of them with diamond-cut red eyes. (82–83)

The story ends with an interruption by someone standing over the narrator, saying he is going out to buy a newspaper, that he is distressed by the war. "Curse this war; God damn this war! . . . All the same, I don't see why we should have a snail on our wall" (83). The narrator responds with the story's last line: "Ah, the mark on the wall! It was a snail" (83). Here, as in many of Woolf's larger works, from *Jacob's Room* to *Between the Acts,* war has intruded on a peaceful medita-tion—and it bears out the danger of allowing "men of action" to continue to rule the world and implies the opposition between war and both feminist and environmental values. The hope for social change is perhaps as small as that mark on the wall. A mark that the story has been trying to read, as if it were the first mark of a written message; but as the last line reveals, it is a fragment of nature, a snail. The snail is, after all, an ancient image for slow but definite progress; in this story it is also a hieroglyph in the book "laid upon the landscape."

Notes

1. For a recent discussion of the idea of "Reading the Book of Nature," see St. Armand. For a late-nineteenth- and early-twentieth-century secular exploration of the concept, see Burroughs.

2. New writings have begun to appear, such as Beer's exploration of Woolf's interest in science, Abbott's discussion of Woolf's essay "The Plumage Bill," and Cantrell's and Westling's essays. A few earlier works, such as essays by Moore and Naremore, proposed to focus on aspects of nature in her work, but in fact did so rather tangentially.

3. See, for instance, Beer.

4. Qtd. in St. Armand 29. Virginia Woolf devotes an entire 1923 essay to the work of Sir Thomas Browne, making clear that she has read his work thoroughly. She comments admiringly on Browne's statement, "We carry with us the wonders we seek without us; there is all Africa and her prodigies in us," and remarks that he inspires us "to extraordinary flights of speculation as to what we are, where we go, and the meaning of all things" (qtd. in *Essays* 371).

Works Cited

Abbott, Reginald. "Birds Don't Sing in Greek: Virginia Woolf and 'The Plumage Bill.'" *Animals and Women: Theoretical Explorations. Virginia Woolf.* Ed. Carol J. Adams and Josephine Donovan. Ann Arbor: U of Michigan P, 1995. 263–86.

Beer, Gillian. *Virginia Woolf: The Common Ground.* Edinburgh: Edinburgh UP, 1996.

Burroughs, John. "Reading the Book of Nature." *Ways of Nature.* Boston: Houghton Mifflin, 1905. 231–38. Rpt. in Walker, *Art of Seeing Things.*

Cantrell, Carol. "'The Locus of Compossibility'": Virginia Woolf, Modernism, and Place." *ISLE: Interdisciplinary Studies in Literature and Environment* 5.2 (1998): 25–40.

Freedman, Ralph, ed. *Virginia Woolf: Revaluation and Continuity.* Berkeley: U of California P, 1980.

McNees, Eleanor, ed. *Virginia Woolf: Critical Assessments.* Vol. 4. East Sussex: Helm Information, 1994.

Moore, Madeline. "Nature and Community: A Study of Cyclical Reality in *The Waves.*" Freedman 219–40.

Naremore, James. "Nature and History in *The Years.*" Freedman 241–62.

Sackville-West, Vita. "The Landscape of a Mind," *Encounter* 2 (Jan. 1954): 70–72, 74. Rpt. in McNees 267–71.

St. Armand, Barton Levi. "The Book of Nature and American Nature Writing: Codex, Index, Contexts, Prospects." *ISLE: Interdisciplinary Studies in Literature and Environment* 4.1 (1997): 29–42.

Walker, Charlotte Zoë, ed. *The Art of Seeing Things: Essays by John Burroughs*. Syracuse: Syracuse UP, 2000.

———. [Charlotte Walker Mendez]. "Creative Breakthrough: Sequence and the Blade of Consciousness in Virginia Woolf's *The Waves*." *Women's Language and Style*. Ed. Douglas Butturff and Edmund L. Epstein. Akron, OH: U of Akron, 1978. 84–98. Rpt. in McNees 56–74.

———. [Charlotte Walker Mendez]. "I Need a Little Language." *Virginia Woolf Quarterly* 1.1 (1972): 87–105.

———. [Charlotte Walker Mendez]. "Language, Mystery, and Selfhood in the Novels of Virginia Woolf." Diss. Syracuse U, 1972.

———. [Charlotte Walker Mendez]. "Virginia Woolf and the Voices of Silence." *Language and Style* (spring 1980): 94–112.

Westling, Louise. "Virginia Woolf and the Flesh of the World." *New Literary History* 30 (1999): 885–75.

Woolf, Virginia. *Between the Acts*. 1941. San Diego: Harcourt Brace Jovanovich, 1969.

———. *Collected Essays*. Vol. 3. Harcourt, Brace & World, 1967.

———. *Collected Essays*. Vol. 3. Ed. Andrew McNeille. London: Hogarth, 1988.

———. *The Complete Shorter Fiction of Virginia Woolf*. Ed. Susan Dick. San Diego: Harcourt Brace Jovanovich, 1985.

———. *The Diary of Virginia Woolf*. Ed. Anne Olivier Bell. Vol. 4, 1931–1935. New York: Harcourt Brace Jovanovich, 1982.

———. *The Essays of Virginia Woolf*. Ed. Andrew McNeillie. Vol. 3. San Diego: Harcourt Brace Jovanovich, 1987.

———. *To the Lighthouse*. 1927. San Diego: Harcourt Brace & Company, 1981.

———. "A Sketch of the Past." *Moments of Being: Unpublished Autobiographical Writings*. Ed. Jeanne Schulkind. New York: Harcourt Brace & Jovanovich, 1978. 61–137.

———. *The Waves*. 1931. New York and London: Harcourt Brace Jovanovich, 1979.

———. *The Years*. 1938. New York and London: Harcourt Brace Jovanovich, 1965.

Nature, Gender, and Community: Mary Wilkins Freeman's Ecofiction

Terrell F. Dixon

Early Nature Stories

Despite all of the nature—the birds and flowers, the dogs, cats, and farm animals, and the trees and woodlands—featured in Mary Wilkins Freeman's short fiction, and in spite of her geographical and chronological closeness to the Concord of Ralph Waldo Emerson and Henry David Thoreau, nature has figured mostly at the margins of how we have understood Freeman's work. With few exceptions, her depiction of nature has been seen simply as one component of her regionalism, one way in which she created what we call "local color." [1] When read from an ecocritical perspective, however, many of her short stories are nature stories that investigate nonhuman nature and our human relationship to it. As these narratives unfold, they often also explore related issues of gender and community.

Although these themes appear as early as Freeman's initial published short story collection, [2] they first find full expression in an important story from *A New England Nun and Other Stories* (1891): "Christmas Jenny." Jenny Wrayne lives on a mountainside where she earns a subsistence living by making Christmas wreaths for sale to the nearby villagers. She also uses her home to shelter injured birds and other woodland creatures until she heals and releases them, and so she becomes Mary Wilkins Freeman's first fully realized example of what the contemporary English novelist of nature John Fowles terms "the green woman" (38). The green woman, or green man, has the power, Fowles says, of "melting" into the trees, of fitting into the forest. This green man or woman exists, at least potentially, in all of us, and he or she can help us bypass a narrowly scientific, utilitarian, and analytic view of nature. The green woman part of the self connects with the natural world in ways that keep nature from becoming "frontiered and foreign, *separate*" (Fowles 78).

As Jenny enters the story so laden with wreaths that she looks like a "broad greenmoving bush," she becomes Freeman's version of this green woman figure (*Nun* 339–40). Jenny's ecological commitment, however, is challenged by the town fathers. The threats originate, as frequently happens in Freeman's fiction, through a misunderstanding growing from gossip. The townspeople, who cannot understand her unconventional life, move toward a witch-hunt, spreading rumors that Jenny starves the small animals and birds caged in her house and that she mistreats the deaf boy who lives with her. Such stories trigger an official visit from two representatives of the town patriarchy, the minister and Deacon Little. The emotional distance they travel from their normal habitat is measured by their walk. To visit Jenny they must first go up the road from the village and then continue on a wilderness path to her mountain home, a weathered place covered with grapevines and with a tall pine in front. Their policing visit is unannounced, and Jenny is out. When they go into her home anyway, their distance from the natural world is emphasized by bewilderment at her home and its curious "sylvan air" of heaped greenery. Nor do they know what to make of the happy boy who is sitting in the midst of evergreens, twining them into wreaths, and who is "dressed like a girl in a long blue gingham pinafore" (169). When they see the caged birds, however, the town fathers think they have the evidence they expected.

What transpires next has been set in motion by events that occurred when Jenny's nearest neighbors were frozen in a comic family quarrel. Jonas Carey has gone down an icy slope to get water for his wife, Betsey; three times he has made the trip, and three times he has fallen. The third time ends in a tantrum with Jonas sitting silently, resolutely refusing to notice either the birds around him struggling to find food or his wife's frantic entreaties to tell her if he is hurt. Jenny comes on this scene, gives him a little push with her basket, checks to insure there are no broken bones, and starts to solve Betsey's problem. Suspecting that the selfish Jonas will not want Jenny to stay for breakfast, she tells Betsey to start cooking. It works, and he comes inside. Jenny leaves after revealing that she will spend her dress money on food to help the birds survive winter.

Jenny's insight into Jonas has helped Betsey deal with a bullying husband, and now—when the town fathers' lack of comprehension threatens the green woman—Betsey's loyalty to her friend becomes crucial. Although it is hard for the mild-mannered, anxious Betsey to confront the town patriarchy, she does challenge them. Standing in front of the two men "like a ruffled and defiant bird" (171), Betsey explains what is really before them, informing them that the cages are for wildlife rehabilitation and telling them about Jenny's sacrifices for the birds. The forces of wrongful, patriarchal authority opposing the green woman are thus turned back, and the story ends when Jenny—after another series of comic failures by the still childish and bullying Jonas—has the Careys to her home for Christmas dinner.

As the title indicates, "Christmas Jenny" is a holiday story, one of many such magazine stories Freeman wrote for a specific occasion. It is also a story in which Freeman's fiction has come to embody a full-fledged ecofeminist vision—depicting a world where women and nature suffer abuse from a patriarchal power structure.[3] Jonas and the officers of church and village refuse to notice the world of nature beyond themselves and their kind, and they discredit those, such as Jenny, who choose to live in harmony with nature and to protect it. Although there is a comic element in Jonas's behavior, the inability to see and the willingness to bully present a threat to women and nature. It is only the combination of Jenny's wisdom and helpfulness along with Betsey's loyalty and hard-won courage that prevents serious injustice; together they create a small female community that preserves Jenny's power to protect and heal nature. There is, perhaps, in the character of the boy working with the wreaths and wearing Jenny's old dress some suggestion that the next male generation could change and adopt ecological values.[4]

The feminist component of Freeman's achievement has by now become a familiar part of how we understand her fiction. Feminist criticism has fittingly argued that women writers such as Mary Wilkins Freeman became marginalized because of gender, and feminist critics have worked successfully to restore important writers, including Freeman, to their rightful place in American letters.[5] However, with this work now accessible, we can begin to see how issues of place and nature have been implicated in this exclusionary, canon-making process, sometimes institutionalizing a double bias. The term "regional writer," for example, is frequently paired with or used interchangeably with the phrase "local color." Both terms ostensibly refer to a focus on the landscapes and the culture of a specific region. In practice, both phrases are often reductive rather than descriptive. "Local color" carries the suggestion that material so designated is merely "colorful" or quaint rather than of real significance, something apart from and less than serious literature. The term "regional," which could be neutral or even positive, has come to mean not worthy of national interest, restricted in its appeal.[6] Both terms figure in a reductive code of reference, one applied to Mary Wilkins Freeman or Sarah Orne Jewett but not to a John Steinbeck or a William Faulkner.

With Freeman—as with Jewett—the reductive regionalist label has thus marginalized them in an additional way. It has obscured and diminished work expressing their love for the natural world, their resolve to protect it, and their desire to inculcate a love of nature in their readers.[7] The importance of nature in their short fiction suggests that the expansion of ecocriticism can add another dimension to the ongoing recovery of important American literary texts as it helps us understand how thoroughly environmental concerns pervade our literature.

Understudies

The twelve stories brought together in *Understudies* (1901), the collection that constitutes the second stage of Mary Wilkins Freeman's nature fiction, feature a writer secure in a well-established reputation, enjoying a wide readership, and confident enough to try a bold experiment. Part of the change comes with Freeman's decision to devote this collection entirely to nature fiction. She takes the concern with nature that had been a crucial, but by no means the only, theme of her previous work and moves it to center stage: our human relationship with the rest of nature becomes the theme. This change is accompanied by a stylistic shift, a broadening of the realism that largely dominated her earlier fiction. Although this change has been described as the manifestation of her stated wish to write with "more symbolism, more mysticism,"[8] it seems more to the point that in these stories Freeman begins adapting the Emersonian doctrine of correspondences to her own creative vision; the stories stress physical likenesses between plants and people and between animals and people to emphasize our shared existence on the planet. To help express this view, she starts blending elements of fable into her familiar narratives of village realism. The result is often a workable hybrid, a narrative that serves well both as short story and as a type of ecological teaching tale. This collection of twelve stories, six focused on animals and six on plants, constitutes her first volume of ecofiction.[9]

"Arethusa" and "Mountain Laurel," two stories placed side by side in *Understudies,* embody complementary explorations of gender, nature, and community. "Arethusa" features Lucy Greenleaf, a young woman and a reclusive beauty who corresponds to the wild marsh orchid of the title. Unlike Jenny, this version of the green woman lives with her mother. As the only daughter of a protective, widowed woman, Lucy is trained "to regard a husband like rain in its season, or war, or a full harvest, or an epidemic." The mother, however, is also determined that her innocent daughter will have the protection of marriage after her death (153). The mother encourages Lucy's suitor, the handsome Edson Abbot; Lucy, who does not like men, merely acquiesces in her mother's wishes. Edson maintains a strong masculine will and an interest in scientific agriculture, and he prefers hothouse plants over wild ones. Edson wants to pick the orchid for Lucy (thus taking over and harming nature as he wishes to control her), but Lucy stops him by making it clear that she will refuse to marry him if he does pick the orchid. They are married, but his wish to possess her remains thwarted; the strength Lucy draws from visiting the wild orchid enables her to sustain her independence, to be "forever her own" (169). The reciprocal, beneficial influences of orchid and woman resist the patriarchal, scientific forces that wish to possess and destroy them.[10]

In "Mountain Laurel," Freeman extends her explorations of gender and nature by creating a version of the green man, thus beginning to expand her ecofeminist sense of environmental community across gender lines. It is an important step for her fiction; because for all the creativity, significance, and power of the green woman stories, such narratives by themselves could have confined Freeman's work within an essentialist view of gender and nature, one that, instead of breaking free from patriarchal notions of hierarchy, dominance, and dualism, simply continued these notions in a new guise. Moving from the set of essentialist hierarchical dualities prevalent in the culture—nature as separate from and inferior to human culture, women as close to nature and inferior to men—to a reversed set of still essentialist and still hierarchical dualities—females as automatically close to nature and therefore superior to males and culture who are alienated from nature—would not allow room for choice or change.[11] By bringing the green man into her nature stories, Freeman works her fiction free from containment in such dualities and extends her sense of environmental community across gender lines, thus opening up greater possibilities for individual and societal change.

Samuel Ladd, the last member of the once-large Ladd family, is living the life of an imaginative solitary in an isolated area past the end of a rough road on a rocky mountainside of Mt. Ladd. Although he owns the mountain, Samuel is "land poor in the fullest sense" (174), for the fertile valley land his family owned has been sold off; what is left is land where only mountain laurel grows. Disappointed in the one romantic love of his life, Samuel sustains his happy spirit with the sight of the sunrise over the mountain, the memory of the young beauty he loved, the writing of his fulfilling although unaccomplished poetry, and the laurel that grows so close to his house that all of its rooms exist in a beautiful "green twilight" (189). Samuel's other laurels, those symbols of societal accomplishment, however, come only because he nobly commits himself to his poetry, despite his lack of talent. Samuel's green masculinity, although benevolent, remains isolated and passive. The figure of the green man, at this point in Freeman's career, is without either Lucy's determined resistance or the energy and the incipient sense of reforming community activism seen in Betsey and Jenny's partnership.[12]

The six animal stories that make up the first half of *Understudies* extend community in a different way than the flower stories. "The Monkey" directly addresses the central question that informs these narratives: what is the right relation of humans to the other members of the animal kingdom? The philosophy set forth by a Dickensian pet shop owner introduces the negative side of this theme. The Bird-Fancier, a name the shop owner shares with his shop, does not care at all for the creatures he sells, but he is fond (despite the fact that no one listens to him) of declaiming his theory of animals to all those around him. His homespun philosophy embodies a reductive, antievolutionary view of animals, one in which all the creatures in his shop—the cats, birds, and monkeys—are "men and women run out," by which the Bird-Fancier means they are in decline.

Lesser humans, ones whose souls have shrunk through "living no-account lives," become animals; the Monkey in his shop, for example, is according to his theory "just as likely as not one of the Bible Pharaohs run out" (29).

Other attitudes toward animals are expressed by the women customers who treat the animals as children and by the owner's wife and her cousin who clean the birdcages but who do not think about the animals at all. However, it is the Boy who loves the Monkey that embodies the values set forth in these stories. The Boy, whose face resembles the Monkey's, is lonely, poor, and unsuccessful at both books and sports. He visits the Monkey every day, and they communicate by mouth and hand movements through the cage bars. After the Monkey destroys some of the other shop animals and thus some of his profits, the Bird-Fancier gives him to the Boy. The two leave the shop with the Boy enlivened by "the ownership of this tiny life of love" (36) and bent over, head toward the Monkey, communicating with him. Although the questions about the human ownership of animals threaded throughout this collection are raised rather than resolved in this story,[13] it is clear that, for Freeman, an appreciative, loving sense of kinship should prevail over a reductive, commodifying view of animals. Like an older version of the boy in "Christmas Jenny" and the baby girl in "A Gatherer of Simples," the Boy in "The Monkey"—distinguished by his love for the Monkey and his sense of kinship with it—offers hope for the future.

Another crucial aspect of animal lives and our human relationship with them emerges in the animal story with a female human protagonist, "The Parrot." The parrot who lives with Martha in her otherwise lonely house is "a superb bird— a vociferous symmetry of green and gold and ruby red, with eyes like jewels" (65). The bird seems so attuned to Martha's feelings that she frequently suspects, even though it runs deeply counter to what her religion teaches her, that the bird has a soul. This relationship of woman and parrot is embedded in a familiar Freeman narrative, one featuring courtship and betrayal staged within the confines of a village. Martha, a New England woman shaped by a stern training, lives in a scrupulously clean house, where she was "as securely caged by her training and narrowness of life as was the parrot by the strong wires of his cage" (67). Until the handsome and dashing village minister begins courting her, Martha has resigned herself to a life without marriage.

The minister deserts Martha, however, and she must struggle to keep the village gossips from suspecting her disappointment. When the minister compounds his betrayal by bringing his bride to Martha's house, the parrot destroys the bride's feathered bonnet in a "whirlwind of feathered rage" (82). It is a wonderfully dramatic scene, and the parrot's expression of Martha's repressed rage convinces her of the bird's comradeship, equality, and—despite the teachings of the church—soul. Martha, like the Boy, now subscribes to the central belief inculcated in the animal stories of *Understudies:* the hierarchical worldview in which humans use religion as a reason to assume selfish dominion over animals needs to give way to one that recognizes kinship and acknowledges partnership.

What Freeman does in *Understudies* is to challenge and revise the patriarchal culture's standard sense of nature's hierarchy. The stories make clear that nonhuman nature—here embodied in animals and flowers—should not be marginalized or given secondary citizenship on a planet where we assume that humans alone occupy center stage. As members of nonhuman nature, animals and flowers are, as the stories underline this irony in the collection's title, not less important understudies but equally meaningful players.[14] Although the literary quality in this first book of ecofiction is somewhat inconsistent, many of the stories are excellent, and *Understudies* plays a key part in Freeman's evolving environmentalism. This collection's insistence on the stature of animals and its movement away from a confining essentialism make it clear that the focus on narratives of nature in this stage of Mary Wilkins Freeman career enables her to expand her ecofiction in substantial ways.

Six Trees

With the publication of *Six Trees* (1903), her second and final collection devoted entirely to ecofiction and the book that constitutes a third stage in her nature fiction, Mary Wilkins Freeman's approach to this type of ecofictional exploration changes again. This time she focuses on one aspect of nature—trees, and she limits herself to six stories, thus achieving both a greater impact for each story and a consistently high quality throughout the collection. In these stories, Freeman also moderates (with the exception of the final narrative) the amount of fable mixed into her usual village realism. Although the stories of *Six Trees* are still within the realm of the ecological teaching story she developed in *Under-*

studies, they rely more on the personalities and situations of everyday village life that Freeman knows best.[15]

Paired narratives—"The Balsam Fir" and "The Great Pine"—form the structural and thematic center of this collection. "The Balsam Fir," like "Christmas Jenny," is a holiday story that places at its core the human relationship to the rest of nature. Martha Elder, however, is a different kind of green woman than Jenny. At first, Martha is one of the saddest of Freeman's older woman characters, marginalized by personal history, poverty, and attitude. The man expected to marry Martha married her sister instead, and over the years she has become progressively more isolated and bitter about all aspects of her life. On Christmas Day, Martha can lament to a visiting, even poorer, deaf relative: "It ain't much Christmas to me" (113).

Change comes through a surprising and powerful defense of the balsam fir tree in Martha's front yard. When a woodsman begins to cut down the tree, Martha runs out to protect it by grabbing the axe and running him off. In doing so, Martha not only saves the tree but she changes her life. By defending nature, she frees her green woman self. Martha can now acknowledge her love for nature by remembering how her life intertwines with that of the fir and by enjoying the tree's fragrance and beauty. Christmas Day has become a celebratory occasion; Martha feels grateful for the gift of the tree, and she begins to build community by asking her relative to come live with her.

Unlike the green women in Freeman's earlier stories, Martha Elder does not enter this narrative as a fully formed green force. She is also a much more ordinary character, living the restricted, quiet existence of a poor, village woman. Martha's transformation into a less exotic, less solitary, and altogether more everyday version of the green woman makes her an important part of the evolving green woman figure in Freeman's fiction, one who helps extend her ecofiction away from essentialism.

Six Trees pairs Martha's story with one about a man who is equally isolated. Unlike Martha, however, the man in "The Great Pine" has actively betrayed those closest to him by running away to sea, leaving behind the hard work of farming, his wife, and a young daughter. The narrative opens on a mountainside where he rests beneath a great pine. Now a wayfarer without resources and with hints of a criminal past, this former sailor is so removed from nature that he cannot notice the bird above him in the tree. His speculation that the great pine would make a good mast if only it were harder wood indicates that when he does see nature it is only as potential commodity. The man struggles twice to cross the mountain, only to lose his way and come back to the tree both times. Enraged, he starts a fire at the base of the tree and leaves it to burn as he heads yet again for his former home.

On the way, he changes. He sees the flames from the mountain above and scrambles down once again, but this time he puts out the fire and saves the pine. The man now sees the tree "like a prophet with solemnly waving arms of bene-diction," and it is clear that he is different, tuned to "a higher place in the scale of things" (78–79).

This transformation finds expression the return to his home valley. Anticipat-ing a warm, welcoming reunion, he bursts into the little house only to learn that great changes have taken place. His now deceased wife assumed him dead and married a neighbor who is himself now dying of consumption. His daughter struggles alone with the backbreaking housework and caring for the children from his wife's second marriage.

Dick, the name the dying second husband now uses to address him, sets out to establish his new life by caring for the children and by cleaning, cooking, and working the farm. Saving the great pine has changed him so thoroughly that he amazes the visiting village doctor with his commitment to hard work and good deeds. Dick's transformation also illustrates how far Freeman's fiction has moved from Samuel Ladd's passive greenness in "Mountain Laurel." Dick's commit-ment to nature and to his human family, as evidenced by his embracing the once detested farm work, embodies a sustained commitment to the natural world, demonstrating that males as well as females now can choose to participate in ecological community.

The fiction of *Six Trees* also contains another significant shift in Freeman's ecofiction—a change in the reliance on wilderness. Even though nearby nature is always an important part of her stories, in much of Freeman's earlier ecofic-tion, green personhood is sustained chiefly by wilderness connections. Aurelia, Jenny, and Arethusa all move back and forth along pathways that connect the wilderness of forest, mountain, or swamp to the more settled locales of village or farm; and Samuel Ladd sustains his greenness by remaining on his wild mountainside. Ecological commitment and actions thus are dependent on constant nourishment from frequent wilderness connection. With the stories of Dick and Martha in *Six Trees,* however, a spontaneous performance of individual environmental action generates its own ongoing green commitment within the context of ordinary life. Although Dick first meets the great pine in the wilderness, it eventually dies a natural death and Dick nonetheless continues his work on the valley farm. His changed life and Martha's action to save the balsam fir in her village yard show that, for Freeman, active ecological commitment now extends also to ordinary people in routine situations; green personhood is sustainable in everyday life through connection with nearby nature as well as through wilderness experience.

This spirit also pervades "Apple Tree," the story that concludes both *Six Trees* and the third stage of Freeman's ecofiction.[16] In comparison to the more tumultuous stories of individual transformation, its meaning emerges more from contrast than change. The Maddoxes are a young couple distinguished by four children who are very much at home playing in the dirt, by a lack of concern about tidiness, and by a yard that contains a beautiful apple tree. In this allegorical story, the woman across the street—Sarah Blake—provides contrast. She is an old woman, obsessed with the tidiness and the constant cleaning that, for her, constitute goodness.

The narrative, one that explores the ecological dimensions of the most symbolic tree in Freeman's culture, sets forth a different view. On the one hand, sin becomes the narrowly utilitarian, harsh commodification of nature seen as Sarah trims her pear tree so closely that it cannot bear fruit. Salvation, on the other hand, resides in the Maddoxes' regard for nature, represented by their resolutely untrimmed apple tree and the reverence for natural process that their choice embodies. Neither husband nor wife ever even pick apples, choosing, instead, to let the children eat the fruit as it falls. Unlike their neighbor, the couple delights in the beauty of the tree and the natural world. "The wind blew, and a wonderful breath of fragrance came from the apple-tree and they inhaled it. 'Lord, it's a dreadful pretty world, ain't it?' said Sam Maddox, and on his face was a light of unconscious praise. 'Yes, 'tis,' said Adeline, and her face looked like her husband's" (206–7).

This connection of the tree to the spiritual world shows, as commentators have noticed,[17] Mary Wilkins Freeman's ties to the transcendental heritage of nearby Concord. It needs to be emphasized, however, that her nature stories incorporate Emersonian transcendentalism into stories that address her own concerns. Emersonian and Thoreauvian preoccupations with Spirit and solitude, respectively, give way to different themes in Freeman's fiction. Her short stories do feature a nature-spirit connection, and they reject a religious orthodoxy that would ignore or subjugate the natural world. But Freeman's fiction is much more likely to pay attention to the physical and the social world than to speculate about abstract Spirit, and it is more inclined to depict the pain of isolation than to valorize solitude. In their persistent, thoughtful explorations of nature, gender, and community, Mary Wilkins Freeman's short stories present an expansive, evolving ecofeminist vision—one that avoids essentialism and that creates green women and green men who love and defend nature while engaged in ordinary life. Her important, complex ecofiction thus complements the nonfiction of her famous predecessor neighbors and remains a rich source of meaning for its readers a century later.

Notes

1. In her introduction to the *Mary Wilkins Freeman Reader*, Mary R. Reichardt refers briefly to the central role that nature plays in the stories. Robert M. Luscher's essay in *ATQ* looks at the intersection of Emersonian self-reliance with Freeman's "nature mysticism."

2. In *A Humble Romance and Other Stories*, the story "A Gatherer of Simples" features Aurelia Flowers, a forest-dwelling herb woman who is a prototype for Freeman's green women characters, but—unlike "Christmas Jenny"—this earlier sketch does not give this green woman a convincing ecological role in its perfunctory plot.

3. See Gaard, "Living" 4.

4. In "Evelina's Garden," published in *Silence and Other Stories*, Freeman resolves the nature-gender conflict in a negative way. The young Evelina must attack and destroy her garden to marry the man she loves. Josephine Donovan provides a Lacanian reading of this story in her essay "Silence or Capitulation."

5. See Reichardt for discussion of these shifts in reputation (*Web* 39–42).

6. There are signs that with the growth of ecocriticism, literary regionalism may be rehabilitated as part of the larger environmental movement's focus on the importance of bioregions.

7. Although these stories are described as mapping "the geography of gender" (see Tichi; Glasser 215–16), they also map relationships between gender and nature.

8. See letter no. 441 in Kendrick 381–82 and Reichardt, *Web* 39.

9. A tendency in the developing field of ecocriticism has been to see ecofiction as a contemporary phenomenon, as what happens when current environmental concerns become manifest through the short story talent of a Rick Bass, Pam Houston, Nancy Lord, or Kent Nelson. When we begun to look at American literary history from an ecocritical viewpoint, however, it is clear that environmental fiction, like feminist fiction, has appeared throughout American literature.

10. Although various other Freeman short stories have been linked to the works of Jewett, the interwoven themes of control, collection, science, masculine will, and marriage tie this Freeman story most closely to Jewett's "A White Heron."

11. This section of the essay is much indebted to an illuminating discussion of these issues in Armbruster.

12. Among the other plant stories in the second half of *Understudies*, the two most interesting are "Bouncing Bet" and "Peony." The first raises questions about nationalism and the colonization of nature. The second reverses the usual economic substructure for the stories; its protagonist, Arabella, has some financial security and thus can be free from the fear of poverty that haunts many characters in the stories. But Arabella is prodigal in her gifts of money and possessions, thereby corresponding to the largesse of nature expressed in her yard's abundance of peonies. Other stories, "Prince's Feather" and "Morning Glory," feature male protagonists who fall far short of their youthful promise. In both, the correspondences between protagonists and flowers are strained and separate from the unfolding of the story.

13. Other stories interrogate the ownership of nature from different angles. "The Squirrel," for example, focuses on the squirrel's right to English walnuts that fall from the trees, as opposed to the human farm "owners'" sense that they own the walnuts. "The Lost Dog" looks at human treatment and ownership of pets, at how the loyalty given a human can be unearned; and "The Doctor's Horse" examines questions of wildness, domesticity, and human ownership. In "The Cat," human notions of ownership are undercut by the cat's prevailing sense of partnership.

14. For the argument that the clever title works because plants and animals are lower organically than humans, see Westbrook 116.

15. David Ransom in "The Elm Tree" and Joseph Lynn in "The White Birch" are, like many characters in Freeman's short stories, old and alone, the last members of their families. Ransom is an aged widower made poor by a bank failure, whose life on the margins has made him bitter. When he is wrongly accused of burning down the

home which his wife loved and which he had been forced to sell, the village elders plan to move him forcibly to an unpleasant boarding home for oldsters. Lynn is an old man who has fallen in love with a young woman. She loves a younger man but plans to marry Lynn for financial reasons until he learns the truth and withdraws from the wedding. Each man comes back from crisis after a transformative encounter with a special tree, and each then formulates a new notion of himself and of what constitutes home. For both men, nature's solidity and durability replace shifting and unreliable socioeconomic constructions of home.

16. Although she would continue to write significant stories that feature nature, this is the last time she dedicates an entire volume to ecofiction.

17. See Luscher.

Works Cited

Armbruster, Karla. "Buffalo Gals, Won't You Come Out Tonight: A Call for Boundary-Crossing in Ecofeminist Literary Criticism." Gaard and Murphy 97–105.

Donovan, Josephine. "Silence or Capitulation: Prepatriarchal 'Mother's Gardens' in Jewett and Freeman." *Critical Essays on Mary Wilkins Freeman.* Ed. Shirley Marchalonis. Boston: G. K. Hall, 1991. 151–56.

Fowles, John. *The Tree.* 1979. New York: Ecco, 1983.

Freeman, Mary Wilkins. *A Humble Romance and Other Stories.* 1887. New York: AMS, 1970.

———. *A New England Nun and Other Stories.* 1891. Ridgewood: Gregg Press, 1967.

———. *Silence and Other Stories.* 1898. Freeport: Books for Libraries, 1969.

———. *Six Trees.* 1903. Freeport: Books for Libraries, 1969.

———. *Understudies.* 1901. Freeport: Books for Libraries, 1969.

Gaard, Greta. "Living Interconnections with Animals and Nature." *Ecofeminism: Women, Animals, Nature.* Ed. Greta Gaard. Philadelphia: Temple UP, 1993. 1–12.

Gaard, Greta, and Murphy, Patrick D., eds. *Ecofeminist Literary Criticism: Theory, Interpretation, Pedagogy.* Urbana: U of Illinois P, 1998.

Glasser, Leah Blatt. *In a Closet Hidden: The Life and Work of Mary E. Wilkins Freeman.* Amherst: U of Massachusetts P, 1996.

Kendrick, Brent L. *The Infant Sphinx: Collected Letters of Mary E. Wilkins Freeman.* Metuchen, N.J.: Scarecrow, 1985.

Luscher, Robert M. "Seeing the Forest for the Trees: The 'Intimate Connection' of Mary Wilkins Freeman's *Six Trees.*" *ATQ* ns 3 (December 1989): 363–81.

Reichardt, Mary R., ed. *Mary Wilkins Freeman Reader.* Lincoln: Nebraska UP, 1997.

————. *A Web of Relationship: Women in the Short Stories of Mary Wilkins Freeman.* Jackson: UP of Mississippi, 1992.

Tichi, Cecilia. "Women Writers and the New Woman." *Columbia Literary History of the United States.* Ed. Emory Elliott. New York: Columbia UP, 1988. 590–98.

Westbrook, Perry O. *Mary Wilkins Freeman: Revised Edition.* Boston: Twayne, 1988.

The Great Rainbowed Swamp: History as Moral Ecology in the Poetry of Michael S. Harper

Elizabeth Dodd

Profit, Pleasure, and Ecocriticism

I want to consider the absence of black writers from existing ecocritical discussion. Leonard Lutwack says flatly, "American wilderness writing ignores the black, because of his association with agriculture" (72). I suspect that African American writers may not have embraced nature writing (creative writing in the autobiographical naturalist tradition) since what Robinson Jeffers called Inhumanism (the literary attempt to deflect attention away from human beings, or what Glen A. Love calls ego-consciousness) might not be appealing for writers who already feel politically, economically, and socially marginalized. Further, academic inquiry, including the work of ecocritics, already expects black literature to focus on the social realm; literary studies categorizes black literature as offering an interest in environment similar to the interest in socioeconomic environment that characterized naturalist novels at the close of the nineteenth century.

As ecocritics articulate the complex and often conflicted attitudes toward the North American continent that contribute to a sense of place, we should not overlook black writing whose obvious focus is sociopolitical. An examination of the underlying attitudes toward nature that are encoded in literary works can contribute to what Neil Evernden calls "what it feels like to have a territory" (97)—or what it feels like not to. As Lutwack notes, "[human] use of the earth's resources, [our] alteration of places in every corner of the globe, must proceed now with a view not only to present profit and pleasure but to the survival of the very next generation" (2). African American writers who focus on this continent's long relationship with slavery have a unique perspective on both profit and pleasure, and an examination of their work from an ecocritical perspective can illuminate previously unrecognized aspects of the work, increasing our understanding of how sense of place and ethical awareness intersect.

In the poetry of Michael S. Harper, race and gender are clearly primary interests. Born in Brooklyn in 1938, Harper began a rapid sequence of publishing in 1970, with six collections appearing by 1975. Selections from these books appear with groups of newer poems in *Images of Kin: New and Selected Poems* (1977). An early poem entitled "Brother John" begins:

> Black man:
> I'm a black man;
> I'm black; I am—
> A black man; black—
> (1–4)

Yet Harper's interests are wider than might be supposed. As an editor once said dismissively of Norman MacLean's stories (qtd. in Love 255), Harper's later poems "have trees in them." Living in the New England countryside, in a house dating to the early nineteenth century, Harper sees that each tree holds in its woody tissue the literal and figurative bones of history. Place—the material world of a particular locale—is infused with the ethical consequences of historical actions. In Harper's eye, landscape becomes history, history becomes landscape, and the ecocritic can find in this intermingling some important challenges to the destinies that Western imperialists once declared manifest. Harper unpeels the layers of social history involved in the American view of land as commodity. His work offers a rich nexus for environmental history and ecocriticism as well as social history and the enduring value of modernist poetic technique.

History as Moral Ecology

Harper was a relative newcomer to Rhode Island when he joined the faculty at Brown University in 1971, having moved from Brooklyn as a teenager to southern

California. He attended high school and college in Los Angeles, earned an M.F.A. at the Writers' Workshop at the University of Iowa in 1963, and held a number of short-term positions at schools along the Pacific coast before moving to Barrington, Rhode Island. Harper soon turned his work toward the study of New England history while he explored the fields and cemeteries surrounding his new home. Learning the untold aspects of colonial history as well as those more familiar is a way to root himself in his new home place, a form of what Gary Snyder calls "reinhabitation: moving back into a terrain that has been abused and half-forgotten" (178). Michael Harper has said, "with luck we are learning animals, but we are in the ecology, and probably falsely at the 'deified' godhead of the triangle; without a certain ruthless ingenuity our wreckage might have been less."[1]

We see this reinhabitation enacted vividly in Harper's poem "History as Apple Tree," which appeared in *Song: I Want a Witness* in 1972. The larger poem sequence focuses on the locale of Dighton, Massachusetts, and constitutes a part of Harper's ruminations on—and rootings into—New England. For three dense and highly allusive stanzas, he recounts details from early Puritan settlement of the colony, but he claims connection not with Massachusetts Colony's John Winthrop and Rhode Island Colony founder Roger Williams, nor with the early settler and trader Richard Smith, but instead with the indigenous Narragansetts and their chief sachem, Canonicus. As Harper notes, African slaves sometimes found freedom in the wilderness by escaping their European masters and joining native communities, a fact more widely recognized among the Seminoles of Florida (whom Harper mentions elsewhere).[2] Harper implies the bitterly ironic contrast to the greater religious freedom enjoyed in the early colony (compared with the Puritan stronghold of Massachusetts), for Rhode Island had a slave population in colonial times. Indeed, at his death in 1692, Richard Smith left a sizeable estate, including eight African slaves (Bailyn 59). By 1708, the colony levied a tax on slave importation as a source of revenue; from roughly 1725 until 1807, a period when commerce far exceeded agriculture in the economy, Rhode Island relied heavily on slave trading. One historian explains that Rhode Island was the only colony where the slave trade "assume[d] long-term social and economic significance" to the extent that it "was the principal American carrier" (Coughtry 5–6).

Further, Harper complicates reader expectations of a polarized racial relationship. Rather than a clear tension of whites versus people of color, Rhode Island's history contains another irony. While Williams's banishment from Massachusetts Colony in 1635 followed from his religious differences with the Puritan establishment, he also protested the method of land acquisition through royal charter, which ignored Native American land rights altogether. Williams's published criticisms (which do not survive) incurred the protestations of both John Winthrop and John Cotton, who each voiced a version of the Anglo immigrants' attitudes. Winthrop claimed that land lying "common, and hath never been replenished or subdued is free to any that possess or improve it"; Cotton wrote derisively of Native American land use, "We did not conceive that it is a just title to so vast a continent, to make no other improvement of millions of acres in it, but only to burn it up for pastime" (qtd. in Gaustad 32). In contrast, Williams maintained a close relationship with the Narragansett sachems Canonicus and Miantonomi, learning their language and publishing *A Key into the Language of America,* a dictionary focusing significantly on the words and phrases needed to establish Anglo–Native American trade. In 1962 Perry Miller declared, "Williams could treat Indian culture with respect. He was the only Englishman in his generation who could do so" (52).

While Harper's poem introduces these historical details, he claims that knowledge requires physical contact as well as abstract comprehension. This is the kind of assertion already familiar to ecocritics and wilderness writers. Harper recounts a legend of how a huge apple tree grew over Roger Williams's grave until two centuries later

> dust and root grew
> in his human skeleton:
> bones became apple tree.
>   (37–39)

Harper then describes his need to touch both place and past in order to take hold of his own presence and belonging.

> As black man I steal away
> in the night to the apple tree,
> place my arm in the rich grave . . .
> take up a chunk of apple root,

let it become my skeleton . . .
my arm the historical branch,
my name the bruised fruit . . .
(40 – 42, 44 – 45, 47 – 48)

The poem's title, "History as Apple Tree," suggests that history can become as matter; the living presence of a tree holds the body of the past in its tissue, while by taking root, Harper allows both the place and its past inhabitants to live in him. Yes, this is a symbolic family tree, but it is very much a real tree, more akin to Robert Frost's apple or beech trees than to William Faulkner's metaphoric family trees of white patrimony, for example. Further, it calls to mind Toni Morrison's notion that, beyond the mind's capacity to recall events and their locations, "rememory" means that, as the ex-slave Sethe explains in *Beloved*, "Places, places are still there. . . . What I remember is a picture floating around out there outside my head. I mean, even if I don't think about it, even if I die, the picture of what I did, or knew, or saw is still out there. Right in the place where it happened" (36). Actions become embodied in the landscape, surviving their actors and remaining in their original location. Morrison, as do Harper and Faulkner, emphasizes the physical durability of moral consequences, in opposition to the notion common in contemporary white society that the damaging injustices of centuries of slavery should no longer play a tangible role in contemporary black-white relations or in black social structures.

Most significant to the ecocritic are the formal and thematic surprises this poem holds. Purporting to be condensed narrative, an historical account, "History as Apple Tree" abruptly abandons narrative for metaphoric epiphany. This is not an Emersonian transcendental epiphany; instead, its epiphany descends to the ground beneath one's feet. Simultaneously, while appearing to consider social and political questions of race in America—Native American, African, and European—the poem subtly suggests that social history has an inescapable effect on physical environment. Thus racism becomes not only a cultural legacy that gets handed on but, through its connections to trade and both Roger Williams's and Richard Smith's early Rhode Island settlements in the form of trading posts, it becomes part of the land, with an ecological legacy that envelops the culture that follows.[3] In the context Harper surveys, the religious struggle that prompted early white Rhode Islanders to leave Massachusetts takes on socioeconomic importance as well, resonating in the poem's intriguing line *"How does patent not breed heresy?"* (5, emphasis in original).

Uplift from a Dark Tower

The significance of mercantilist and capitalist trade, which find their logical extreme in the commodification of people—what Harper elsewhere calls, in a chillingly layered allusion, "sex fingers toes / in the marketplace" (*Images of Kin* "Dear John, Dear Coltrane" 1–2)—is further explored in a series of four poems titled collectively "Uplift from a Dark Tower" and included in *Images of Kin: New and Selected Poems.* I want to supply detailed close reading of a few individual poems and then return to consider the poems' contribution toward a more fully American ecocriticism. Harper's exploration of what W. E. B. Du Bois called "the problem of the color line" (xxiii) has important implications for our urgently needed development of an environmental ethic. While Harper's title *Images of Kin* emphasizes human interconnectedness, the quiet role of place in the "Uplift" series extends beyond questions of transracial and transgenerational kinship. In Harper's moral ecology, thoughtful examination of social history entails attention to the treatment of both persons and places. His interest is similar to that of Annette Kolodny, when she argues that the marriage of Pocahontas to John Rolfe was "a kind of objective correlative for the possibility of the Europeans' actually possessing the charms inherent in the virgin continent" (5). As Kolodny makes clear, the personification of place ("virgin continent") and the objectification of persons (especially in this case, Native American women) are closely connected in the myth of American settlement.

Harper's "Uplift" poems make clear reference to the fact that he composed them during his stay at Yaddo, the well-known writers' colony in Saratoga Springs, New York. During his use of the tower studio in the mansion-style, nineteenth-century house, Harper is an indirect beneficiary of Spencer Trask and Katrina (Kate Nichols) Trask, a wealthy couple who purchased the estate in 1881 and eventually set up a trust to establish the colony. As Katrina Trask described her vision for the estate to her husband, "Yaddo is not to be an institution, a school, a charity: it is to be, always, a place of inspiration, a delightful, hospitable home where guests may come and find welcome. . . . At Yaddo they will find the inspiration they need. . . . Look, Spencer, they are walking in the woods, wandering in the garden, sitting under the pine trees—men and women—creating, creating, creating!" (193).

The exhilarated tone seems indicative of Katrina Trask's enthusiastic and romantic sense of life; it is decidedly in contrast to the fact-packed syntax in Harper's poems. The Trasks were eccentric idealists, dedicating their home at Yaddo to the pursuit of their notion of chivalry, full of medieval pageantry and literary allusion. Although the majority of Katrina Trask's memoir, *Yaddo: The Story of Yaddo*, details parties, masques, and other social events of her time as "Katrina Regina, Queen of Yaddo," Harper finds it to be one of several sources that inform the poems he writes during his stay in the tower, originally Katrina Trask's library-study.

The layering of geography with history, people with place, and economy with ecology takes its most developed form in the last poem of the series, "Psychophotos of Hampton." Earlier poems in the "Uplift" series have contemplated Booker T. Washington's problematic belief in economic uplift for African Americans through industrial education at his Tuskegee Institute—which, incidentally, received funding from philanthropists such as George Foster Peabody, a close friend of Spencer Trask and Katrina Trask (and Katrina's second husband after Spencer's death). Here Harper goes further back, to Washington's education at Hampton Institute in Virginia.

The layering takes form in stanza-long sentences, piling clause against clause without clear grammatical connectives. In the fourteen-line opening stanza, Harper takes us halfway across the continent, from Yaddo's comfortable room and board and across the Adirondacks to Canada—where "French/Indian alliances" are based on the currency of beaver pelts (8). We then cross the western plains, where the buffalo were slaughtered, and on to Utah, where "runaway bigamists" settle at the Great Salt Lake (11). By now the page is littered with corpses, from beavers trapped for the European pelt market to bison shot for hides, tongues, or in pursuit of extermination of the Plains Indians, whose culture depended on the great herds.

I find this a dizzying journey, especially since it is made not only in the company of Harper but also Etienne, an African who served in the Trask household in 1881. Trask, whom Harper briefly quotes, mentions Etienne in her *Story of Yaddo*, speaking of having tutored him prior to his training for "missionary service" and describing how he doubled as her "guardian and protector" since she had no other "man-servant."

> One night after midnight, I opened my door, thinking I heard a noise downstairs: there, just outside the threshold, lay Etienne, a most startling sight. He was the blackest black man that could be imagined: he lay on his back, stretched to his full length, sound asleep, and in his hand was a large carving knife! The fear that had impelled me to open the door was as nothing compared to my sudden fear of Etienne, the son of a cannibal, a carving knife in his hand, at my door! It was true no one could pass him to come to me—but it was also true I could not pass him to escape, if his hereditary tendencies should assert themselves. . . . Etienne's pride lay in the pure strain of his cannibal ancestry. His mind was quick and altogether unexpected: he learned very fast and had most amazing opinions about life. Once, when I was talking with him of the African race, he said a very true thing: he said it was merely a question of the sun on his outside—"My body may be black, but my soul is white." Candour compels me to confess that, after having sharpened his wits at our American institutions, his missionary zeal failed to develop, and he went back to Africa as—a trader! (Trask 78–79)

While no more than three pages of the 214-page monograph address Trask's "long interest" in "the colored race," these few paragraphs contribute significantly to Harper's history of Yaddo. It is a history filled with ironies, which Harper presents without explanation. However, Harper has clearly intended readers to find contexts: he even notes that the Trask memoir is privately printed, as if to help in our interlibrary loan searches (*Images of Kin* 27).[4]

The "having sharpened his wits" and "cannibal ancestry" from Trask's prose are syntactically fused in Harper's "Psychophotos of Hampton," becoming "his cannibal ancestry sharpened by" the combination of landscape and history that follows in lines 7–14. Not only did Etienne learn quickly, Harper implies, he learned thoroughly from the Trasks, whose fortune came from Spencer's skill as an investment banker. Despite his missionary-sponsor's intentions, Etienne learns that the true lesson America teaches is capitalism, where anything can be converted to commodity. Booker T. Washington also learned this lesson, Harper suggests; the poem begins with an epigraph noting that Washington owed his career to the white founder of Hampton Institute, General Samuel Chapman Armstrong, with whose enthusiasm he launched the project of Tuskegee—uplift through industrial education.

Education continues as a theme for the poems, as "Psychophotos" focuses more closely on Hampton Institute. Although the institute began under the auspices of the Freedman's Bureau for former slaves (the first classes are said to have been held under a great oak, the Emancipation Tree), the United States pursued its long policy of assimilation of Native Americans here as well. In Harper's words, "At $68/head, the great Dakotah nation went to college"—line 28 opens with the language of commodity, so many dollars per unit. As Harper "walk[s] out over swampgrounds, campsites" (33), the poem turns toward elegy or memorial, listing sixteen names of the dead, "their souls finally saved / from the highlands where they were born" (74–75). These are young people, ranging in age from infancy to twenty-two—most are in their teens. Nearly all are Sioux, from the Dakotas; two are from Arizona pueblos; and one is from South Africa.

We have thus returned to a mingling of nations of color, red and black, treated in the earlier "History as Apple Tree." In the next stanza of "Psychophotos," Harper moves beyond the specific extinctions of spirit listed among the dead young people. We find "the common man of Andrew / Jackson" (99–100) seeking in the wars of 1816–1818 to exterminate the Seminole nation in Florida, largely because the tribe had a significant black population living in a freedom that would, by its proximity to southern plantations, weaken the institution of U.S. slavery.

After these glimpses at assimilation and extermination as major U.S. policies toward nonwhites, Harper turns to the nineteenth-century novelist Herman Melville and his "scrimshaw tales" (126). Scrimshaw is an art form carved on the bones from the bodies of whales slaughtered for oil production; originally a leisure pastime for whaling sailors, it derives directly from capitalist slaughter. Harper implies that the paradigm has a close similarity to the way "the Renaissance [was] built on slave trading" (137). It also parallels Katrina Trask's buoyant but ironic wish for artists to engage in leisured, elegant creating on the grounds of her estate. For, in another poem of Harper's "Uplift" series, "Dining from a

Treed Condition, An Historical Survey," we learn that the first white owner of the land was Jacobus Barhyte, a Revolutionary War officer who was an "American patriot" (33); he was also a slaveholder. The ease and luxury Trask described will rest atop the labor—and so the bodies—of those eighteenth-century slaves who worked the land.

By now the poem's journey is nearly over, and Harper stands at "the terrace overhang" for a "last view" (132–33). The vista is, of course, the handsome gardens and grounds of the Yaddo estate; yet this created order and beauty do not have the last say. Instead, the poem turns deliberately away from the mood Trask had hoped for artists in her beloved tower. In her memoir she wrote of her delight there: "My high Tower was a consummation! O room of rooms, where my mountains and the spurs of three other ranges may be seen; the glorious colours of the sunrise flush it at Dawn, and at Even the vivid splendour of the sunset. To this Tower the chosen came [but] . . . [a]lthough the Tower is a shrine to friendship, it is also a room for work" (27). Later she describes the view the room affords her: "The great eastern window in the Tower commands the thirty miles of rolling valley, and the wondrous range of mountains from whence my help [hired servants] has come through all these changing years" (154).

Harper articulates a different mood and view both of and from the tower. The time frame is unspecific, and, toothbrush in hand (in a playful gesture toward Booker T. Washington's insistence on hygiene, especially the brushing of teeth), Harper observes:

> the talk was of politics,
> rhetoric, and the literature of the great
> rainbowed swamp from the vision of the black tower.
>
> (143–45)

This could be a conversation among writers at the colony during his stay, but it carries a layered sense of the nineteenth-century Trask dinner table as well. Trask titled one chapter "Table Talk at Yaddo," and she makes clear that both George Foster Peabody (financial supporter of both Hampton and Tuskegee) and Booker T. Washington were guests there. Beyond the "rhetoric" and "politics," however, Harper focuses finally on dinner table discussions of literature—Melville's *Moby Dick,* perhaps, and the work of other Americans, contemporary and historic. Harper means as well his own work, no doubt. Had Washington's politics won out, Harper's oeuvre would not exist, including the poem under question. Washington's priority was economic enfranchisement, at the expense of both learning for its own sake and political enfranchisement; his emphasis on industrial education required that reading and writing be firmly linked to the learning of trades. Further, agriculture was to be the trade of choice at Tuskegee, with an eye to promoting higher crop yields and market production to ensure economic profit. In the words of one historian, who quotes Washington, "Instead of producing 'the proud fop with his beaver hat, kid gloves, and walking cane,' industrial education would return the rural youth to his home community unspoiled and dedicated to its uplift" (Harlan 161).

The Great Rainbowed Swamp

Harper's poems investigate the interrelationships among education, capitalism, and racism, grounding these questions specifically in a sense of place that recalls and interrogates Washington's role as the great enthusiast for social uplift for post–Civil War blacks. In *Working with the Hands,* Washington wrote, "Our pathway must be up through the soil, up through swamps, up through forests, up through the streams and rocks; up through commerce, education, and religion!" (29). His statement alludes to the linking of slavery (and therefore African Americans) with agriculture, and it invokes swamps as both literal challenges to successful farming and as figurative impediments to self- and race-improvement. It also suggests the figure of Etienne, who "went back to Africa as—a trader." Further, the relationship between land and commerce, past and future, and oppression and uplift that Washington assumes is the one that Harper examines, using some of the same language.

For Washington, swamps were a small part of the terrain over which the descendants of slaves must travel to achieve the transcendence of uplift. "Psychophotos of Hampton" presents more, and increasingly complicated, references to swamps: the "mosquitoed swamp near Fort Monroe" (29); "swampgrounds, campsites" (33); and the "literature of the great / rainbowed swamp" (144–45). Like the places from Sethe's past in Morrison's *Beloved,* which still exist despite intervals of time and distance, the swamps in Harper's poem are remnants from the continent's—and the nation's—past; yet they are still accessible as he "walks out" among them. For Harper, the swamp is both tenor and vehicle, a place of both natural and historical processes. His diction implies the importance of connotative and denotative nuance in the poem's moral ecology.

Not only among environmentalists, the term "wetland" has largely replaced "swampland," conferring a changed set of attitudes and political policies. The *Oxford English Dictionary* defines "swamp" as first occurring in reference to colonial North America, specifically Virginia; the combination "dismal swamp" was a frequent appellation for wet, low-lying regions, implying dreary and possibly evil connotations. Early uses of the term "swamp" suggest richness of soil yet unsuitability for agriculture. The history of the word, therefore, is woven with Anglo-colonial attitudes toward land—as a resource to be exploited, with any hindrances amounting to either negative costs on the balance sheet or divine evidence of Native American misuse.[5] "Wetland," however, shows the shift in attitude that results from the twentieth-century scarcity of swamp ecosystems. An 1847 usage of "wetland" reflects the utilitarian attitudes we saw with "swamp": "Wet land . . . by judicious cultivation . . . rapidly improves in fertility." Examples of usage from 1979, 1980, and 1985 show a swift progression of connotation, emphasizing "plans to protect the Somerset wetlands," intentions to "preserve this swamp area in its natural state . . . for wetland flora [and] birds and animals," and legal codification of those attitudes where "[u]nder state law construction cannot take place on a wetlands unless there are plans to replace the wetlands," respectively.

Harper's poem depicts the swamps, devoid of late political protections, as the literal testing grounds for American economic identity and race policy. Further, these swamps are indeed places of death and decay, ecological monuments to the past. Yet Harper identifies the kind of connection to the past that promises a future: spiritual or cultural "fertility." And like the places from Sethe's past that still exist, despite intervals of time and distance, these swamps from the nation's past are still accessible, as the poet "walks out" among them.

The poem's mansions are also still in existence, from the grounds of Yaddo to the Franklin Delano Roosevelt estate at Hyde Park (near, incidentally, the magnificent Vanderbilt estate) to Robert E. Lee's mansion at Arlington and back again to Yaddo. Significantly, Harper details aspects of their placement and history that connect to his contention that "the Renaissance [was] built on slave trading" and his interest in the connections among red and black people in North America. He refers to Roosevelt's mansion as being situated near Esopus, New York, a place named for the indigenous inhabitants, the Esopus (although it is usually called by the family's name, Springwood, or placed at Hyde Park). Harper notes that the handsome mansion at Arlington, built originally as a memorial to George Washington, "sprouted with Union graves" at the "doorstep" (36, 37) when Secretary of War Edwin Stanton approved General Montgomery Meigs's suggestion that the grounds become a military cemetery; a tomb containing 2,111 unknown soldiers was constructed in the estate's rose garden. Although the poem makes no mention of the fact, the grounds around Arlington became Freedman's Village, a camp for former slaves including not only a tent city but an industrial school aimed, like Tuskegee, at teaching trades. Initially located on low-lying land, a portion of the village was moved when its water supply was found to be contaminated by adjacent marshes (Peters 23–31). Harper does refer to Wiltwyk School for Boys, a home for troubled youth established on land the Roosevelt family donated. Again, the connection is implied between these young people and the young dead of the Native American graveyards such as that found at Hampton.[6]

Stark Black Dearth

The repeated contrast of swampland to mansion in "Psychophotos of Hampton" provides a structure both literal (evoking not only place names but the features of the land) and thematic (exploring the ironies and injustices of the historical devotion to trade). This connection, arising from Harper's interest in American history and the places it has played out, is one familiar to ecocritics from the work of Aldo Leopold, who, although his main focus is ecology, also suggests the linking of human morality—and commodification—with ecological outcomes. Leopold opens his famous essay "The Land Ethic" with a description of the ethical consequence of treating human beings as chattel, or property: the hanging of a dozen slave girls suspected of wrongdoing. "This hanging involved no question of propriety. The girls were property. The disposal of property was then, as now, a matter of expediency, not of right and wrong" (201).

Leopold looks back three thousand years to Odysseus and ancient Greece, but Harper reminds us that we need look no further than the nineteenth century and no farther than the land we inhabit. Harper also focuses more specifically on the ethical effects of capitalist commodification and the pursuit of economic profit, not merely the ethical questions of property rights. Leopold and Harper arrive at a similar viewpoint, despite their different directions of approach. Eco-critics would do well to consider the implications this convergence of ethics connotes.

First, we are reminded that issues of race in ecological theory or politics extend well beyond where landfills or toxic industries are located, although these are important factors. Second, and more important for literary studies, we must continue to develop the examinations of both genre and aesthetics for what Lawrence Buell defines as an "ecological text" (7–8). Even as critics have begun to note that inner-city and urban residents may not feel the appeal of wilderness literature, we should not inadvertently ghettoize black literature. Harper does not invoke W. E. B. Du Bois's notion of the "talented tenth" and its emphasis on fostering keen intellectual education for the "exceptional" rather than uniformly endorsing technical or industrial education for all. Yet the poems clearly share Du Bois's criticism of Washington's exclusive focus on industrial education, while they condemn the pursuit of capitalist profit.

Censure and praise both take shape in these poems through implication. As in the modernist tradition, Harper relies on juxtaposition and inference rather than rhetoric or narrative, and he demands an extraordinary amount of work from his readers. Indeed, much of the aesthetic body of each poem depends on its relation to other poems and the way a careful and informed reader will see connections and ironies. This technique is often seen as academic, but despite its inter- and intra-textual allusiveness, Harper reminds us that he does not live—or write—in an ivory tower. Although Harper may sometimes write with resonance to Ezra Pound or T. S. Eliot, he writes of Booker T. Washington and Etienne as well as all the fallen dead of Hampton Institute, Arlington, and beyond.

Herein lies Harper's important contribution to contemporary poetry, combining a modernist use of allusion with criticism of the cultural tenets that modernism so often endorsed. His is the "literature of the great / rainbowed swamp," and it recalls Robert Browning's poem "'Childe Roland to the Dark Tower Came'":

> Names in my ears
> Of all the lost adventurers my peers,—
> How such a one was strong, and such was bold,
> And such was fortunate, yet each of old
> Lost, lost! one moment knelled the woe of years.
>
> (194–98)

As the swamps provide natural monuments to the dead, the poem's allusions provide an elegiac structure that is based in history and literature; yet it is also bathed in private, personal detail. The Dark Tower implies contrast with the ivory tower academic writers are said to inhabit as well as correction to the leisured privilege of the Trask mansion. Who are "the lost adventurers my peers" for Harper? They are the dead—both black and Native American—who repeatedly surface, ghosts or conjured presences, throughout the poems. Not all are named as directly as the dead at Hampton. Harper's friend and fellow poet, the late Robert Hayden, joins him in "Psychophotos of Hampton," although most readers may not realize this. Harper says that he and Hayden visited the grounds of Hampton Institute together, and they stood under the Emancipation Tree as they talked about poetry.[7]

Standing in America's swamps, Harper may think of himself as a corrective to the Trasks' self-congratulating chivalry, surveying the surroundings like Browning's knight in "'Childe Roland to the Dark Tower Came'":

> Then came a bit of stubbed ground, once a wood,
> Next a marsh, it would seem, and now mere earth
> Desperate and done with; (so a fool finds mirth,
> Makes a thing and then mars it, till his mood
> Changes and off he goes!) within a rood—
> Bog, clay and rubble, sand and stark black dearth.
>
> (145–50)

The Great Rainbowed Swamp ~ 191

Yet the poem looks forward as well as back: Harper's oldest son is named Roland, as is the knight in Browning's poem.

Thus I find the poems in the "Uplift" series, despite their elegiac tendencies, to offer more hope than much of Harper's earlier work. The swamps are full of the submerged history of this nation, and Harper has made a point of quoting William Carlos Williams that this history "begins in murder and enslavement, not discovery" (*TriQuarterly* 119). However, the "great rainbowed swamp" is not the colorless swamp of Browning's poem. It is a site of aesthetic beauty, of unity among people of color, and of guarded promise. Beyond the "rubble" and "dearth" of Browning's dismal allegory, beyond the all-too-physical mire of Washington's symbolic obstacles, Harper's emphasis on the swamp's "literature" calls on readers to preserve the swamp's accumulation of memories. Place matters, he implies, both for itself and for the historic and emotional meaning it has accrued for people who lived and died there: Place can bear witness if we pay attention.

Notes

1. Letter to the author in August 1999.

2. See "Healing Song" and "Psychophotos of Hampton" in *Images of Kin* 14, 34. For a treatment of the inclusion of African Americans in Native American tribes, see Katz.

3. The major towns of Providence and Newport indicated the importance of trade in defining the economy and land use patterns of the colony (and then the state). The effects on forest and big game due to colonial-British trade exchange was similar to the rest of New England: by 1850 the tree cover of Rhode Island had been reduced from 95 percent to 32 percent. The beaver fur trade decimated not only the beaver population but also species who depended on the beaver-pond ecosystems for survival. Specific to Rhode Island, changes in the land were distinctly linked to the seaport emphasis on trade. By 1828, the Blackstone canal was constructed along the Blackstone River to connect Wooster with Providence and Newport. See Merchant 66–67, 193–95, 225.

4. In "The Battle of Saratoga" (Springs) Revisited," Harper mentions "a private printing / of a history of *Yaddo*" (*Images of Kin* 3–4).

5. *The Oxford English Dictionary* cites Captain John Smith in Virginia, 1624: "Some small Marshes and Swamps there are, but more profitable than hurtfull."

6. In a telephone conversation with this author, Harper said, "I feel certain that the land is an old Indian graveyard," although I have been unable to confirm his claim.

7. Telephone call with the author in May 1997.

Works Cited

Bailyn, Bernard. *The New England Merchants in the Seventeenth Century.* Cambridge: Harvard UP, 1955.

Browning, Robert. *The Poems.* Ed. John Pettigrew. Vol. 1. New Haven: Yale UP, 1981.

Buell, Lawrence. *The Environmental Imagination: Thoreau, Nature Writing, and the Formation of American Culture.* Cambridge: Belknap-Harvard P, 1995.

Coughtry, James. *The Notorious Triangle: Rhode Island and the African Slave Trade, 1700–1807.* Philadelphia: Temple UP, 1981.

Du Bois, W. E. B. *The Souls of Black Folk.* New York: Random House, 1996.

Evernden, Neil. "Beyond Ecology: Self, Place, and the Pathetic Fallacy." Glotfelty and Fromm 92–104.

Gaustad, Edwin S. *Liberty of Conscience: Roger Williams in America.* Grand Rapids: William B. Eerdmans, 1991.

Glotfelty, Cheryll, and Harold Fromm, eds. *The Ecocriticism Reader: Landmarks in Literary Ecology.* Athens: U of Georgia P, 1996.

Harlan, Louis R. *Booker T. Washington: The Making of a Black Leader, 1856–1901.* New York: Oxford UP, 1972.

Harper, Michael S. *Dear John, Dear Coltrane.* Pittsburgh: U of Pittsburgh P, 1970.

———. *Debridement.* Garden City: Doubleday, 1973.

———. *History as Apple Tree.* San Francisco: Scarab, 1972.

———. *History Is Your Own Heartbeat.* Urbana: U of Illinois P, 1971.

———. *Honorable Amendments.* Urbana: U of Illinois P, 1995.

———. *Images of Kin: New and Selected Poems.* Urbana: U of Illinois P, 1977.

———. Interview with David Lloyd. *TriQuarterly* 65 (winter 1986): 119–28.

———. Letter to the author. 13 August 1999.

———. *Nightmare Begins Responsibility.* Urbana: U of Illinois P, 1975.

———. *Song: I Want a Witness.* Pittsburgh: U of Pittsburgh P, 1972.

————. *Songlines in Michaeltree: New and Collected Poems.* Urbana: U of Illinois P, 2000.

————. Telephone interview. 31 May 1997.

Jeffers, Robinson. *The Double Axe and Other Poems.* 1948. New York: Liverwright, 1977.

Katz, William Loren. *Black Indians: A Hidden Heritage.* New York: Atheneum, 1986.

Kolodny, Annette. *The Lay of the Land: Metaphor as Experience and History in American Life and Letters.* Chapel Hill: U of North Carolina P, 1975.

Leopold, Aldo. *A Sand County Almanac and Sketches Here and There.* New York: Oxford UP, 1987.

Love, Glen A. "Revaluing Nature: Toward an Ecological Criticism." Glotfelty and Fromm 225–40.

Lutwack, Leonard. *The Role of Place in Literature.* Syracuse: Syracuse UP, 1984.

Merchant, Carolyn. *Ecological Revolutions: Nature, Gender, and Science in New England.* Chapel Hill: U of North Carolina P, 1989.

Miller, Perry. *Roger Williams: His Contribution to the American Tradition.* New York: Antheneum, 1962.

Morrison, Toni. *Beloved.* New York: Knopf, 1987.

Peters, James Edward. *Arlington National Cemetery: Shrine to America's Heroes.* Kensington, MD: Woodbine, 1986.

Snyder, Gary. *The Practice of the Wild.* San Francisco: North Point, 1990.

Trask, Kate [Katrina] Nichols. *Yaddo: The Story of Yaddo.* Privately printed. Boston: The Thomas Todd Co., 1923.

Washington, Booker T. *Working with the Hands.* 1904. New York: Arno, 1969.

Anti-Pastoralism, Frederick Douglass, and the Nature of Slavery

Michael Bennett

If we separate the term "ecocriticism" into its two components, its parameters seem clear: "criticism," engaging in analytical reading practices, and "ecological," focusing these practices on environmental concerns. In theory, then, ecocriticism could be applied to any cultural artifact since every cultural text issues from, and envisions, a particular relationship with its environment. In practice, however, ecocriticism has tended to focus on the genre of nature writing, a designation usually reserved for essays about the two environments most removed from human habitation: the pastoral and the wild. This narrowed focus of most ecocritics is reflected in Glen A. Love's summary of ecocriticism as a "new pastoralism" (210).

But of what use is ecocriticism if the culture under consideration has a different relationship with pastoral space and wilderness than the ideal kinship that most nature writers and ecocritics assume or seek? This question is foregrounded in the following effort to provide an ecocritical reading of *The Narrative of the Life of Frederick Douglass, an American Slave,* a text central to the development of an anti-pastoral African American literary tradition. By focusing on Frederick Douglass's 1845 narrative, I will show that the method of ecologically informed reading pivotal to ecocriticism can be productive within African American studies, but that the perspective offered by the discipline of black studies challenges ecocritics to expand and reconceptualize the boundaries of the ecological. I begin by tracing the contours of African American anti-pastoralism, before reading Douglass's narrative in this context and suggesting that the nature of slavery in the United States created the link between anti-pastoralism and African American culture that has been operative from Douglass's day to our own.

Pastoralism, the literary and social valorization of country life, has come to refer to "all literature that celebrates an ethos of rurality or nature or wilderness over against an ethos of metropolitanism" (Buell 439). But as Raymond Williams notes in the appendix to his classic work *The Country and the City*, the word "pastoral" originally came into common usage in English for "shepherds from the fourteenth century, and has an almost contemporary analogical meaning for priests" (307). The problem with using this term in relation to the origins of African American culture should be obvious. African Americans in the antebellum United States were much more likely to be referred to in the lexicon of slavery as sheep rather than shepherds—as soulless creatures excluded from the flock ministered to by those men of the cloth who were part of what Frederick Douglass called the "*slaveholding religion* of this land" (326). It is this fact that motivated Douglass's scathing critique of American Christianity in the appendix to his narrative, where he argues that slaves were considered as lower than sheep by the pro-slavery clergy: "They would be shocked at the proposition of fellow-shipping a *sheep*-stealer, and at the same time they hug to their communion a *man*-stealer, and brand me an infidel, if I find fault with them for it" (328).

The quintessential space of contemporary ecocriticism, the wilderness, has also had an antithetical relationship with African American culture, for the most part. Melvin Dixon reminds us that African American spirituals exhorted slaves to "go in de wilderness / To wait upon the Lord" and to find "free grace in de wilderness." Dixon uses such songs as evidence that "during slavery blacks depicted the wilderness as a place of refuge beyond the restricted world of the plantation" (3); however, he also points out that one only travels through the wilderness to reach the other side—a sanctified community waiting with open arms. The slaves also sang, "I'm so glad I come out de wilderness" and "a rock cried out de wilderness / 'No hiding place!'" So if the wilderness could be a temporary place of spiritual reflection it was also a space of terror and loneliness without the welcoming community waiting in the celestial city on the other side.

I do not wish to totally discount Dixon's argument that the wilderness—along with the underground and the mountaintop—has been a major topographical feature of African American literature. However, Dixon's analysis treats these spaces as "metaphors" for the search for identity. If ecocriticism has taught us anything, it has taught us to view "settings" not just as metaphors but as physical spaces that inform, shape, and are shaped by cultural productions. Lawrence Buell notes that it has been one of ecocriticism's central projects to restore the "referential dimension" to literary criticism by insisting, for instance, that the setting of a novel is not just a formal technique but an embodiment of "nature-responsiveness" (86, 113). Although the physical spaces invoked in early spirituals and slave narratives may have inherited a certain meaning from biblical typology, the topographical meaning that Douglass and other slave narrators gave them was often a different matter. The apparent freedom of the wilderness—valued by and available to someone in Henry David Thoreau's subject position when he issued the famous ecological dictum that "in wildness is the preservation of the world" (609)—was not available to slaves or even most free blacks, who tended, with reason, to flee the countryside for life in the city. Or again, the mountaintop seen by Dixon to be a "figure for personal triumph and witness" providing a "moment of transcendence" (19)—not a place actually to be occupied or experienced but a metaphor for divine revelation—has little in common with Aldo Leopold's famous ecological essay "Thinking Like a Mountain." Dixon is interested in figurative mountains, while Leopold focuses on mountains as part of a "biotic community" (225) to which we are ethically bound by ties that are strengthened through our efforts to empathize with nature—to make the attempt to literally think like a mountain or a wolf or a deer.

Although the geography of slavery as Douglass depicts it is not a matter of metaphoric settings, to which space is often reduced in nonecological literary criticism, it is also not in accordance with the ecocritic's lyrical evocation of natural spaces. For a runaway slave, the Ohio River is neither simply the metaphor of renewal that a river becomes for Dixon nor the rejuvenating presence that it might be in an eco-friendly text such as *A River Runs through It;* it is the border between the North and the South that, although it may be overwritten as the River Jordan in African American spirituals, represents the very real boundary between slavery and freedom. Whatever we think of Dixon's metaphors of wilderness, mountains, and rivers or of these physical spaces, African Americans and their culture have, since the time of Frederick Douglass, increasingly been involved in a process of urbanization.

Reversing the well-known narrative progression of the pastoral from corrupt city to revitalizing nature, *The Narrative of the Life of Frederick Douglass* traces its author's efforts to leave behind the cruelty he encounters in rural nature for the relative safety of the urban environment. Douglass suggests that the proximity of other eyes and ears in the city stayed the hand of slaveowners who were given free reign on rural plantations—out of sight and sound of their fellow citizens. In this sense, Douglass's *Narrative* can be read as a fascinating anti-pastoral that both draws on and calls into question the conventions of American nature writing. The trajectory of Douglass's slave narrative speaks to the relevance of eco-criticism for African American studies generally and particularly for a black literary tradition that, from its inception, has constructed the rural-natural as a realm to be feared for specific reasons and the urban-social as a domain of hope. As H. Bruce Franklin argues, Douglass's narrative foregrounds the "dialectic between rural and urban existence," contesting the dominant vision of the relationship between country and city in most European American antebellum fiction as a conflict between "rural innocence" and the "infernal city" (12–13). For Douglass, according to Franklin, the city is the favored term in this dialectic because it "represents consciousness and the possibility of freedom; the country represents brutalization and the certainty of slavery" (13). And so pastoral space and wilderness represent something different for Douglass than they do for either traditional literary critics such as Melvin Dixon or mainstream ecocritics such as Glen Love.

Gesturing toward the racialization of pastoral space that excluded African Americans from such supposedly Edenic environs, Douglass's narrative points to a flaw at the heart of pastoralism that has been evident since its origins in classical Greece. From Hesiod in the ninth century B.C.E. to the present, the pastoral has always imagined some past golden age from which we have fallen. Raymond Williams provides ample instances of this constant pastoral lamentation not just from our industrialized and jejune twentieth-century context but from Hesiod, who complains that three ages had intervened since the time when mortal men "had all good things, for the fruitful earth unforced bare them fruit abundantly and without stint" (14). Hesiod's lament for the fallen state of his own "iron age" is part of the long tradition that includes the Christian story of Adam and Eve's expulsion from their perfect pastoral precincts, on which Douglass comments.

The pastoral continually recedes to an always vanishing mythic horizon—a vista even more distanced from the landscape African slaves inhabited in the New World. It is not hard to see why the only consistent pastoral vision in early African American culture is of the Promised Land waiting beyond this mortal coil. But for early African American authors such as Frederick Douglass, this distant pastoral vision offers little solace for confronting the real travails of this world, which are obfuscated and kept in place by a mythic understanding of the relationship between humans and their environment. The world Douglass lived in is one in which the myth that "the fruitful earth unforced bare . . . fruit abundantly and without stint" can only be maintained by the erasure of the slave labor that brought the fruits of southern agriculture and husbandry to the tables of the white ruling classes. Thus the mechanism of the pastoral in the antebellum South was anathema to efforts by Frederick Douglass, and other slave narrators, to be seen as more than part of an idealized scenery.

Frederick Douglass's 1845 Narrative

The early chapters of Frederick Douglass's narrative establish the pastoral qualities of the plantation on which he was raised and then proceed to lift the veil over this picturesque scene to reveal the cruelty and deprivation the beautiful landscape has hidden. The narrative begins, "I was born in Tuckahoe, near Hillsborough, and about twelve miles from Easton, in Talbot county, Maryland. I have no accurate knowledge of my age, never having seen any authentic record containing it. By far the larger part of the slaves know as little of their ages as horses know of theirs, and it is the wish of most masters within my knowledge to keep their slaves thus ignorant" (255). And so the first few sentences of Douglass's narrative indicate that he was born in slave country several miles from the nearest town and that he was robbed not only of his birthright but even of his birth by a system that assigned him the same worth as horses and other property of the plantation owner. It was on this isolated plantation that Douglass first witnessed the brutal whipping of a slave—an incident that he calls "the blood-stained gate, the entrance to the hell of slavery"—and it was here that he "received [his] first impressions of slavery" (258, 259). Douglass highlights the inadequate food, clothing, and provisions his surroundings yielded, noting that he received little

direct physical abuse while on Colonel Lloyd's plantation but that the environment provided punishment enough with its lack of sustenance and warmth (271).
The definition of the slave as property makes it difficult for Douglass to have a
positive relationship with the southern landscape since he is legally part of that
landscape.

One of Douglass's most interesting evocations of his physical environment
comes when he creates an allegory of the plantation as an apparent Garden of
Eden. Colonel Lloyd's garden is described as "the greatest attraction of the place"
(264), drawing crowds of sightseers from the far-off cities of Annapolis and Baltimore. The fruit of this garden proves to be too great of a temptation for the
plantation's hungry inhabitants, until Colonel Lloyd hits on a scheme to capture
those who disobey his dictate not to eat of the fruit of his garden. The good
colonel has tar put on the fence surrounding his garden and then orders that any
slave "caught with any tar upon his person" is deemed guilty of trespassing in
the garden and is to be "severely whipped by the chief gardener" (264). This plan
proves to be so successful, Douglass reports, that "the slaves became as fearful of
tar as of the lash" for "they seemed to realize the impossibility of touching *tar*
without being defiled" (264).

The obvious resonances with the story of Adam and Eve's expulsion from the
Garden of Eden are complicated by the racialization of the story and its apparent
confluence with two other biblical stories describing punishments for transgressions against law and custom. The significant detail that those who broke Colonel
Lloyd's commandment were marked with tar calls to mind God's punishment for
the first sin committed after Adam and Eve's expulsion from the Garden of Eden,
when God placed a mark on Cain after he slew Abel (Gen. 4:15). In Douglass's
time, this biblical story was used to suggest that the darker races were those which
had been marked as the descendants of Cain and were thus deserving of ill treatment. A similar use was made of the story of Noah's son Ham, whose descen-
dents were likewise cursed for their forbear's transgressions. The biblical typology
applied to the outcast and the enslaved was directly mapped onto those marked
as trespassers in Colonel Lloyd's garden of forbidden fruit.

Even this telling allegory of the Garden of Eden does not provide the most
compelling reason for the validation of city life and concomitant devaluation of

country living that one finds in Douglass's narrative. As William Lloyd Garrison reminds us in the preface to Douglass's narrative, "no slaveholder or overseer can be convicted of any outrage perpetrated on the person of a slave, however diabolical it may be, on the testimony of colored witnesses, whether bond or free" (251). On the basis of this legal principle, slaveholders and overseers on plantations, far removed from the eyes of white witnesses, attempted to wield complete control over the bodies of the enslaved. Douglass tells the story of a slave named Demby who fled a whipping by his overseer, Mr. Gore, and sought refuge in the middle of a creek, where Gore confronted him:

> Mr. Gore told him that he would give him three calls, and that, if he did not come out at the third call, he would shoot him. The first call was given. Demby made no response, but stood his ground. The second and third calls were given with the same result. Mr. Gore then, without consultation or deliberation with any one, not even giving Demby an additional call, raised his musket to his face, taking deadly aim at his standing victim, and in an instant poor Demby was no more. His mangled body sank out of sight, and blood and brains marked the water where he had stood (268).

Not only does this passage provide another twist in the complicated relationship between slaves and rivers, it illustrates the danger faced by slaves whose masters were cut off from any social pressures to regulate their conduct. This is not, of course, to say that the lives of slaves in the city were free of abuse, but this incident shows that Douglass and other slaves were well aware of how entirely plantation life put them at the mercy of individuals with no laws to bar the most outrageously cruel behavior. We learn that Mr. Gore's "horrid crime was not even submitted to judicial investigation" because "it was committed in the presence of slaves, and they of course could neither institute a suit, nor testify against him; and thus the guilty perpetrator of one of the bloodiest and most foul murders goes unwhipped of justice, and uncensured by the community in which he lives" (269). This grisly scene reminds us that even the most inviting physical environment cannot be considered separately from the sociopolitical structures that shape its uses and abuses.

Given the vagaries of plantation life and the evident dispensability of the lives of the slaves who lived there, the seven-year-old Douglass is overjoyed at the prospect of being sent to live with a relative of his master in Baltimore. He refers to the period between the time he learned that he would be heading to the city and the moment of his transport to Baltimore as "three of the happiest days I ever enjoyed," and he reveals that he "spent the most part of all these three days in the creek, washing off the plantation scurf, and preparing myself for my departure" (271). While Glen Love speaks of contemporary urban nature writers "slough[ing] off their New York or L.A. skins when they confront western landscapes" (209), the process is reversed for Douglass. Leaving the rigid confines of rural life, Douglass works to scrub the "plantation scurf" off his body before he deems himself worthy of the adventures that await him in the city. Douglass does admit that there was something a little naïve about this preteen vision of his. He ascribes much of the awe that he felt for the city to the stories his cousin Tom told him: "I could never point out any thing at the Great House, no matter how beautiful or powerful, but that he had seen something at Baltimore far exceeding, both in beauty and strength, the object which I pointed out to him. Even the Great House itself, with all its pictures, was far inferior to many buildings in Baltimore" (272). It is hard not to notice the irony that Douglass launches his trip from Colonel Lloyd's plantation to one of the South's largest cities with a reference to the greater luxury of objects in Baltimore. Douglass as narrator is aware of this irony that the young Freddy is about to become one of the pieces of property that will take on a grander aura by association with the great city.

Despite the bemusement with which Douglass greets his youthful enthusiasm for urban living, the older and wiser narrator is earnest in his belief that were it not for his experience of life in the city he would have remained forever a slave:

> It is possible, and even quite probable, that but for the mere circumstance of being removed from that plantation to Baltimore, I should have to-day, instead of being here seated by my own table, in the enjoyment of freedom and the happiness of home, writing this Narrative, been confined in the galling chains of slavery. Going to live at Baltimore laid the foundation, and

opened the gateway, to all my subsequent prosperity. I have ever regarded it as the first plain manifestation of that kind providence which has ever since attended me, and marked my life with so many favors. (273)

In a sense, Baltimore becomes Douglass's celestial city, the place where Providence awaits him on the other side of the wilderness through which he must travel. On a more practical level, Baltimore is a realm of freedom for Douglass because "a city slave is almost a freeman, compared with a slave on the plantation" (275). In particular, Douglass points out that a city slave is better fed and clothed as "few are willing to incur the odium attaching to the reputation of being a cruel master; and above all things, they would not be known as not giving a slave enough to eat" (275). And so Douglass portrays the city as providing the things that his plantation environment most lacked—sustenance and warmth. The same social pressures that compel better treatment of city slaves make it less likely that a city slave would be beaten or otherwise mistreated, although Douglass is quick to add that there were "painful exceptions to the rule" (276). But for Douglass the city is not just relatively more free than the country, it is also a place that offers hope of the ultimate freedom: escape. He notes that "the chances of success [for runaway slaves] are tenfold greater from the city than from the country" (285), indicating that freedom is figuratively and literally closer to the slave's grasp in an urban environment.

Not only does Douglass's new urban environment provide him with the components needed to gain his physical freedom (food, warmth, and proximity to the thoroughfares leading north), it also supplies him with literacy, the skill Douglass credits with contributing the mental freedom he needed to even begin his escape to the North. Douglass praises his Baltimore mistress, Sophia Auld, with teaching him the ABCs before her husband intervenes on the grounds that educating young Freddy would "forever unfit him to be a slave" (274). Douglass takes these words to heart, writing that "from that moment, I understood the pathway from slavery to freedom" (275). The connection between freedom and literacy Douglass forges in this passage has been much discussed, but critics have overlooked the role that Douglass's urban environment plays in his achievement of mental freedom. Douglass writes that the education Mrs. Auld began was completed by "little white boys whom I met in the street" (277)—hungry urban youth who are willing to teach Freddy to read in exchange for a few pieces of bread. And so Douglass literally gets his education from the city streets, for the city of Baltimore provides the physical and social environment that enables Douglass's journey from slavery to freedom.

When Douglass is forced to return to the country after his master's death, he is more aware than ever of his "degraded condition" as a plantation slave (281). His recalcitrance in accepting this role causes him to be sent to the "nigger-breaker" Mr. Covey, who is depicted as an omnipresent part of the plantation environment: "He was under every tree, behind every stump, in every bush, and at every window, on the plantation" (291). The characterization of Mr. Covey as "the snake" whose "forte consisted in his power to deceive" as he skulked through the woods and "appeared to us as being ever at hand" (291–92) recalls the mysterious stranger, "he of the serpent" (55), who appears and disappears at will in the haunted woods of Nathaniel Hawthorne's story "Young Goodman Brown." The men in these two narratives are clearly figurations of the devil, who is associated in nineteenth-century iconography with wild spaces that are seen not as places of spiritual rejuvenation but as threatening domains of sin and suffering. Only by confronting Mr. Covey, the devil incarnate, is Douglass able to face down his internal demons and resist the temptation to become the "brute" that his environment dictates (293). Refusing to be whipped by Covey, Douglass fights him to a draw, claiming that this moment of resistance means that "the day had passed forever when I could be a slave" (299). Thus the rest of the narrative is presented as a fait accompli because once Douglass is able to free himself from the clutches of Mr. Covey and his own plantation mentality, Douglass is determined to once more return to his beloved Baltimore and effectuate his escape.

Ultimately, Douglass self-consciously describes his escape as a sort of inverted pastoral, whereby he leaves behind the deadening influence of the country for the rejuvenating forces of the city. Eventually returned to the "care" of the Aulds, it is from the port city of Baltimore that Douglass makes his successful escape to the North, running away (as did other slave narrators) along commercial routes. Thus the trade mechanisms that enabled slavery to continue by transporting rural goods to urban centers also make possible Douglass's "glorious resurrection from the tomb of slavery, to the heaven of freedom" (299). Once safely established in New York, Douglass looks back to his time as a slave and uses the same animalistic imagery to describe the slaveowner as that which had been applied to him as a slave. In the course of one paragraph, Douglass refers to his former slaveowners, and their agents who would try to capture him and return him to the South, as "a den of hungry lions," "ferocious beasts," "hideous crocodile[s]," "wild beasts," and "monsters of the deep" (320). While others have seen this passage as Douglass taking on the moral authority denied him as a slave or inverting the commodification of the slave as an animal by showing the similar effect on the slaveowner (Franklin 17), an ecocritical perspective highlights how Douglass is also responding negatively to the wilderness and its inhabitants. Those "money-loving kidnappers" who would return him to slavery "lie in wait for the panting fugitive, as the ferocious beasts of the forest lie in wait for their prey" (320). Or again, these men attempted to seize runaways "as the hideous crocodile seizes upon his prey!" (320). Douglass ties into an active strain of anti-pastoral discourse that circulated in the antebellum United States, depicting the wilderness and woods as dangerous and frightening spaces. The specific context of American slavery racialized and concretized this discourse in Douglass's narrative, which thus, along with other slave narratives, helped to launch a tradition of anti-pastoralism within African American culture.

The Nature of Slavery

The kind of spaces that most mainstream environmentalists and ecocritics validate—the pastoral and the wild—were not likely to be appreciated by Douglass and other slaves whose best hopes lay with negotiating an urban terrain. Slavery changed the nature of nature in African American culture, necessitating a break with the pastoral tradition developed within European American literature. In a speech given the title "The Nature of Slavery" in the appendices to Douglass's 1855 version of his narrative, *My Bondage and My Freedom*, Douglass reiterates one of the fundamental reasons for this difference between African American and European American visions of the landscape: "A master is one who claims and exercises a right of property in the person of a fellow-man" (272). Slavery created a system whereby those of European descent controlled a pastoral landscape that included those of African descent as part of their property. Is it any wonder that this fact gave rise to an anti-pastoral discourse that continues to the present day?

This discourse was only strengthened during the postbellum period; the steady urbanization of African Americans after the Civil War ensured that the city would increasingly become more central to African American culture than was the country. More than forty thousand former slaves and free blacks moved north, most from the rural South to the urban North, each decade between 1870 and 1890. More than double this number moved north and west in the 1890s, during the build up to what has been called the Great Migration—the period during the first half of the twentieth century when the African American population shifted so dramatically that the majority of blacks in this country were no longer found in rural southern locales but in northern urban areas, not to mention the increasing urbanization within the South (Osofsky 18). This massive population shift was part of a trend that has continued to the present day, such that 82 percent of African Americans now live in urban areas—a greater percentage than any other ethnic group (Rosler 24). The resulting cultural outgrowths of these dramatic geographical developments shaped a twentieth-century inheritance of the anti-pastoral qualities of slave narratives such as Douglass's.

In the twentieth century, the most obvious translation of the Great Migration into African American culture was provided by the Harlem Renaissance, an urban phenomenon during the early decades of the century. In the pathbreaking essay "The New Negro," which served as his introduction to the influential volume of the same name, Alain Locke frames the Harlem Renaissance as a manifestation of a new generation shaped, first and foremost, by the "shifting of the Negro population" not only "toward the North and the Central Midwest, but city-ward and to the great centers of industry" (5). Locke traces the huge importance of this development not just to a geographic transposition but to an accompanying sociohistorical transformation, "a deliberate flight not only from countryside to city, but from medieval America to modern" (6). The forties and fifties witnessed a growing investment in urbanism by African American writers, such that the country recedes into the background of the two most famous African American novels of this period: Richard Wright's *Native Son* and Ralph Ellison's *Invisible Man,* which explore the cultural topography of Chicago and

New York, respectively. The anti-pastoral strain within African American culture was kept alive through the era of the Black Power movement. Drawing on the words of Elijah Muhammad, Malcolm X made repeated references to "this wilderness of North America" (Haley 193, 197). The urban riots of this period challenged but did not extinguish the efforts of African American writers to explore the parameters and possibilities of city life. As James DeJongh puts it, "the poets of the Black Arts movement were seeking an inner city of the spirit in the ashes of a riot" (208). This anti-pastoralism continues to the present day. The two best-known explorations of the relationship between African American literature and geography—Melvin Dixon's *Ride Out the Wilderness* and Charles Scruggs's *Sweet Home*—both end with explorations of the complex relationship between country and city in the Nobel Prize–winning fiction of Toni Morrison as paradigmatic of what Scruggs sees as the balance of utopian and dystopian images of the city evident in African American fiction throughout the last half of the twentieth century. Distrust of rural environments is still deeply associated with images of southern violence and lynchings. The historical memory of slavery and its aftermath includes a forest of trees that were used to enforce southern lynch law, as we are reminded in cultural images from Billie Holiday singing "Strange Fruit" to Speech, of Arrested Development, rapping about "trees my forefathers hung from" in "Tennessee."

Having built an argument about a certain trajectory within African American culture from slavery to the present, I need to note that the anti-pastoral discourse at work in each of these historical moments circulated with its dialectical opposite. The urbanicity of the Harlem Renaissance gave rise to the valorization of the country in Jean Toomer's *Cane*. The appeal to African civilization in the Black Power movement sometimes traveled under the guise of imagining Africa as an untroubled Eden. The cautionary tale about trees in Arrested Development's "Tennessee" is balanced with a genuine celebration of life in the slow lane (the song reminds us that the trees that Speech's "forefathers hung from" are the also the trees that his generation climbed on as kids). And, as Raymond Williams reminds us, the country and the city are not diametrically opposed but construct one another. To return to the era of slavery, urban centers such as Boston, Washington, D.C., and Atlanta established the economic and governmental policies that oiled the machinery of the peculiar institution. So although slaves such as Frederick Douglass may have experienced city life as infinitely preferable to plantation living, the former enabled the latter.

Despite these qualifications, I still argue that a main current within African American culture has, from Frederick Douglass to Toni Morrison, expressed a profound antipathy toward the ecological niches usually focused on in ecocriticism: pastoral space and wilderness. This fact challenges ecocritics to train our methods of reading and theorizing on African American cultural texts that question mainstream assumptions about the universal appeal of "unspoiled" nature. Just as a careful reading of Douglass's 1845 *Narrative* reveals an inversion of the usual ecocritical value assigned to Edenic solitude, so attention to the African American–led environmental justice movement has caused an inversion in the priorities of many environmentalists. By focusing on the challenges confronting black urban communities and questioning the valorization of wilderness spaces and wildlife within the mainstream environmental movement, the environmental justice movement has "transformed the pastoral face of green politics" (Ross 103). A similar transformation of ecocriticism and ecologically informed reading practices is needed to account for the topography of contemporary African American culture.

Lawrence Buell gestures toward such a connection when he suggests that the depiction of the countryside within African American literature as "an area of chance violence and enslavement" might help to explain "the tepid African American interest to date in environmentalist causes" (17). But Buell has it backwards. The vibrancy of the environmental justice movement, which has quickly become one of the most active social movements in the country, indicates a decidedly nontepid African American interest in the "environment" when that term is not conceptualized as solely a domain of nonurban space. Instead of using the few studies that have been conducted on the "ethnic differences in landscape preferences" (17) to show that blacks just do not get the importance of wilderness aesthetics, perhaps Buell and other ecocritics should learn from these same studies, and from the history of anti-pastoralism within African American culture, that the wildness of the world cannot be preserved unless and until we have broken down some of the racial, class, and gender barriers that distance wilderness and pastoral space from those outside the upper echelons of our society. In short, the long history of the dominant culture's romanticization of the wilderness will have limited appeal until the generations since Frederick Douglass have an equal stake in the dispensation and appreciation of landscape, which has, for most of our history, been written over rather than by them. It would behoove all of us interested in the fate of our shared planet to work for an ecocriticism and an ecological movement that accounts for and is accountable to this vision of environmental justice.

Works Cited

Buell, Lawrence. *The Environmental Imagination: Thoreau, Nature Writing, and the Formation of American Culture.* Cambridge: Harvard UP, 1995.

DeJongh, James. *Vicious Modernism: Black Harlem and the Literary Imagination.* Cambridge: Cambridge UP, 1990.

Dixon, Melvin. *Ride Out the Wilderness: Geography and Identity in Afro-American Literature.* Urbana: U of Illinois P, 1987.

Douglass, Frederick. *My Bondage and My Freedom.* 1855. Ed. and Intro. William L. Andrews. Urbana: U of Illinois P, 1987.

———. *Narrative of the Life of Frederick Douglass, an American Slave.* 1845. *The Classic Slave Narratives.* Ed. Henry Louis Gates, Jr. New York: NAL Penguin, 1987. 243–331.

Franklin, H. Bruce. *Prison Literature in America: The Victim as Criminal and Artist.* New York: Oxford UP, 1989.

Haley, Alex. *The Autobiography of Malcolm X.* New York: Ballantine, 1992.

Hawthorne, Nathaniel. "Young Goodman Brown." *The Portable Hawthorne.* Ed. Malcolm Cowley. New York: Penguin, 1983. 53–68.

Leopold, Aldo. *A Sand County Almanac and Sketches Here and There.* New York: Oxford UP, 1987.

Locke, Alain. "The New Negro." 1925. *The New Negro.* Ed. Alain Locke. New York: Atheneum, 1977. 3–16.

Love, Glen A. "Revaluing Nature: Toward an Ecological Criticism." *Western American Literature* 25.3 (1990): 201–15.

Maclean, Norman. *A River Runs through It and Other Stories.* Chicago: U of Chicago P, 1976.

Osofsky, Gilbert. *Harlem: The Making of a Ghetto. Negro New York, 1890–1930.* New York: Harper and Row, 1963.

Rosler, Martha. "Fragments of a Metropolitan Viewpoint." *If You Lived Here: The City in Art, Theory, and Social Activism.* Ed. Brian Wallis. Seattle: Bay Press, 1991. 15–44.

Ross, Andrew. *The Chicago Gangster Theory of Life: Nature's Debt to Society.* London: Verso, 1994.

Scruggs, Charles. *Sweet Home: Invisible Cities in the Afro-American Novel.* Baltimore: Johns Hopkins UP, 1993.

Thoreau, Henry David. "Walking." 1862. *The Portable Thoreau.* Ed. Carl Bode. New York: Penguin, 1983. 592–630.

Williams, Raymond. *The Country and the City.* New York: Oxford UP, 1973.

The Novels of Toni Morrison: "Wild Wilderness Where There Was None"

Kathleen R. Wallace and Karla Armbruster

Why read Toni Morrison's novels from an ecocritical perspective? One compelling reason is that Morrison's profound engagement with the natural world has thus far been overlooked by most of her critics, with the prominent exceptions of Barbara Christian, Vera Norwood, and Jhan Hochman.[1] In this essay, though, our purpose is not simply to draw attention to Morrison's lyrical descriptions of the green world but rather to suggest how her complex representation of African American experiences with nature can productively complicate American environmentalist discourse and the practice of ecocriticism.

The fundamental dynamic through which all Morrison's novels engage with this discourse is strikingly illustrated in *Tar Baby,* a novel set primarily on the Caribbean estate of Valerian Street, a white American who acquired a fortune manufacturing candy using sugar and cocoa produced in the region. The novel begins when Son, a rough-and-tumble wanderer living on the boundaries of mainstream culture, shows up at the estate. A complex and disturbing character, Son displays an empathetic awareness of the fate of so much of nature's wildness at the hands of dominant Western culture. For example, he muses on the transformation of ocean water into bathwater, noting that "The triumph of ingenuity . . . had transformed the bored treachery of the sea into a playful gush of water that did exactly as it was told. And why not? Wilderness wasn't wild anymore or threatening; wildlife needed human protection to exist at all" (221).

In these observations, Son echoes some of the attitudes of mainstream American environmentalism: a sense of regret that so much of nature is not wild anymore and that anything "wild" that remains depends on human protection for its existence. But just as remarkable as these environmentalist expressions is how

Morrison represents the perspective of nature itself, which she describes else-where as a kind of chorus "thinking and feeling and watching and responding" to the action of the novel ("Rootedness" 341). Indeed, after a brief introduction to the story of the human characters, *Tar Baby*'s first chapter begins with a scene of environmental destruction from the viewpoint of the natural residents of the place—clouds, fish, parrots, thousand-year-old daisy trees, and even a river—that are destroyed, evicted, or altered by the construction of "a collection of magnificent winter houses on Isle des Chevaliers" (9). Morrison returns to this nonhuman perspective repeatedly throughout the novel, emphasizing that al-though nature is profoundly affected by human activities, it also has a life and perspective of its own.

In drawing our attention to the plight of wilderness and reminding us that wild nature, although vulnerable to our actions, has its own independent being, Morrison displays a consciousness quite compatible with the values and concerns of the American nature writing tradition and mainstream environmental move-ment.[2] However, in *Tar Baby* and her other novels, Morrison also repeatedly confronts us with perspectives on nature and wildness that complicate those val-ues and concerns. When Street fires his Caribbean servants, Gideon and Thérèse, for stealing apples, Son is appalled that Street "had been able to dismiss with a flutter of the fingers the people whose sugar and cocoa had allowed him to grow old in regal comfort" (202–3). Son's rage grows into a rant against the uncon-trolled greed and wastefulness of white, Western culture: "[T]hey had not the dignity of wild animals who did not eat where they defecated but they could defecate over a whole people and come there to live and defecate some more by tearing up the land and that is why they loved property so, because they had killed it soiled it defecated on it and they loved more than anything the places where they shit" (203). In his invocation of the dignity of wild animals, Son reflects Morrison's recognition of a natural world in some ways separate from human culture and possessing its own logic, a world he contrasts with the physically and spiritually destructive behaviors of dominant Western culture that defy order and logic. However, Son steps beyond such a standard environmentalist critique of the human drive to dominate nature when he links the destruction of Isle des Chevaliers to the ideology that sanctions the oppression of the marginalized people who call it home.[3]

Son's insight here exemplifies the most significant way Morrison's treatment of nature moves beyond mainstream nature writing and environmentalism: all her novels resonate with the profound awareness that despite the fact that nature exists beyond human perceptions, perceptions are all we have—and they have powerful implications, for both humans and nature. Morrison's work as a whole may suggest that a respect for the dignity of wild things is superior to the drive to control nature, but what is even more notable is her focus on the different and often conflicting interpretations of nature espoused by various human communities and the ways dominant groups use these interpretations to control and subjugate both human and nonhuman others.[4] By consistently representing clashing cultural perceptions of the natural world, Morrison emphasizes that any human perception of nature is a culturally mediated one rather than an inherent truth about the world.

Morrison's body of work also suggests that her African American characters are especially likely to understand how nature is interpreted, mediated, and used because they themselves have so often been dominated and oppressed through whites' uses of nature. Feminist standpoint theory has described such a phenomenon, contending that those who are subjugated may be especially attuned to cultural dynamics fostering dominance and oppression.[5] Building on this theory, Donna J. Haraway argues that the perspectives of the subjugated should not be exempt from critical reexamination, but she maintains that they "are least likely to allow denial of the critical and interpretive core of all knowledge. . . . 'Subjugated' standpoints . . . seem to promise more adequate, sustained, objective, transforming accounts of the world" (584–85).

In representing the subjugated standpoint of African Americans, Morrison is notable for exploring how the natural world has been used as an instrument of oppression but has simultaneously provided a source of sustenance and comfort. In doing so, she both challenges and ultimately enriches mainstream American environmental discourse, including the ecocritical discourse that has to some degree grown out of it. In this essay, we focus on her treatment of wildness, a concept central to the dominant tradition of American environmental thought. This tradition often values nature most for its wildness, interpreted as its separateness from human culture, whether it is viewed as an escape, complement, or challenge to that culture. Morrison's treatment of wildness overlaps with this tradition, and yet, by providing a range of specifically African American perspectives on the concept, it also offers a compelling revision.

Morrison's Revision of Dominant Cultural Conceptions of Wildness

One of the strongest dimensions of all definitions of wildness is its status as outside or exceeding the boundaries of human culture(s). Henry David Thoreau equated it with "the raw material of life" but also emphasized that it is a quality that "no *culture,* in short, can give" (611, 616). This sense that wildness stands outside culture informs the U.S. Wilderness Act of 1964, which defines wilderness as "an area where the earth and its community of life are untrammeled by man, where man himself is a visitor who does not remain" (Callicott and Nelson 121). Most contemporary environmental thinkers concerned with wildness see it as most pure when untainted by human intervention; for them, "Wildness is out there" (Turner 125).[6] Even Gary Snyder, who insists that wildness is an integral aspect of human identities, bodies, and cultures, still sees it as "out there" in the sense that it eludes and exceeds culturally created categories and structures.

Until the mid-nineteenth century, American views of wildness and wilderness were typically negative, equating them with the uncivilized, uncultivated, chaotic, violent, and destructive.[7] As wilderness became more rare, though, the notion began to take root that wildness might be valuable to human culture—that, as Thoreau wrote, "in Wildness is the preservation of the World" (609). More recently, contemporary thinkers such as Turner and Snyder have celebrated the ways in which wildness can destabilize and potentially revitalize human culture. Today, the valorization of wildness and wilderness is fundamental to American environmental discourse, just as the protection of wilderness areas remains a priority for many mainstream environmental organizations.[8]

While affirming such view of wildness as an irrepressible force that destabilizes culture, Morrison's novels also demonstrate how African Americans' relationships to wildness and wilderness have been shaped by a cultural history different from that of most white environmental activists and writers.[9] Many of Morrison's characters—particularly the former slaves of *Beloved*—struggle to reconcile the beauty they see in nature, and their love for it, with their personal and communal history as property and the ways nature has been used both physically and conceptually to help enslave and oppress them. For example, Paul D. hears the song of doves as he endures the dehumanizing horrors of a prison camp in Alfred, Georgia, and he realizes that he has "neither the right nor the permission to enjoy it because in that place mist, doves, sunlight, copper dirt, moon—everything belonged to the men who had the guns" (162). Eighteen years after her escape with her children from a Kentucky farm called Sweet Home, Sethe still struggles with the realization that "It never looked as terrible as it was and it made her wonder if hell was a pretty place too. Fire and brimstone all right, but hidden in lacy groves. Boys hanging from the most beautiful sycamores in the world" (6). In this image, Morrison identifies nature as an instrument through which whites oppress and even kill blacks; she makes this point even more forcefully through her treatment of animality.[10] In a graphic example, Sethe describes how the two white boys who violate her take the milk from her breasts as if she were "the cow, no, the goat, back behind the stable" (200), and Morrison makes clear that they can do so only because they have been taught she is less than human. As Vera Norwood notes, "the green world cannot save Sethe from the violence of slavery" (189). The construction of nature as refuge so prominent in mainstream environmental thought simply does not hold true for Morrison's characters.

While *Beloved* gives us the greatest insight into the history of African Americans' experiences with nature under slavery, Morrison's other novels explore how this history affected subsequent generations. She emphasizes how their experiences of nature, wilderness, and even wildness are profoundly mediated by cultural interpretations and priorities; moreover, because Morrison's novels focus on humans as part of communities, her characters rarely encounter the natural world in the extreme, unpeopled form recognized by the Wilderness Act.[11] For these characters, wildness at once exceeds human culture and materializes in human communities and individuals. Morrison's African American characters are also necessarily less eager to embrace the aspects of wildness—its openness, lack of final identity, and resistance to cultural control—that contemporary environmentalists and wilderness advocates are likely to celebrate. Rather, these characters are often occupied with achieving a more stable sense of identity (as individuals and as communities) and exercising some degree of control over their surroundings because historically they have been denied such agency.

In producing a dense web of overlapping, sometimes contrasting perspectives on wildness, Morrison's novels draw our attention to wildness that has nothing to do with nature and possesses no redeeming aspects: it manifests in chaotic human behavior that destroys all in its path. This wildness is culturally induced, a product of the crippling effect of oppressive, hate-filled environments on natural desires for love, growth, and fulfillment. Morrison also recognizes another kind of wildness, an expansive wildness that can resemble the wildness valorized in mainstream environmental thought. Unlike culturally induced wildness, expansive wildness emanates from outside human culture and exceeds human control and comprehension. While such wildness can have a positive, revitalizing effect on human individuals and communities, Morrison is careful to point out that it can also destroy if not carefully integrated into human communities through ritual and tradition.

"Unnatural" Wildness Induced by Cultural Oppression

In *Song of Solomon,* the protagonist Milkman Dead initiates and then ends an affair with his cousin, Hagar, who retaliates by repeatedly trying to kill him. Confronting Hagar, Milkman's mother, Ruth Foster, recognizes a kind of wildness in Hagar's thoughts and actions, realizing "that there was something truly askew in this girl. That here was the wilderness of Southside. Not the poverty or dirt or noise, not just extreme unregulated passion where even love found its way with an ice pick, but the absence of control. Here one lived knowing that at any time, anybody might do anything. Not wilderness where there was system, or the logic of lions, trees, toads, and birds, but wild wilderness where there was none" (138). Hagar's wild reaction to Milkman's rejection is precisely the type of behavior that whites might label "unnatural"—irrational behavior befitting nonhuman animals and thus not "natural" for humans. Morrison's novels repeatedly illustrate how dominant (white) American culture has employed the concepts of natural and unnatural to reinforce ideological boundaries between the human and the less-than-human, often in the service of denying African Americans their full humanity.

But rather than simply asserting African Americans' place on the human side of that boundary, Morrison deconstructs the boundary itself. Ruth, for example, differentiates the wildness she sees in Hagar from the wildness of nature's wilderness. Like Son, who contrasts the dignity of wild animals with the self-destructive, chaotic impulses of Western imperialism and capitalism, Ruth recognizes that nature's wildness has a certain system and order, while Hagar's is truly chaotic and deadly to herself as well as others. Morrison implies Hagar's behavior has little to do with nature or anything outside of human culture. Hagar's murderous frenzy grows out of a culturally dictated lack of self-worth and a resultant lack of self-control: her kind of wildness, represented again and again throughout Morrison's novels, is culturally induced, catalyzed by the hateful environment created by dominant cultural forces.

In these portrayals of culturally induced wildness, Morrison reinterprets the concepts of natural and unnatural, insisting that it is the oppression and hatred that spawn this wildness that are unnatural, rather than the behavior of the person exhibiting it. This point is illustrated most directly by Milkman's friend Guitar, who joins a secret retribution society called The Days, which randomly kills one white for every black killed by whites. Guitar justifies this practice by contending that "There are no innocent white people, because every one of them is a potential nigger-killer, if not an actual one. . . . White people are unnatural. As a race they are unnatural" (155–56). Ultimately Guitar displays a culturally induced wildness when he projects his murderous anger against white culture onto Milkman, but his recognition that hatred and discrimination are unnatural is supported throughout Morrison's novels.

While emphasizing the cultural interpretation and deployment of concepts such as natural and unnatural, Morrison simultaneously displays a sense that a natural order exists outside of human perception and suggests that humans—whether they realize it or not—are constrained and shaped by this natural order. As Barbara Christian notes, Morrison views humans as part of nature and nature as part of human beings; consequently, each person has an inherent need for growth, love, and fulfillment, and this need "will manifest itself either in natural terms or in derangement" (62). Many of Morrison's novels dwell on the tragic results of denying these natural human needs. *The Bluest Eye*, for example, details the damage wrought by an "unnatural" belief system that "creates a hierarchy in which just a few can be worthy of love and happiness" (Christian 52); Jadine, the sophisticated niece of Street's house servants in *Tar Baby*, struggles with a culturally induced alienation from her African American roots; and *Paradise* illustrates the costs of an all-black community's tradition of suppressing all natural tendencies toward growth and change.

Ultimately, Morrison shows us that the conditions that produce "wild" behavior such as Hagar's and Guitar's are unnatural because they warp fundamental human needs by forcing a race of people to repeatedly assert its humanity. Stamp Paid, a member of the newly freed black community in *Beloved*, affectingly expresses this dynamic:

> Whitepeople believed that whatever the manners, under every dark skin was a jungle. Swift unnavigable waters, swinging screaming baboons, sleeping snakes, red gums ready for their sweet white blood. In a way, he thought, they were right. The more coloredpeople spent their strength trying to convince them how gentle they were, how clever and loving, how human, the more they used themselves up to persuade whites of something Negroes believed could not be questioned, the deeper and more tangled the jungle grew inside. But it wasn't the jungle blacks brought with them to this place from the other (livable) place. It was the jungle whitefolks planted in them. And it grew. It spread. In, through, and after life, it spread, until it invaded the whites who had made it. (198–99)

Stamp Paid evokes the perniciousness of a planted wildness polluting all it touches and inevitably spreading back into the white culture that created it. Such wildness is not the wildness of dominant environmental discourse; rather, it is an unnatural wildness instigated by twisted cultural standards.

Expansive Wildness that Exceeds Culture

Beloved revolves around an act that could be interpreted as an example of culturally induced wildness: Sethe's killing of her "crawling already?" daughter.[12] However, the multiple narrative perspectives Morrison provides on Sethe's action reveal it as an expansive, extracultural wildness that cannot be classified as wholly positive or negative. When Schoolteacher, the overseer of Sweet Home, finds Sethe after she has experienced just twenty-eight days of freedom across the Ohio

River, she attempts to kill her children to save them from slavery, succeeding in the case of her older daughter. However, her murderous act differs in an important way from Hagar's or Guitar's homicidal tendencies. Rather than lashing out for revenge, Sethe is attempting to protect her children, to put them "where no one could hurt them" (163). There is a desperate logic to her action, although it is a logic that evolves in response to an unbearable, twisted cultural institution.

From Schoolteacher's perspective, Sethe has "gone wild" as a result of a beating one of his nephews gave her shortly before she escaped (149). He interprets her actions as "testimony to the results of a little so-called freedom imposed on people who needed every care and guidance in the world to keep them from the cannibal life they preferred" (151). While this reaction dismisses Sethe as less than human, it also signals a subtle but significant shift from his earlier perception of Sethe as a domestic animal, a piece of property unproblematically available for use by whites. This change of analogy—from domestic to wild animal—along with his decision not to take Sethe back to Sweet Home can be seen as a grudging if not completely conscious recognition of Sethe's new-found freedom to act in her and her children's interests. Stamp Paid also recognizes the power of Sethe's wildness by likening her to a wild animal, describing her as "snatching up her children . . . like a hawk on the wing; how her face beaked, how her hands worked like claws" (157), a parent acting on the natural impulse to save her children. Likewise, when Sethe describes the moment to Paul D., she characterizes herself as having been propelled by "Little hummingbirds [who] stuck their needle beaks right through her headcloth into her hair and beat their wings," a wild force that catalyzes her reaction: "if she thought anything, it was No. No. Nono. Nonono. Simple. She just flew" (163). Her drastic decision expresses a wildness that exceeds human categories and value judgments. It is positive in its ability to defy and frighten dominant culture; it is destructive, too, leaving a child dead and its mother to face a lifetime of regret and guilt.

Expansive wildness resonates throughout Morrison's novels, expressing itself in human characters and actions, yet always exceeding the boundaries of human culture. In *Jazz*, a rural community experiences this force through an enigmatic figure known as Wild, a black woman believed to live in the fields and woods on the town's outskirts. Human, yet without speech, clothing, or any other trappings of civilization, she exists on the boundary between nature and culture. Joe Trace comes to believe that she is his birth mother, while the folklore of the community describes her as everywhere and nowhere—"somewhere in that cane field—at its edge some said or maybe moving around in it. Close . . . and probably looking at them" (166). Their sense of Wild's presence encapsulates an aspect of Morrison's sense of expansive wildness that corresponds to the wildness that Thoreau and other environmental thinkers prized. Morrison's wildness is likewise full of vitality and complexity, and its seeming chaos is always organized according to its own constantly changing and evolving order. While Morrison's wildness clearly exceeds culture, though, it finds full expression not only in wilderness but also in the realms of myth and the supernatural. In contrast to mainstream environmental thinkers, Morrison cannot unreservedly celebrate the notion that this wildness is neither inherently good nor bad. Like these thinkers, she recognizes expansive wildness as a necessary force of revitalization for human culture, but she is more wary of its excessive nature, recognizing its power to destroy when not carefully integrated into a community's cultural structures.

The most extreme, unadulterated manifestation of expansive wildness in Morrison's work is the character Beloved and the wild realm beyond death and time from which she comes. Materializing in the body of a young adult woman, she is clearly the ghost of Sethe's oldest daughter, but she is also, as Sethe's second daughter, Denver, succinctly puts it, "more" (266), carrying the collective memory of those killed through the systemic cruelty of slavery. Her desires—whether for sweets or Sethe's company—are uncontrolled; her powers are supernatural; and one by one the other characters realize that "She was not like them. She was wild game and nobody said, Get on out of here, girl, and come back when you get some sense" (242). They recognize that Beloved cannot be domesticated and integrated into their human community. Her return confirms Sethe's belief that "nothing ever dies," that events and people continue to exist unchanged in a realm outside of time "not just in my rememory, but out there, in the world" (36), even after they are finished, dead, or destroyed. Returning from this realm after eighteen years, Beloved seems untouched by time, still demonstrating the psychological state of a young child. She is also outside of the symbolic order in many ways, unable to speak when she first appears and pre-Oedipal in her lack of individual identity.

Beloved's status outside of culture is also marked by an association with wild nature—for example, she first emerges as a physical presence from the water. Supernatural and natural often overlap in this way in Morrison's novels, exemplifying, as Norwood notes, African traditions that "include in the natural world space for 'the dangerous ghosts of men who have been lost, or drowned, or burnt alive'" (192, quoting Geoffrey Parrinder). For Morrison's African American characters, the supernatural permeates not just the natural but also the cultural; Beloved's return first as a ghost and then a physical presence is no great shock to the other characters.[13] Still, they sense the distance between the cultural and natural spaces they inhabit and the remoteness of the borderland between natural and supernatural where presences such as Beloved belong. As Ella, a member of the community, expresses it: "As long as the ghost showed out from its ghostly place—shaking stuff, crying, smashing and such—Ella respected it. But if it took flesh and came in her world, well, the shoe was on the other foot. She didn't mind a little communication between the two worlds, but this was an invasion" (257).

Transgressing the boundaries between the living and the dead, the past and the present, the natural and the supernatural, the infant and the adult, and the one and the many, Beloved's wildness challenges the most fundamental ordering concepts of human culture; in doing so, she represents one of the defining qualities of expansive wildness. Many of Morrison's most memorable characters do likewise: *Sula*'s title character, who defies communal and societal norms to seek fulfillment on her own terms; Milkman Dead's aunt Pilate, whose rejection of dominant cultural standards encourages him to question his father's materialistic compulsion to objectify and control both people and property; and Son, "[a] man without human rites" (165) who challenges the other characters to examine their customary, often dysfunctional, self-images and relationships to each other.

Morrison has described these transgressive characters as possessing "a nice wildness . . . [that] has bad effects in society such as the one in which we live. It's pre-Christ in the best sense. It's Eve. . . . Opposed to accepted notions of progress, the lock-step life, they live in the world unreconstructed" (Tate 126). As Morrison's statement suggests, such wildness often leads to disaster because most characters who experience it are unable to integrate it into their lives or communities in productive ways. Sula's wildness, which Christian terms her "fluidity" (60), ultimately leads to her death because she lacks connections, except to her childhood friend, Nel. Pilate is unable to create an environment where her granddaughter Hagar can develop an adequate sense of self-esteem because they live apart from any coherent community that shares their values—a failure that leads to Hagar's suicide. Virtually none of the characters in *Tar Baby* accept the challenge Son brings to their lives, and his eventual abandonment of the world of human culture for a folkloric realm suggests that his extreme wildness cannot find a positive outlet in modern society.

The paradox of expansive wildness is that it is necessary to individuals and communities for change and growth, but it can also destroy them. Morrison's most recent novel expresses her most complex and focused exploration to date of this paradox. *Paradise* tells the story of an all-black community in Oklahoma founded by ex-slaves in 1889 in response to an environment of race hatred, which the community members characterize as "Out There."[14] In reaction, they attempt to maintain their town, Haven, as an earthly garden of paradise, truly an orderly haven divorced from the culture outside by inflexible traditions and rituals. When their efforts begin to fail, they create and move to a new town, Ruby, in 1943. But by 1976, Ruby is in danger of dying out, both literally and spiritually. No one has died in the town since its establishment, and births are few: in the aftermath of their move from Haven, "the fertility shriveled" (193).

Morrison's message is clear: as a community, Ruby is in stasis, trapped between birth and death, past and future, because its impermeable boundary between Out There and In Here has cut it off from expansive wildness. Expansive wildness, however, proves irrepressible, and it eventually infiltrates Ruby. This wildness primarily manifests itself through a group of women living seventeen miles outside of town in an old mansion known as the Convent. These women, "Bodacious black Eves unredeemed by Mary" (18), follow no rules, strike up tenuous relationships with various inhabitants of Ruby and with outsiders, and seem capable of cross-fertilizing Ruby with much-needed sexual, spiritual, and cultural diversity. However, Morrison does not present these women's wildness as unproblematically positive. Just as the stagnation created by Ruby's insistence on control threatens to destroy the community, the untempered, disconnected wildness of the Convent women proves unsustainable as well.

The expansive wildness of Morrison's novels can resemble the wildness celebrated within mainstream environmental thought, but Morrison problematizes
that association. Acutely aware that wildness exceeds culture, Morrison also
shows how wildness can destroy human individuals and communities. In order
to rejuvenate, wildness must be integrated into and expressed through living ancestral traditions and folk culture rather than left untempered or forced into
static embodiments of cultural and natural history. In Morrison's novels, expansive wildness most threatens individuals and communities lacking vibrant cultures tied to an ancestral past. As Morrison explains, "It was the absence of an
ancestor that was frightening, that was threatening. . . . [S]olace comes, not from
the contemplation of serene nature as in a lot of mainstream white literature"
but through the recognition of ancestral ties and knowledge ("Rootedness" 343).
Shortly before they die at the hands of men from Ruby, the women of the Convent reinvent an ancestrally based, vital tradition, a months-long story-telling
ritual seemingly based on the Brazilian candomblé religion, a syncretic mix of
Catholicism and African spirituality that one woman remembers from her girl-
hood in Brazil. This hybrid ritual helps the women confront wounds from their
pasts and teaches them to love themselves. Christ-like, the women reappear after
their deaths to those who love them, and Morrison ends the novel with signs that
their sacrifice may have taught Ruby the way to redeem itself by making room
for wildness rather than walling it out.

While the women in *Paradise* must reinvent the kind of vital communal tradition that can successfully integrate wildness into culture, Milkman Dead encounters an existing tradition of this type when he experiences a hunting ritual
in the rural community of Shalimar, Virginia, the ancestral home of his father's
family. Listening to the men and their hounds as they hunt, Milkman undergoes
an epiphany of sorts:

> No, it was not language; it was what there was before language. . . . Language
> in the time when men and animals did talk to one another. . . . And he was
> hearing it in the Blue Ridge Mountains under a sweet gum tree. And if they
> could talk to animals, and the animals could talk to them, what didn't they

know about human beings? Or the earth itself, for that matter. It was more than tracks [a fellow hunter] was looking for—he whispered to the trees, whispered to the ground, touched them, as a blind man caresses a page of Braille, pulling meaning through his fingers. (278)

Surrounded by his ancestral community and wrapped in darkness, Milkman experiences hunting as an ennobling tradition through which a community can reconnect itself to a primeval state "before language." By passing this vital tradition—along with that tradition's sacred place—from one generation to the next, the residents of Shalimar have incorporated wildness into their community without letting it destroy them or turning it into an extraneous and life-defeating ritual.

Morrison makes clear that not all expressions of expansive wildness can be incorporated into human cultures in revitalizing ways, though. The most tragic example of a wildness too far outside of human culture to be assimilated is Beloved. Her disruptive influence does have revitalizing aspects: her appearance shakes her mother and sister, Denver, out of a narrow, isolated routine where their only future is "a matter of keeping the past at bay" (42). Yet it is also clear that Sethe's revitalization would not have occurred without the intervention of the women of the community, who rally around Sethe in a hybrid ritual of exorcism after Beloved has nearly drained the life from her. This is not, however, a ritual that incorporates wildness into the community; rather, the ritual expels it. Beloved's wildness is so extreme that only her disappearance allows her revitalizing influence to be felt.

Morrison ends the novel not with the hopeful image of Sethe, Denver, and Paul D. moving on to "some kind of tomorrow" (273) but with a poignant description of Beloved, the "girl who waited to be loved and cry shame" who becomes "a loneliness that roams" (274), lingering outside the bounds of culture, on the wild fringes of nature and also in the wild, subconscious realm just below the memories of those who knew her. Thus, Morrison finishes by reminding us of Beloved's human dimension while simultaneously emphasizing that Beloved's brand of wildness cannot be assimilated into the living human community: "Disremembered and unaccounted for, she cannot be lost because no one is looking for her. . . . Although she has claim, she is not claimed" (274). By ending with this tragic image of a being with nowhere to be, the novel brings us back to the idea that Beloved, once a human child, was condemned to this fate through the unnatural culture of slavery. While Morrison's work consistently shows that expansive wildness such as Beloved's has great power to affect human cultures for good or ill, the ending of this novel also testifies to the power that cultural forces hold to warp or destroy what is natural in humans as well as in their environment.

Conclusion

Considering Morrison's novels alongside mainstream American environmentalism and nature writing productively highlights the racially inflected character of those traditions. Her representation of African American experiences with nature reminds us that, as culturally and historically positioned subjects, we all identify with particular constructions of nature; our perceptions and valuations of nature are not simply "natural" responses to the green world but responses that rest on underlying racial politics.

The valorization of wildness is just one major aspect of mainstream American environmental thought that Morrison's works can productively problematize. Another feature is the widely held assumption that land ownership necessarily objectifies nature and leads to its degradation. In *Song of Solomon*, Milkman Dead travels from his affluent, urban home to his father's rural birthplace, where he learns that his grandfather was renowned as one of the best farmers in the county. For a freed slave such as Macon Dead Sr., land ownership meant rising above the legacy of being owned by others, a significance he marked by naming his farm Lincoln's Heaven. According to Morrison's narrator, this farm signified volumes to the community, exhorting them to "Stop picking around the edges of the world. . . . We live here. On this planet, in this nation, in this county right here" (235). The passage goes on to show how the community shares in Dead's prosperity ("if I got a home you got one too!") and ends with a call to "Grab it. Grab this land! Take it, hold it, my brothers, make it, my brothers, shake it, squeeze it, turn it, twist it, beat it, kick it, kiss it, whip it, stomp it, dig it, plow it, seed it, reap it, rent it, buy it, sell it, own it, build it, multiply it, and pass it on— can you hear me? Pass it on!" (235). However, the next line—"But they shot the top of his head off and ate his fine Georgia peaches"—shows just how precarious land ownership could be for blacks. Morrison suggests, though, that the jealous possessiveness that leads Dead's white neighbors to murder him is different than the possessiveness the farm itself articulates in the passage above. There, the environmental violence suggested by the verbs "take," "beat," and "sell" is mitigated by the farm's command to pass the land along, to build a placed community.

The ability to pass land on, along with its ancestral and monetary value, is a missing, vital element in many communities in Morrison's novels, from the Bottom in *Sula* to Ruby in *Paradise.* In her essay "Touching the Earth," African American writer bell hooks recounts her grandparents' love of the land and the environmental and psychological damage resulting from the loss of those connections. Hooks writes, "When we love the earth, we are able to love ourselves more fully. I believe this. The ancestors taught me it was so" (21). Hooks's remarks and Macon Dead Sr.'s pride in his farm show us how loving the land can result from a stewardship made possible by legal ownership, a helpful reminder to environmental thinkers, nature writers, and ecocritics who have too quickly equated ideologies of land use with land abuse.

And finally, we end by returning to the subtitle of our essay, "'Wild Wilderness Where There Was None,'" taken from the passage in *Song of Solomon* in which Ruth Foster describes Hagar's culturally induced wildness. In the context of this essay, we interpret this phrase as expressing how Morrison's representations of nature and wildness are themselves "wild," both in their complexity and their challenges to critical perceptions that African American literature lacks a tradition of attention to the natural world.[15] By revealing the potent yet often invisible cultural biases underlying such representations, she leads us to consider how culturally specific histories of slavery and oppression affect all Americans, not only in how we construct and experience cultural institutions but also in how we construct and experience nature and wildness. In the process, Toni Morrison articulates a rich tradition of African American experiences with the natural environment, a tradition where it was once thought there was none.

Notes

1. Christian discusses the centrality of nature to Morrison's human communities in *The Bluest Eye, Sula,* and *Song of Solomon;* Norwood explores Morrison's use of

plants and animals in *Beloved*, and Hochman focuses on trees in *Beloved*. To the best of our knowledge, our essay—the foundation for a book—is the first critical treatment of Morrison's approach to nature and environment in her novels as a group.

2. For overviews of the American nature writing tradition, see Buell, Fritzell, and Lyon. For discussions of American environmentalism, see Gottlieb, Sale, and Shabecoff. Both American nature writing and U.S. environmentalism resist easy categorization, but certain shared perspectives operate as tropes characterizing mainstream American environmental thought.

3. Son parallels the insights of the environmental justice movement (see Bullard, Di Chiro, and Hofrichter), which has critiqued mainstream American environmentalism for prioritizing preservation of wild, unpopulated areas over concern for environments where people (particularly people of color) live.

4. See Christian for an extensive discussion of contrasting communal interpretations of nature in *The Bluest Eye, Sula,* and *Song of Solomon*.

5. See Hartsock and Collins.

6. Wilderness advocates disagree on how best to preserve the wildness of wilderness; activist groups such as the Wildlands Project lean toward scientific management, while purists such as Turner believe that human intervention is antithetical to true wildness.

7. See Nash for a history of American attitudes toward wilderness; and see both Oelschlaeger and Snyder for broader discussions of human perceptions of wilderness.

8. While the valorization of wildness and preservation of wilderness areas continue to characterize mainstream environmental thought and activism, the concept of wilderness as an idealized natural place untouched by humans has recently come under fire for detrimentally separating nature from human culture and denying the historical reality of indigenous inhabitation of wilderness areas. See Callicott and Nelson for a wide selection of readings on American perspectives on and debates over wilderness.

9. For a wide-ranging discussion of this history and its implications, see Anthony.

10. For a more detailed discussion of Morrison's use of animal images and the concept of animality in *Beloved*, see Norwood.

11. The fact that Morrison's characters rarely experience unpeopled wilderness may also relate to a cultural avoidance of wilderness among African Americans induced by a history of being abused and terrorized in isolated settings (see White).

12. We find it significant that our reading of this pivotal scene, which grows out

of our focus on various types of wildness in Morrison's work, so closely parallels Norwood's, which revolves around examining Sethe's associations with plants and animals.

13. As Morrison explains in "Rootedness," "Black people . . . are very practical people, very down-to-earth, even shrewd people. But within that practicality we also accepted what I suppose could be called superstition and magic, which is another way of knowing things" (342).

14. The parallel between this characterization and Turner's statement that wildness is "out there" is suggestive, for in attempting to isolate themselves from the cultural environment of race hatred that we argue catalyzes culturally induced wildness, the citizens of Ruby also cut themselves off from expansive wildness.

15. A number of critics, including ecocritics, have assumed that the lack of scholarly attention to representations of nature in African American literature stems from a lack of interest in nature on the part of African American writers. As our essay suggests, the evidence does not bear out this assumption. A growing number of conference papers, essays—including the contributions by both Bennett and Dodd to this collection—and books have begun to map this tradition, often by exploring built as well as natural environments. See, for example, Dixon, hooks, Stein, Wallace, and selected paper presentations at the 1995, 1997, and 1999 conferences of the Association for the Study of Literature and Environment.

Works Cited

Anthony, Carl. "Ecopsychology and the Deconstruction of Whiteness." *Ecopsychology: Restoring the Earth, Healing the Mind.* Ed. Theodore Roszak, Mary E. Gomes, and Allen D. Kanner. San Francisco: Sierra Club, 1995. 263–78.

Buell, Lawrence. *The Environmental Imagination: Thoreau, Nature Writing, and the Formation of American Culture.* Cambridge: Belknap-Harvard P, 1995.

Bullard, Robert D. *Confronting Environmental Racism: Voices from the Grassroots.* Boston: South End, 1993.

Callicott, J. Baird, and Michael P. Nelson. *The Great New Wilderness Debate.* Athens: U of Georgia P, 1998.

Christian, Barbara. "Community and Nature: The Novels of Toni Morrison." *Black Feminist Criticism: Perspectives on Black Women Writers.* New York: Pergamon, 1985. 47–63.

Collins, Patricia Hill. *Black Feminist Thought.* London: Unwin Hyman, 1990.

Di Chiro, Giovanna. "Nature as Community: The Convergence of Environment and Social Justice." *Uncommon Ground: Toward Reinventing Nature.* Ed. William Cronon. New York: Norton, 1995. 298–320.

Dixon, Melvin. *Ride Out the Wilderness: Geography and Identity in Afro-American Literature.* Urbana: U of Illinois P, 1987.

Fritzell, Peter. *Nature Writing and America: Essays upon a Cultural Type.* Ames: Iowa State UP, 1990.

Gottlieb, Robert. *Forcing the Spring: The Transformation of the American Environmental Movement.* Washington, DC: Island P, 1993.

Haraway, Donna J. "Situated Knowledges." *Feminist Studies* 14.3 (1988): 575–99.

Hartsock, Nancy. *Money, Sex, and Power: An Essay on Domination and Community.* Boston: Northeastern UP, 1983.

———. "The Feminist Standpoint: Developing the Ground for a Specifically Feminist Historical Materialism." *Discovering Reality: Feminist Perspectives on Epistemology, Metaphysics, and Philosophy of Science.* Ed. Sandra Harding and Merrill B. Hintikka. Dordrecht, Neth.: Reidel, 1983. 283–310.

Hochman, Jhan. "A Peculiar Arborary: *Beloved.*" *Green Cultural Studies: Nature in Film, Novel, and Theory.* Moscow: U of Idaho P, 1998. 93–107.

Hofrichter, Richard, ed. *Toxic Struggles: The Theory and Practice of Environmental Justice.* Philadelphia: New Society, 1993.

hooks, bell. "Touching the Earth." *Orion* 15.4 (1996): 21–23.

Lyon, Thomas J. "A Taxonomy of Nature Writing." *This Incomperable Lande: A Book of American Nature Writing.* Ed. Thomas J. Lyon. New York: Penguin, 1989. 1–7.

Morrison, Toni. *Beloved.* New York: Knopf, 1987.

———. *The Bluest Eye.* New York: Plume-Penguin, 1970.

———. *Jazz.* 1992. New York: Plume-Penguin, 1993.

———. *Paradise.* New York: Knopf, 1998.

———. "Rootedness: The Ancestor as Foundation." *Black Women Writers (1950–1980): A Critical Evaluation.* Ed. Mari Evans. New York: Doubleday, 1984. 339–45.

———. *Song of Solomon.* New York: Knopf, 1977.

———. *Sula.* New York: Plume–New American Library, 1973.

———. *Tar Baby.* New York: Plume-Penguin, 1981.

Nash, Roderick. *Wilderness and the American Mind.* 1967. 3rd ed. New Haven: Yale UP, 1982.

Norwood, Vera. "Writing Animal Presence: Nature in Euro-American, African American, and American Indian Fiction." *Made from This Earth: American Women and Nature.* Chapel Hill: U of North Carolina P, 1993. 172–208.

Oelschlaeger, Max. *The Idea of Wilderness: From Prehistory to the Age of Ecology.* New Haven: Yale UP, 1991.

Parrinder, Geoffrey. *African Traditional Religion.* London: Sheldon, 1974.

Sale, Kirkpatrick. *The Green Revolution: The American Environmental Movement, 1962–1992.* New York: Hill and Wang, 1993.

Shabecoff, Philip. *A Fierce Green Fire: The American Environmental Movement.* New York: Hill and Wang, 1993.

Snyder, Gary. *The Practice of the Wild.* San Francisco: North Point, 1990.

Stein, Rachel. *Shifting the Ground: American Women Writers' Revisions of Nature, Gender, and Race.* Charlottesville: UP of Virginia, 1997.

Tate, Claudia, ed. Interview with Toni Morrison. *Black Women Writers at Work.* New York: Continuum, 1983. 117–31.

Thoreau, Henry David. "Walking." 1862. *The Portable Thoreau.* Ed. Carl Bode. New York: Penguin, 1957. 592–630.

Turner, Jack. *The Abstract Wild.* Tucson: U of Arizona P, 1996.

Wallace, Kathleen R. "'All Things Natural Are Strange': Audre Lorde, Urban Nature, and Cultural Place." *The Nature of Cities: Ecocriticism and Urban Environments.* Ed. Michael Bennett and David Teague. Tucson: U of Arizona P, 1999. 55–72.

White, Evelyn C. "Black Women and the Wilderness." *The Stories that Shape Us: Contemporary Women Write about the West.* Ed. Teresa Jordan and James R. Hepworth. New York: Norton, 1995.

Part III

Expanding Ecocriticism
across Genres and Disciplines

Literary Place Bashing, Test Site Nevada

Cheryll Glotfelty

Nevada! . . . Abomination of desolation presides over nine-tenths
of the place. The sun beats down on a roof of zinc, fierce and
dull. Not a drop of water to a mile of sand. The mean ash-dump
landscape stretches on from nowhere to nowhere, a spot of
mange. No portion of the earth is more lacquered with paltry,
unimportant ugliness.
—Unidentified novelist, early 1900s, quoted in Lillard,
Desert Challenge

We came to the great gambling and marriage destruction hell,
known as Nevada. To look at it from the air it is just that—hell
on earth. There are tiny green specks on the landscape where
dice, roulette, light-o-loves, crooked poker and gambling thugs
thrive. Such places should be abolished and so should Nevada. It
never should have been made a State.
—Harry S. Truman, 1955

In 1989 the literary scholar and Nevada resident Ann Ronald wrote an important
essay with a provocative title, "Why Don't They Write about Nevada?" Ronald,
whose specialties include nature writing about western deserts, noticed the curious fact that almost none of the well-known nature writers have written about
Nevada. Think of the many writers who have written lyrical prose about deserts—John C. Van Dyke, Mary Austin, Joseph Wood Krutch, Wallace Stegner,
Edward Abbey, and Ann Zwinger. Who among them has hoisted a pen in praise
of Nevada? In the essay, Ronald answers her title question by explaining that

nature writers have been drawn to the same kinds of desert scenery: colorful canyons, red rock wilderness, "arches, alcoves, glens and grottoes" (215–16). Such places are apparently more aesthetically hospitable and more emotionally stirring than Nevada's alkali playas and sagebrush plains. "Photogenic scenery has always taken precedence over barren wastes," Ronald reasons, "so nature essayists flock to intellectually appreciable locales rather than inhospitable sites" (222).[1] Ronald concludes that people "don't write about places like Nevada because traditional modes of appreciation are inappropriate there" (223). Nevada has been by this account decidedly beyond nature writing.

While Ronald is correct that until recently Nevada has not stimulated nature writers to rhapsodize, nevertheless, it possesses a rich literary tradition of condemnation. Indeed, with a few notable exceptions such as Walter Van Tilburg Clark and Robert Laxalt, most of Nevada's best-known writing pillories the state and might be categorized as Nevada bashing. Historian Richard G. Lillard claims that "Nevada's scenery has been damned more than that of any other state" (36). Nevada may top the charts, but it certainly is not alone in being the object of literary contempt. New Jersey, Nebraska, and North Dakota have all suffered from bad press at one time or another, as have a multitude of unfortunate cities and landscapes across the country.

Despite the fact that many fine works of literature disparage various places, no one to my knowledge has devoted serious critical attention to this phenomenon. This essay, then, expands the boundaries of ecocriticism by opening an inquiry into the nature and significance of literary place bashing. Who writes "place bashers," and why? How are place bashers received by readers? Do unflattering literary representations of a place have real-life consequences? This essay focuses on Nevada; nevertheless, the generalizations that emerge from this case study may apply to other maligned places as well.

Poisoned prose about the Silver State predates Nevada's statehood and begins with the first white explorers and emigrants to cross what was then the western half of the Utah Territory.[2] In 1826–27 Jedediah S. Smith, a fur trapper, was the first white man to venture across what is today Nevada. Of central Nevada, Smith writes, "the general Character and appearance of the country I have passed is extremely Barren. High rocky hills afford the only relief to the desolate waste for at the feet of these are found water and some vegetation While the intervals between are sand barren Plains" (178). Another early fur trapper, Peter Skene Ogden, searching for beaver in northern Nevada in 1828, concludes that "it is a barren country destitute of everything" (389). Explorer John Charles Frémont, traveling through Nevada in 1843 and 1844, kept a journal in which he describes southern Nevada as "desolate and revolting . . . where lizards were the only animal, and the tracks of the lizard eaters the principal sign of human beings" (688).

Why did these explorers write place bashers? In the cases of Smith and Ogden, fur companies such as the Hudson's Bay Company required that their trappers keep daybooks, noting routes, describing the country, and, in particular, recording the daily beaver take. Frémont's expedition was funded by the U.S. government, which expected him to publish a report of his explorations. Taken as a whole, these early descriptions are not unremittingly negative but, rather, are surprisingly dispassionate, reporting the good with the bad in a matter-of-fact tone. Disappointment and physical hardship may account for the bleakest passages. Smith and Ogden enjoyed only limited success at beaver trapping. Frémont did not find the mythical Buenaventura River, which was said to provide a water route across America to the Pacific. All early explorers and their animals suffered in Nevada, and some lost their lives. To generalize, then, in the literature of exploration, place bashing occurs when the explorer's party suffers physically and when it fails to find what it sought.

Smith's and Ogden's accounts were not available to readers of their day. Frémont's report was widely read, and it inspired some emigrants to head west to Oregon and California. Not only did Frémont prove that such a crossing could be and had been successfully made but his report provided maps and useful information about the route. Frémont's chronicle may also have deterred some prospective emigrants who realized how difficult and dangerous the trip would be. Thanks to the place-bashing aspects of reports such as Frémont's, virtually no one fantasized about Nevada as a destination for settlement. Until the discovery of the Comstock Lode launched the gold and silver rush to Washoe in 1859, Nevada remained the province of its indigenous people.

While only a handful of whites took up residence in Nevada before 1859, some 350,000 journeyed across it in the quarter century between 1841 and 1866 (Porter vii). Emigrants on the Overland Trail realized they were taking part in a historic and magnificent movement of people. For the majority, the overland journey was the bravest undertaking and the most memorable event of their lives. Many felt the call to record their experience. It is estimated that there are between five thousand and ten thousand written accounts of this crossing in the form of notes, diaries, letters, and narratives, about twenty-five hundred of which have been published (Porter viii). In this body of literature, Nevada figures as a hellish expanse of wasteland that tests the weary travelers to the utmost of their endurance. Nevada's forty-mile desert (today's Carson Sink) was the most dreaded leg of the odyssey. As the overland crossing takes on symbolic importance in the journey of life, Nevada is transfigured in emigrants' memories as an almost typological obstacle where the weak perish and where a pilgrim's faith is tested and affirmed. Forty-niner Sarah Royce traveled to California with her husband and their two-year-old daughter, Mary. Thirty years later, at the request of her son Josiah Royce, a philosophy professor at Harvard University, Sarah wrote a memoir of that family odyssey entitled *A Frontier Lady*. Perhaps in response to her son's secularism, Royce inflects her story with mystical Protestantism, particularly in her recollection of the Carson Sink, in which she "seemed to see Hagar, in the wilderness walking wearily away from her fainting child among the dried up bushes, and seating herself in the hot sand" (49). In the heat of noonday, like Moses, Royce sees a burning bush, and later, with bowed head, she worships "the god of Horeb" for her deliverance.

If one were to construct a taxonomy of place-bashing literature, emigrant accounts would be identifiable by distinctive field marks, one of the most prominent of which is intense homesickness. Passages describing Nevada almost unconsciously slip into a list of the things the traveler misses about home. Nevada is thereby rendered as a land not of presence but of absence. Judge J. Quinn Thornton, for example, an emigrant from Illinois bound for Oregon in 1848, waxes nostalgic as he recalls the miseries he and his ailing wife endured along the Applegate Trail in northern Nevada:

> The country over which we had passed was dreary beyond description. There were in it no diversities of color or form, to relieve the mind by their variety. . . . Here was none of the living luster of a gay and beautiful spring, dressed in robes of the richest green, smiling upon the wooded hills and the grain-covered valleys, or laughing and dancing along the brooks and rivers.

Here were none of the rich glories of autumn, laden with delicious fruits. There were neither sounds of melody to charm the ear, nor sights of beauty or grandeur to please the eye, and delight the heart. (179)

In this passage Thornton paints an evocative picture of what is not there. As the literary critic Terry Caesar observes about American writers abroad, travel writing "has enabled the representation of home; moreover, enabling this domestic representation has finally been the purpose of the travel" (5). It would be inaccurate to claim that emigrants traveled west in order to represent the homes they left behind; nevertheless, their travel through Nevada often did cause them to realize what they had at home, even as they receded farther from it. In this instance, bashing Nevada becomes a vehicle for writing about home.[3]

Emigrant narratives are a particularly well-defined subgenre of literary place bashers. The great majority of their authors are not professional writers. The overriding purpose of these written accounts seems to be to preserve the memory of a historically important event that the writer participated in firsthand. Most of the accounts are intended for a readership of friends and family back home, also including future generations. Why bash Nevada? Clearly, emigrants did suffer physically in Nevada almost beyond their ability to endure it. Added to this physical distress was raw fear. They witnessed a trail lined with the bloated bodies of dead oxen and horses, littered with discarded household belongings and abandoned wagons, and punctuated with makeshift gravesites; and they wondered if they would be next. Whereas much of the Overland Trail was uncomfortable and tedious, in Nevada an emigrant stood a good chance of dying. "The fearful crossing," as it was called, was anticipated with much trepidation, endured in a state of protracted anxiety, and recalled with a shudder. It made for a great story! It added drama and created a natural climax in the narrative. Nevada made the journey's end—Oregon or California—appear to be the Promised Land, indeed.

These accounts were eagerly read by the folks back home. Some books were self-published in limited quantities, some were published by the major eastern publishing houses. It is questionable what effect emigrant writing might have had on the land of Nevada. As in the case of explorers' reports, emigrant writing certainly did not encourage readers to want to sink roots in Nevada, but, rather, it perpetuated its reputation as a desert wasteland, a place to hurry across, or, better yet, to avoid entirely. Thanks to its reputation as a desolate wasteland, Nevada remained a pristine wilderness until well into the nineteenth century.

Professional writers first turned their attention to Nevada in 1859, with the discovery of the Comstock Lode, one of the richest ore bodies in world history, ultimately producing tens of millions of dollars worth of silver and gold. The Comstock led to the permanent Caucasian settlement of Nevada and to its statehood in 1864. Nevada's mining boomtowns attracted writers such as J. Ross Browne, Fred Hart, James W. Gally, Dan de Quille, Sam Davis, and Bret Harte, many of whom supported themselves by their pens when efforts with pick and shovel failed to strike paydirt.[4] While in the Nevada Territory, working for Virginia City's famous newspaper, *The Territorial Enterprise*, Samuel Clemens launched his writing career and adopted the pen name Mark Twain. Ten years after returning to the East, Twain penned *Roughing It*, a rambunctious account of his western travels. Of his approach to Carson City, Twain writes:

> Visibly our new home was a desert, walled in by barren, snow-clad mountains. There was not a tree in sight. There was no vegetation but the endless sage-brush and greasewood. All nature was gray with it. We were plowing through great deeps of powdery alkali dust that rose in thick clouds and floated across the plain like smoke from a burning house. We were coated with it like millers; so were the coach, the mules, the mail-bags, the driver — we and the sage-brush and the other scenery were all one monotonous color. . . . [W]e moved in the midst of solitude, silence, and desolation. (177)

John Muir spent three summers exploring the Great Basin in the late 1870s. In a series of five essays written for the *San Francisco Evening Bulletin* and later collected in *Steep Trails*, Muir strives to appreciate and describe Nevada's natural endowments. But, in contrast to his Sierra manuscripts, Muir's Nevada writing is best—most vivid, powerful, and memorable—when he stoops to the occasional bash, such as the following: "Nevada seems one vast desert, all sage and sand, hopelessly irredeemable now and forever" (154). Later, in the great American tradition of the negative catalog, Muir continues, "No singing water, no green sod, no moist nook to rest in—mountain and valley alike naked and shadowless in the sun-glare" (160).[5] Entering the state from the west, Muir contrasts

Nevada's mountains to his beloved Sierra: "From the very noblest forests in the world [the traveler] emerges into . . . dead alkaline lake-levels. Mountains are seen beyond, rising in bewildering abundance, range beyond range. But . . . these always present a singularly barren aspect, appearing gray and forbidding and shadeless, like heaps of ashes dumped from the blazing sky" (164).

Like the explorers and emigrants before them, Muir and Twain have no permanent investment in Nevada. Twain lived in Nevada for three years and Muir for one summer. Neither man came intending to stay. Rather, they adventured in Nevada, drawn by curiosity and, in Twain's case, avoidance of the draft during the Civil War. Their accounts take the form of travel writing and are directed to an audience unfamiliar with the places about which they write. Both writers rely on comparison to highlight their topic; thus, Muir, writing for the *San Francisco Evening Bulletin,* compares Nevada to California, and Twain likens Nevada to his naïve romantic fantasies of what the West would be like. For Twain, place bashing is done for the sake of humor, just as he simultaneously makes fun of himself, the callow pioneer, full of illusions and brimming with ignorance. Muir's technique in his reports is to begin each essay by bashing Nevada but then to proceed to note the area's subtle beauty, or surprising fertility, or fascinating geology. Muir is philosophically committed to loving wilderness, however arid, and his essays trace the evolution of his thought from initial repugnance, through close observation, and to eventual appreciation. Despite the fact that Muir's Nevada essays inch toward admiration, he seems to be most sincere and is most forceful in his opening bashes, which is probably why he is remembered as having hated Nevada.

As a literary target, Nevada sits in double jeopardy. Writers of the nineteenth century found its wildlands repulsive, while writers of the twentieth century have thought its cities revolting as well. Since World War II, bashers have struck a veritable mother lode in Las Vegas. In a travelogue of the late 1980s entitled *The Lost Continent: Travels in Small-Town America,* Iowa native Bill Bryson begins his chapter on Nevada this way:

> Here's a riddle for you. What is the difference between Nevada and a toilet? Answer: You can flush a toilet.
> Nevada has the highest crime rate of any state, the highest rape rate, the

second highest violent crime rate . . . the highest highway fatality rate, the second highest rate of gonorrhea . . . and the highest proportion of transients—almost 80 percent of the state's residents were born elsewhere. It has more prostitutes than any other state in America. It has a long history of corruption and strong links with organized crime. And its most popular entertainer is Wayne Newton. So you may understand why I crossed the border from Utah with a certain sense of disquiet. (244)

In *The Lost Continent*, Bryson, who now lives in England, deploys an armada of snide comments on America's towns, based on his 13,978-mile drive through all but ten of the lower forty-eight states. His book reads like a three-hundred-page stand-up comedy routine, deriding American people, culture, and institutions. No town escapes entirely unscathed, especially Bryson's native Des Moines, which, he jokes, has a sign outside of town that says, "WELCOME TO DES MOINES. THIS IS WHAT DEATH IS LIKE" (3). Although Bryson's chapter on Las Vegas begins with the flush of a toilet and a list of unflattering statistics, he then confesses that Las Vegas "dazzled" him—it was an "ocular orgasm" (245)—and that the casinos appealed to his insatiable greed. Gorged on the "heap of tasteless goo" that he ingested at the Caesar's Palace buffet, Bryson with the "distended abdomen" (248) staggers back to his hotel room, heading west into the desert on Interstate 15 the next morning. In Bryson's reading, Las Vegas, a neon temple to the seven deadly sins, represents just another perversion of American taste, different but no worse than the hundreds of other towns on his itinerary; it is but one stop on his extended place-bashing American road tour.

In another contemporary slam, Ellen Meloy, a California native who summers in Utah's canyon country and winters in Montana, recalls her arrival in Las Vegas:

> At the Nevada state line we cast aside Utah's wholesome aura for its nemesis. Behind: Leave it to Beaver. Ahead: Sodom and Gomorrah. In dusk that sizzles at 103 degrees, the land sprawls in bowls of creosote bush cupped by serrated ribs of rock. Over a long rise, past a convoy of trucks afloat in mirages of diesel and heat, we top the crest of the final ridge and behold the valley below, an island of neon capped in sludgy brown smog, ringed by a rabid housing boom. Las Vegas. The Meadows. (181)

Why does Meloy include a chapter she titles "The Flora and Fauna of Las Vegas" in her book *Raven's Exile: A Season on the Green River*? The book traces the natural and human history of Desolation Canyon in Utah, and Meloy describes a summer with her husband, Mark, who works as a river ranger on the Green River. Meloy experiences the Green River as part of her "bloodstream" and writes that "no other life but River Life seems worthwhile" (16, 19). In her Las Vegas chapter, Meloy argues that "For every river rat this visit is mandatory. We cannot know the River until we know this place" (182), for, thanks to the Hoover Dam, Las Vegas is powered and watered by the Green and Colorado Rivers. Meloy, a nature writer with an incisive sense of humor, has only contempt for this profitable city: "In Las Vegas the best survival strategy is a wholesale reduction of Self to imbecilic dipstick, easily managed in these clockless, windowless mazes of flashing lights and blaring gaming devices with nary a molecule of The Environment allowed across the transom. The idea is complete disconnection from Earth, a realignment of the senses through a techno-collage of myths and fantasies conjured by corporate hacks" (184). The disconnection and disorientation Meloy feels in Las Vegas serves to underscore the sense of belonging and sensory engagement she experiences on the river. Las Vegas's lack of real flora and fauna—all the potted plants are fake—contrasts sharply with the Green River's abundance. Here, Las Vegas stands for things man-made and artificial, a hellish perversion of natural resources. Meloy's narrative hastens back to its source, the river.

Despite their different intents, the most important thing to note about the two preceding examples of twentieth-century place bashers is that, like *Roughing It* and *Steep Trails* of the nineteenth century, they are written by non-Nevadans for an audience of non-Nevadans, or, in other words, by outsiders to outsiders. For these writers, Nevada sometimes serves as a foil character, highlighting by contrast the nature of their primary subject. For example, Bryson's sketch of Las Vegas is done in colors that contrast with his portraits of small-town America, while Meloy's excursion to Las Vegas throws Utah's Green River into greater relief. As a literary genre, then, place bashing is generally written by and for outsiders; it frequently takes the form of travel writing; and it relies on juxtaposition for its effect, which is often humorous.

Laughter creates camaraderie, and making fun of places allows an author to establish a rapport with the reader, who learns to share the author's low opinion of the godforsaken place. Indeed, literary place bashing may serve the same function for author and reader that insulting other people does for youth gangs: defaming others reinforces group solidarity. Insult establishes an us-them distinction—or, for places, a here-there sharpness—that downplays differences within the group by magnifying differences among groups. Thus, despite their various antagonisms, New Yorkers, Californians, Nebraskans, and Floridians find common ground in deriding Nevada, even as they flock to its gambling resorts for vacation.

From the reader's perspective, surely one of the undeniable pleasures of reading a well-written place basher is the reassurance that at least one does not live there. Literary place bashers remind us of the ugly places we do not have to live, just as books such as Upton Sinclair's *The Jungle* and Rebecca Harding Davis's *Life in the Iron Mills* help us remember the horrible jobs we do not have to do. While we may pity the poor souls who are trapped in these lives, still, we take comfort in the knowledge that those lives are not our lives. In the case of literary place bashers, we savor the prose precisely because we are spared the place.

The response of locals to literary bashing of their place is mixed. Among some locals, place bashers enjoy a certain notoriety. These amused readers relish a well-aimed barb in the same way that some folks enjoy reading satire, laughing at their own flaws. Many of these readers are new to Nevada, and they delight to see their first impressions of the place confirmed in print.[6] Nevada readers who enjoy Nevada bashing often identify more strongly with the values of the dominant culture than with Nevada, which they may regard as somewhere they just happen to live for now. Reading Nevada bashers, especially over a cup of latté, is a way for the exiled to maintain their membership in the cultural elite.

Nevada's chambers of commerce are likewise sanguine about best-selling place bashers because they understand that negative press is infinitely better than no press and that many tourists are attracted to Nevada because of its tainted reputation. In this spirit of turning insult into profit, the tourism industry has managed to get the state legislature to name Nevada 50 "The Loneliest Road in America" and, more recently, Nevada 375 "The Alien Highway." Finally, in a reversal of chamber of commerce logic, there are Nevadans such as myself who enjoy seeing Nevada's negative image perpetuated in print, because, fearing population growth and crowding of their favorite outdoor recreation spots, they want to keep "the real Nevada" top secret.

On the opposite end of the local reader-response spectrum are the angry readers, people who are outraged and personally offended to see their home represented so ignominiously. Irate readers identify with a place as passionately as many people identify with their families. These readers are quick to point out inaccuracies in a text's factual content or geographical detail, hoping, perhaps, that exposing mistakes will undermine the author's authority and discredit the work. Believing that it takes a lifetime—or even several generations—to truly know a place, these readers are furious that the rest of the world will get its impression of Nevada from the writings of a tourist. It does not seem fair to them that the writer enjoys more fame, respect, and power than the resident, who feels disenfranchised.

Angry readers believe that their state or county is being victimized by the rest of the country, and they see a direct connection between literary place bashing and political policy making. The critic Edward W. Said argues convincingly in *Orientalism* that colonial rule in Asia was justified in advance by the textual attitude of orientalism, that is, by the way that literature depicted Asia as exotic and foreign. By similar logic, textual attitudes of Nevada as a wasteland or a Sodom and Gomorrah have justified a history of domestic colonialism, beginning with unrestricted mining and continuing today. For more than a decade, America tested its nuclear bombs by dropping them on the Nevada Test Site, and, currently, in a congressional bill known locally as the "Screw Nevada Bill," America is taking steps to make Nevada the nation's nuclear waste dump.[7] In this light, literary place bashing is not innocent fun at all; it is a form of domination.

Indeed, it is instructive to compare place bashing to people bashing. What if instead of funny excerpts about Nevada, this essay quoted some witty passages about how ugly, stupid, and subhuman black people are? Although such jests were standard fare in earlier centuries, most contemporary readers find them highly offensive. While today's readers still chuckle at Twain's withering descriptions of the Nevada landscape, most people find his insulting portrayal of the "Goshoot" Indians—"the wretchedest type of mankind I have ever seen" (166)—almost unreadable. If racial slurs are now considered offensively racist, should place bashing be considered insultingly "placist"? Are the two cases analogous? Some people complain that political correctness has gone too far. Maybe it has not gone far enough.

So what is a bashed place to do? One direct-action response has been to fight back. Challenge the image head on. A common bumper-sticker in Nevada is red, white, and blue, stating simply, "Nevada Is Not a Wasteland." The three-lobed symbol for radioactivity frames the word "waste," a visual pun that underscores the connection between imagining a place to be a wasteland and treating it as a nuclear waste dump.

While some groups protest the wasteland image and corresponding mistreatment of Nevada, other people work to create alternative imagery, perhaps in the hope that if Americans learn to reimagine Nevada's landscape, they will not be so ready to abuse it. Ann Ronald is among this group. Six years after she speculated on the dearth of purple prose about the Silver State, Ronald rose to her own challenge by becoming Nevada's first nature writer. Her book *Earthtones: A Nevada Album*, with stunning photographs by Stephen Trimble, evokes in painterly prose the subtle wonders and striking wildness of Nevada's outback, teaching readers how to see beauty where an earlier generation saw only barren waste:

> Teal sky and a sea of purple sage. Mountain mahogany, white fir, a crimson mass of claret cup cactus. Rawhide springs and Green Monster Canyon. A bobcat tiptoeing along Corn Creek. Desert tortoise, a marmot whistling for his mate, a nesting long-eared owl. The Black Rock playa, Lake Lahontan. Currant Mountain and Duckwater Peak, Rainbow Canyon and Calico Hills. Limestone, sandstone, and tuff. One stone wall, a few broken bricks; dry alfalfa, an empty irrigation ditch. A dust-blown sunset, vermilion and orange and gold. "One vast desert?" Not exactly. One vast deserted landscape of color and shadow and aesthetic dimension. (4–5)

Thanks to *Earthtones* and other recent literary cousins such as Stephen Trimble's *The Sagebrush Ocean* and Rebecca Solnit's *Savage Dreams*, Nevada is well on its way to becoming "The Next Best Place."[8]

Given this revisionist trend, Nevadans may ask, Is this what we want? Do we want Americans to be attracted to our scenery? Do we want nature writers to extol Nevada's beauty? One shudders to think of the touristification of Moab, Utah, in the wake of Edward Abbey's *Desert Solitaire*. As Ellen Meloy observes,

"Anyone who writes a deep map of Place fears her words will detonate that place. Incited by books of love, thousands already adore Utah's canyon wilderness to death" (255). There is reason to fear the environmental impact of nature writing as well as of place bashing, for these two contrasting literary modes are different sides of the same coin, drawing attention to places that may have been better off overlooked.

Notes

1. Until books such as Van Dyke's *The Desert* appeared, all western deserts were generally considered inhospitable barren wastes. For a history of attitudes toward deserts of the American West, see Limerick. See Teague, who traces a history of desert aesthetics. For a history of images of Nevada, see Shepperson.

2. Native Americans had lived in Nevada for millennia before European Americans "discovered" it. In Paiute, Shoshone, and Washoe stories, the land figures as home. Literary place bashing of Nevada thus begins with the first whites.

3. One of the motives behind Thornton's writing was to get even with Jesse Applegate for persuading his party to try the Applegate cutoff. The party suffered greatly, and Thornton became furious with Applegate for duping them into leaving the established route. Depicting the scenery along the trail in the worst possible light thus serves Thornton's purpose of discrediting the route and defaming the man.

4. See Emrich for a delightful sampling of the literature of Nevada's early mining period.

5. Muir (and Thornton earlier in this essay) is establishing a western version of the classic litany of America's deficiencies vis-à-vis Europe, a negative catalog pioneered in the East by Crevecoeur, Irving, Cooper, Hawthorne, and James, noting—with pride, defensiveness, or regret—America's lack of aristocrats, castles, ruins, great music, great art, refined manners, and a storied past.

6. I recall my glee, when, as a newly hired professor at the University of Nevada, having recently graduated from an Ivy League university back East, I encountered Tom Wolfe's description of veteran gamblers: "[O]ne of the indelible images of Las Vegas is that of the old babes at the row upon row of slot machines. There they are at six o'clock Sunday morning no less than at three o'clock Tuesday afternoon. Some of them pack their old hummocky shanks into Capri pants, but many of them just put on the old print dress, the same one day after day . . . . They have a Dixie Cup full of nickles or dimes in the left hand and an Iron Boy work glove on the right hand to

keep the callouses from getting sore" (6–7). The snobbish tone of Wolfe's description perfectly matches the revulsion and profound alienation I felt in the downtown casinos of Reno.

7. This bill, passed in 1987, is an amendment to the Nuclear Waste Policy Act of 1982. In the amendment—Title 5, Energy and Environmental Program, Subtitle A, Nuclear Waste Amendment—all other potential sites for a national long-term nuclear waste storage facility are eliminated, leaving only Nevada's Yucca Mountain to be studied. An environmental impact statement is currently being drafted for the site, which, if the impact statement is approved, will become the permanent dumping ground for America's high-level radioactive waste.

8. Montana, which prides itself on being "The Last Best Place," is being upstaged in popularity by Nevada, which for more than five years has registered the highest population growth in the nation.

Works Cited

Abbey, Edward. *Desert Solitaire: A Season in the Wilderness.* 1968. New York: Ballantine, 1971.

Bryson, Bill. *The Lost Continent: Travels in Small-Town America.* 1989. New York: Harper Perennial, 1990.

Caesar, Terry. *Forgiving the Boundaries: Home as Abroad in American Travel Writing.* Athens: U of Georgia P, 1995.

Emrich, Duncan, ed. *Comstock Bonanza.* New York: Vanguard, 1950.

Frémont, John Charles. *The Expeditions of John Charles Frémont.* Vol. 1. *Travels from 1838–1844.* Ed. Donald Jackson and Mary Lee Spence. Urbana: U of Illinois P, 1970.

Lillard, Richard G. *Desert Challenge: An Interpretation of Nevada.* New York: Knopf, 1942.

Limerick, Patricia Nelson. *Desert Passages: Encounters with the American Deserts.* Niwot: UP of Colorado, 1989.

Meloy, Ellen. *Raven's Exile: A Season on the Green River.* New York: Henry Holt, 1994.

Muir, John. *Steep Trails: California, Utah, Nevada, Washington, Oregon, The Grand Canon.* Boston: Houghton Mifflin, 1918.

Ogden, Peter Skene. "The Peter Skene Ogden Journals: Snake Expedition, 1827–28 and 1828–29." Ed. T. C. Elliott. *The Quarterly of the Oregon Historical Society* 11.4 (1910): 355–99.

Porter, Lavinia Honeyman. *By Ox Team to California.* Rpt. in *Westward Journeys:*

Memoirs of Jesse A. Applegate and Lavinia Honeyman Porter Who Traveled the Overland Trail. Ed. Martin Ridge. Chicago: R. R. Donnelley & Sons, 1989.

Ronald, Ann. *Earthtones: A Nevada Album.* Photographs by Stephen Trimble. Reno: U of Nevada P, 1995.

———. "Why Don't They Write about Nevada?" *Western American Literature* 24.3 (1989): 213–24.

Royce, Sarah. *A Frontier Lady: Recollections of the Gold Rush and Early California.* Ed. Ralph Henry Gabriel. New Haven: Yale UP, 1932.

Said, Edward W. *Orientalism.* New York: Vintage, 1979.

Shepperson, Wilbur S., with Ann Harvey. *Mirage-Land: Images of Nevada.* Reno: U of Nevada P, 1992.

Smith, Jedediah S. *The Southwest Expedition of Jedediah S. Smith: His Personal Account of the Journey to California, 1826–1827.* Ed. George R. Brooks. Glendale, CA: Arthur H Clark Co., 1977.

Solnit, Rebecca. *Savage Dreams: A Journey into the Landscape Wars of the American West.* New York: Vintage, 1994.

Teague, David W. *The Southwest in American Literature and Art: The Rise of a Desert Aesthetic.* Tucson: U of Arizona P, 1997.

Thornton, J. Quinn. *Oregon and California in 1848.* 1849. 2 vols. New York: Arno, 1973.

Trimble, Stephen. *The Sagebrush Ocean: A Natural History of the Great Basin.* Reno: U of Nevada P, 1989.

Truman, Harry S. *Off the Record: The Private Papers of Harry S. Truman.* Ed. Robert H. Ferrell. New York: Harper and Row, 1980.

Twain, Mark. *Roughing It.* 1872. Ed. Hamlin Hill. New York: Penguin, 1981.

Van Dyke, John C. *The Desert.* 1901. Salt Lake City: Peregrine Smith, 1980.

Wolfe, Tom. *The Kandy-Kolored Tangerine-Flake Streamline Baby.* New York: Farrar, Straus and Giroux, 1965.

Heading Off the Trail: Language, Literature, and Nature's Resistance to Narrative

Rebecca Raglon and Marian Scholtmeijer

The assumption that language plays an important role in constructing reality has achieved the status of a truism: something so obvious that it is well on its way to becoming the invisible underpinning of all literary discussion. To think otherwise is to be either naïve or ironic, for references to nature should never be thought of as literal or unproblematic. According to this viewpoint, language is a powerful force that directs our perceptions, shaping it into coherent forms, or categories (Nadeau 5). Nature itself is such a category, and according to the most extreme expression of this point of view, nature does not exist apart from our language. This makes nature a thoroughly human product, much like soap, cars, and computers, for nature, "like everything else we talk about, is first and foremost an artifact of language" (Cawley and Chaloupka 5).

Accompanying this preoccupation with language is a sociological strain of criticism that concentrates on language's culpability in creating categories that are in turn responsible for a variety of social and environmental ills. What these viewpoints share is the idea that literature, language, and culture have much to answer for when faced with environmental catastrophe and human misery. Because language and literature direct our perceptions, they are guilty participants in the destruction of the world.

But does language only imprison us in concepts of our creation? Is literature really a culpable part of what we term an "environmental crisis"? Or is there another role that language and, in particular, literature can play in helping us negotiate changes in our relationship with the natural world? As set out below, this essay looks at the contemporary preoccupation with language, but it extends this absorption to include examples of literature that begin to gesture toward the rediscovery of a powerful natural word, one that resists our narratives. This essay thus takes the position that literature not only imposes categories on the natural world but can also be a flexible and vibrant agent of change.

Under the uncompromising instruction of the natural world, literature is capable of making amends for past mistakes. We are able to create new stories and fresh meanings. The modern era is replete with examples showing us that many of our past stories of nature were misguided. The silence of extinction, for example, provides us with a corrective to beliefs that nature is forever abundant and immutable—that great story of nature we told ourselves for centuries, almost as if we were in a collective trance. We convinced ourselves that nature was forever abundant as we beat the last passenger pigeons from their roosts, and then we were faced with nature's uncompromising answer—a terrible and profound silence. When we get our stories wrong in this way, we are given incentives—by nature—to correct our beliefs, to make redress, to confront nature's resistance to our impositions.

This essay will first look at the idea of literature's ability to make these adjustments, and then we present three examples we draw from twentieth-century writers who employ nature's resistance within their narratives. We discuss the implications of this resistance, and we conclude by suggesting that while contemporary critical preoccupations with language provide a necessary caution, in terms of our relationship to the world, it is in the far corners of certain stories that we can find moments when nature's incandescent strangeness is made available to us again.

Literary Balancing Acts

In one of the more interesting recent reassessments of the role of literature in society, Seamus Heaney looks at poetry not as something that contributes to oppression but, in a more refreshing way, as a "balancing act," a form of redress, or countervailing gesture. That is, while literary critics may be correct in their belief that language to some extent molds our impressions of reality to conform to existing oppressive tendencies, the best literature is simultaneously at work forming countervailing gestures that frustrate the inclination to be content with common expectations and complacency. Heaney writes, "This redressing effect of poetry comes from its being a glimpsed alternative, a revelation of potential that is denied or constantly threatened by circumstances" (4).

Heaney takes it for granted that poetry not only operates through a "self-delighting inventiveness" but, in addition, works to represent things in the world (5). In discussing one of John Clare's sonnets, for example, Heaney makes the point that in Clare's evocation of a butterfly "rarely has the butteriness of butterfly been so available" (71). Good writing can make available what formerly might have been masked, hidden, or constructed by less adept or clumsier uses of language such as propaganda or polemic. It is frank acknowledgment of the differences between good literature and literature of a lesser quality that is lacking in most postmodern criticism. Heaney emphasizes the vital distinction that must be made between good writing and writing that somehow misses the mark. It is less talented authors who expose the clumsy underpinnings of language and who impose a linguistic experience on the world. Others, more skillful, can do the opposite by revivifying and renewing our experience of the world.

In an earlier study of the relationship of language to reality (or nature), C. K. Stead suggests that any piece of literature must be viewed as existing within a tension among a writer, his or her audience, and reality (11–12). If a writer, for example, has a relationship that is too close to his or her audience, and too far from reality, the result is a literature that will appear stifled, or strangely distorted, to succeeding generations. Stead's concerns are with imperialist, propagandistic poetry written before the First World War, but his comments could apply to any period of piety and orthodoxy, including our own.

Discussions such as Stead's and Heaney's, which make distinctions between literature of the first rank and literature that is of a lesser quality, comprise a positive first step in clarifying literature's role in society, as well as its relationship to a broader reality. Writing that is about nature offers a special case in these discussions since genres such as nature writing so clearly have their roots in modern scientific observation, which holds a privileged role in its ability to describe reality. Here we would like to proffer a caution and point out that much writing that is ostensibly about the natural world—primarily nonfictionalized accounts such as nature writing—can display the same foibles as any other genre if literary concerns are submerged by the polemical needs of the moment. Early in the twentieth century, the nature study advocate Neltje Blanchan Doubleday, for example, writes that the American goshawk is a "villain of the deepest dye," a "murderer," the "most destructive creature on wings . . . bloodthirsty, delighting in killing what it often cannot eat" (Strom 65). Doubleday's contemporary reader is left to marvel not at the murderous goshawk but at the human preconceptions that inform her 1903 accounts about the bird. Writing at a later date (1954), and in a far more scientistic vein, Fred Bodsworth, a noted Canadian journalist keenly interested in the natural world, describes the Eskimo curlew's dramatic bipolar flight but is careful to tell readers that the bird's "instinctive behavior code, planted deep in his brain by the genes of countless generations, told him only what to do, without telling him why. His behavior was controlled not by mental decisions but by instinctive responses to the stimuli around him" (36). While there is no villain here, the allusion to an "instinctive behavior code" in retrospect appears as unidimensional as the attribution of anthropomorphic claims. Neither example functions to redress harmful human conceptions of nature. Both examples demonstrate a relationship that is too close to an intended audience: moralistic on one hand, scientistic on the other. From a distance, it is possible to see how both examples have dated, absorbing the textures of their times, so that the nature presented is hardly recognizable to today's readers. Language, rather than imposing a hegemonic view on the world, here seems to have preserved these interpretations as if they were so many curios in a cabinet.

The idea that language constructs reality, when pushed to its logical conclusion, reveals a disturbing human arrogance and one-sidedness. What seems more productive is to view Doubleday's failure as a striking example of how nature evades human attempts to construct reality. Clearly, the living goshawk—the bird that is still available to us today—resists Doubleday's narrative. That we recognize Doubleday's villainous bird as little more than an early-twentieth-century construction speaks to the fact that not only does language attempt to impose on nature but that nature has the power to resist this imposition. In this case, far from shaping reality, the use of this type of language reveals its failure to impose its logic on the world and thus its failure to construct reality or to exist solely as a mental artifact. Such failures are far from providing evidence of the power of language, and they speak instead to nature's powerful resistance to our narratives.

Furthermore, such resistance can manifest itself not only when we glance back at what we have here termed "failures" but also expresses itself in the best writing—although in a different way. The difference between such failures as Doubleday's and writing that can help redress the terrible imbalance in the human relationship to the world exists in the fact that the best writing about nature builds into its narrative allusions to nature's resistance. That is, rather than merely giving nature symbolic or metaphoric roles, something literature of all eras has done, we believe that the best stories about nature are those that have sensed the power of nature to resist, or question, or evade the meanings we attempt to impose on the natural world.

Looking for the Literature of Nature

We are perhaps being too literal-minded if we believe that the answer to Henry David Thoreau's question, "Where is the literature which gives expression to Nature?" ("Walking" 120) is to be found primarily in nature writing, or in realistic descriptive passages, or even nature poetry. "He would be a poet who could impress the winds and streams into his service, to speak for him; who nailed words to their primitive senses," Thoreau muses, concluding that little in English literature gives adequate expression to the subject (120). Thoreau spent a lifetime pressing metaphor into expressing his sense of the wild, bending language almost as far as it can be bent, in order to adequately express nature. Thoreau's tastes led him to believe mythology came closer than any other genre to expressing the original vigor of nature.

That a literature that gives expression to nature might not fit neatly defined genres nor follow along narrative trails human desires have laid down for the order and control of nature seems obvious. As such, some of the best narratives about nature emerge in rather unexpected places. It is not just in nature writing, or nature poetry, or descriptive prose where examples of redress, or resistance, are found. Many different narratives convey the strangeness of life and the elusiveness of nature—and often with far more precision than do works that are more ostensibly about nature (that is, nonfiction nature writing, field guides, first person essays, and semi-scientific accounts). Weak narratives of nature, such as Doubleday's, reveal nature's resistance in retrospect, but strong narratives, such as Thoreau's, incorporate the idea of resistance into the narrative. Any literature that alludes to a natural order that exists apart from human control contains within it the elements of a strong narrative of nature, and it is less likely to display the weaknesses we associate with more overt and superficial constructions of the natural world. This fact can invert our expectations: some strong, fanciful narratives can provide insights into the natural world, while others, claiming to have science on their side, can appear to be a species of weak fiction. Thoreau makes a similar point when he remarks in his journal that he is finding the language of science restrictive, and that he prefers the skill of ancient writers who "left a more lively and lifelike account of the gorgon than modern writers give us of real animals" (*Journal* 12 18 February 1860).

Stories can, of course, turn the tables and show nature rebelling against human dominance. There are enough movies of this "revolt-of-nature" (Newman) variety to indicate a fondness in Western culture for witnessing a scripted assault on humankind by the natural world. Worms, reptiles, birds, sharks, bears, tornadoes, earthquakes, comets, and even vegetation rise up to attack us, and we enjoy watching. These days, it is not even necessary that humankind triumph in the end. We feel sufficient guilt over our relations with the environment that a victory for nature now and again is not only tolerable but welcome. As narratives, however, stories in the revolt-of-nature mode follow the usual path: escalating assaults, a crisis, and then some sort of resolution. The narrative line is left unaffected by the presence of natural phenomena, and we are not really obliged to think about the natural world except as it temporarily impinges on the continual quest for human happiness.

Similarly, writers can incorporate elements of the natural world in their work without really expressing much in terms of nature's resistance. John Hawkes's *The Frog* is a case in point. In the novel, a frog climbs out of a lily pond and into a boy's mouth and lives inside the boy's stomach for the remainder of the boy's life. As the boy Pascal grows to manhood, the frog emerges to give Pascal's father a fatal heart attack and to pleasure numerous women. At the end of the story, it turns out that all of the inmates in the asylum where Pascal has lived have acquired frogs of their own. A novel such as *The Frog*, while interestingly murky, has more to do with psychoanalysis than with nature. Once the frog-penis connection occurs, the only strangeness with which the reader is left to cope is how Pascal's penis manages to fly across the room or how even the female inmates of the asylum can possess frogs. A reader is not required, ultimately, to ponder the nature of literal frogs.

The genre of nature writing has tended to show nature eluding human control by minimizing the human presence and focusing attention on the nonhuman world. Works of fiction that successfully integrate nature and natural phenomena into human stories, however, are of greater interest to contemporary readers because they allow nature to change the shape, direction, and outcome of the narrative. The South African novelist Nadine Gordimer's "The Termitary" ends with the narrator's contemplation of her mother's power, and yet nature controls the story. If one is looking for a story with the "earth clinging to its roots" (Thoreau, "Walking" 120), "The Termitary" is a fine example. Indeed, when the woman who tells the story recalls her nine-year-old self coming home to find the floor beneath the Axminster rug in her family's parlor ripped up and the earth below exposed, we are all reminded that our solid, secure houses are built on the good earth. "The thought of that hollow, earth-breaking dark always beneath our Axminster thrilled me," the speaker says (115).

Workmen have ripped up the floor of her home because termites are destroying it. The workmen are earthy: "All had the red earth of underground clinging to their clothes and skin and hair. . . . These men themselves appeared to have been dug up, raw from that clinging earth entombed beneath buildings" (117). The work of the three exterminators throws into chaos both home and daily routine. This home is one of those attempts by the British to import British rules and values into colonized South Africa—a home containing an Axminster rug and a Steinway piano, a home where tea is served in china cups and children are taught proper deportment, and where the mother complains of her husband in that familiar Western manner of the 1930s to 1950s: "I haven't got a husband like other women's. . . . I haven't got a home like other women" (115). The three earthy workers intimidate this English woman who is queen of the household.

The object of the excavation is the queen of the termite colony, mother of all the termite thousands, the one who must be eradicated in order to destroy the colony. Gordimer gives us a brief nature lesson: "[T]he queen cannot move, she is blind; whether she is underground, the tyrannical prisoner of her subjects who would not have been born and cannot live without her, or whether she is captured and borne away in a shoe-box, she is helpless to evade the consequences of her power" (119). Gordimer reminds us that not only the earth but other kingdoms exist beneath our homes. As the speaker's mother is doing that most motherly of chores, mixing a cake, the workers come in bearing the termite queen in a shoe box. The children are fascinated and horrified. "We all gazed at an obese, helpless white creature, five inches long, with the tiny, shiny-visored head of an ant at one end. The body was a sort of dropsical sac attached to this head; it had no legs that could be seen, neither could it propel itself by peristaltic action, like a slug or worm. The queen. The queen whose domain, we had seen for ourselves in the galleries and passages that had been uncovered beneath our house, was as big as ours" (118).

The termitary is an impressive domain, chambered, dotted with food fungus, composed of "tunnels for conveying water from as much as forty feet underground [and an] elaborate defence and communications system" (120). Once the queen is removed from her domain, the termites abandon the termitary. "We lived on, above the ruin" (120), the narrator observes. Human-British order reasserts itself.

Now it is easy enough to read the termite queen and the termites as symbolic, to take the queen as symbol of bloated, powerful-powerless white South Africa and the termites as African people compelled to serve the colonizers—caught in some weirdly symbiotic colonial relationship. Since the story ends with the observation that the mother of the household, many years later, is dead and "the secret passages, the inner chamber in which she was our queen and prisoner are sealed up, empty," one can also take the termite queen as a symbol of the mother in her children's minds and memories, and the termitary as a metaphor for their socialization. Certainly, the idea of breaking through the artificial niceties of daily life and exposing the dim, chaotic underground has a symbolic, psychoanalytical quality. The implication that the termite queen the workers display might well be a fake, simply the same termite queen conveyed from house to house and triumphantly shown to the home owner, also lends itself to ironic interpretation. Perhaps the mother has the same iconic significance.

Regardless of the conclusions one might make about the correspondence between the human situation and life in the termitary, the point is that the originating experience is the termitary and not the human situation. In Western culture, we have sought in nature analogies to the human state; in "The Termitary," however, the exposure of the termites' underground world provides the inspiration, the reason, for contemplation of humanity, not vice versa. The termitary renders the corresponding human relationships deep, freighted with mystery. Without it, the mother and the home are merely cultural stereotypes.

Because the termitary thrills the narrator, and because it has had an impact on the mind of the author, the narrative takes an original shape. In a way, it is more of a meditation than a narrative. The ambiguity surrounding the authenticity of the termite queen leaves the possibility open that the termitary might still be intact, unconquered—despite the fact that the termites abandon it. The termitary remains a living place in the imagination. Decades are summed up in the last paragraph of the story, all with the one episode of breaking open the termitary as their foundation in memory. The narrator considers herself free; her memories are more spacious than her mother's. "Why should I remember? I, who—shuddering to look back at those five rooms behind the bow-window eyes and the front-door mouth—have oceans, continents, snowed-in capitals, islands where turtles swim, cathedrals, theatres, palace gardens where people kiss and tramps drink wine—all these to remember" (120). While the sense of liberty she expresses appears to cast the termitary in the symbolic negative, the idea of breaking out is initiated by the revelation of the termite's labyrinthine dominion existing under her childhood home. All of these features: the time frame, ambiguities, various possibilities in symbolic reading, and naturalistic information— preserve the termitary as a potent place that cannot be subsumed by the narrative. Here we find an example not of literature's culpability but of a gesture of redress toward the natural world.

Another example of narrative that acknowledges nature's ultimate resistance to our stories is *Turtle Diary* by Russell Hoban, an American-born, British-based author. The conventional view of turtles has little to do with freedom; one is inclined to think of tortoises, land turtles, burdened with heavy shells and achingly slow of movement. The graceful underwater flight of the swimming turtle may come to mind for people who watch nature programs, but turtles have been constructed socially in Western culture as models of ponderous deliberation and vulnerability—the proverbial sitting ducks. Perhaps it is this convention that renders the power and grace of the swimming turtle a thing of beauty. There can be little doubt that Hoban took inspiration from the freedom of marine turtles for his novel. Indeed, one could speculate that in *Turtle Diary* Hoban has transferred to three characters his desire to liberate turtles from a zoo, and he has used fiction as the means to satisfy that desire.

In some respects, *Turtle Diary* is a conventional narrative. Plotlines converge to move steadily toward the release of the turtles, the turtles are released, and then the two characters who have performed the deed go their separate ways and deliver the dénouement. William G. and Neara H., who alternate as narrators throughout the story, have other experiences besides the central one with the turtles. Nevertheless, the narrative exists to enable contemplation of human relations with the natural world.

Following the release of the turtles, Neara observes: "The sea was wherever it was, and the turtles. It could not be done again. Of those who did the launching there were no survivors" (157). She is feeling the bleakness of life, the radically coincidental nature of all the world's phenomena. More than that, her observation that there were no survivors suggests that her narrative has been vacated with the launching of the turtles. Once Neara and William have served their purpose as the means of the turtles' release, the aimlessness of their lives becomes apparent to them. They lack the purposiveness that the turtles possess. The zookeeper who has abetted William and Neara comments, "'Nothing to be done really about animals. Anything you do looks foolish. The answer isn't in us. It's almost as if we're put here on earth to show how silly they aren't'" (158). "The answer isn't in us"—this could well be the ultimate finding of *Turtle Diary*.

Perhaps some of the observations about turtles and other animals could have been made in a piece of nature writing. Nevertheless, because *Turtle Diary* is a fictional narrative, and particularly a first-person narrative with two narrators, all thoughts on nature are conditional and contested rather than final and authoritative, as they might be in other genres. The expectation we bring to nature writing as a genre is that it can give us information, and it can tell us the facts. We might put up with an amusing or obstreperous nature writer—but even with the loosest of definitions, our expectation of nature writing does not allow a writer, a writer's emotions, or a writer's conflict with meaning to become our main concern. We bring different expectations to fiction, however. In the novel, Neara is free to imagine herself as another being and to pass judgment on her confessional musing. "What I do is not as good as what an oyster-catcher does. Writing and illustrating books for children is not as good as walking orange-eyed, orange-billed in the distance on the river, on the beaches of the ocean, finding shellfish" (49). Neara is free to wonder, on contemplating a water beetle in an aquarium, "If someone were to buy me, have me shipped in a tin with air-holes, what would I be a specimen of?" (76).

Granted, when William notes the "[t]housands of miles in [the turtles'] speechless eyes [and] submarine skies in their flipper wings," a nature writer might have said the same. It takes the added dimension of a fictional character, however, to give primacy to the emotional sense of lostness that William discovers in himself when he realizes that the turtles are not lost. "Could I abolish the human condition? Could I swim, experience swimming, finding, navigating, fearlessness, unlostness? Could I come back with an answer? The unlostness itself would be the answer. I shouldn't need to come back" (72).

William continues with the theme as he drives the van with the three turtles in their crates toward the coast:

> Looking at them I couldn't think there was any expectation in them. When they felt themselves once more in ocean they would simply do what turtles do in the ocean, their readiness was whole and undiminished in them. If permitted to live they would navigate by the sun, by chemical traces in the water, by the imprint in their genes of an ancient continent sundered. They were compacted of finding, finding was embodied in them (134).

The turtles' story, whatever it might be, is separate from the human story. And although a reader does become involved in the stories of William G. and Neara H., Hoban's technique of alternating between them means that no one human story in this novel determines the meaning of the release of the turtles. The openness of the two narrators to considering that nature points up the unreality of human life is repeated in the structure of the novel. The turtles can be free because all we have before us are the thoughts of two people. These people may be wrong, or they may be right. We may find their ideas congenial, or we may not. But both in themselves and in the way they are presented, the thoughts of these characters do not bind the turtles. Hoban's awareness that nature does not conform to our narratives necessitates the dual narrators because, as he writes, "The answer isn't in us."

A final example demonstrating nature's resistance comes from Franz Kafka. Much inclined to experiment with the world in stories such as "The Metamorphosis" and "The Hunger Artist," Kafka again turns the tables on our expectations in "A Report to an Academy." In the story, an ape, who by his own account has become human, observes human acrobats at a variety show. "What a mockery of holy Mother Nature! Were the apes to see such a spectacle, no theater walls could stand the shock of their laughter" (253). Given that Kafka's general theme is often humankind's lack of freedom, there is irony in the liberties he takes with the world, regularly employing phenomena of the natural world to destabilize the idea of humanity. In the process, Kafka compels his reader to think about nature.

Although rarely recognized in critical assessments of his work, the natural world is foundational to Kafka's stories. A vegetarian who felt empathy for animals, particularly animals held in zoos, Kafka suffered under a tyrannical father who called his son enough animal names so that Franz was obliged to wrestle with the idea of his own animality. All of Kafka's stories are strange, and so one cannot argue that nature alone is the force that caused him to produce enigmatic narratives—unless one means nature in the abstract. Nevertheless, when natural elements—usually animals—appear in his works, Kafka's habitual eccentricity reinforces the awareness that nature does not conform to our constructions.

"A Report to an Academy" is among the more intelligible of Kafka's stories. The frame for "A Report to an Academy" is a meeting of presumably learned men and women, although they are given no voice as the speaker tells his tale. The speaker is Red Peter, a chimpanzee who has become human and who solemnly tells his learned audience how he went about achieving this conversion. According to Red Peter, when he found himself in a tiny cage in the cargo hold of ship, his only way out of the cage was to become human. "There was nothing else for me to do, provided always that freedom was not to be my choice" (258). Becoming human means mastering a series of tricks: drinking schnapps, smoking a pipe, uttering words, and acquiring information about European culture. While clearly a commentary on the human condition, Red Peter's story also makes one think of how apparent successes in teaching apes to manipulate our semiotic systems convince some biologists that they are our kin.

Nature's invasion of culture could not be more thorough than it is in "A Report to an Academy." Kafka does not allow the assembled academics to question Red Peter's assertions. What do they see when they look at him? A performing chimpanzee, however talented? A squat, hairy raconteur? Either way, Red Peter has seized control of this story. Although he denies that choice was involved in his decision to become human—or to mimic humanity—it is clear that through Red Peter, nature and Kafka deconstruct the human image. Red Peter is "not appealing for any man's verdict." "I have only made a report," he says at the close of his speech (259). In an odd and ironic way, Kafka's chimpanzee is more himself ontologically than chimpanzees in other stories. Red Peter is not allegorical or metaphorical; he is not separate from ourselves, as are "natural" chimpanzees; and yet he remains immune to human construction. We have seen a situation like this, one that Gordimer creates with her termitary and its termite queen: the relationship between the natural phenomenon and human culture defies explanation.

Granted, one will not find in Kafka's stories what one is used to in conventional nature writing. Mice who sing, or appreciate singing, or what seems to them to be singing ("Josephine the Singer, or the Mouse Folk"); a dog who speculates that his species might be the only real entity in the world ("Investigations of a Dog"); a paranoid burrow dweller, possibly a badger, who is plagued by an invisible, whistling enemy ("The Burrow"); and a traveling salesman transformed into a gigantic cockroach ("The Metamorphosis")—little of this is recognizable as nature. Where are the trees and lakes? Where are the insouciant animals and their curious habits? Why are we not learning about bioregions? The least that can be said is that Kafka shakes us out of our customary ways of thinking about life, and this, we think, is the redress literature can offer us in the face of an environmental crisis. These are the kinds of stories that lead us to something that is, finally, "beyond nature writing."

Conclusion

Gordimer, Hoban, and Kafka place nature in the domain of the imponderable. They open up the narrative form so that nature can remain ambiguous, enigmatic, and resistant to the imposition of human meaning-making exercises. They accomplish this by constructing narratives that allude to nature's ultimate resistance to the human. This is not to say that nature is hostile to humanity but that it exists on its own terms. This fact alone can challenge our most dearly held beliefs, and contemporary authors have been quick to explore it.

We began our discussion by noting that much literary criticism is informed by the idea that language molds our perceptions of the world. This is a corrective to earlier concepts that held that certain unproblematic correlations existed between the natural world and language. Unfortunately, this insight has been distorted by those who are willing to proclaim that there is no relationship between language and the world and that all meaning is human meaning.

If we are to find creative responses to what we call an environmental crisis, we suggest it is important to keep our minds open to other possibilities. Tired slogans and old cliches (how tedious it is to hear for the one hundredth time that "man is a part of nature"?), while perhaps having served their purpose in an earlier period, are not what is needed now. Thinking and writing about nature and the environment is a grown-up task, and it requires all the subtlety, complexity, and sophistication writers can muster.

As a way to illustrate these points, we have examined three writers who have used some aspect of nature in their work. In the process, each writer has confronted something that is resistant to human meaning. While we might attempt to make a symbol of Gordimer's termite queen, or Hoban's turtle, or Kafka's chimpanzee, ultimately each of these creatures eludes capture by the author. While each story can work on a symbolic, metaphoric, or psychological level, for our purposes we have found that in each story's deepest level all such meanings fall away, and we are left to contemplate the unknowable, mysterious aspect of termite, turtle, or chimpanzee.

It is at this point that we recognize nature's resistance to our stories, and this recognition calls into question all the constructs we have built in our attempts to cement over the living earth. That fiction might be better situated to accomplish this than other genres is also something we have tentatively proposed. Our sense is that the environmental crisis is a crisis of meaning, and to recover what we have lost we need new stories about nature. As we continue to probe and manipulate all facets of the natural world, it is a timely moment to remind ourselves of that ultimate mystery of which we, too, are a part. Good stories, we believe, are able to do just that.

Works Cited

Bodsworth, Fred. *Last of the Curlews*. 1954. Toronto: McClelland and Stewart, 1963.

Cawley, R. McGreggor, and William Chaloupka. "The Great Wild Hope." *In the Nature of Things*. Ed. Jane Bennett and William Chaloupka. Minneapolis: U of Minnesota P, 1993. 3–23.

Doubleday, Neltje Blanchan. "How to Attract the Birds and Other Talks about Bird Neighbors." 1903. Strom 52–66.

Gordimer, Nadine. "The Termitary." *A Soldier's Embrace: Stories by Nadine Gordimer*. Harmondsworth, Middlesex: Penguin, 1980. 113–20.

Hawkes, John. *The Frog*. New York: Penguin, 1996.

Heaney, Seamus. *The Redress of Poetry*. London: Faber and Faber, 1995.

Hoban, Russell. *Turtle Diary*. London: Pan, 1977.

Kafka, Franz. "A Report to an Academy." 1917. Trans. Willa Muir and Edwin Muir. *Franz Kafka: The Complete Stories*. Ed. Nahum N. Glatzer. New York: Schocken, 1971. 250–59.

Nadeau, Robert. *Readings from the Book of Nature*. Amherst: U of Massachusetts P, 1981.

Newman, Kim. *Nightmare Movies: A Critical History of the Horror Film, 1968–1988*. London: Bloomsbury, 1988.

Raglon, Rebecca, and Marian Scholtmeijer. "Shifting Ground: Metanarratives, Epistemology, and the Stories of Nature." *Environmental Ethics* (spring 1996): 19–38.

Stead, C. K. *The New Poetic: Yeats to Eliot*. London: Hutchinson & Co., 1964.

Strom, Deborah, ed. *Birdwatching with American Women*. New York: Norton, 1986.

Thoreau, Henry David. "Walking." *The Natural History Essays*. Salt Lake City: Peregrine Smith, 1980. 93–136.

———. *Journal 12*. Ed. Bradford Torry. Boston: Houghton Mifflin, 1906.

The Non-Alibi of Alien Scapes: SF and Ecocriticism

Patrick D. Murphy

Introduction

A leading journal in the field of critical analyses of science fiction (SF) is *Extrapolation*. Its title identifies a basic orientation toward defining the relationship between the genre of science fiction and literary realism and referentiality. The application of the concept of extrapolation to science fiction insists that the writing and reading of SF are intimately linked to, and based on, getting people to think both about the present and about this world in which they live. SF stories that emphasize analogy between imagined worlds and the reader's consensual world encourage such thinking as well (see Suvin, *Positions* 37, *Metamorphoses* 28–29). The encouragement of that type of critical thinking provides a linkage between science fiction and nature-oriented literature (see Murphy). Rather than providing the alibi of fantasy, extrapolation emphasizes that the present and the future are interconnected—what we do now will be reflected in the future, and, therefore, we have no alibi for avoiding addressing the results of our actions today.

Certainly, SF is not nature writing, in the sense of that genre's definition as being scientifically based, personal observation written in nonfiction prose. What it can be, however, is nature-oriented literature, in the sense of its being an aesthetic text that, on the one hand, directs reader attention toward the natural world and human interaction with other aspects of nature within that world, and, on the other hand, makes specific environmental issues part of the plots and themes of various works. SF also at times shares with both nature writing and other forms of nature-oriented literature detailed attention to the natural world found in the present as well as to the scientific disciplines that facilitate such detailed attention (Van der Bogert 58). Large-scope SF novels and series, such as *Dune* and its sequels, often combine a wide array of scientific disciplines that bear on perceiving, interpreting, and understanding the world (see Gough).

Extrapolations and Cautionary Tales

Any prediction of environmental disaster that has been made in recent years has been prefigured in science fiction in one way or another. Until the resurgence of the environmental movement in the United States in the 1970s, the greatest threat to the natural world in the minds of most people was that of nuclear war. While activism against nuclear war centered around the possible extinction of humankind, there were many who also recognized the environmental threats nuclear weapons posed. Pat Frank's *Alas, Babylon* (1959), for instance, portrays a limited nuclear war in which the good people of small American towns survive by relying on Jeffersonian agrarian values. At the novel's end, the U.S. military is going to help such people get back on their feet, but it is clear that their allegiance has shifted to the local community and away from the nation state.

While some ecocritics and environmental philosophers doubt that it is possible to be anything but anthropocentric, others argue for the need to become, at least intellectually if not instinctively, ecocentric or biocentric. From that perspective, literary works, then, that are anti- or de-anthropocentric can be understood as environmental literature. In John Brunner's *Bedlam Planet* (1968), he emphasizes that the only hope for the colonists' survival is to allow themselves to undergo adaptation to the ecosystem of the planet on which they land. While making a claim for the necessity of becoming inhabitants through transforming these individuals from exogenous to indigenous human beings, Brunner conveniently works with a planet with no competing sentient life. Unlike Brunner, Ursula K. Le Guin in *The Word for World Is Forest* (1972) pits an indigenous sentient species against human interlopers, who consider themselves superior because they know how to exploit the planet. As these two novels suggest, SF has a strong potential to function as parable addressing the issue of how people become inhabitants and what it means to be indigenous in relation to environmental responsibility and the mutual adaptation between humans and the rest of nature (see Suvin, *Metamorphoses* 30).

In one of his most famous novels, *The Sheep Look Up* (1972), Brunner depicts what happens when people do not learn to become inhabitants but continue to try to live on the borrowed time of environmental depletion and pollution proliferation. Brunner, developing a kind of if-then extrapolation, describes in extensive detail a United States awash in hazardous waste sites; killer smog; and high security, sterile suburbs. Eventually, the intensification of despoliation reaches a trigger point and the American masses begin to revolt. While Brunner spins out his extrapolation close to home in *The Sheep Look Up,* Le Guin has usually not set her SF novels close to the present, and only rarely are they set on Earth. These distances make it easier for her to generate a what-if, rather than if-then, type of SF. For instance, in *The Dispossessed* (1974), the action takes place in another solar system a century or two in the future. Here, Le Guin generates a novel that matches up the working out of an anarchist society with conditions of environmental scarcity. Near the end of the novel, Le Guin introduces the Terran ambassador to Urras, who tells the protagonist Shevek about conditions on Earth, "a planet spoiled by the human species" who "multiplied and gobbled and fought until there was nothing left, and then [they] died" (279). In response to the devastation, the surviving people had to submit to total centralization and rationalization of all resources. Devastating the planet will lead, Le Guin argues, not only to human self-destruction but also to the loss of human freedom.

Brunner provides what might be labeled a dystopian cautionary tale, while Le Guin provides a eutopian cautionary tale. In *The Sheep Look Up,* people come to awareness as a result of environmental crises. Le Guin posits the world of Anarres as a place where human beings are working out a sustainable relationship with the rest of nature, where culture and economy are being adapted to environmental constraints. And it is that possibility with which Le Guin wants readers to identify in contrast to the blighted landscape of Earth that the ambassador describes. But in a way, Le Guin might be providing a loophole, in that the Anarresti are able to work out this new nature-culture relationship on a planet where there are no other sentient beings to challenge their right to settle and transform the environment even as they adapt to it. As with Le Guin's *The Word for World Is*

Forest and Brunner's *Bedlam Planet*, this right to settle another planet issue will need to be revisited when considering Kim Stanley Robinson's Mars trilogy.

But before doing that, I want to take a look at two novels published contemporaneously with Robinson's *Red Mars* (1993), *Green Mars* (1994), and *Blue Mars* (1996). While both of these novels address environmental issues, each suffers from certain problems if viewed ecocritically.

Meta-meteorology and Indigenous Cloning

Bruce Sterling's *Heavy Weather* (1994) provides an example of nature-oriented literature written in the highly popular cyberpunk style. Well known as one of the founding authors of cyberpunk, Sterling fills this novel with high-tech wizardry and focuses on a team of nomadic tornado chasers. This iconoclastic team headed by Dr. Jerry Mulcahey is out in an environmentally devastated southwestern United States, which has been wracked by the greenhouse effect and the agribusiness practices that contributed to it. The Storm Troupe is on the lookout for the mega-tornado, the F-6, that their leader has been predicting. Eventually, in 2031 it arrives. Prior to that readers are gradually educated about some other likely effects of global warming, but such education often gets overshadowed by attention to the troupe's gadgetry. As Noel Gough remarks, *Heavy Weather* dramatizes "the ways in which our knowledge of climate change is constructed by the global networks of satellites, weather stations, supercomputers, meteorologists, and broadcasters that produce the images, models, and simulations that materially represent such knowledge" (413).

But, perhaps inadvertently, Sterling also demonstrates how unreliable and limited such knowledge remains. When the F-6 arrives, the story of its appearance gets mixed up with the plot of a group of terrorists who use it as a cover to become independent of their anonymous superiors. It remains unclear whether the F-6 is the inevitable freak of nature that human eco-destruction has unleashed or if it is the result of meteorological manipulation by a secret terrorist organization that has attempted to lessen human impact on the world through sabotage and assassination. But actually, in either case, the F-6 is the consequence of human manipulation of the environment gone awry. It is precisely the awry part that casts doubt on the idea that we are witnessing "the end of nature" (see

McKibben), since even at the novel's end neither Dr. Mulcahey nor anyone else can accurately predict, much less control, the weather.

This is a rather pedestrian lesson for a novel that runs over three hundred pages. Sterling, however, provides other lessons, all of which I find troubling. First is the lesson Jane Unger suggests in an exchange with Jerry about the F-6. Jerry points out that its winds could scour the planet and become a permanent fixture in the atmosphere, but Jane discounts such fears: "Things can get totally awful, but then something else comes up that's so amazingly screwy that it makes it all irrelevant. There never was any nuclear war or nuclear winter. There's never gonna be one. That was all just stupid hype, so they could go on ruining the environment, so we'd end up living just like we're living now, living with the consequences" (207–8). Despite the tortured logic, the point seems to be that warnings about catastrophes are just public relations and do not play a role in changing mass consciousness to enable the averting of forecasted disasters. A second message is that no matter how bad it gets humanity will muddle through. Is such a message a positive or helpful one at this point in time? Does it encourage people to muddle toward a more ecologically sustainable human culture or does it provide them with an alibi to continue living their lives without assuming responsibility for the health of the biosphere?

Another significant moment in the novel occurs when a reporter asks the members of the Storm Troupe, "When do you think the human race conclusively lost control over its own destiny?" (243). The members give a variety of answers, but Jerry and Jane basically query the question by doubting that humanity ever controlled its own destiny. Jerry remarks that "the atmosphere is a chaotic system. . . . That begs the question of when we lost control of our destiny. We have none now; I doubt we ever had any" (245). And Jane concludes that "I'm real sorry that we did this to ourselves and that we're in the fix we are in now, but so-called Mother Earth herself has done worse things to the planet. And believe it or not, the human race has actually had things worse" (246). These conclusions, while true in regard to humans' lack of control over "destiny," undercut the value of environmental activism in the present. If something might not make any difference, why should people sacrifice to do it? Certainly one can reply that sacrifices for environmental health ought to be undertaken because they are what we understand to be the moral course of action to take today, and they may make a positive difference, but will that argument be persuasive to the average American consumer? Or will the argument that Sterling is making at the novel's end have greater appeal?

At the end of *Heavy Weather*, Jerry has received a lucrative research appointment and settled down to academic life. He and Jane have married and she is a happy homemaker and mother. At least for the professional middle class and the rich in the United States, "heavy weather" is just another inconvenience that cannot halt the continued striving for the post–World War II suburban American dream even in the warmer-globe years of the 2030s. Perhaps what I find so chilling about the conclusion is just how realistic its portrayal seems to be for so many Americans at the end of the 1990s. And yet, at the same time, I can see it from another angle in which the ability to weather the storms that environmental irresponsibility spawned in the twentieth century may mean the gradual development of a widespread ability to ameliorate and redress the damage in the next, without cataclysmic destruction of human life. I do not think the novel ends on any such note of ambiguity, but an ecocritical reading of *Heavy Weather* can pursue such ambiguity in terms of whether the novel's conclusion is a pessimistic one regarding environmental accountability or an optimistic one regarding human adaptability to environmental change.

Kathleen Ann Goonan's *The Bones of Time* (1996), like Sterling's *Heavy Weather*, is set on Earth in the 2030s. But the prologue begins in 1887, introducing the story of the last princess of Hawai'i. Of the authors discussed so far who write near-future SF set on Earth, Goonan is the only one to engage any culture in-depth other than a dominant white one. The near-future world is one in which schools recommend genetic engineering of children; multinationals control the genetic marketplace; and Hawai'i continues to be controlled for the benefits of the military, agribusiness, and tourism to the detriment of the lives and culture of its indigenous people. The protagonist, Lynn Oshima, accidentally comes into contact with a Hawai'ian Homeland movement to clone an ancient leader, Kamehameha, a movement under attack from those who would lose if an independence movement were to make any gains. Intertwined with Lynn and the efforts to kill the Kamehameha clones is the story of another Hawai'ian, a brilliant mathematician who discerns how to travel in time in an effort to save Princess Kaiulani. Eventually these strands are brought together.

Throughout, Goonan provides information about the environmental destruction of Hawai'i and the exploitation and oppression of the colonized Hawai'ians. She also introduces the perspective that there are other forms of scientific thought than the Western laboratory model, such as Polynesian navigation. But Goonan's attention is focused on the survival of indigenous cultures and the possible knowledge that they may have to offer the rest of humanity. And yet, curiously enough, Goonan has this knowledge and environmental sensibility brought to bear not on the reclamation and recovery of the Hawai'ian islands but on the seizing of an interstellar spaceship. This spaceship becomes a new ark taking five thousand human beings and various animals on a voyage across the vast stretches of space rather than the vast stretches of the Pacific. Earth is left behind as a new voyage of discovery is initiated in which an indigenous people will find an uninhabited planet to call home. The implication is that such a quest will be an inversion of European voyages of discovery and decimation; but I wonder. Left unsaid is how the new voyagers will know that they are not colonizing a planet already inhabited, perhaps by less intelligent and self-conscious species or ones so different that their intelligence cannot be recognized. Left unsaid, also, is what will come of Hawai'i as its most adventurous and most brilliant children leave the islands.

While Goonan's *The Bones of Time* may be the most multicultural SF novel of the nineties, it is also a highly romantic assessment of the history of human impact throughout the Pacific. It ignores the devastation of the ecologies of islands, such as Rapa Nui; the extinction of species by first settlers; and the problems of population pressures, historically and in the present day. Invariably the image of a fresh start is at once highly appealing and deeply flawed if readers are to experience the kind of cognitive estrangement necessary to rethink their relationship to nature and culture in the present, on an earth where there are no more locations for fresh-start beginnings. Unless, of course, they are being encouraged to believe that the solution to Earth's environmental problems lies in human expansion, or departure, to other planets.

The Ethics of Colonizing the Dead

In Kim Stanley Robinson's massive Mars trilogy, he addresses almost every major question of environmental ethics and does so from a variety of persuasive positions. And it appears likely that many of these questions will move from the what-if to the we-can-but-will-we realms in the lifetimes of most of the people who will read this essay. (The voyage of the landing party of one hundred in *Red Mars* takes place in the year 2026, when I will be seventy-five years old.) That Robinson is generating an extrapolation more than a thought experiment is suggested by NASA's end-of-the-millennium launching of spacecraft toward Mars to analyze the climate and search for ice (Dunn 3).

One of the first ethical questions that arises among the one hundred is whether or not to terraform the planet to adapt it to human inhabitation or to require that humans adapt to Mars as it is. These options become the extreme Green Mars and Red Mars positions until the ill-fated revolution of 2061. Although the scope and character of terraforming is debated for thirty-five years in dichotomous terms, it is initiated on the basis of the argument that Mars is an inorganic mass and therefore environmental ethics do not apply to it, since such ethics only apply to biospheres and without indigenous organisms there is no ecology—a crucial philosophical question that Robert Sparrow addresses in the fall 1999 issue of *Environmental Ethics*. But a second argument also develops, which could be depicted as one between terraforming and terragouging. In the former case, a Martian biosphere would be developed sufficient to sustain human life without people having to wear spacesuits, but higher altitudes would remain virtually unchanged. In the latter case, whatever necessary would be done to facilitate extraction of raw materials for earthly consumption.

Robinson employs throughout the trilogy a semi-omniscient narrator with the story told with different characters selected as focalizers for each chapter, so that various points of view are represented in internally persuasive discourses. Also, the point of attention is adjusted to vary the attitude toward and concern with Mars, the people on it, and their activities in line with such shifts in point of view. As a result, not only do we hear the debate over whether or not to terraform from opposing viewpoints but we also hear debates about the relationship between terraforming Mars and changing the human culture on its surface. A Russian, Arkady, for instance, argues for the need to have a new architecture representative of the physical, chemical, and mineral properties of Mars as part of a necessary social and psychic transformation of its settlers.

In the context of the same general argument, an American, Sax Russell, suggests that terraforming will change the human beings on Mars in an evolutionary way. But Arkady disagrees by distinguishing evolution from history. He argues that the former consists of "environment and chance," while the latter involves "environment and choice" (88). In particular, Arkady strenuously argues that the decisions about social change should be made by the people on Mars and not the people on Earth. Later in the novel, the term "aeroform" will be introduced to suggest this process by which human beings are transformed by and on Mars (253). Aeroforming would become a form of history in which conscious choices are made about fundamentally planned decisions with an effort to realize intended results at the level of social transformation. And in this context, such social transformation is interdependent and mutually inter-serving with environmental transformation.

This argument is developed from a sociopolitical perspective by a Russian scientist in reaction against the pragmatic apolitical perspective of an American scientist. But Robinson also provides a third perspective, which is a mystical, ground-based spirituality spearheaded by a Japanese agronomist, Hiroko. It is perhaps telling that she is the leader of the team establishing greenhouses, because soil proves to be one of the most difficult materials to generate on Mars since it requires such interdependent action between the organic and the inorganic. It is Hiroko who claims that Mars will tell them what it wants and then they will have to do it (115). Terraforming, then, not only has to be reactive to the specificities of the landscape but also reactive to the particularities of the spirit of place. It may be that Robinson has chosen a Japanese character for this role, since she and later Japanese settlers speak of Martian *kami* or local spirits in an application of Shinto to their locale (229). Noteworthy here is that Shinto finds *kami* in both organic and inorganic matter, trees and rocks, animals, and rivers. Such a spirituality contradicts the argument the terraformers initially make that Mars has no ecology since it has no organic matter (205), although Hiroko's viewpoint does not rule out all terraforming.

In the character of Nadia, readers begin to learn how one might appreciate Mars as Mars and be open to large-scale terraforming. Early in the novel Nadia suddenly realizes that she is learning to see Mars when she recognizes how utterly alien it is (141–43). To see it as such and not as analogous to Earth requires a fundamental shift of consciousness. And as the novel progresses, it is suggested that the people who have the ability to become inhabitants are the ones who learn to see Mars' environment as distinct from Earth's as much as possible, rather than those who are always trying to explain it through earth terminology, symbols, and metaphors.

Unfortunately, while the original one hundred are having marvelous debates about terraforming, the United Nations decides to support mega-terraforming and sends fifteen hundred more colonists (202). As the second decade of settlement proceeds, it becomes clear that the UN is little more than a front for the transnational corporations—"metanationals"—who want to exploit Mars for resources and send temporary workers who are not supposed to become inhabitants. Such a position runs directly counter to considerations of settlement based on arguments about the carrying capacity of the extremely limited and fragile ecosystem and atmosphere being developed (309). With such pressure on them from Earth, the one hundred begin to talk about the need to establish a different kind of economic system on Mars, one that will work with the environment and contribute to cultural change rather than cultural and economic recidivism. Thus Robinson links the issue of inhabitation with that of environmental transformation and engineering, cultural change, and political and economic change.

The various factions within the one hundred join with their children and later settlers and begin to form two major parties and a variety of lesser ones. The major two are the Red Mars Party, which seeks minimal terraforming, and the Green Mars Party, which favors large-scale terraforming for the benefit of the inhabitants not the metanationals. Both favor independence from Earth (370–79). These political developments are accelerated by strong pressure from Earth to increase immigration to Mars to relieve population pressures, while the transnationals' exploitation of Mars is facilitated by the large corporations taking control of smaller countries to utilize their political access to the planet. Members of the one hundred realize that a place will change people only if that place is given the time to do its work on people committed to learning to inhabit it and the place is not overwhelmed by settlers seeking to recreate the world they have left behind. But with time running out, the Red and Green parties attempt a revolt and are crushed. The last 150 pages of *Red Mars*, then, are concerned with the failed revolt of 2061 and how its suppression results in unleashing major natural forces that accelerate terraforming beyond the wildest dreams of its most ardent proponents.

The first part of *Green Mars,* the second book of the trilogy, is titled "Aeroformation," indicating that even though the revolt was crushed, human adaptation to Mars will continue. That process, however, will necessarily develop in a complex way since the place is undergoing rapid and fundamental changes: "And terrain is a powerful genetic engineer, determining what flourishes and what doesn't, pushing along progressive differentiation, and thus the evolution of new species. And as the generations pass, all the members of a biosphere evolve together, adapting to their terrain in a complex, communal response, a creative self-designing ability" (2). This assessment clarifies two points. One, the planet has a biosphere now; it is an ecology and therefore environmental ethics have to be thought through differently than they were before. Two, while human beings make history through making choices, that history is made in the context of evolution, which means chance; therefore, while there are choices, plans, and intentions, there is no condition of control and no point of inevitability.

Hiroko early in this part of *Green Mars* makes a crucial claim that bears acutely on the issue of human colonization of other planets, whether they are dead such as Mars or alive such as the planets that Brunner and Le Guin imagine, and perhaps such as the one discovered in the summer of 1998 thirty thousand light-years from Earth:

> There's a constant pressure, pushing toward pattern. A tendency in matter to evolve into ever more complex forms. It's a kind of pattern gravity, a holy greening power we call viriditas, and it is the driving force in the cosmos. Life, you see. . . . We are its consciousness as well as our own. We rise out of the cosmos and we see its mesh of patterns, and it strikes us as beautiful. And that feeling is the most important thing in all the universe—its culmination. . . . [A]nd our task in this world is to do everything we can to foster it. And one way to do that is to spread life everywhere. (9)

How is this position fundamentally different from the pragmatist position that Sax Russell takes when he claims that humans impute beauty and give meaning to Mars? Robinson certainly seems to think there is a difference as their perspectives are developed as nonidentical throughout the trilogy. And I think he is right.

Hiroko does not claim that humans provide the beauty and the meaning but rather that they are entities, and not necessarily the only entities, who recognize the beauty and the meaning and are able both to express and to foster them. Our responsibility is not to do what we want with Earth or with Mars but rather to determine who might best assume responsibility for fostering life on these planets in all its forms and permutations. The problem, however, is that such a position may lead to similar conclusions as the ones the scientific pragmatists and the transnationals reach, which is to explore and colonize other planets. But is such colonization ethical? As *Green Mars* develops, it becomes clear that this ethic of fostering life wherever it may become rooted applies not only to Mars and how human beings from Earth treat life there but also to Earth and how Martians handle the struggle for life on the home planet.

A significant portion of *Green Mars* is given over, on the one hand, to describing the transformations of the Martian landscape that the violence of 2061 unleashed, and, on the other hand, to efforts to establish an alternative form of economics combining features of gift and barter economies to develop an "eco-economics," along with efforts to transform the metanational corporations on Earth into cooperatives in the post–nation state decades. It is important to note for people unfamiliar with the trilogy that Robinson has scientists on Mars discover a longevity gene therapy that enables him to keep some of his main characters alive through the approximate two hundred years that the trilogy covers. At the same time, he introduces characters and their viewpoints from succeeding generations and shows how different perspectives can be between people born and raised on Mars and the first settlers, as well as new settlers. Also in *Green Mars* Robinson gives attention to the increasingly multicultural character of the new settlers populating the planet. As a result, even as he is working on the alternative economics to go along with a new biosphere, he is also able to develop an argument about cultural syncretism, concluding that survival requires cultural cross-fertilization.

By the end of *Green Mars*, there is a fairly clear picture of the pace and character of terraforming with an understanding to leave at least 30 percent of the planet as originally Martian as possible, to promote and develop an alternative economics, and to form a type of government that will best support an ecoregional, cooperative, and community-based sense of identity—a politics of place, centered around the locations that people call home. All that is needed is independence! And the opportunity for that comes when there is an environmental catastrophe on Earth. With their attention diverted, the governments and corporations of Earth cannot prevent the second Martian revolution from succeeding in achieving the goal of planetary independence. While the first volume, then, concludes with the noise of defeat and chaos, the second volume ends on a note of triumph and also chaos: "At the heart of any phase change there was a zone of cascading recombinant chaos. But there were methods to read it, to deal with it" (559). And part of the reading and dealing involves making appropriate compromises. Domestically on Mars that means negotiating the degree of terraforming that will be acceptable to all parties on the planet and the rate of immigration that will continue to be allowed from Earth. To protect what they have gained the new free Martians have to work out the ways in which they will help Earth with its population and environmental crises.

In a sense, these two arenas of compromise become the background issues driving the plot of the third book of the trilogy, *Blue Mars*. This volume also affords Robinson the opportunity to describe in detail the multiplicity of en-natured cultures and communities developing out of the environmental, economic, political, and cultural transformations occurring on Mars, cultures and communities that he believes could be developed on Earth with the right phase changes and the appropriate compromises. In *Blue Mars* Robinson also considers the problem plaguing almost every political revolution intent on creating a new society: what happens to the ideology when political power shifts from the revolutionary generation to the next one and the one after that, particularly when by the third generation the conditions of scarcity, pioneering experience, and intensity of collective self-sacrifice have dissipated and the heirs of the fruits of struggle experience relative prosperity?

Robinson continues a strong focus on the development of political practice in a rapidly evolving postcapitalist era on both Mars and Earth. He also depicts the transition of Mars from being largely alien wilderness for the first generation to familiar garden for the second and third generations, who have known nothing else. With more and more of Mars becoming developed and populated, Robinson's major characters representing the Red and Green positions sustain their debate on the issue of maintaining wilderness as enclave or park (134). One of the key political innovations represented throughout *Blue Mars* is the establishment of an "environmental court," which functions as the equivalent of the Supreme Court in deciding significant cases about development, population, settlement, and terraforming—both its pace and characteristics (155). Clearly, such an idea is one that Robinson does not envision as being applicable only to Mars.

While *Green Mars* depicts acts of ecotage as part of the struggle for independence, it casts the most extreme forms of such action in a negative light. In *Blue Mars* arguments against ecotage are developed with Robinson's position appearing to be to accept it tactically but not strategically and to favor the promotion of alternative communities instead (271–72). The feasibility and sustainability of such alternative communities is seen to rest with the firm establishment of a cooperative dominated economy.

Again, as in the preceding volumes, Earth's population problem and the pressures of immigration to Mars generate political crises. But Robinson demonstrates convincingly that human emigration to other planets will never address Earth's population problems because of the logistics and equipment involved in moving large numbers of people through space (348). Mars functions, then, more as a symbol of possibility and as a safety valve rather than a practical solution to a dilemma that must be solved on Earth—the balancing out of human society in relation to the carrying capacity of the planet.

As *Blue Mars* moves toward the third Martian revolution, in which the political errors of its young government are corrected, Robinson trims down the successes and achievements of individuals, especially the original one hundred, to counter the romantic tendency to see individuals as heroes determining the outcome of events. He also counters the romantic tendency to see technology and science as the determining forces in the successful establishment of a new society on a new planet. Further, Robinson has major characters modifying their ideological positions. What becomes key in the last pages of the trilogy is the development of the following: "to learn to feel it oneself . . . love of planet. Love of a planet's life" (639, ellipses in original). And that feeling must include a multigenerational perspective: "Better to die thinking that you're going to miss a golden age, than to go out thinking that you had taken down your children's chances with you" (728). This sentence demonstrates with startling explicitness that SF can thematically be very much about the present time and place.

Conclusion

Some of the works that I have discussed in this essay provide what I would call alibis, invoking Mikhail Bakhtin's notion of the non-alibi. By that I mean they provide loopholes to justify ethically questionable behavior or else to sidestep ethical questions. Brunner does that with *Bedlam Planet,* Sterling does so in *Heavy Weather,* and Goonan effects this in *The Bones of Time.* In contrast, the strengths of works such as Le Guin's *The Word for World Is Forest* and Robinson's Mars trilogy are that they provide no *deus ex machina* alibi. Human beings have to act in ethically responsible ways while realizing that they are not ever in control of the overall situation and that what they understand to be ethically justified or technically correct today may prove to be erroneous tomorrow. Such works can turn readers' attention toward the major socioenvironmental issues facing humanity today. Especially through near-future extrapolation, SF can orient readers to think about ethical questions rapidly coming into sight, such as the colonization of Mars.

Works Cited

Bakhtin, Mikhail. *Toward a Philosophy of the Act.* Ed. and trans. Vadim Liapunov. Austin: U of Texas P, 1993.

Brunner, John. *Bedlam Planet.* New York: Del Rey, 1968.

———. *The Sheep Look Up.* 1972. New York: Del Rey/Ballantine, 1982.

Dunn, Marcia. "NASA Looking for Ice on Mars." *The Indiana Gazette* 4 Jan. 1999: 3.

Frank, Pat. *Alas, Babylon.* 1959. New York: Bantam, 1960.

Goonan, Kathleen Ann. *The Bones of Time.* New York: Tor, 1996.

Gough, Noel. "Playing with Wor(l)ds: Science Fiction as Environmental Literature." *The Literature of Nature: An International Sourcebook.* Ed. Patrick D. Murphy. Chicago: Fitzroy Dearborn, 1998. 409–14.

Herbert, Frank. *Dune.* 1965. New York: Ace, 1990.

Le Guin, Ursula K. *The Dispossessed.* 1974. New York: Avon, 1975.

———. *The Word for World Is Forest.* 1972. New York: Berkeley, 1981.

McKibben, Bill. *The End of Nature.* New York: Random House, 1989.

Murphy, Patrick D. *Farther Afield in the Study of Nature-Oriented Literature.* Charlottesville: UP of Virginia, 2000.

Robinson, Kim Stanley. *Blue Mars.* 1996. New York: Bantam, 1997.

———. *Green Mars.* 1994. New York: Bantam, 1995.

———. *Red Mars.* New York: Bantam, 1993.

Sparrow, Robert. "The Ethics of Terraforming." *Environmental Ethics* 21 (fall 1999): 227–45.

Sterling, Bruce. *Heavy Weather.* 1994. New York: Bantam, 1996.

Suvin, Darko. *Metamorphoses of Science Fiction: On the Poetics and History of a Literary Genre.* New Haven: Yale UP, 1979.

———. *Positions and Presuppositions in Science Fiction.* Kent: Kent State UP, 1988.

Van der Bogert, Frans. "Nature through Science Fiction." *The Intersection of Science Fiction and Philosophy: Critical Studies.* Ed. Robert E. Myers. Westport: Greenwood, 1983. 57–69.

Discomforting Creatures:
Monstrous Natures in Recent Films

Stacy Alaimo

The cover of the June 1998 *Audubon* provocatively asks "Who's Eating Whom?" As if in response, Peter Benchley writes that "for every human being killed by a shark, 10 million sharks are killed by human beings" (55). He claims that despite the fact that *Jaws* put his children through college, he "couldn't possibly write *Jaws* today. We know much more about sharks—and just as important, about our position as the single most careless, voracious, omnivorous destroyer of life on earth—that the notion of demonizing a fish strikes me as insane" (56). Despite Benchley's shift in perspective, he denies the cultural impact of his creation: "I have no sympathy with the few shrill critics who have long asserted that the appearance of *Jaws* abetted the destruction of sharks" (56).

If we take *Audubon*'s question to the movies, we find that humans, despite the overwhelming evidence to the contrary, are the endangered species. In analyzing several recent films, I would like to examine why, when humans are the "most careless, voracious, omnivorous destroyer of life on earth," that it is a myriad of other creatures who are demonized as such. Since, unlike Benchley, I believe that representations have material consequences, I think it is important to explore the cultural work of these discomforting creatures.

Ecocriticism, for the most part, has ignored monstrous natures, directing its attention toward texts that portray nature more favorably. Monster movies, however, could be the single most significant genre for ecocriticism and green cultural studies. Many of these films wrangle in messy but piercing ways with the fundamental issues of green philosophy and politics. Furthermore, the widespread appeal of these films suggests their cultural potency. Monster movies offer sometimes stunning insights into how the arguments, images, and rhetoric of environmentalism have been received; moreover, these films shape contemporary responses to environmentalism.

On one level, the environmental implications of monstrous natures are obvious—such representations vilify nature, justifying the slaughter of creatures we construct as repulsive. Carrollton, Texas, for instance, recently slaughtered thousands of egrets during their nesting season, calling the massacre Operation Remove Excrement. The "plot" of this incident echoes not only Alfred Hitchcock's *The Birds* but a slew of horror films featuring monstrous natures that must be eradicated. As Donna J. Haraway argues, "[m]onsters have always defined the limits of community in Western imaginations" (*Simians* 180). When films such as *The Beast, The Island of Dr. Moreau, DNA, Congo,* and *Mimic* portray nature as monstrous—as something that literally threatens human life and figuratively threatens the bounds of human subjectivity—they insist on solid divisions between nature and culture. Notwithstanding Jhan Hochman's provocative argument that culture is monstrous when it tries to "weld nature to itself through force and fantasy" (185), many recent monster movies conclude not with a smothering embrace but with a triumphant expulsion. Even though the monster movies of the late 1990s perform in some surprisingly subversive ways, the plots, settings, and camera work of most of these films distance humans from discomforting creatures. They undertake a kind of border work, dramatically distinguishing "man" from nature. Such plots, although they entertain the fear that humans are part of the nature they destroy, ultimately reassure us with a vertical semiotics, signaling that humans are free to float above the nature of the beast. *Habitat* and *Safe* undertake no such flight but instead dissolve the boundaries that demarcate safe spaces. Monstrous natures pose challenges not only for environmental politics but also for ecocriticism and theory since the very thing these creatures embody as horrific—the collapse of boundaries between humans and nature—is what many theorists, such as Val Plumwood, Carolyn Merchant, and Donna Haraway, promote. How effective can stressing the continuities between humans and nature be when popular films represent this kinship as beastly?

Making Men: A Cautionary Tale

Although Benchley asserts that he "couldn't possibly write *Jaws* today" because "the notion of demonizing a fish strikes [him] as insane," his 1996 film *The Beast* is a shameless remake of *Jaws*. The beast, in this case, is a giant squid rather than a huge shark, but the plot, several of the scenes, and the central characters remain the same. The gender dynamics of *The Beast*, however, are even more apparent than those of *Jaws*. The film opens with three scenes in which women, clearly, have far too much power, which sets up the "problem" that the film works to correct.

What is fascinating about this not-at-all-compelling film is that it contains a metacritical moment that critiques *Jaws* and nearly unravels the plot. At the town meeting, Dalton argues persuasively (at least to environmentalist ears) that they should just leave the beast alone, especially since killing the beast would also destroy all the fish—the source of the town's economy. He proceeds with an environmentalist moral: "It's payday folks. We trapfished our waters clean. The squid's natural source of food is gone. It's got nothing to eat so it's going after us. It's not a monster. It's just a hungry animal trying to survive." Imagine the film ended here. The townspeople wish their fellow creature well, stay out of the water for a while, and resume their lives after it departs. Or suppose that the film, midway through, gathered its forces and created some other plot, one that did not conclude with the destruction of "the beast." The film could then serve as an incisive rewriting of *Jaws*—a new kind of film that refuses to perpetuate the insanity "of demonizing a fish." Unfortunately for us as well as for the squid, the filmmakers exerted no such imaginative powers. The plot—the struggle to kill the beast—forges ahead, deaf not only to Dalton's words but to environmental discourses that advocate granting fellow predators space rather than obliterating them.

It is not just a failure of the imagination that propels the plot. Nor is it merely a recognition of the suspense, excitement, and sense of closure that such kill-the-beast plots proffer, since the pivotal issue, it turns out, is masculinity. When Dana, Dalton's daughter, accuses her father of being a coward, he somehow forgets what he had so passionately advocated a few scenes before and promptly enlists in the squid hunt. Dalton's determination to prove his manhood is purchased at the expense of an environmental ethos, which is blithely cast away like so much bycatch. Predictably, he kills the squid and becomes the town hero. Despite the machismo of organizations such as Earth First!, this film suggests that environmentalism is not a manly stance; leaving the beast alone does not a hero make, especially when masculinity is supposedly besieged by female power. And the beast, with her monstrous clitoral beak, is unmistakably female. Patriarchal order is magically reestablished once this unruly female nature is slain. The final scene rights the power "imbalance" that the first three scenes demonstrated, restoring "order" to the workplace and family. *The Beast* illustrates the prevalent practice of using nature as a site for man making, warning that it is crucial for environmentalism to interrogate dominant notions of masculinity—because the cost of producing such men is certainly too high.

While *The Beast* warns against dreadfully dilated female power, the 1996 *Island of Dr. Moreau* exposes how even diminutive females may be harboring beastly natures. Stranded at sea, Edward Douglas (David Thewlis), a United Nations peacemaker, is rescued and taken to an island by Montgomery Moreau (Val Kilmer). At first Edward finds the place much to his liking, inhabited as it is by an enchanting woman who whiles away the hours by dancing seductively. Soon, however, Edward stumbles upon a laboratory of caged animals, fetuses in jars, and a grunting, furry female—with rows of breasts—giving birth to a monstrous baby. Running from this scene, he tries to escape, only to encounter more humanish creatures sporting animal features—fur, claws, snouts, whiskers, and fangs. Dr. Moreau informs Edward that the island is populated with his "children," whom he created by fusing human and animal genes. The woman who so captivated Edward turns out to be Moreau's daughter and also, literally, "a real pussycat," as Montgomery had earlier quipped. As Edward falls in love with the daughter—an "absolute angel" according to her father—he reiterates that she is not like the others. As her teeth lengthen into fangs, however, she realizes she is "regressing," and she begs Edward to find the serum that will keep her more human. Ironically, Moreau had brought Edward to the island to serve as a source for this serum. The film concludes with a revolt of the beasts in which she is killed and Edward flees intact. Dr. Moreau's plan, however, suggests a more ominous ending: her humanity was supposed to have been secured by his death. This shadow conclusion suggests that women's humanity is—if not a fundamental impossibility—at least a serious threat to male subjectivity. Women, it seems, must serve as the border zone between nature and culture, keeping nature safely at bay in order that men can be fully human.

Escaping the Beast, or Vertical Visions

Such border work is common in contemporary horror films, which erect rigid distinctions between "man" and nature. Since the plots of many of these films are predicated on genetic engineering, it seems that they both express and ward off the fear that genetic manipulation will diminish the differences between humans and nonhumans, betraying how we, like other creatures, are an array of genes that can be reshuffled into disturbing configurations. Genetic engineering, like Darwinism, evokes tremendous anxiety about the fact that humans are inextricably bound to nature. Just as misreadings of evolution restore humans to the "top," where we stand as the pinnacles of a teleological process, monster movies work to reassert solid differences between humans and nature by visually mapping a vertical terrain. This semiotics of the vertical, which seeks to reestablish the difference between the "low" and the "high," is achieved primarily through setting and camera work. The vertical becomes a visual axis of meaning, a way to understand or amplify the significance of the plot. If, as J. P. Telotte argues, the "horror film functions best in its ability to toy with our vision" (389), one way in which recent monster movies control our sight is to grant us a transcendent gaze—most often employed in the conclusions—that removes us from the horror of the monstrous natures below. For example, several films conclude with comforting, triumphant scenes that visually distance the protagonists and the viewers from nature, rendering nature a nicely framed landscape that is not only distant but, significantly, below. Landscapes, unlike monsters, are devoid of agency; they neither chase us nor devour us, but instead, they remain quietly in the background. These visions of transcendence are no doubt impelled by the nagging fear that there is no escape from environmental devastation. This delusory cartography, however, has devastating implications for environmental politics since it suggests that humans need not worry about environmental woes, because escape is just around the corner.

The preferable vehicle for escape is the helicopter, which is able to fly straight up. *The Beast,* for example, begins and ends with a helicopter, and it is a helicopter that delivers protagonists from death. In *Carnosaur 2,* the contained space of the helicopter allows humans not only to literally escape from the perils of nature and technology but, more symbolically, to visually demarcate an unadulterated human subjectivity.[1] *DNA,* set in "a province of northern Borneo," depicts Balakai, a creature of indigenous myth whom Western scientists bring back to life. In order to obtain a rare beetle, a crucial ingredient in the resurrection of Balakai, the scientists must break down a solid wall that the indigenous people say should never be transgressed. One could be tempted to read Balakai as representing the horrors of Western weapons technology, since the scientists intend to sell it as a weapon (they liken it to the atomic bomb). However, the camera, early on, insists that nature is the source of Balakai's horror. The camera gazes straight down on a newly discovered skeleton, the bones of Balakai barely emerging from the earth. Indistinguishable from nature, the live Balakai mirrors the human in that its dinosaur-like head emerges from a two-legged, anthropomorphic body. The film conjures up the spectacle of this border creature—who disrupts the boundaries between human and animal, technology and nature, Western science and "primitive" beliefs—only to destroy it. Early scenes evoke a vertical semiotics, demonstrating that the ground is not only the origin of the monster but a dangerous place for humans, as an African American man is lowered underground in a cage in order to serve as bait for the creature.[2] A specular semiotics also establishes the significance of the ending, in that throughout the film we glimpse Balakai's jungle-immersed perspective—a strange, warped, neon-colored view in which the natural world is vertiginously immediate. Balakai's vision argues, by contrast, that humans cannot understand or maneuver without distance. The final scene promises "normal" vision: our vantage point begins above the tree line, and, significantly, we rise higher as we move further back. Helicopters, the quintessential symbol of transcendence, come into view at eye level, linking our superior vision to our technological advances and rendering nature a pleasant background.

Although the protagonists of *Congo* escape in a balloon rather than a helicopter, transcendence remains the answer to the "problem" of nature. *Congo* features Amy, a boundary-transgressing cyborg-gorilla—seemingly conjured by the theorist Donna Haraway's keyboard. Amy paints, looks at books, and, more important, speaks, as a virtual reality glove renders her bodily movements into words. Professor Peter Elliot (Dylan Walsh), a primatologist, explains that "what separated humans from animals" is "speech," but now "animals can talk." Peter hopes that Amy will be able to translate the thoughts of wild African gorillas; she may be a conduit for communication across heretofore unspeakable distances. Once Peter, Amy, and their entourage arrive in Africa, it is Amy who can get them across the border because the Africans "are afraid of being seen in an American movie being cruel to a gorilla." Amy—artist, translator, international ambassador—distinctly disrupts "the certainty of what counts as nature" (Haraway, *Simians* 142).

The patronizing depiction of Amy, whose virtual reality voice is that of a human child, and who repeatedly says things such as "Amy mother" (when she is not), contains her potentially subversive difference within a familiar familial structure; she is, at once, a good girl and an altruistic mother (nature). The plot, however, reveals that Amy remains a threat, despite her cloying portrayal, since Peter aims to restore Amy to her "natural" home in the Congo. When Peter removes her virtual reality glove in order to make her seem less odd to wild gorillas, the film begins to restore borders. Even more provocative, however, the film insists on the necessity of such borders by creating a species of killer gorillas that must be eradicated. Such monsters serve as Amy's shadow, warning us that the evils of nature forever lurk. When the group of humans encounter killer gorillas in the jungle, they must erect literal borders, "perimeter protectors," invisible and high-tech walls that repel nature's threats and demarcate a safe circle of culture.

Part of the horror of these evil gorillas is that they seem to live in a kind of "civilization," inhabiting rows of recesses within a cave and guarding diamonds in the center, similar to a panopticon reminiscent of the ruins of the Roman coliseum. When humans enter this domain, they are the ones who are seen, and being seen means vulnerability, usually death. Despite this temporary reversal of visual power, and notwithstanding the gory deaths of many of the humans, the film ends transcendentally. The evil gorillas are destroyed; Amy is now "home" with the good gorillas; and the protagonists float away in a balloon. The final scene restores the power of vision to humans, as they look down on Amy, who is now indistinguishable from the other gorillas. The boundaries between humans and nature are once again intact, as nature becomes a mere landscape, an expanse of visual pleasure that humans float above. *Congo*'s ultimate landscape, like that of *DNA*, is colored by the racist and colonialist assumption that nature is coextensive with the "third" world, a playland for tourists. One may visit nature for scenery or even adventure, but every trip concludes with leaving it far behind.

In *Mimic*, nature occupies the subterranean world of the New York subway system. The proximity of this monstrous nature to (American) humans makes even more urgent the plot to demarcate firm boundaries. The film begins by informing the audience that cockroaches (creatures who sneer at borders) were responsible for an epidemic that had killed thousands of children. Dr. Susan Tyler (Mira Sorvino), an entomologist, exterminated the roaches by genetically engineering a new species, the Judas breed. Three years later, Dr. Tyler talks with children in her laboratory, explaining "why she likes bugs so much." "Just imagine that you are one of them." The kids interject with a "normal" sense of disgust for insects—"eating furniture and stuff—that's got to suck." She protests, "No, no, no, don't judge them too quickly. These guys were building castles while dinosaurs were still wimpy little lizards." As they look at an ant colony, its tunnels exposed by the glass and its inner chambers revealed by video cameras, Dr. Tyler marvels that it is "perfectly balanced, and it's very beautiful." Aesthetic appreciation, however, is contingent on scientific vision, which offers a sense of control. For in the next scene, the illuminated ant tunnels become the deceptive darkness of the subways, and a woman mistakes a monstrous creature for a man.

Having evolved into a mimic, the Judas lurks around the subways, looking like a tall man in a long black raincoat. Its "face" is really a human-looking mask concealing its insect features; its coat is actually a pair of wings. The horror here is that this monster is frequently mistaken for a man. Even Dr. Tyler misjudges the Judas for a man, asking him for the time before he snatches her off to his den. Once below with the creatures, Dr. Tyler discovers to her horror that they have evolved lungs, making them less insect and more human. She tells her husband, Peter Mann, the policeman Leonard, Manny the shoe polisher, and his child Chuy, who have all ended up underground, that "the Judas evolved to mimic its predator—us." "These things can imitate us. They can infiltrate us and breed a legion before anyone would notice." Mimicry confuses categories in a particularly discomforting way, for instead of displaying their otherness, the creatures mirror back a human "self." Fearing that humans will fail to notice that their fellow subway goers are really giant insects, the group decides to destroy the Judas before it spreads further. Ironically, however, as they hole up in an old subway car, they must cover themselves with the odor of the Judas, rubbing the revolting scent organs all over their bodies in order to olfactorily code themselves as insects. The humans are forced to mimic the insects because "they won't attack you if they think you are one of them." In this underground world where the homeless live as "moles," and all people become prey to this man-like insect, the boundaries between humans and nature threaten to become imperceptible.

The film, of course, works to reestablish these boundaries. For example, despite the awkwardness, two of the six main characters are named "man"—Peter Mann and Manny. (The African American character, significantly, is not graced with this appellation.) Furthermore the vertical semiotics of *Mimic* charts a hierarchical relationship between humans and nature. Although the subway is a human creation, it is not only associated with the ant tunnels but is represented as dark, wet, and cave-like—a mysterious urban wilderness. The characters are terrified to fall down shafts and through broken floors into deeper levels of the subway system. Although the insect can fly, it is often represented as threatening from below. In contrast, the characters are recurrently rescued by being pulled upward, barely escaping the creatures' grasp. Notably, several characters voice their amazement that the Judas's excrement hangs from the ceiling—an aberration from the "natural" order in which feces, like insects, belong down low.

In one extraordinary vertical scene, Dr. Tyler screams up into a long pipe that leads to the street above. She can see people walking over the transparent cover, but they cannot hear her outcry. As she screams, the camera travels up higher and higher in the pipe, following her voice as it ascends, seemingly carrying it to freedom. But when the camera reaches the top, it reverses to look down on Susan, making her seem pitifully small. Notwithstanding Carol J. Clover's contention that "horror is far more victim-identified than the standard view would have it" (8), this scene joltingly severs that identification, catapulting the viewer upward in a kind of visual thrill ride. By privileging the viewer with this ascendant perspective, the camera distances us from the protagonist, reassuring us that Susan's predicament is not something we need fear and already suggesting a transcendent "normalcy" before the creatures have even been exterminated. Perhaps this nightmarish scene is also punitive, in that Dr. Tyler is the creator of these creatures. Manny, for example, is outraged to learn that she has created the Judas, "How could you do this? You take something and make it like a man who is not a man but a thing." The film punctuates Manny's sentiments as the creatures then attack, the horror screaming out the difference between a "man" and a "thing."

Where "woman" fits within this dualistic ontology is somewhat unclear, especially since the film counterposes Dr. Tyler's reproductive capacities with her ability to scientifically create creatures. In the beginning, for example, one of the Judas bugs in a jar haunts the foreground as her husband suggests they "have a couple babies of their own." The fetus-like Judas bug appearing in the next scene, however, hints that her scientific offspring supplant her ability to procreate. By associating Dr. Tyler with her monstrous progeny, the film can discipline her scientific pretensions while invoking woman as the uneasy, unstable, border zone between man and beast. The plot, though, graphically restores her maternal status when she stabs herself in the hand in order to lure the Judas away from Chuy, the boy. She rescues Chuy; Peter Mann blows up the tunnels and kills the beasts; and the three meet again on top, embracing as a reconstituted family. The triumphant embrace signifies an implosion of value, a smug turning away from all that is deemed outside the domain of the family. Such a conclusion no doubt plays to this era of "family values," which encourages us to ignore all that threatens outside the walls of the home.

No Place Is *Safe*

Habitat and *Safe* dramatize that the home, the sanctuary from supposedly external threats, is itself a monstrous place. Although they are quite different—*Safe* is serious and artful while *Habitat* is wonderfully silly—both films dramatize the impossibility of demarcating protected places and thus serve as potent counterpoints to prevalent kill-the-beast plots, vertical visions, and transcendent conclusions. *Habitat* is set in the future, after humans have destroyed the ozone layer and "the species that survived had to adapt to a life sheltered from the sun." "One of those species," the opening scene informs, "is us." The film begins with a scientist named Hank (Tcheky Karyo) lamenting that the world has gone from a "paradise to a wasteland in less than a century." Hank, determined to remedy the lack of green spaces, decides to "bring nature indoors."[3] Tinkering with powerful molds and viruses in his damp basement, he rants against ascendant aspirations: "fools, reaching for the stars when in every basement there's a garden of Eden." Hank manages to transform the house into an Edenic dwelling, a dense jungle overflowing with all manner of plants, flowers, vines, fungi, and insects. The house later transforms into a corporeal creature with walls of flesh, a being who defends itself against hostile forces by enveloping them. Nature dramatically demolishes the division between itself and culture, as the walls of the home—boundaries ordinarily meant to keep nature out—become the stuff of actively evolving life-forms. It is impossible for humans to transcend nature, not only because the home is rendered a "habitat" but because, as Hank's wife Clarissa (Alice Krige), who has a Ph.D. in microbiology, reminds us, our own bodies are teeming with creatures. We are covered with microscopic beings; our skin flakes are, in effect, miniature ecosystems, crowded with dust mites that "look like dinosaurs" or like "crocodiles with eight legs." While the film does depict a battle against the monstrous nature of the house, those who wage this battle are portrayed as fools. In a remarkable contrast to the transcendent narratives that firmly delimit a coherently "human" subjectivity, Clarissa and Hank disperse into the air, becoming disaggregated "swarms," "scattered throughout the elements." Although the house is demolished at the conclusion, "a whole new ecosystem" grows from its ruins.

Like *Habitat*, *Safe* demonstrates the futility of demarcating boundaries. *Safe* presents suburban housewife Carol White's environmental illness and her search, in vain, for a place that is "safe" from toxins. *Safe* may seem an odd film to include here, since it is certainly not a monster film in any conventional sense.

Yet, *Safe* can be viewed as a "muted version of the horror film" (Reid 34) and can be read as a critique of the plots, themes, and vertical semiotics of contemporary monster movies. The film even suggests its own oblique relation to monster movies when Carol (Julianne Moore) and Greg White (Xander Berkeley) listen to their son Rory read his report on gangs. Rory recites: "Rapes, riots, shooting innocent people, slashing throats, arms and legs being dissected, were all common sights in the black ghettos of L. A. Today black and Chicano gangs are coming into the valleys in mostly white areas more and more." As young Rory reads his report with an authoritative air, their Latina maid works quietly in the background, visual evidence that people of color are hardly a threat to upper-class Anglos. Carol does not notice the racism, but she objects to how "gory" his essay is, which, in a sense, echoes the essay's sentiments—just as whites do not want "others" intruding on their safe spaces, Carol does not want gore brought into her immaculate home. The film is only minimally gory—a few drops of blood, a couple of convulsions. The horror here is invisible, which certainly poses challenges for the filmmaker, Todd Haynes, who draws on techniques of the horror film to import anxiety into this staid and seemingly empty environment. In an early scene, the suspense builds and Carol screams, "Oh my God!" We wonder, along with Roddey Reid, whether Carol has "discovered the blood-spattered body of her stepson in the spotless décor." But no, it is "just an aesthetic horror. The wrong furniture had been delivered" (35). Since it is difficult to fix our terror on a sofa, the anxiety disperses, littering the entire space of the screen.

Carol's pristine home—not the black and Latino gangs—become the real threat. Even though a viewer attuned to issues of environmental racism will notice that it is people of color who work most directly with chemicals, Carol is the one who becomes violently ill. Her husband's deodorant, hairspray, and cologne; traffic exhaust; her perming solution; and even her new, but, as it ends up, "totally toxic" couch are all culprits. Although suburbanites may be obsessed with fear about encroaching and dark "others," their supposed refuges, the glaringly bright houses of Carol and her friends present the real danger. The houses stand as metonyms of a kind of toxic affluence, a late-twentieth-century glut of chemical consumption. Environmental illness epitomizes that humans are inseparable from their environments—there is no safe place, no possibility of transcending from the nature that is wracked with poison. Even when Carol flees to Wrenwood, a chemical-free desert retreat for the environmentally ill, she discovers that a highway is nearby.

What is most visually arresting about this film is its depiction of environment. The multitude of distance shots, in which Carol and other characters inhabit the background or the edges of a scene, emphasize rooms, empty spaces, and human habitats. In contrast to the vertical semiotics of monstrous nature films, *Safe* insists on the horizontal. The rooms within Carol's house are wide, flat, and long; the ceiling beams exaggerate the horizontal dimension. When Carol drives on the crowded southern California highways, we see the other cars from a driver's-eye view, not from above. When Carol has her first major attack, choking from truck exhaust, she heaves in the distance, as we witness the low, horizontal spaces of the parking garage. Whereas Reid argues that "space implodes" (42), I see the long, wide spaces expanding outward, denying the characters a place of shelter, even when, or especially when, they are within their own homes. The film also denies viewers their desire to demarcate or transcend. We are immersed within these unsafe spaces, where the threats cannot be seen or securely known. As Reid asserts, "Carol's multiple chemical sensitivity registers the collapse of modernist geography that was confident it could locate, make visible, and thus control social, biological, and ideological dangers" (42). Just as viewers cannot confidently find and thus command manifold dangers, we cannot securely classify or understand the protagonist, who dwells at the margins of the screen. Moreover, because it is difficult to identify with such a vacuous protagonist, the film encourages us to dwell, self-reflectively, within spaces, or environments. The almost complete lack of character development forces our attention outward in diffuse paths.[4]

That Carol hardly exists as a character forces us to attend to environments and deters our psychological analyses. Haynes plays up the vacuity of the character not to demean her but to criticize viewers' desire for psychological explanations. When we arrive at Wrenwood, the criticism of New Age psychobabble becomes much more pointed, as Peter Dunning (Peter Friedman), the Founder, forces his guests to admit that they made themselves sick through self-hatred, guilt, or refusing to forgive. The film ends with Carol moving into a safe house, the igloo-like shape of which denies all relationship to the desert environment. Carol, inside her supposed refuge, looks into the mirror and recites an affirmation: "I really love you. I love you." This creepy conclusion is an apt critique not only of the contemporary cult of the individual that seeks personal, rather than political, solutions for systemic problems but of monster films that quest to reinstate a clearly demarcated human.

Of Wandering Snouts and Muddled Middles

While it is important to recognize how *Habitat* and *Safe* counter recent monster movies, I do not want to conclude by leaving these two films in opposition to the rest, for monstrous natures may be more green than they seem. To be sure, films that represent nature as monstrous present a particular threat to environmentalism, as they directly contradict the ethos of environmentalism. For whereas most environmentally oriented advertisements, television programs, or direct-mail campaigns encourage us to realize our connection to and to take responsibility for ecosystems as far away as the Amazon or the Arctic, monstrous natures demand just the opposite. Natural creatures become the threat against which humans must defend themselves and from which they must distance themselves. The relentless verticality of films such as *Mimic* and *DNA,* which culminate in myths of triumphant transcendence, is particularly pernicious in that it applauds anthropocentric delusions of grandeur and the smug denial that humans are inextricably part of the nature we blithely destroy. Perhaps so many plots conclude with this notion of transcendence because these false borders must be continually shored up—the knowledge that economic, information, and environmental systems are global makes such borders impossible to sustain.

But as much as the border work of these films is fraught with a kind of bad faith, it does call into question one of the major strategies of environmentalist philosophy, the dismantling of the nature-culture divide. Val Plumwood, for example, argues for a recognition of "both the otherness of nature and its continuity with the human self" (160). Carolyn Merchant's "partnership ethic" is "grounded in the concept of relation" as a "mode of connection," recognizing both "continuities and differences between humans and nonhuman nature" (217). Donna Haraway's cyborgs, primates, coyotes, and "material-semiotic" actors all disrupt the boundaries between humans and animals, subject and object, culture and nature. But, as many monster movies dramatize, "not everyone likes being likened to lichen" (Manes 22). How effective can emphasizing the continuities between human and nonhuman nature be when so many popular films console by distancing and firmly demarcating?

Driven by escape plots and vertical visions, these films nonetheless are inhabited by remarkably potent creatures who embody—with a vengeance—the agency that much environmental philosophy emphasizes. As these creatures run, rampage, and scheme, they dramatize nature as an active, purposeful force—neither a benign landscape for quiet contemplation nor a passive, empty resource for human consumption. In a time when we are all too familiar with the dismal "images of ecology"—the "seabirds mired in petrochemical sludge" or the "fish floating belly up" (Ross 171)—perhaps monstrous natures are born from an identificatory desire to see nature not as pathetically damaged but as vigorously alive.

Focusing on the creatures—while they live on the screen—directs us to attend to the muddled middles of monster movies rather than to the tidy conclusions. As Cary Wolfe and Jonathan Elmer argue, "What horror suggests for ideology critique, then, is that the ideological 'point' of fictions may lie not so exclusively with the reimposition of ideological norms in the fiction's ending but rather with its complicated and contradictory middle, where identificatory energies are released and invested" (143). Even though *The Island of Dr. Moreau* ultimately insists on rigid borders, for example, much of the film seduces us with melting boundaries. Moreau explains that in order to eradicate the "monstrous elements in the human psyche," we must accept a "snout or hoof here or there." The odd snout or hoof, when emerging from an otherwise human form, reminds us that humans are animals. Notwithstanding that the film renders such a recognition horrific, the voyeuristic energy of the film depends on exhibiting an array of animal-human admixtures. If the film is at all compelling, it is the fur, the snout, and the hoof here and there that compels. Perhaps part of the specular pleasure comes in glimpsing "social and bodily realities in which people are not afraid of their joint kinship with animals" (Haraway, *Simians* 154). While these hybrid creatures are certainly spectacles, and while audiences have been trained to practice a distancing gaze, there is also a sense in which the viewer may experience a pleasurable sensation of identification with these creatures. The horror of the film depends on it. As Linda Badley contends, the "language" of horror is "somatic," in that horror is "a loss of ego in cellular chaos" (10). Viewers may experience a sort of visceral identification in which the boundaries of their own bodies seem to dissolve. As Elizabeth Grosz explains, "The melting of corporeal boundaries, the merging of body parts, the dripping apart of all the categories and forms that bind a subject to its body and provide it with bodily integrity" is an experience that "alarms and horrifies, and, at the same time, entices to the highest possible degree" (292). Perhaps, in the muddled middles of these films, viewers can experience a kind of corporeal identification with the monstrous natures—with Moreau's beastly humans, the two-legged Balakai, and the Judas bugs, insects who mimic and thus dissolve a stable sense of what constitutes a human being. Perhaps the horrific but pleasurable sense of the "melting of corporeal boundaries"—the visceral remembrance of a wandering snout—can catalyze some sort of resistance to the desire to demarcate, discipline, and eradicate monstrous natures.

Notes

1. See my article "'Endangered Humans'? Wired Bodies and the Human Wilds" for an in-depth analysis of the *Carnosaur* films.

2. Incidentally, this character does not make it out alive. The racial politics of many contemporary horror films are hardly subtle: African American women are nearly nonexistent and African American men meet gruesome fates.

3. See my book *Undomesticated Ground: Recasting Nature as Feminist Space* for an analysis of *Habitat* as a critique of environmental consumerism, "family values," and women's enclosure within the domestic.

4. See Roddey Reid for a more extensive analysis of how Todd Haynes works against "Hollywood's manipulation of the process of viewers' desires to identify with characters" (32).

Works Cited

Alaimo, Stacy. "'Endangered Humans'? Wired Bodies and the Human Wilds." *Camera Obscura* 40–41 (May 1997): 226–43.

———. *Undomesticated Ground: Recasting Nature as Feminist Space.* Ithaca: Cornell UP, 2000.

Badley, Linda. *Film, Horror, and the Body Fantastic.* Westport: Greenwood, 1995.

The Beast. Dir. Jeff Bleckner. Universal, 1996.

Benchley, Peter. "Swimming with Sharks." *Audubon* 100.3 (1998): 52–57.

Carnosaur 2. Dir. Louis Morneau. New Horizons, 1994.

Clover, Carol J. *Men Women and Chain Saws: Gender in the Modern Horror Film.* Princeton: Princeton UP, 1992.

Congo. Dir. Frank Marshall. Paramount, 1995.

DNA. Dir. William Mesa. Interlight, 1996.

Grosz, Elizabeth. "Animal Sex: Libido as Desire and Death." *Sexy Bodies: The Strange Carnalities of Feminism.* Ed. Elizabeth Grosz and Elspeth Probyn. New York: Routledge, 1995. 278–99.

Habitat. Written and Dir. René Daalder. Matarans, 1998.

Haraway, Donna J. *Primate Visions: Gender, Race, and Nature in the World of Modern Science.* New York: Routledge, 1989.

———. *Simians, Cyborgs, and Women: The Reinvention of Nature.* New York: Routledge, 1991.

Hochman, Jhan. *Green Cultural Studies: Nature in Film, Novel, and Theory.* Moscow: U of Idaho P, 1998.

The Island of Dr. Moreau. Dir. John Frankenheimer. New Line, 1996.

Jaws. Dir. Stephen Spielberg. Universal City Studios, 1975.

Manes, Christopher. "Nature and Silence." *The Ecocriticism Reader: Landmarks in Literary Ecology.* Ed. Cheryll Glotfelty and Harold Fromm. Athens: U of Georgia P, 1996. 15–29.

Merchant, Carolyn. *Earthcare: Women and the Environment.* New York: Routledge, 1995.

Mimic. Dir. Guillermo Del Toro. Buena Vista Home Entertainment, 1997.

Plumwood, Val. *Feminism and the Mastery of Nature.* New York: Routledge, 1993.

Reid, Roddey. "UnSafe at Any Distance: Todd Haynes' Visual Culture of Health and Risk." *Film Quarterly* 51.3 (1998): 32–44.

Ross, Andrew. *The Chicago Gangster Theory of Life: Nature's Debt to Society.* London: Verso, 1994.

Safe. Dir. Todd Haynes. The Chemical Films Limited Partnership, 1995.

Telotte, J. P. "The Movies as Monster: Seeing in *King Kong*." *The Georgia Review* 42.2 (1988): 388–98.

Wolfe, Cary, and Jonathan Elmer. "Subject to Sacrifice: Ideology, Psychoanalysis, and the Discourse of Species in Jonathan Demme's *Silence of the Lambs*." *Boundary 2* 22.3 (1995): 141–70.

Robert Frost, the New England Environment, and the Discourse of Objects

Kent C. Ryden

It is a common experience for walkers in New England forests to stumble across insistent material evidence of exactly what they were probably hoping to escape by taking to the woods in the first place: human manipulation of the natural world. Stone walls, cellar holes, barn foundations, and other such relict artifacts provide mute testimony to the agricultural history of the New England country-side, a landscape whose current green aspect was only made possible as farming became less and less viable in the region and farmers abandoned their fields to the advance of second-growth forests. To some observers, coming across something such as an old stone wall—a crafted artifact, an emissary of culture—may shatter any sense of sojourning in a natural environment. Looked at another way, however, a vernacular artifact such as a stone wall does not erase nature but rather helps us understand nature—or, more particularly, the attitudes toward and relationships with nature held in the minds of the people who create that artifact. As a cultural creation, an artifact is a material text just as a poem is a verbal text, and therein lies its ecocritical significance: as something created from natural materials that places people in a certain physical and imaginative relation-ship with the natural world, the artifact offers a window into human understand-ings of nature just as literature does. In addition, artifacts and literature can work together in mutually enriching ways. When writers include in their works both vernacular artifacts and the landscapes and cultural contexts within which those artifacts were created, they allow readers to appreciate not just particular well-rendered places, not just an author's valuation of the natural world, but the en-vironmental attitudes of entire groups of people and the understandings of na-ture that are encoded in the landscape itself. By writing realistically about artifacts that express specific cultural relationships to nature, authors serve as interpreters of material texts, providing ecocritical glosses on local understandings of nature and culture as made manifest in individual acts of making, building, and using.

Robert Frost affords a particularly instructive example of such an author. Frost, of course, wrote famously about New England stone walls in "Mending Wall" and also considers the implications of other kinds of vernacular artifacts in poems such as "The Ax-Helve." In these two poems, as well as in others from his long career, Frost creates poetic texts commenting on material texts, enabling readers to gain a deep and subtle perspective on those New England landscapes where nature and culture are so inextricably tangled. The meaning of the poem draws on the meaning of the artifact, and the artifact's significance is broadcast by the poem; in apprehending either, the reader grasps the other, as both work together to illuminate the complex intersection of life and landscape in a particular time and place.

Seeing Frost in this way also makes it less counterintuitive to include him in a book dedicated to moving "beyond nature writing." After all, many of Frost's poems focus on natural scenes and on the encounter of the human imagination with those scenes, and prominent ecocritics such as John Elder and Ian Marshall have written about him at length in their recent books. Poems such as "Birches" and "Desert Places," for example, use images and phenomena in the New England landscape—a tree bent under the previous winter's ice storms, a field filling with snow—to comment on aspects of human existence both heartening and sobering. In "The Most of It," Frost muses on the separation of humans from nature, noting that the universe does not offer "counter-love, original response," but rather a sort of powerful indifference as embodied by an enormous buck that swims and strides past the poem's longing human observer without acknowledging him in any way—"and that was all." Through both his subject matter and the range of attitudes he expresses toward it and explores within it, Frost could be counted as a nature poet without inspiring much argument from readers and critics.

And yet the poems on which his academic and popular reputation rests tend to concentrate not on the reflections of a solitary observer in the New England countryside but on the social world of rural New England, on the psychological and interpersonal conflicts and concerns of the men and women who live in that region's scattered farms and villages. As such, Frost focuses not so much on a separate and pristine natural world as on the social and cultural aspects of nature in New England. Significantly, Frost's 1914 collection *North of Boston*—which contains such oft-analyzed and frequently anthologized poems as "Mending Wall," "The Death of the Hired Man," "Home Burial," and many other dramatic monologues and dialogues—is subtitled "This Book of People," emphasizing that one of Frost's goals here (and in subsequent works) is to analyze and assess—sometimes critically, other times in celebration—the tenor of individual and collective life, thought, and character in his adopted northern New England homeland. As the critic John C. Kemp has commented, "his is not a world of orchards and pastures only. There is a social world, too, composed of men and women who struggle unsuccessfully to live and work together" while also experiencing "the good and bad of rural life, its joys and satisfactions, its fears and limitations" (127, 133). In crafting poems from his experiences and observations in New Hampshire and Vermont, Frost emerges as not so much a nature poet as a poet of the individual mind within the small local community. His countryside supports an entrenched rural population and is alive with the sound of human voices. Rarely does Frost simply present scenes of nature for their own sake; they always come to the reader filtered and mediated through some aspect of human presence, perception, and culture, be it that of a first-person speaker or of some other character or group of characters.

At the same time, the figures whom Frost includes in his "Book of People," as well as in his other New England poems, are grounded and located people; they are firmly embedded in a specific regional landscape by the circumstances of their lives and work and as such cannot be fully understood apart from it. Nature is everywhere in Frost's poetry, even when it is not the sole or even the primary focus of his work, but it is a nature that is deeply implicated in patterns of local life and economy. Any attempt to analyze the presence and meaning of nature in Frost's poetry must therefore do so within the context of, and in conjunction with, the specific regional culture that Frost draws on and depicts in his New England poems. And insofar as Frost portrays members of the rural New England working class, he creates figures who interact with their environment not only with their minds but also with their hands. As such, one central aspect of regional culture that figures repeatedly in Frost's poetry, and that has important implications for understanding his portrayal of New England cultural relationships with and attitudes toward the environment, is the traditional material culture of the rural landscape.

The New England that Frost constructs through words and images is to a great extent a world of objects, vernacular artifacts, material items built according to traditional standards of form, appearance, and use of the sort that were common visual elements in the regional world of which he wrote—stone walls, houses, barns, and tools, as well as other, temporary artifacts of farm operation such as haystacks and woodpiles. Moreover, these objects are not simply scenery, props that are scattered about in order to give an air of regional authenticity to poems that could otherwise have been set anywhere; in many cases, they are integral simultaneously to the action and the meaning of the poem. Frost's vernacular artifacts figure in his poems by recapitulating within those poems the same purposes they served within the local neighborhood cultures that produced them: not only the strictly functional purposes of accomplishing a specific task—shelter, boundary marking, some aspect of farm work—but the less immediately obvious purposes of communicating cultural values from maker to viewer or user and mediating simultaneous social and environmental relationships within the local landscape and community. Vernacular artifacts encode shared standards of seeing, thinking, and acting, and the extent to which individuals within the poems recognize these standards when they see or use those artifacts marks the degree of their membership in or estrangement from both the local society and the landscape in which that society lives. Seeing the ways in which Frost both recognizes this aspect of vernacular artifacts' meaning and builds poems around it provides another clue to our understanding of how his poetry was grounded in the textures of traditional New England life within a specific New England environment.

Think of the material, humanly constructed world of Frost's New England poems, one whose typical features are listed in the titles of poems such as "Mending Wall," "The Ax-Helve," "The Wood-Pile," "The Grindstone," "The Old Barn at the Bottom of the Fogs," "The Black Cottage," and "A Star in a Stoneboat." Consider, too, representative features that appear elsewhere as well, such as the loads of hay that Silas was so proud of building in "The Death of the Hired Man," or the old cellar holes in poems such as "The Generations of Men" and

"Directive." Independent of how such objects might be analyzed in more strictly literary contexts, material culture scholarship provides some theoretical frameworks for interpreting vernacular artifacts as cultural phenomena, frameworks that in turn shed light on the culturally precise ways in which Frost uses those artifacts in his poetry.

Vernacular artifacts—particularly the tools, buildings, stone walls, and other material culture found in rural agricultural communities of the sort that figure in many of Frost's poems—have much more than a basic utilitarian meaning. They can be seen not only as functional objects but as environmental texts of a sort, interpretive expressions of a local culture's working relationship with a particular geographical setting. Through their form and their use, they indicate cultural relationships with the landscape in several ways. Tools, shaped and reshaped over time to more efficiently work the land, encode a community's cumulative experiential understanding of the qualities, textures, and limitations of that land. In addition, any act of building implies an environmental ethic, a set of assumptions about what is right and proper to do to the nonhuman environment. Finally, the products of building serve to separate people from the world around them both physically and conceptually as they shelter themselves, exercise control over natural materials, and convert wild places into productive cultural landscapes. In addition to performing practical functions, then, these kinds of artifacts also communicate meanings and relationships. Through what the material cultural scholar Bernard L. Herman calls "the discourse of objects," they incorporate an "expressive or textual aspect" (5) directly into their physical fabric, a fabric drawn materially from the local environment that mediates both tangibly and imaginatively between its human makers and the natural world. And for an object to be discursive, it must not only communicate but also be easily understood; thus, in the vernacular world in which it was originally made and used, the artifact's discursive element would have been recognized as a matter of course, built into it in the process of its making, and read unself-consciously by its users. Interpreting the rural material culture of Frost's poems thus involves several aspects at once: recognizing its original social context as an interpretive framework, using the material object as a means of grasping larger cultural worlds, and studying an artifact's form and substance in order to see how a group of people located themselves both physically and imaginatively within their environment. The artifact connects people experientially to the landscape they inhabit; at the same time, as an aspect of culture, as an expressive text implying a receptive audience, the artifact connects them to the other people with whom they share that landscape.

Of course, artifacts such as buildings and tools and fences are not just disembodied expressions of culture, with their meaning locked in the realm of the purely symbolic. They are created to be seen, used, entered, and exchanged by the maker and his or her neighbors and thus figure crucially and directly, not just symbolically, in the fabric of daily life and work. In the face-to-face rural agricultural communities of the New England past of the sort Robert Frost observed and transmuted into poetry, one important aspect of artifacts was the role they played in negotiating, enabling, and expressing social interaction, and thus much of their meaning lies in, as Herman puts it, "the ways in which people employ objects in the organization of everyday social relationships" (8). They brought about, mediated, and facilitated social interactions and relationships by virtue of performing practical functions in the community, functions that took place in the context of local working and economic relationships as people entered each other's buildings, made or mended or lent tools, or helped each other design or build new farm structures. Material life and social life were thus inextricable in such farm neighborhoods. Artifacts figured directly in social process, acting as material catalysts to the negotiation of social relationships, thereby in the eyes of the neighborhood incorporating their discursive element directly into their physical fabric. A barn was more than just a barn, and a tool was more than just a tool. In deriving from and communicating relationships to the local landscape, the barn or the tool expressed a body of environmental perceptions and understandings; in being created according to shared formal and aesthetic standards, it provided a link to a collective way of looking at and thinking about the local world; and in being used in the course of daily life, it enabled one to claim a place simultaneously in the local environment and in the local social web of people whose cultural identity was closely tied to that environment.

This sort of framework for interpreting vernacular artifacts bears directly on an ecocritical reading of Robert Frost's poetry, a reading grounded not in abstract ideas about "nature" but in the specific ways in which nature, culture, and society interacted in the world of which he wrote. Many of Frost's New England poems center on questions of simultaneous social and environmental relationships, on a speaker or character negotiating a connection with, or demonstrating his distance from, a local rural culture grounded in and dependent on the New England landscape. Vernacular objects figure centrally in some of these poems, such as "Mending Wall" and "The Ax-Helve," insofar as they communicate cultural values and mediate social and environmental relationships, mirroring within the poems the function that they played in rural New England life. Speakers may express and negotiate relationships in language, but the poems contain a simultaneous discourse of objects as well as language, a material reference to a world of intertwined social interaction and environmental knowledge beneath the words of the poems, a cultural as well as physical reality against which the thoughts, actions, and verbal expressions of the speakers play off. Language and objects combine to form a single unified discourse, inviting an ecocritical approach that reads artifacts in order to read poems, that interprets material texts in order to more fully understand verbal texts. A poem such as "Mending Wall" lends itself well to a material culture approach to literature, in that a cultural analysis of one class of New England vernacular artifact, the ubiquitous stone wall, can be fruitfully applied to a reading of the poem. Whatever else the poem is about, it has a firm grounding in the circumstances of vernacular material and social life in the region, playing integrally on the local environmental relationships that lay at the heart of the regional culture that Frost attempted to grasp in poetry.

Stone wall building was a common part of rural New England material folk culture, and, in addition to their immediate functional purpose, walls carried two primary meanings within the communities in which they were made, seen, and used. First, the New England stone wall enacted and objectified the New England farmer's desire and ability to master his physical environment. Plucking from the ground the stones that made plowing and cultivation so difficult, the farmer made them obedient, turning them into a crafted artifact and converting them into an important part of the farm's operation. Walls enabled New England farmers to control and reshape the environment so that it would support an agricultural economy and be subservient to human needs and desires, and walled-in fields embodied order and cultural control over natural materials and processes. And just as stone walls expressed both physical and imaginative relationships between New England farmers and their environment, so too did they communicate and facilitate social relationships within the agricultural world that depended on that environment. Most New England farmers in the nineteenth century, when most walls were built, practiced a system of mixed agriculture under which they raised both crops and livestock, an arrangement whose success depended on keeping the animals and the plants strictly separate. This separation was vital not only to the operation of individual farms but also to their larger neighborhoods; if everyone was raising both crops and livestock, both agricultural success and civil order depended crucially on everyone cooperating to keep the animals from eating what was growing in the fields. In this atmosphere, a neat and strong stone wall carried practical, legal, and moral significance. It maintained social order and thus, in the historian Susan Allport's words, "was looked on as an index of a good and well-ordered settlement, a measure of a farmer's worth and capabilities" (20). Good fences, in this case, literally made good neighbors. Surrounded by these deeply significant objects, New England farmers were free to go about the rest of their daily lives, bound together by a world of artifacts created in the service of a shared environmental vision.

Read in this light, the speaker of "Mending Wall" is not just talking about a wall, not just musing on his relationship with his neighbor and with humankind in general, but is also revealing his relationship with a local and regional culture and the environment in which that culture is embedded. The poem's titular wall is richly symbolic, deeply metaphorical, but at the same time it has literal presence as an actual stone fence of the sort that was built all over New England, fences that communicated intertwined social and environmental meanings. The poem, of course, centers on a stone wall and on the speaker's questioning the need to repair it every year. Clearly, it no longer seems to serve the practical purpose for which it was created: as the speaker puts it,

> There where it is we do not need the wall:
> He is all pine and I am apple orchard.
> My apple trees will never get across
> And eat the cones under his pines, I tell him.
>
> (23–26)

The neighbor, however, famously replies, "Good fences make good neighbors." We know nothing of the specific past of these farms. Perhaps the wall's position between orchard and woodlot is a vestige of earlier New England pasturing practices whereby cows were often turned loose in the woods to forage but still had to be kept out of other people's property; or maybe an old pasture or field has become reforested after being taken out of production at some point in the past. Still, neither farm has an active dairying operation anymore, and so the wall's original purpose within a neighborhood system of mixed agriculture has vanished, as the speaker fully recognizes. He imagines himself saying to his neighbor, "*Why* do they make good neighbors? Isn't it / Where there are cows? But here there are no cows." The speaker's comments are fully accurate within the functional circumstances under which New England stone walls were originally created, and in his eyes, since those circumstances no longer apply, the wall is drained of meaning.

The speaker's approach to this particular artifact, then, is basically utilitarian—he judges it according to how well it does its job, or, in this case, whether it does a job at all—and it is locked in the immediate present. Since there are no longer any cows around, the wall is useless, a nuisance, a relic from an earlier time, and rebuilding it seems to serve no practical purpose. The speaker feels justified in completely dissociating the wall from the context of farm work and rural life by referring to the present-day act of repairing it as "just another kind of outdoor game, / One on a side. It comes to little more." Since the speaker sees the wall as having outlived its usefulness and its time, as having become freed from its original framework of meaning, it becomes available, in his mind, for him to assign meanings to it of his own, to transform it from a material, contextually situated wall into pure metaphor, a symbol standing for barriers between individuals in general.

> Before I built a wall I'd ask to know
> What I was walling in or walling out,
> And to whom I was like to give offense.
> (32–34)

The speaker's interpretation of the wall becomes decontextualized and highly individualistic, as he uproots the vernacular artifact from its landscape and freely bends it to his imaginative purposes. If he cannot find utility and positive meaning in the wall, it stands to reason that no other intelligent person should be able to either.

And yet, there is that neighbor on the other side of the fence, for whom it seems likely that the wall has significance not as an obsolescent farm tool but as a marker of local cultural identity and membership in a geographical place and a vernacular social system with deep roots in the past. His reiterated phrase, "Good fences make good neighbors," is perhaps more significant than the poem's speaker thinks it is. The speaker chides his neighbor (although not to his face) for not going, as he sees it, "behind his father's saying," but he is guilty of that same sin of omission, of seeing the aphorism as yet another outdated relic, as uselessly clung to as the wall, and he acknowledges no additional cultural significance supporting it. If "good fences make good neighbors" is, in fact, the neighbor's father's saying, it is possible that the neighbor is not clinging mindlessly to the outmoded, petrified forms of the past for no good reason but is keeping important aspects of the local past alive in the present. He maintains both traditional material practices toward the landscape and the environmental attitudes behind them while also renewing past structures of mutual work, interaction, and social obligation, even in the face of changing historical conditions. The immediate purpose behind the wall of both constraining nature and maintaining social order in a neighborhood system of mixed agriculture may no longer seem to be fully relevant in the eyes of the speaker. But repairing the wall's fabric keeps that vernacular way of seeing alive for those who understand the full range of the artifact's meaning, maintaining its legibility as a text for those who participate in the local culture.

And that participation is traditionally active: stone walls provided the ongoing necessity and opportunity for neighboring farmers to order nature together for their mutual benefit, to be not just two separate and independent husbandmen but partners. Through the act of maintenance and repair, neighbors were brought together in space, their mutual membership in the local community and culture emphasized and reiterated to them through the shared act of applying their shaping hands to the landscape, overcoming the natural forces that tear walls down by bringing the recalcitrant stones under control once more, and redrawing straight lines on the rugged land. As it provided a meeting point and a site of mutual labor, the wall literally made good neighbors, constructed neighborly relationships as an agent in an active process, and this was part of the meaning it expressed through its material form. This function of the vernacular artifact, its role in creating and maintaining local social structures through rein-forcing a common recognition and renewal of traditional relationships with the local environment, is still available in the world of the poem. And if the taciturn neighbor is sufficiently tradition-minded to say "Good fences make good neigh-bors" in the course of working, it is not unreasonable to think he might also be sufficiently tradition-minded to know the full depth of meaning behind that phrase, to link the phrase and the act of mending wall to the vernacular world and the regional landscape in which he and his father lived and to the environ-mental understandings that they shared.

Even if the neighbor is not that tradition-minded, the opportunity for creating neighborly links, forging connection to local society and claiming membership in a local culture remains, but the speaker of the poem refuses that opportunity. The wall is a cultural communication that he lacks the skills to read, and there-fore, both wall and neighbor remain incomprehensible to him. If he understood either the artifact or its maker, the other would make sense as well, but the speaker disdains even the possibility of understanding. Evidently there is such a thing in this neighborhood as "spring mending-time," a traditional part of the calendar year and the local round of work, and the speaker observes it to a de-gree. Ironically, the speaker is the one who lets his neighbor know when it is time to fix the wall again—but he does not seem to really know why, and he seems to have little interest in being there. The act of mending wall is an empty ritual to him, a deed with no social or environmental meaning; it actually seems socially destructive to him, symbolic only of erecting figurative barriers between people rather than forging and strengthening social links and environmental control as was central to its original local function. The wall remains unreadable to him rather than expressing a specifically place-based meaning and facilitating social relationships. In his illiteracy, the speaker demonstrates the imaginative distance at which he stands from the local New England landscape that surrounds him, as well as from the society and culture rooted there.

The speaker signals this distance elsewhere in the poem as well, of course, mostly in the tone and substance of his behavior toward and comments about his neighbor. He wonders if he "could put a notion in his head," but he seems unwilling to speak to him directly and to try to understand him, hoping he will say the desired things for himself. He sees the neighbor as almost simple-minded, repeating his favorite phrase only because "he likes having thought of it so well." Tellingly, he condescendingly and dismissively compares his neighbor to "an old-stone savage armed" who "moves in darkness as it seems to me." The phrase "as it seems to me" is important, for these subjective comments are wholly a matter of the speaker's interpretation; he decontextualizes and projects meaning onto his neighbor just as he does onto the wall, removing them from their time and place and reducing them to abstract ideas. In so doing, he distances himself from more than just a single New England neighbor. He holds himself apart from an entire environment and its attendant system of social and material discourse; he separates himself from a complex world of meaning in which vernacular artifacts such as stone walls played an important role, where the natural landscape was intimately known and carefully controlled, and in which handmade objects, in the process of embodying and transmitting this knowledge, perpetually made and re-made good neighbors. The speaker is a placeless person, alienated from his environment, and he is willfully ignorant of the meanings lodged in the landscape and in the artifacts that have been built from this landscape and that give it a human shape.

Even outside of established social networks, artifacts can be used as a physical means of transmitting environmental knowledge and establishing connections and relationships by virtue of their being passed from one person to another. Handmade vernacular artifacts are individual expressions even as they are contained within collective traditions; they are cultural communications passed from their creator's mind through his or her hands and released into the social world for others to grasp in their turn, using the artifact as a means of connecting physically, imaginatively, and socially with its maker. The artifact also connects people to nature, as its form is constrained by the maker's awareness of the capabilities and limitations of wood or stone or metal, a set of qualities and body of knowledge that are then implicitly communicated to the recipient as the artifact is passed from hand to hand. Frost places this complex process, the vernacular artifact acting simultaneously as an embodiment of natural knowledge and a means of establishing and expressing social connection, at the center of his poem "The Ax-Helve." The poem begins with the speaker being stopped in the act of splitting firewood by his French Canadian neighbor Baptiste, a man whose heavily accented speech marks him as an outsider in this Yankee neighborhood.

And yet the speaker, too, seems only slightly connected to the place. He is confused at first by Baptiste's actions, revealing how barely acquainted he is with his neighbor.

> I didn't know him well enough to know
> What it was all about. There might be something
> He had in mind to say to a bad neighbor
> He might prefer to say to him disarmed.
>
> (14–17)

The speaker's turn of phrase in these last two lines betrays a guilty suspicion that he might in fact be the bad neighbor in question. It turns out that Baptiste stopped the speaker because he could tell at a glance the poor quality of his machine-made ax handle and wanted to prevent an accident. He invites the speaker to his house, where he has never been before, in order to give him a good homemade ax-helve. The speaker accepts, although he retains at first his distance and diffidence: he agrees that his ax handle might snap at any moment, but then asks, "and yet, what was that to him?"

As it happens, safety is the least of Baptiste's concerns. His real desire is to develop a social relationship with his neighbor, to be more to each other than simply people who own adjoining property. And Baptiste does so through bestowing on his neighbor a handcrafted artifact that grows out of and demonstrates his awareness of the properties of the natural world around him, an ax-helve that he had carved with his own knife and his own hands. Baptiste is a skilled worker, a man who "knew how to make a short job long / For love of it, and yet not waste time either." Through long practice with local materials, he knows how to fit his carving to the grain of the wood in order to achieve the greatest possible strength, and—nervously, eager to please—he picks out his best piece from a bundle of handles to give to his neighbor, a piece that "[H]ad beauties he had to point me out at length / To insure their not being wasted on me." To the speaker, it may on the surface be just another ax handle, but Baptiste introduces him into his deep knowledge of wood and the aesthetic and technical standards that derive from that knowledge, the ways in which the handle is most meaningful to him as a craftsman. Through giving his neighbor the handle, Baptiste also reveals to him a facet of his mind, bestowing on him a segment of his working and imaginative life. Ax handles are meant to be gripped by their users, and so the gift is also a literal, tactile connection between one hand and another, a means of bringing those hands symbolically together. And the speaker by the end of the poem appreciates both

> the curves of his ax-helves and his having
> Used these unscrupulously to bring me
> To see for once the inside of his house.
>
> (87–89)

Once indoors, they have engaged in a conversation about knowledge and education, each perhaps now knowing and being educated about the ways of the other as well. Through his vernacular craft, Baptiste discloses himself to be deeply rooted in place, as rooted as the trees from which he carves his ax handles, and certainly more rooted than his neighbor who barely knows the family next door and gets his ax handles from a factory. By passing both an artifact and the environmental awareness behind that artifact to the speaker, then, by bestowing his gift and explaining its form and meaning, Baptiste also helps root his neighbor more firmly in place—materially, imaginatively, and socially. Here too, as in the case of stone walls, the vernacular artifact performs its neighbor-making function; drawn from the local environment, the artifact communicates cultural relationships both to that environment and to the people who live within it, inviting people to share in those relationships if they so choose.

Frost developed a version of nature poetry that was true to the place in which he lived, a place where notions of nature and culture were inextricable and in which eloquent material environmental texts lay thick on the ground. In such a world, his job as writer was to meld the material and the poetic text as completely as he could, providing close and sensitive readings of artifacts made from and found within the New England landscape. The ecocritical reader does well to approach Frost's work with the same sort of critical awareness of how words and things can inform each other when landscapes are transmuted into literature. In writing about vernacular objects in situations that approximated the ways they were actually used in their time and place, Frost gives those artifacts a voice within his poetry, recognizing their intrinsically discursive nature and allowing them to express the traditional roles and meanings they took on within a regional cultural context. Drawn and shaped directly from the landscape, objects such as stone walls or carved ax handles grow out of direct tactile relationships with the environment at the same time that they offer people a way of understanding and participating in a local social and cultural system that is firmly grounded in place. Those people in Frost's New England poems who remain deaf to the discourse of objects seem disconnected from both their physical and social environment, while those who grasp the meaning of artifacts inhabit the landscape deeply in imagination as well as enter more fully into a local society whose ways of living, and of getting a living, are grounded there. Understanding vernacular material culture helps us recognize the environmental perceptions and values of the people who make it, and, by looking at objects as material texts and seeing how a writer such as Frost incorporates them in turn into his poetic texts, we come to realize one significant way in which a "book of people," and the things that those people make with their minds and hands together, can also be read as a book about landscape, environment, and place.

Works Cited

Allport, Susan. *Sermons in Stone: The Stone Walls of New England and New York.* New York: Norton, 1990.

Elder, John. *Reading the Mountains of Home.* Cambridge: Harvard UP, 1998.

Frost, Robert. *The Poetry of Robert Frost: The Collected Poems, Complete and Unabridged.* Ed. Edward Connery Lathem. New York: Holt, Rinehart, and Winston, 1969.

Herman, Bernard L. *The Stolen House.* Charlottesville: UP of Virginia, 1992.

Kemp, John C. *Robert Frost and New England: The Poet as Regionalist.* Princeton: Princeton UP, 1979.

Marshall, Ian. *Story Line: Exploring the Literature of the Appalachian Trail.* Charlottesville: UP of Virginia, 1998.

The Poetry of Experience

John Elder

Entering the Field

"Go to grass. You have eaten hay long enough. The spring has come with its green crop." So Henry David Thoreau exhorts us in "Walking" (127). Both our institutions and we ourselves always require the refreshment of nature's present moment. Revelation subsides into theology and insight ossifies into a curriculum as surely as the newly gathered grass turns into hay. High time, once more, to walk back out into the mysterious, unmown field.

Over the past decade, many teachers and scholars have been trying to reconnect the study of literature with the living earth. The evolution of this project may be tracked by looking at certain terms that have dominated the conversation at different stages. "Nature writing" identified a lineage that ran from Gilbert White and Thoreau up through contemporary authors like Edward Abbey, Barry Lopez, and Terry Tempest Williams. By calling attention to the deeply rooted history as well as the continuing power of the genre, this term has helped literary studies to go beyond the conventional categories of poetry, fiction, and drama. It has celebrated a rich American tradition of reflective nonfiction, grounded in appreciation of the natural world yet also open to the creation's spiritual significance. The example of nature writing has also established a firmer connection between literature and the natural sciences, bridging the "two cultures" and fostering the development of interdisciplinary environmental studies programs in our colleges.

Nature writing continues to flourish, both as a form of writing and as a rewarding field of study. It has become clear, though, that this is not as comprehensive a genre as the name might suggest. It refers to just one variety of the personal essay rather than to the whole range of imaginative writing about the earth. In addition, for reasons the social history within Lawrence Buell's book *The Environmental Imagination* suggests, nature writing is a form that has been practiced largely by white writers. By using the more inclusive term "environmental literature," a number of scholars have sought to broaden the conversation. This has allowed for connections between Thoreauvian nature writing and treatments of nature in other genres. It has also called attention to many authors of color—including Zora Neale Hurston, Langston Hughes, Rudolfo Anaya, and Leslie Marmon Silko—who powerfully depict and reflect on nature in their novels and poems.

Another reward of this greater inclusiveness has been a fresh look at canonical literature in English. Increasingly, critics are investigating the place of landscape and natural history within mainstays of English literature such as Shakespeare, Milton, Wordsworth, Tennyson, and Woolf as well as in the work of Americans like Melville, Whitman, Dickinson, and Fitzgerald. The term "ecocriticism" has recently been adopted by some of these scholars, in preference to "environmental literature." It avoids any implication that "environmentalism," in the current American sense, was a concern for writers before the twentieth century. It also initiates a dialogue between literature and the science of ecology that offers critics a fresh perspective on topics such as metaphor and narrative form.

This progression in our language reflects both the ambition and the healthy self-criticism of this burgeoning scholarly field. It does leave out something crucial, though: the role of natural experience in the study of literature. However, such experience has not been lacking. Many of us who teach nature writing delight in outings with our classes, in order to ground our discussions in observations like those the writers themselves made. We have arrived at a point, however, where we need to begin integrating this experiential dimension of teaching and scholarship in a more strategic way. The increasing refinement of our critical terminology can be complemented now by an equally deliberate pedagogy. It may well be that the study of poetry, as the most distilled form of literature, will provide the best context for this next stage of development.

An emphasis on experience may protect against one danger in ecocriticism's emergence as a form of literary theory. Contemporary theory has certainly proven to be a valuable source of insight into literature. But it can also suffer from jargon, self-referentiality, and a narrow professionalism that are the opposite of nature writing's original, liberating impulse. This is why scholars and teachers must now undertake a determined, unceasing effort to ground criticism and teaching alike in the natural experience from which so much of the world's great literature has emerged. Authors such as Thoreau or Mary Oliver can inspire us to ventilate and invigorate the merely academic world. Carrying our reading, reflection, teaching, and writing out under the sky can remind us that this scholarly adventure is not about competing with other academic specialties and critical schools. Our central purpose should be renewing literary education and enhancing the vitality of our culture.

Scything

We gather just after sunrise on a morning in July, beside a dewy field of timothy in Craftsbury, Vermont. This introduction to handmowing is the opening session of Sterling College's Robert Frost Day. It has been organized by Sterling faculty member Ross Morgan, in order to offer participants a personal experience of this traditional mode of labor that figures in several of Frost's poems. Our instructors are Roger Shattuck, a noted literary scholar and critic from Lincoln, Vermont, and his son Marc, a welder from Richmond, Vermont, who is a champion mower in annual contests around the state. Roger became interested in handmowing over thirty years prior to this July morning, when he was looking for a way to keep down the tall grass around his family's cabin. He bought a scythe and became acquainted with the local community that preserved and passed along the art of using such a tool. He also discovered that he had both an aptitude and an appetite for this rhythmic, physically rigorous, and surprisingly effective way of sheering off ripe stems of grass and grains.

The Shattucks demonstrate to our group how to cut a swath. Plant your feet so that you are facing directly toward the row to be mown, then advance in a slow shuffle. The blade passes through an arc that leaves a cleanly mown edge a foot or more to your right and gathers each stroke's sheared grass into a windrow about the same distance to your left. Skilled scythers achieve a surface as close and smooth as any push mower or power mower could accomplish. And while mechanical mowers do their best work when the grass is totally dry, it has always been the practice of hand mowers to go out after a rain or, as we are doing now, just after dawn when there is a heavy dew. The wet stalks are heavier and less likely to bend before the scythe's sweep. Our teachers pronounce three watchwords as the rest of us pick up our scythes and try to imitate what we have just observed: "polish," "slice," and "pivot."

Both the point and the heel of the blade are always held in contact with the ground, with no tilt and no lift for a backswing. This continuous motion burnishes the blade's bottom surface and sends a vibration up through your arms as you move forward. The grass is sliced, not chopped, with the blade sliding through the stems at an angle, from point to heel, rather than meeting them squarely edge on. Then it rustles back over the stubble at exactly the same height in preparation for the next slice. This dialogue with the grass makes a rhythmic, sibilant sound that is one of the distinctive pleasures of handmowing.

"Pivot" refers to another sensual attraction of such work. The power comes not from the movement of your arms but from twisting back and forth at the waist. Turning your torso smoothly left and right, you shuffle forward with knees springy and slightly bent, leaving two dark, shiny tracks in the shorn grass between windrows. This is the whole dance, with the work always out in front, the harvest collecting to your left, and the scythe's whisper music pulling you farther and farther into the mystery of the grass. After we have been practicing for a while, a few of us line up side by side, although staggered to give safe clearance to our blades. We advance together like Vermont contradancers, leveling a smooth floor within the field.

In the discussion that followed, after we had taken a break for breakfast, several of Frost's poems were considered, including that wonderful one "The Tuft of Flowers." But the poem that was most enriched for me by the experience of handling a scythe in the dewy grass was "Mowing," from Frost's 1913 volume *A Boy's Will:*

> There was never a sound beside the wood but one,
> And that was my long scythe whispering to the ground.
> What was it it whispered? I knew not well myself;

Perhaps it was something about the heat of the sun,
Something, perhaps, about the lack of sound—
And that was why it whispered and did not speak.
It was no dream of the gift of idle hours,
Or easy gold at the hand of fay or elf:
Anything more than the truth would have seemed too weak
To the earnest love that laid the swale in rows,
Not without feeble-pointed spikes of flowers,
(Pale orchises), and scared a bright green snake.
The fact is the sweetest dream that labor knows.
My long scythe whispered and left the hay to make.

(*Early Poems* 24)

Though I had long loved this poem, the experience of mowing the hayfield in Craftsbury helped me enter into it and appreciate it in a new way. As we learned to keep the blades of our scythes down, we advanced from the percussiveness of swinging and chopping to a continuous, beautiful rustling. This subtle sound was the surest guide to effective technique. The words "whispering" and "whispered," which Frost employs in the second, third, sixth, and fourteenth lines of his sonnet, are arguably the most important in the poem. Most readers surely feel their mystery, their suggestion of meanings just out of earshot that the poet, with his chosen stance of "enigmatic reserve," will never make wholly plain. But the experience of working with a scythe helped me to relate that mystery to the subtle pulse of a keen blade sliding along the ground.

In the 1987 "Voices and Visions" documentary on Frost, Seamus Heaney expresses his admiration for the whispering scythe of "Mowing": "It's not writing school proficiency of mimicking the movement of a mower by the line breaks. It's a deeper rhythm of labor . . . the slightly lulling, consoling rhythm of a repeated motion." "What was it it whispered?" evokes with a special precision the mower's experience of pivot and reverse, with its shift of syntax and direction between the word "it" and its reiteration. Heaney singles out this question in Frost's third line for special appreciation, commenting, "It's colloquial. It does have the spring of spoken English about it." Heaney's connection here between the rhythm of mowing and the spring of language reflects the fact that he, like

Frost, is a poet who knows the countryside through physical labor as well as through language. But Frost's eloquent formulation penetrates even more deeply for me now that I can bring my own physical experience to bear—remembering mowing in the glow of my back and arms and in the throbbing pulse that echoed an hour spent wading through those subtle waves of sound.

The notable emphasis on sound in this poem is of course set up by the first line: "There was never a sound beside the wood but one." This line also highlights the solitary state of the mower. When Frost was farming in the early years of the twentieth century, haying in the main fields would already have been carried out by a cutting machine pulled behind a team of horses. By the 1920s and 1930s, such a cutter would more frequently have been pulled behind a tractor. Wet ground, low ground, uneven ground, and little strips of meadow between the woods and a road would have been relegated to an individual worker with a scythe. It was the fact of working away from the clash of machinery and the roar of motors that allowed the solitary speaker of "Mowing" to clear the whispering and to reflect on the significance of this dialogue between scythe and ground. Such an experience must be rare for most of Frost's readers today. Our own work out of doors so often involves the noise of engines, and our experience of solitude in nature is, conversely, more often associated with recreation than with work.

The urgent physicality of labor powered by muscles, not gasoline, is implied by the fourth line: "Perhaps it was something about the heat of the sun." The day is already far enough advanced for the sun to be warming the scene. In part, though, this remark about the heat may be a token of the muscular effort associated with the speaker's "long scythe whispering to the ground," as he bends over, holding the handle away from his body and pivoting back and forth from the waist. It is also a reminder that the haying must be done before the grass is so dry that it will not shear off cleanly and so that the windrows will still be able to bake in the sun when the mower leaves "the hay to make."

After that morning in Craftsbury, I was incautious enough to mention to one Frost scholar that the experience of mowing had opened up new dimensions of the poem to me. His rejoinder was, "The scythe in that poem means one thing and one thing only." And of course it is true that Frost is continually alert to shadows of mortality. Whenever I hear the phrase "Et in Arcadia ego"—death's warning not to be lulled into a carefree state by the beauty of a pastoral land-scape—it is always in that poet's dry Yankee accents. But the fact remains that a scythe is a tool as well as a symbol, that it was used by the poet himself in hand-mowing, and that its sound and technique informs both the music and the emotional tone of the poem.

There is a tricky balance to observe here. In the same "Voices and Visions" documentary about Frost, William H. Pritchard calls attention to the period that decisively separates the sonnet's last two lines: "The fact is the sweetest dream that labor knows. / My long scythe whispered and left the hay to make." The poem transcends the experience of labor, as Pritchard insists: "The scythe is just going on, just making its sound, finishing its task . . . . It's really the poet who makes poetry. Not nature, not scythes" (Pritchard 27, 28). My purpose in the present reading is certainly not to reduce the poetry to its germinating instance. Rather, it is to suggest the value of cultivating, in our physical experience, an appreciation of the soil from which the art has sprung. William Meredith, who is also interviewed in the documentary, refers to Frost's characterization of poetry as "the transition from delight to wisdom." This is a helpful way of formulating the never resolved yet intimate relationship between a finished poem, with its tempered complexity, and the surges of impulse and experience that inspired it and that are perpetuated within it.

Frost's line "The fact is the sweetest dream that labor knows," with its Shake-spearean resonance, sums up the importance placed on work in "Mowing." Neither the lure of idle hours nor a fantasy of fairies would be satisfying to "the earnest love that laid the swale in rows." Frost understands the erotics of work—exertion pressing forward to culmination. Satisfaction lies—and lays—in finishing the job at hand, not escaping from it into a pastoral illusion. Any reading of Frost's poetry that reduces the physicality of the landscape or the labor of farmers to nothing more than intellectual argument or abstract music is a fantasy in this sense—an escape from the texture and solidity of fact. Both work and nature are more than tropes for this poet. They are the world, one in which poetry is grounded and by which it is inspired. Through the music and mystery of poetry we are enabled to re-enter nature with renewed senses and with a heightened capacity for wonder.

Once the experience of handmowing had enhanced my sense of the sonnet's achievement, by placing me in the wet field at dawn, I found that the specific ecology of that New England scene also emerged with comparable concreteness. Frost is one of the most gifted and precise naturalists among our poets in English. Over the past twenty-six years of living and teaching in Vermont, I have come increasingly to rely on him as a guide to the geology, forest history, agricultural history, and what Linnaeus would call its "floral calendar." An allusion in Frost's poetry to a flower is never merely decorative or incidental, despite what many critics seem to assume. It tells an ecological story and evokes a particular living community.

An example comes in the lines "Not without feeble-pointed spikes of flowers, / (Pale orchises), and scared a bright green snake." I looked up pale orchises in my *Newcomb's Wildflower Guide,* since it was not a plant with which I was familiar. I found that the Tubercled, or Pale Green, Orchis *(Habenaria flava)* raises a slender flower spike above a couple of well-developed basal leaves and that it grows in moist meadows during late spring and summer. A swale is the older, more poetic name for a wet meadow or low ground. It describes both the sort of terrain where a solitary hand mower would have been called for during Frost's early years as a farmer in northern New England and the environment in which this flower, with its "feeble," sinuously slender stem, would have grown. The "bright green snake" is a similarly precise and telling reference. Vermont has relatively few reptiles—and no native lizards at all. The green snake *(Opheodrys vernalis)* was a fairly common sight until the latter part of the nineteenth century—often spotted by scythe wielding mowers as it slithered ahead of them into the still-uncut grass. With the advent of mowing machines, green snakes have become much rarer. They are not fast enough to elude those mechanical blades with the same success they had in staying ahead of a shuffling, deliberate human laborer.

Pale orchises and bright green snakes are the "facts" that Frost labors to encompass in his verse, along with the ecosystem and the agricultural economy in which they would likely be encountered. Marianne Moore described poems as imaginary gardens with real toads in them. But Frost's swale, snake, and orchis are at once concrete, closely observed, and precisely related to the human labor proceeding around them and in their midst. Because his poetic landscapes resolutely avoid "anything more than the truth," they can balance and sustain the ambiguity, and ambivalence, about spiritual meaning that is so central to his poetry.

Windrow

A single morning's workshop on scything could never make anyone a competent mower. But my purpose has been to show that even a brief exposure of this sort can illuminate a poem such as "Mowing." One implication may be that those of us who teach writers as sensitive to the living landscape as Frost should systematically integrate field trips and other outdoor experiences into our courses. This could simply be an occasional outing with our students to experience some phenomenon that figures in the literature we are reading. Excursions of several days would be even better although harder for most teachers to manage during the regular academic term. Regardless of the length of a class's time outside, however, the goal would be the same: to experience personally the images and rhythms we meet again on the page. We dwell in a poem so that the world, with all its other poems, may be renewed. Just so, we can return to poetry with fresh appreciation once we are regrounded in the earth. As John Dewey insisted, the most vital education grows out of the "play of mental demand and material supply" (107).

Such play becomes especially striking when Frost couples his close observation of the New England countryside with pointed allusions to the English poets. Robert Faggen suggests, for example, that there is a connection between the imagery of "Mowing" and a line in Samuel Coleridge's "Christabel": "When lo! I saw a bright green snake" (*Early Poems* 265). Frost's line is enriched both by the poetic echo and the precise and appropriate placement of this snake in the unmown grass of a New England swale. A similar effect of compounding can enhance the experience of readers as well. Just as natural phenomena can reground a poem's language for us, so too can poetry mediate and heighten our awareness of the living earth.

An even more intriguing connection arises between the fourth line of "Mowing" and the first stanza of a song from *Cymbeline:*

Fear no more the heat o' the sun,
Nor the furious winter's rages;
Thou thy worldly task hast done,
Home art gone, and ta'en thy wages;
Golden lads and girls all must
As chimney-sweepers, come to dust.
(qtd. in Kenner 121)

As Anne Ferry has discussed, Frost was particularly devoted to Francis Palgrave's *Golden Treasury*, often imitating, responding to, or alluding to lyrics in this collection. The fact that this selection from Shakespeare was included in Palgrave's anthology (under the title "Fidele") thus heightens the possibility that Frost intended such an echo within his poem. I take a special interest in this association because of a story Hugh Kenner relates to the same stanza from *Cymbeline*. After celebrating the song's evocation of golden youth and its passing, Kenner goes on to tell that

> in the mid-20th century a visitor to Shakespeare's Warwickshire met a countryman blowing the grey head off a dandelion: "We call these golden boys chimney-sweepers when they go to seed."
>
> And all is clear? They are shaped like a chimney-sweeper's broom. They come to dust when the wind disintegrates them. And as "golden lads," nodding their golden heads in the meadows around Stratford, the homely dandelions that wilt in the heat of the sun and would have no chance against the furious winter's rages, but need never confront winter because they turn to chimney-sweepers and come to dust, would have offered Shakespeare exactly what he needed to establish Fidele's death in *Cymbeline* as an easy, assimilable instance of nature's custom.[1] (122)

In reading Shakespeare's verse today, as in reading Frost's, most of us run the risk of missing an entire range of concrete reference, because of our separation from the seasonal rhythms and tasks that informed the poets' lives. When we do experience these things for ourselves, however, we discover even in poems we have lived with for years that the metaphors become more satisfyingly extended, the descriptions more sharply focused and arresting.

The importance of natural experience within the total meaning of a poem is shown especially clearly by Frost's "The Need of Being Versed in Country Things." The best-known lines in this poem come at its characteristically round-about ending: "One had to be versed in country things / Not to believe the phoebe wept" (*Early Poems* 263). The poem as a whole is as sly and irreducible as any by this supremely cagey poet, being at once a meditation on the emotional meaning of nature and a stringent insistence that such meaning reflects our basic ignorance of nature. Standing beside an abandoned house—so naturally associated for us with the sadness of loss, separation, and departure—we too easily hear in birdsong the weeping of former inhabitants or the sighing of visitors like ourselves. We project a human presence on the otherness of nature. But conventional academic readings of Frost, which delight in the poet's sardonic debunking of the pathetic fallacy, too often stop there.

Frost's art circles around and around between the essential unknowability of the world and the perpetual suggestiveness of natural phenomena. Appreciation of this quality of suspension within his poetry depends on registering his natural details in their concrete particularity. As far as the standard, reductive reading goes, the word "phoebe" could as well be replaced by "birdy." "Robin" or "starling" would also do, if rhythm were all. But the fact is that those other birds would not do. Here is where a late spring or summer field trip to one of the sugarhouses, hunting camps, or abandoned farmhouses that dot the New England woods might enhance students' experience of the poem.

Frost places the phoebe *(Sayornis phoebe)*, as he did the orchis and the green snake of "Mowing," in exactly the habitat where it belongs. It likes to nest under the eaves of buildings far from the road and close to the woods. Phoebes are easy to observe, and students will note their nervous habit of wagging their tails, their frequent shiftings from perch to perch, and the constant, plaintive up and down of their songs: FEE-be, fee-BE. The phoebe is an unostentatious bird. The feathers of its head, back, and wings are brown with an olive cast and those of its breast are creamy. A robin may have a name that would satisfy a critic looking for no more than a trochee in that line of verse. But its vivid red breast makes it much more of a visual presence and its full-throated, melodious song could never be mistaken for weeping, no matter how melancholy the human observer or the scene.

The nondescript phoebe, by contrast, has a reedy repetitiveness that can sound heartsick, or even desperate, to a susceptible human. Being "versed in country things" can help us remember that this call is most likely a territorial assertion—translatable as something like "I am here now." Without having heard the phoebe's distinctive song, though, a reader might miss the poem's emotional tension and subside into the equally "unversed" sentimentality of hearing no bird beyond the one on the page. Just as our projections onto nature are invariably skewed, so too our readings abstracted from nature are impoverished. Frost offers us the experience of particular natural environments as provocations to our own perpetually personal utterances. With his beloved Virgil, Frost finds in the world "the tears of things, mortal affairs that touch the mind." He knows that the tears may have less to do with nature than with the particular human stories that surround an onlooker—as is also true in the *Aeneid.* But the mortality, and the manifold individuality, of the natural creation are much more than projections.

Frost is piqued by the disjunction between suggestions of weeping in a bird's call and the otherness of the bird's life, just as he is by the insistent but untranslatable conversation between the scythe and the ground. Robert Penn Warren declared that to be a poet was to stand in the rain every day, in the knowledge that sometimes lightning would strike. Frost's poems include both the lightning strike and its afterimages against retina and optic nerve. To be alert and receptive readers of his poetry, we too need to venture out under the sky, into rain and sun. We need to hear the distinct calls of specific birds, to startle and be startled by snakes appearing at our feet. To confine our readings and reflections to the library or classroom—as if we had neither arms to swing a scythe nor legs to step forward into the mystery of dewy, snake-braided grass—would be an impoverishment. It would be like the diminishment of weeping in a world where no phoebes nest.

Thoreau adds the following remark to his celebration of the spring's green crop: "The very cows are driven to their country pastures before the end of May; though I have heard of one unnatural farmer who kept his cow in the barn and fed her on hay all the year round" (127). Grand enclosures against the weather are an essential part of the agricultural, and the educational, year. But no barn, whether we call it the Western canon, ecocriticism, or environmental studies, should confine us from enjoying our country pastures. Students and teachers must all remember, from time to time, to go to grass.

Note

"The Poetry of Experience" by John Elder originally appeared in *New Literary History* 30:3 (1999): 649–59. Copyright the University of Virginia. Reprinted by permission of the Johns Hopkins University Press.

1. The visitor in question was William Arrowsmith.

Works Cited

Buell, Lawrence. *The Environmental Imagination: Thoreau, Nature Writing, and the Formation of American Culture.* Cambridge: Belknap-Harvard P, 1995.

Dewey, John. *Dewey on Education.* Ed. Martin S. Dworkin. New York: Columbia UP, 1959.

Ferry, Anne. "Frost's 'Land of the Golden Treasury.'" *Under Criticism: Essays for William H. Pritchard.* Ed. David Sofield and Herbert Tucker. Athens: Ohio UP, 1998. 249–65.

Frost, Robert. *Early Poems.* Ed. Robert Faggen. New York: Penguin, 1998.

Heaney, Seamus. "Visions and Voices: Robert Frost." National Endowment for the Humanities and the Annenberg/CPB Project. 1987.

Kenner, Hugh. *The Pound Era.* Berkeley: U of California P, 1971.

Pritchard, William H. *Frost: A Literary Life Reconsidered.* New York: Oxford UP, 1984.

Thoreau, Henry David. "Walking." *The Natural History Essays.* Salt Lake City: Peregrine Smith, 1980. 93–136.

Performing the Wild: Rethinking Wilderness and Theater Spaces

Adam Sweeting and Thomas C. Crochunis

Theatrical realism may seem an odd place to begin a discussion of new ways to imagine and conceive wilderness. With its rows of seats in the audience and its performers on the stage, a conventional realist theatrical space appears far removed from the wild. Indeed, the technologies of order and control that seem necessary in the production of a realist play are diametrically opposed to the apparently unregulated workings of the natural world that creators of official wilderness zones seek to uphold. But when we examine more closely the conventions of both the realist stage and designated wilderness zones, we find parallels that reveal how carefully constructed human performances are essential to both kinds of spaces. As we argue in this essay, ecocriticism, by helping us perceive how these performances unfold, can transform our experience of both theater and the wild.

A few definitions are in order before we begin to explore these parallels. First, when discussing wilderness zones we are considering places that have been carved and framed through legislative or executive action. The largest and best known of these spaces can be found in the fifty-seven million acres currently protected from all future development by the U.S. Wilderness Act of 1964. We view these zones as examples of a space-based notion of wilderness because they locate the wild within specific geographic confines. We then relate this idea of wilderness space to the rhetorical strategies of naturalist and realist theater. Since theater scholars do not consistently distinguish the two terms, we use "realism" to refer to the set of theatrical conventions with which most of us who know Henrik Ibsen's or Arthur Miller's dramas are familiar. We reserve the term "naturalism" for a type of realistic drama whose late-nineteenth-century European proponents—best exemplified by Émile Zola and August Strindberg—articulated a clear political and philosophical program. As we will show, the historical context out of which theatrical naturalism emerged is essential to understanding both why space functions as it does in conventionally realistic drama and why we have chosen to compare these strategies of theatrical performance to wilderness spaces.

At least three structural similarities link the familiar conventions of theatrical realism with space-based notions of wilderness. First, both rely on rigidly dualistic conceptualizations of space. In a typical realist performance, a plane defined by the proscenium (the architectural arch along which the curtain is drawn) separates the audience from the stage, differentiating performance and audience from each other both conceptually and spatially. The audience, playing its role as visitor, views the lives enacted as if through a "fourth wall." Similarly, wilderness zones, by definition, are bureaucratically distinguished from the land from which they have been carved. A second similarity between these spaces stems from the way our experiences of both efface the cultural assumptions and structures that shape our performances, encouraging audiences or wilderness visitors to observe events as though they simply unfold on their own. Theater audiences, for example, are discouraged from noticing how a performance's rhetoric produces conditions that shape how onstage "life" is perceived. Realist performance assumes that both actors and audiences will efface the social logic that brought them to the theater in the first place. Audiences familiar with the rhetoric of acting that emerged from stage realism expect performers trained in the lineage of Stanislavskian or American Method acting to display their professionalism by gesturing and moving across the stage as if their relationship to the audience did not follow strict conventions. And finally, both realist stages and wilderness spaces limit perspective and authorize what audiences are allowed to see and hear. Both employ a rhetoric of space that naturalizes what is seen and heard and that disregards the structures of performance that shape perception. For this reason, the analogy between realist theater and wilderness spaces can raise several important questions about how space functions as part of ecocritical thinking.

Wilderness Space and Theatrical Space

Most critiques of officially created wilderness zones argue that such spaces dichotomize our view of the wild. For example, legislated wilderness zones such as those created by the Wilderness Act of 1964 separate spaces that the culture deems wild from areas that it does not. Spatial divisions such as this resemble naturalist drama's separation of the audience from the performer through the architectural imposition of the proscenium. Moreover, both wilderness zones and naturalist theater divide space into a clear "here" and equally obvious "there" in order to establish the conditions of our gaze. Less remarked on, however, are the ways in which wilderness zones, like naturalist theater, depend on a process of effacement. By assuming the existence of places outside and beyond human effect or interest, the Wilderness Act asks us to turn our backs on the history of human involvement in the landscape, for the things that constitute wilderness—plants, soil, creatures—must be posited to exist in a state that can be legislatively cut off from past or ongoing human influence. When wilderness is envisioned as a place apart, the human audience cannot be seen as part of the performances of the wild without breaking down the dualistic logic that separates what stands "here" from what appears "there."

Some writers sympathetic to environmental concerns have critiqued wilderness zones for what might be called their representational aesthetic, arguing that spatialized wilderness misrepresents the wild. When considering the National Bison Range in Montana, for example, Donald Worster asks whether the protected animals have become "only a marginally wilder version of domesticated cattle" (82). Removed from the larger workings of the land and from some typical influences of human creatures, they become cross sections or observable slices of life, something akin to the characters of naturalist drama. The philosopher Thomas Birch has used even stronger language to condemn what he calls "the incarceration of wildness" that the Wilderness Act brought about by the spatial segregation of the world into sacred and profane spaces (339). While space-based wilderness legislation scales wildness to human dimensions, the costs of space-based thinking are not merely conceptual. Although legislators and activists usually create or defend wilderness zones in response to clear and immediate threats, some commentators have pointed to the questionable impact of wilderness zones on overall ecological health. In part because of what George Sessions names "the pre-ecological" understanding found in the Wilderness Act of 1964 (119), wilderness that is enacted through bureaucratic and congressional action fails to take into account the complexity of ecosystems and human planet-wide, long-term influence. As a result, such zones often introduce a host of problems. For example, the behavior patterns of some large mammals and birds require land access that is incompatible with current allocations. In addition, when we label some areas wilderness and others not, we run the danger of creating habitats that lack the genetic exchange and diversity necessary for ecological health. Finally, without the free movement of genetic information, species become increasingly vulnerable to changes of conditions. From a biological perspective, spatialized ecology seems little more than a large-scale human laboratory experiment, a kind of biological theater. And so we might ask of models of space-based wilderness—including even some of our unexamined ecocritical paradigms—for whom and to what ends is this slice of life being presented?

This is the question that critics have asked of naturalist theater. The legacy of naturalist theater is now most familiar to audiences and general readers in the form of Stanislavskian or American Method acting, a system of professional training that prepares actors to conceal—even from themselves—the complex social purposes of performance. But the philosophical, historical, and cultural origins of naturalist theater provide a suggestive starting point for our discussion of how performance theory and ecocriticism can combine to contribute new ways of thinking about wilderness zones. As Raymond Williams demonstrates, the term "naturalism" is sometimes used simply to denote lifelike or accurate representation, asserting a work of art's rejection of conventional styles in favor of realism. In other cases, the term has scientific associations, suggesting not just accuracy but also methodical, systematic processes of observation and reproduction. In the history of theater, the term "naturalism" has often been used to describe a particular philosophical position in which stage representation does not merely aim at accuracy to real life but also attempts to show through systematic reproduction how social conditions produce human behavior (Williams 203). Émile Zola, the most vehement spokesperson for naturalist theater's political agenda, urged that "environment, the study of which has transformed science and literature, will have to take a large role in the theatre," arguing that drama should illustrate the "inevitable laws of heredity and environment" (qtd. in Brockett 369–70, 431–32). For Zola and other dramatists influenced by nineteenth-century science and social theory, the representation onstage of realistic environments would play an important role in theater's attempt to effect social change.[1]

Theatrical naturalism's institutional practices effectively intensify the imaginative experience of the audience. To discipline its audience's attention, naturalism has to control the experience of the performance, maintaining clear distinctions between what counts as part of the theater event and what is merely circumstantially necessary for the event to occur. In particular, naturalist stage space—functioning as though it were stable and fully present from the opening of the curtain—often represents environments that audiences can scrutinize for both causes and explanations of character behavior. But because these spaces—like naturalist actor performances—are offered as representations and not explicitly as presentations to the spectators, awareness of how theatergoing might be implicated in the social world of the play is suppressed. For example, because it relies on naturalist conventions, Ibsen's *A Doll's House* seems to encourage imaginative identification with the elaborately represented lifestyle of the Helmers. But these same conventions prevent the audience from registering how their pleasure, concealment, and prurient observation are actions that reveal the psychological and social dynamics that drive Nora to exit both home and stage at the play's end. By employing rhetorical structures that provide audiences with absorbing, imaginatively intense experiences in the theater, naturalism nourishes a kind of passivity and, as later theatrical theorists and practitioners such as Bertolt Brecht understand, makes theatrical audiences respond emotionally rather than intellectually to the spectacle of social problems. In this sense, naturalist theater audiences bear some resemblance to the expectant wilderness visitor who craves a satisfyingly intense, wild, natural experience, but who once satisfied can return to a way of living whose effects on the wild go unnoticed. And so, when we see the wild, like theater, as something happening in a specific place, our ongoing consciousness of wildness is blocked.

Realist drama as we know it today still carries on the legacy of naturalism. It is not surprising, then, that the most rigorously upheld convention of realist theater involves the control of the audience's sensory experience of the performance. Not only is the realist stage's representational space contained by a proscenium frame but a clearly defined beginning and end delineates what counts as part of the performance event and what does not. Like the Wilderness Act, which supports activities that frame out or conceal complex socioecological processes, the logic of the realist stage diverts our attention from how performances come into being. But like space-based wilderness, realist theater provides its visitors with a preserve of intense emotional experience that brings us in contact with another world, a slice of life. The gestures of the contemporary realist audience—its entry at a designated time, its silence, its sitting in rows, its rising for scheduled intermissions—are treated as mere social machinery surrounding the clearly defined theatrical sequence. Rarely, if ever, are these pragmatic behaviors considered part of the theatrical event; in this sense, they resemble the apparatus of nature appreciation. Just as we are unlikely to ask what the audience's elaborate process of arrival (advertisement reading, ticket purchase, dressing, driving, parking, finding their seats) contributes to the performance, we might similarly fail to consider how the nature lover's intricate process of arrival (equipment purchase, guidebook reading, cross-country travel, hiking, finding a campsite) fosters the performance of the wild. But for ecocriticism, it is these complex performances and processes that constitute our encounters with the wild within specific historical, cultural, and biological conditions that deserve greater attention.

Questions about how the realist stage uses space to discipline audience experience bring to mind Birch's critique of the incarceration of wildness. The theater critic Bonnie Marranca, for example, argues that the realist stage "entraps" an audience within a predetermined set of experiences of character, history, and action. Realist setting, she claims, "is mere scenery, information, the dressing that frames a play in a set of gestures, speech styles, and moral values" (197). By controlling what an audience sees and where it sees it, such productions rely on a "static view of space" that is overly concerned with causation and motivation. Interestingly, even attempts to challenge these conventions through experimental theatrical practice often fall prey to the underlying assumptions about space that limit realist theater. The environmental theater movement of the late 1960s, for example, attempted to violate the spatial logic the proscenium imposes in the hope of challenging the boundaries that realist theater rigorously upholds between audience and performers.[2] In attempting to undermine the rhetoric of conventional theater space that positions the spectator as psychological observer, environmental theater has actors perform within the audience's space and invites audiences to observe the event from different parts of the performance space. In theory this redrawing of the boundary between performer and audience would change assumptions about theatrical space. But as the theater historian and critic Una Chaudhuri notes, such productions uphold rather than subvert the core ideologies underlying realist uses of space. For Chaudhuri, environmental theater's blurring of the boundary between performer and audience simply extends the tight logical relationship between character and place into "the house" so that the theater space that preexists the audience now contains them.[3] Although physical boundaries may be challenged in such performances, conceptual boundaries are not.

Both conventional stage realism and the experimental productions Chaudhuri describes assume relationships among character and physical and social environment that reinforce a belief that performance environments preexist the entrances of the Nora Helmers or avante garde actors of the world. Space in this model stands inert, a stable environment with which the character or performer interacts rather than a created part of the performance event. As a result, audience members do not acknowledge that all participants—actors and audiences alike—create the space in the course of the unfolding theatrical event. Such productions treat space as a given condition while simultaneously effacing the complex psychological and social processes of theater. Audiences might, for example, draw analogies between their lives and those represented (my life is like or unlike Nora's), but they typically do not think about how as theatergoers they have a much more immediate relationship with the actress playing Nora Helmer or the performers in an experimental play. In a sense, realism and its theatrical heirs use space, as Marranca argues, to separate "human beings from the world, forcing the two into opposition" (197). Clearly, the implications for ecocriticism of such a division based on space are profound. If we understand space not as an inert given condition but as something called into being by human and more-than-human performance, the interconnectedness of seemingly disparate gestures, places, and times will become visible.

Temporality, Wilderness, and the Stage

Two brief examples drawn from twentieth-century theater theory reveal how the effort to think about theater as a temporal process rather than a space for performance might help ecocritics revise the notion that wilderness stands as a place apart. In both cases, critical attention focuses on the sequenced processes through which theatrical events unfold. In *The Actor's Instrument,* for example, the actor-critic Hollis Huston begins his discussion of performance by suggesting that entrance into any place always implies access to its phenomenological history. For Huston, then, a space (particularly a theatrical space) can only be understood as a sequence of perceptual experiences for both actors and spectators. What we conventionally think of as the preexisting objects on a stage—including the actors—take shape for us through our awareness of their movements through time. For Huston, because we experience theater as phenomena in time, actors literally teach space "to those who watch, animating it by foregrounding its sensuous properties" (67). By viewing stage space as a perceptual phenomenon that unfolds in time based on our subjective perceptions of the histories and movements of objects and actors, Huston challenges the static spatial conventions of stage naturalism and urges actors and spectators to remain alive to the emergent perceptual history that we experience in the theater.

In her 1935 essay "Plays," Gertrude Stein anticipates much of Huston's emphasis on the processes of theatrical stage making, but she places even greater importance on the audience's role in creating alternate temporal sequences as they watch a play. Stein writes about the anxiety she feels when watching a play whose events demand that she follow a prescribed temporal order; she worries she may lose track or even grow bored. As an alternative to the enforced sequence of the naturalist stage (where one event must logically unfold from another), Stein conceives of a play as a landscape that opens itself to any number of views or time frames. In such a performance, she claims, "there would be no difficulty about the emotion of the person looking on at the play being behind or ahead" of the action (263), for her imagined viewer could explore freely without following either rigorous sequences or clearly delineated views. Thus, the viewer does not risk losing track of anything but remains perpetually at play in the spatial-visual landscape. This Steinian theatrical landscape moves "always in relation, the trees to the hills the hills to the fields" to create an ever-changing field of perceptual possibilities (265). Although Stein's play-as-landscape still might seem to stand apart from the viewer, it is not a naturalist environment to be read for its cause and effect relationships. Its sequenced story may or may not be followed, but its relation—or narrative performance and juxtapositions—remains continually available to the audience. In such a model, what constitutes the play emerges from viewers' interactions with the play-as-landscape, from the performance of the audience rather than from structures or meanings in the drama or production.

Stein, like Huston, offers rich possibilities for ecocriticism. Although she does not question the present otherness of the play-as-landscape, Stein welcomes variations in audience performance and considers them to be an important part of how theater unfolds. By liberating theater theory from the rigorous causality of realist plot and space, Stein and Huston encourage awareness of the range of performances that together constitute a theatrical event. Such a turn may be one that ecocriticism needs to make in order to move "beyond nature writing." These efforts, however, will depend on the extent to which ecocritics follow Stein and Huston by letting go of the stable perspective that spatial views of the wild provide, so that they may better understand the nuances of the psychological, biological, social, and political processes that create our perceptions of the wild.[4] Just as performance includes far more than spaces, characters, and objects presented on a proscenium stage, ecocriticism—if it is to have much intellectual viability— must find wildness and nature writing outside and beyond the boundaries of a narrowly defined nature. To do anything less would be to confine ecocriticism to a limited space within cultural studies, just as official wilderness zones preserve a sacred place apart from the profanation of society.

One writer who sees ecocriticism's broader possibilities likens natural processes to the creative essay, much as we have been considering the relationship between wilderness and the stage. In *Edge Effects,* an account of living and writing in the midst of an Oregon clear-cut, Chris Anderson claims that "the essay has the structure of an old-growth forest. It's rough and jagged and variously textured, digressive, splintering, apparently unsystematic, a thickness of multiple and indistinct layers." Essays, Anderson goes on to say, "grow from careless seeds, from the varieties of life" (159–60). Done well, they contain a structured looseness. For Anderson, an essay is less a detailed definitive map of a thought space than it is an idiosyncratic, performative ramble along the available paths. While essays begin and end, they possess few conceptual limits. Given the right combination of reader and writer, an essay, like Stein's play-as-landscape, can follow any number of paths. A forest also knows no boundaries. Its edges are diffuse. The ebb and flow of grasses and trees never comes to a stop; this year the trees might advance, next year it will be the grass. Soil erosion, wind, rain, the forester's ax—all may temporarily establish an edge, but none permanently define it. Within the forest, where the grasslands cannot be seen, trees are born and they die, returning nutrients to the earth. Anderson, like Stein and Huston, insists that time can change our view of space: "Understanding the forest means thinking temporally rather than spatially. And thinking in big swaths of time, 200, 300, 400 years" (162). By revising our ways of seeing space and time through perceiving new connections between nature and cultural forms, Anderson shows how we might rethink ecocriticism's relation to cultural studies and critical theory.

The ideas we articulate in this essay are indebted to recent cultural theorists who have described the conceptual, psychological, and social construction of space. Gaston Bachelard, for example, explains how the basic functions (such as the uses of rooms) and the richly emotive associations of one's house perpetually unfold through the interactions among perception, memory, and structure.[5] Taking a slightly different approach, Henri Lefebvre examines the social purposes of conceiving space as inert and analyzes how our social relations produce the seemingly mute substance that we call space.[6] While we, too, wish to challenge the somewhat arrogant assumption that humans can view spaces in which we perform as though they are simply "there," this does not imply that there exists no world beyond human perception. Undoubtedly, for example, something we call the wild endures across time for us to point to, but we must become aware that it is the representational rhetoric of our pointing that obscures from us the particular dance we do with the more-than-human world. We should not ask "when are we in the wild?" but rather "how are we in it at any given moment?" This second question inquires how we participate in the process of space making rather than merely allowing us to imagine ourselves as having a location at any given moment. And so, when Gary Snyder defines wilderness as a "place where the wild potential is fully expressed, a diversity of living and nonliving beings flourishing according to their own sorts of order" (12), we hear his definition as an invitation to ask whether the wild might not exist anywhere and everywhere, in our grandest forests and our dirtiest streets, taking place on many different scales and levels and called into our consciousness through a variety of human performances.[7]

We are in relation to wildness regardless of our geographical location. Ideas about space are part of how we describe patterns of relationships, but often our space-based thinking keeps us from choosing alternative performances in relation to the wild. From an ecological and epistemological view, the notion of spatial separateness on which so much of human inquiry is founded must be called into question. How, for example, can we even separate one species from the next if we understand each organism to always be unfolding toward something else? And we must recognize how, such as in environmental theater, even our impulses to be in the wild are founded on assumptions that the wild is a preexisting space. If we could remove the lines we have drawn, we could perhaps encounter a more-than-human world in which our perceptions turn around a series of pivots. As David Abram suggests, the things of the world "disclose themselves" as "styles of unfolding not as finished chunks of matter given once and for all, but as dynamic ways of engaging the senses and modulating the body" (81). William James's connection of the processes of human consciousness to a stream seems especially apt in this regard. For James, consciousness "is of a teeming multiplicity of objects and relations" (21).[8] To navigate the stream and negotiate the ebb and flow of thought we must, in effect, become skilled and perceptive performers in constantly shifting spaces. We must see that all life— from water lilies to dung beetles to humans—exists within an ever-changing stream of biological, conceptual, and metaphysical relationships that is at once significant and mysterious.

In closing, we want to suggest some possibilities that might emerge when we revise our conceptions of wilderness space in response to alternative models of theatrical performance. One involves notions of scale. A process- or performance-based conception of the wild makes visible how our conventional role as audience contains ecology within the limits of human scale. The Wilderness Act of 1964 specifies five thousand acres as the minimum size of a designated zone, but even wilderness advocates such as Bob Marshall have employed measures for wilderness zones scaled to human performance—for example, the amount of time a generic human would need to cross a space. A wilderness space, Marshall claims in a frequently cited 1930 article, must be "sufficiently spacious that a person crossing it must have the experience of camping out" (qtd. in Zaslowsky 210). This may sound large, but the scale is undeniably human and is defined by recreational activities. One could just as easily measure wilderness by its remoteness from human centers of population (that a person visiting from a city of at least fifty thousand people will have had to travel at least eight hours by car to the entry point). By acknowledging the role of human performance in encountering natural processes and studying it more carefully, we will open up the possibility of envisioning natural processes from the perspective of other scales. If we can conceive of performances that, for example, use an entire city or state as their stage, we can as surely imagine wildernesses in all manner of sizes and shapes. What matters is not so much that other scales can be considered but that the scales on which the wild is perceived influence how we perform in relation to it.

Process- or performance-based conceptions can also help us reexamine the limits placed on space-based environmental thought by temporal scales that emerge from particular human time frames. Thinking of wilderness as human-scaled space often limits ecological thinking to responses that are neither long enough to have sustained effects on developing systems nor pinpoint-accurate enough to intervene in precise contexts. But a greater sensitivity to process could enable us to consider longer-term actions such as traditions of community storytelling about the wild or the interaction of climate change and species habitation. We could also study rapid interventions in specific situations, which often come from individuals or spontaneously formed groups that can combine human and more-than-human actions. Both of these performance-oriented responses center on patterns of activity or responses to perceived features of the environment. Of course, while these actions are also on a human scale, human audiences need to become sensitive as well to the effects of geologic- or cellular-scaled performance and space. For, as changes in the movement of viruses from rain forests have shown, environmental action happens simultaneously on a variety of spatial and temporal scales. Our point is not that legislation and space-based preservation should be abandoned but rather that we can and must consider many more scales, durations, and strategies of performance in relation to the wild to understand and influence change. One might even say that we do not necessarily need yet another strategy for ecological health so much as a new and more flexible consciousness of how we participate in the making of the place in which we live.

Of course, viewing wilderness (or theater) as a process that performance activates rather than as a space or place forces us to reconsider our geographical situations. When wilderness areas are conceived merely as a series of places, we typically stand at a comfortable intellectual distance from them. While walking through Manhattan, we can measure how far we stand from a wilderness place. Such a relationship has a specific spatial content. But the processes of the wild—like those of theater—take place even as we ask ourselves the question about our location. If the wild is a process in which human beings participate, we are in theory never away from it, just as we are potentially never outside places of social performance. Continuing to locate wilderness in space only forestalls the transformed awareness that we need in order to become more than naturalist spectators at an inert world-theater.

Perhaps our critique of spatialized wilderness sounds like an argument against valuing and protecting the wild. It is not. Rather, we are seeking vocabularies, metaphors, and images that might increase the amount of wildness we perceive in the world at large. We can begin by locating wildness in unlikely places—in cities and towns, along highways, on farms, and in office buildings. We can go on to radically alter how we think of the scale and temporal duration of the wild, seeing wildness in a small spring pond formed by backwash, a moving storm front, a run-off ditch, a chain of stopping points for a migratory bird population, or a pile of leaves collected under a highway abutment. But this relocation and rescaling is not enough. We must also explore how we perform in relation to wildness—wildness as idea, as source of perception, and as memory. In addition, ecocriticism can add an important element to culturally based performance theories, reminding us that our performances of the wild are not only psychological and social but also take place through ecological, biochemical, and genetic dialogue that moves across identity boundaries, membranes, and politically defined perimeters. Recognizing such movement across boundaries, we argue, gives fresh meaning to Mikhail Bakhtin's narrowly linguistic notion of the dialogic. If we followed such a course, the multi-vocality of the conversation between the human and more-than-human would more fully inform our awareness of the wild. At the very least, we will have to establish new relations with the more-than-human world to break down the spatial segregation implicit in discourse about wilderness zones. Ecocriticism can and should challenge humans to be more fully in wildness wherever they go rather than sensitively seeking to minimize the amount they encroach on the territory of the wild. Perhaps a sensitivity to the perceptual dance of engagement and retreat is precisely what we need.

Notes

1. Williams identifies several sources for the emergence of naturalism and the associated realism as central rhetorical patterns in European theatrical history. While he relates representations of everyday life in drama to changes in theater audiences, with urban bourgeois audiences responding favorably to plays that reflected back at them familiar situations and conditions (208–10), he notes that changes in the technologies of stage representation also influenced nineteenth-century dramatic subject matter (206–8). For example, changes in stage lighting that British playwright Joanna Baillie proposed as early as 1812 to make theater more psychologically intimate were effected later in the century by August Strindberg in Sweden (Baillie 234–35 n; Strindberg 84–85). Likewise, European methods of scenic representation changed during the eighteenth and nineteenth centuries from employing painted images on sliding panels to using three-dimensional space, onstage furniture, and lifelike props to represent social environments.

2. Although influenced by ecological movements, this urban theater movement dealt mainly with the environment of the theater.

3. Chaudhuri argues that environmental theater continues the containment of the theatrical event, perpetuating what she calls the naturalist and modernist theater's "geopathology." She describes how modern drama grounds both plot and identity in a "symbology of home" that "defines place as the protagonist's fundamental problem" and produces recognition (and perhaps enactment) of "the heroism of departure." For Chaudhuri this thematic pattern is embedded in the use of theatrical space: "The characterization of place as problem—to which I have given the label *geopathology*—is supported by the stage practice of early modern drama, specifically by the spatial arrangements of naturalism, which function according to a logic of *total visibility*" (xii).

4. For a thorough history of how many different cultures have conceived of wilderness, see Oelschlaeger. While *The Idea of Wilderness* studies major trends in cultural discourse, we are concerned primarily with the positions from which individual critics might respond to the wild.

5. In *The Poetics of Space*, Bachelard writes, "In the theater of the past that is constituted by memory, the stage setting maintains the characters in their dominant roles" (8).

6. In *The Production of Space*, Lefebvre writes, "Could space be nothing more than the passive locus of social relations, the milieu in which their combination takes on body, or the aggregate of the procedures employed in their removal? The answer must be no" (11).

7. Of course, Snyder's use of the term "place" is not merely reflexive. Place has come to represent a historically situated space that is both natural and social. The question this essay asks is whether place does not continue to carry within it several of the inherent limitations that have led many to challenge spatialized ideas of environment. It is worth noting that place-based ecological thinking, although it might seem grounded in the spatiality this essay questions, is often more committed to defining communities in terms of their histories—that is, in consideration of performances over time—than in viewing places as spaces.

8. The connections between James's philosophical pragmatism and ecology are discussed in *Environmental Pragmatism,* edited by Light and Katz; see especially Parker, "Pragmatism."

Works Cited

Abram, David. *The Spell of the Sensuous: Perception and Language in a More-than-Human World.* New York: Vintage, 1997.

Anderson, Chris. *Edge Effects: Notes from an American Forest.* Iowa City: U of Iowa P, 1993.

Bachelard, Gaston. *The Poetics of Space.* Boston: Beacon, 1994.

Baillie, Joanna. "To the Reader." 1812. Rpt. in *The Dramatic and Poetical Works of Joanna Baillie, complete in one volume.* London: Longman, Brown, Green, and Longmans, 1851. 228–35.

Birch, Thomas. "The Incarceration of Wildness: Wilderness Areas as Prisons." *Deep Ecology for the Twenty-first Century: Readings on the Philosophy and Practice of the New Environmentalism.* Ed. George Sessions. Boston: Shambhala, 1995. 339–52.

Brockett, Oscar G. *History of the Theatre.* 7th ed. Boston: Allyn and Bacon, 1995.

Chaudhuri, Una. *Staging Place: The Geography of Modern Drama*. Ann Arbor: U of Michigan P, 1995.

Huston, Hollis. *The Actor's Instrument: Body, Theory, Stage*. Ann Arbor: U Michigan P, 1992.

James, William. *The Writings of William James: A Comprehensive Edition*. Ed. John J. McDermott. Chicago: U of Chicago P, 1977.

Lefebvre, Henri. *The Production of Space*. Oxford: Blackwell, 1996.

Light, Andrew, and Eric Katz, eds. *Environmental Pragmatism*. London: Routledge, 1995.

Marranca, Bonnie. *Theatrewritings*. New York: Performing Arts Journal, 1984.

Oelschlaeger, Max *The Idea of Wilderness : From Prehistory to the Age of Ecology*. New Haven: Yale UP, 1991.

Parker, Kelly A. "Pragmatism and Environmental Thought." Light and Katz 21–37.

Sessions, George. "Ecocentrism, Wilderness, and Global Ecosystem Protection." *The Wilderness Condition: Essays on Environment and Civilization*. Ed. Max Oelschlaeger. San Francisco: Sierra Club, 1992. 90–130.

Snyder, Gary. "The Etiquette of Freedom." *The Practice of the Wild*. San Francisco: North Point, 1990. 3–24.

Stein, Gertrude. "Plays." *Gertrude Stein: Writings 1932–1946*. New York: Literary Classics of the United States, 1998. 244–69.

Strindberg, August. "Preface to *Lady Julie*." *Pre-Inferno Plays*. New York: Norton, 1970. 71–86.

Williams, Raymond. "Social Environment and Theatrical Environment: The Case of English Naturalism." *English Drama: Forms and Development: Essays in Honour of Muriel Clara Bradbrook*. Ed. Marie Axton and Raymond Williams. Cambridge: Cambridge UP, 1977. 203–23.

Worster, Donald. *An Unsettled Country: Changing Landscapes of the American West*. Albuquerque: U of New Mexico P, 1994.

Zaslowsky, Dyan. *These American Lands: Parks, Wilderness, and the Public Lands*. New York: Henry Holt, 1986.

Zola, Émile. "From *Naturalism in the Theatre*." *The Theory of the Modern Stage: An Introduction to Modern Theatre and Drama*. Ed. Eric Bentley. New York: Penguin, 1972. 351–72.

⌒ⁿ Beyond Nature/Writing:
Virtual Landscapes Online,
in Print, and in "Real Life"

H. Lewis Ulman

Riven's forests . . . are alive with flying, winking insects and buzzing beetles. Birds casually wheel and call in the sky. The water
shimmers. The effect is so dazzling we could feel the sun's heat on
the back of our necks and the breeze blowing through our hair.
—Joseph O. Holmes, *"Riven,* the Sequel to *Myst"*

Why produce virtual environments at all when we could be enjoying a far more satisfying and beautiful physical reality?
—Margaret Morse, *"Nature Morte"*

. . . soon, lost among electronic representations "just as good" as
the real thing, we'll collectively lose sight of the fact that approximations and reenactments are a kind of lie.
—Mark Slouka, *War of the Worlds*

Approximation: Approaching the Real Thing

The Riven extolled in the first epigraph to this essay is the virtual (and epony-
mous) landscape of a computer game. However, *Riven* differs markedly from
typical arcade games.[1] As the software reviewer Joseph O. Holmes informs us,
"you're dropped into a lavishly detailed, mythical world, free to roam and explore. Follow trails through lush jungles, navigate dark tunnels through mountains, wander along beaches, and explore a primitive village. . . . [A]t the outset,

341

you won't even have a clear idea of exactly what you're looking for or are expected to do in order to achieve your goal. You'll spend your first hours trying to understand this world—how to navigate it, who populates it, and what's going on" (52). To be sure, *Riven* is game-like in that players must solve puzzles to accomplish specific goals, but *Riven*'s popularity with game players and critics alike stems primarily from its stunning multimedia representation of the Riven archipelago. In Holmes's words again, "The illusion of exploring a real, if surrealistic, world remains intact until the end" (53). Is Holmes saying simply that elements of *Riven* are realistic? That the image quality is photographic and the ambient sounds of wind, waves, and animal voices are lifelike? Perhaps, but I think he is also getting at something more—that *Riven* supports a multidimensional (visual, aural, imaginative, and ratiocinative) gestalt through which players sustain a satisfying illusion of existing and acting in the world of Riven.

Virtual reality is currently embodied in several kinds of digital systems—text-based online role-playing games, multimedia computer games online and off, and elaborate simulations supported by equipment that surrounds or is worn by participants. All of these systems seem crude compared to *Star Trek's* holodeck, but critics worry that even now digital virtual reality (VR to the digerati) can divert our attention and allegiance from the real world. Holmes's phrasing is as suggestive as it is paradoxical: the real surreal might refer to any representation that allows us to sustain a satisfying—and seductive—illusion of reality. We experience such representations, at least imaginatively, from the inside out, and we ignore their material embodiment, except when a technological malfunction or critical reflection shatters the illusion and directs our attention to the mediation of print, film, audio technology, or graphics acceleration. Such attention to the media of symbolic representation highlights the unreality of realistic and fantastic representations alike—of an airline flight simulator and *Riven,* for instance, or travel writing and science fiction. In *"Nature Morte:* Landscape and Narrative in Virtual Environments," Margaret Morse represents fantastic and realistic VR as polar opposites bound by their virtuality but distinguished by their motives: "The underworld in which symbols of the once-was, is-not-yet, and never-will-be are given virtual life is poles apart from the ultimate display in which the virtual proves its power over material reality—first by resembling it, then by submitting it to death. These two relations to, or motivations for producing, cyberspaces contrast an open-ended and subjunctive realm of fantasy against the desire to control the material world via a virtual double" (208).

Morse ascribes a sinister motive to realistic VR (and by extension to the illusion of reality that Holmes experiences while playing *Riven*)—a motive that rings true in the context of her argument about digital art and aesthetics but is harder to attribute to realistic VR in other contexts. For instance, extremely realistic VR systems are used to train people for real experiences of both medicine and war (and, of course, the ethics of those uses are complicated in their own right). However, fantasy VR games such as *Doom* are also popularly credited with the power to translate themselves into real life, through their influence over impressionable children, with tragic consequences.

In the face of such complexities, some critics condemn VR in all its forms, a line of argument that, seemingly in spite of itself, often ends up calling all representations into question. Reviewing a famous case of virtual rape in an online role-playing environment, Mark Slouka warns of the seductive power of such virtual communities: "Part of the risk involved in setting up residence in these metaphorical communities, then, was that we might begin to devalue the significance of physical reality" (52–53). How familiar this charge has been in the history of media—including printed text and film! Later in *War of the Worlds: Cyberspace and the High-Tech Assault on Reality,* Slouka distinguishes between the qualities of particular VR systems (realistic or fantastic, peaceful or violent) and the underlying nature of our engagement with representations:

> What's significant here, it seems to me, is not the [qualities of any particular] simulation, but our willingness to buy into it; whether we're growing tomatoes or slicing our way through a crowd with a chainsaw, after all, we're buying into a fake, and that says something about us and our relationship to reality. Simulation games are important, in other words, because they are part of something larger: the wholesale blurring of the line . . . between the original and the representation. (116)

Of course, it is hard to imagine how we might escape representation. Certainly not by turning to books, film, storytelling, or any other analog, offline symbolic medium. Although their modes of mediation differ from digital VR (and from one another), representations in all of these media still stand, in this view, at a symbol's length from any original, material world to which they refer. Whatever the medium or level of sophistication, the original world stands asymptotically separate from the curve of our representations.

Why, then, are so many critics of technoculture so especially concerned with the cultural effects of VR and so seemingly unconcerned with the effects of more traditional media such as print? Slouka argues that before the advent of digital media, "our willingness to believe in copies was kept in check by the inability of our technology to lie convincingly" (123). In this view, representations that approach the asymptote of reality too closely threaten our ability to discriminate between the two. Although it sounds plausible, this answer is surely misleading, as evidenced by fear of imaginative art stretching from Plato's distrust of dramatic poetry to nineteenth-century concerns over the effects of reading novels to current attempts to ban books from schools. History suggests that our experience of representations is as important as their material embodiment in a particular symbolic medium. A more creditable explanation for the blurring of representation and reality, offered by Slouka and others, is that the entire gestalt of VR and real life are often disturbingly alike, at least along some key axes of human engagement. In Slouka's words, "Our world today, by every standard, is more man-made, more synthetic, than ever before. We may not be living in artificial pods quite yet, but increasingly, the sensibility that would interpret that scenario as both grotesque and infinitely sad seems to be fading" (72–73). Such human transformation of the physical world creates what we might call the surreal real or, following Jean Baudrillard, hyperreality—"the substitution of the reproduction for the actual object" (Murray 292 n. 7). Such transformations of the physical world are effected by both artifice and sensibility. After all, belief in magic has in many cultures and times transformed the natural world into a magical place, occupied by real (that is, material) talismans and (to those outside the belief system) imaginary presences. As Janet H. Murray argues, "Postmodern writing about the digital world often assumes that it is intrinsically hyperreal. But hyperreality is less a property of a particular medium than a way of experiencing media in general: a teetering on the border between a powerfully present illusion and a more authentic but flickeringly visible ordinary world" (292 n. 7). In this alternative view, it is the perceived distance of our hypermediated, everyday experience from reality, not the capacity of any specific technology to mimic reality, that poses a threat. Indeed, many critics of technoculture share environmentalists' concern that authentic experiences of the world are becoming increasingly harder to find or define, much less restore or preserve.

However, decrying the existence and seductive allure of digital VR seems futile, for technologies are notoriously difficult to uninvent, and VR will only increase in representational power. Moreover, scapegoating digital media tends to remove it from close critical scrutiny and dulls our critical ability to evaluate representations and reproductions elsewhere. Instead, it behooves us to discover what imaginative and conceptual resources we need to construct ethical and healthy relationships between digital and material worlds, just as ecocritics have been working to establish such relationships between textual and material worlds. Indeed, the blurring and interanimation of symbolic and material worlds raises important questions for ecocriticism. In what sense are computer simulations, textual representations, and managed, constructed, or disturbed landscapes (for example, nature preserves, parks, and cities) all examples of virtual worlds? What range and power does each sort of virtual landscape—simulated, described, and material—afford our imaginations? How do our experiences of material landscapes inform our experiences of symbolic landscapes—and vice versa? How do we distinguish virtual landscapes from real ones and establish ethical relationships in or to both? In sum, how can our symbolic approximations of the material world help us sustain relationships to that world that avoid disastrous or oppressive consequences for ourselves and the other species with which we live?

Restoration: Modeling the Real Thing

Healthy, ethical relationships to a complex system of symbolic and material landscapes require attention to the relationships among those landscapes. When all of the landscapes we typically experience stand at some chronological or qualitative distance from an original landscape, one that embodied sustainable relationships among its parts, we need to do the sort of work that Alexander Wilson, in *The Culture of Nature: North American Landscape from Disney to the*

Exxon Valdez, terms "restoration": recognizing "that once lands have been 'disturbed'—worked, lived on, meddled with, developed—they require human intervention and care. We must build landscapes that heal, connect and empower, that make intelligible our relations with each other and with the natural world: places that welcome and enclose, whose breaks and edges are never without meaning" (17). Wilson challenges us to restore not only physical landscapes but also our relationship to them. Restoration, he argues, involves "working out an idea of nature that includes human culture and human livelihood" (17). Wilson also maintains that conception is especially critical when dealing with the relationships among symbolic and material landscapes, for all of our ideas of nature have been "disturbed" relative to whatever *ur*-relationship to the natural world our species had in our evolutionary past. In the remainder of this essay, I try to imagine how restoration might help us understand the "breaks and edges" separating virtual landscapes from the material world.

Among the most significant breaks in our everyday world are doorways that lead outside—outside our homes, offices, stores, automobiles, and RVs. (Who can forget Edward Abbey entreating visitors to Arches National Monument to get out of their "goddamned upholstered horseless hearse" and "walk—*walk*—WALK upon our sweet and blessed land!" [233]?) But critics of technoculture and ecocritics alike worry that too few of us go outside anymore—except to travel as quickly as possible to another door leading inside. Slouka claims that "we're retreating inside because the world outside our homes has less and less to offer us. . . . We live, many of us, in communities whose planners clearly had little or no interest in integrating the outside world into the lives of future residents" (78). However, my own suburban backyard complicates Slouka's argument. The planners of this neighborhood clearly intended residents to spend time outdoors, if only to service the high-maintenance landscaping! But the yards, although fashioned from living plants and home to squirrels, birds, rabbits, and myriad insects, are virtual worlds nonetheless, intended to recreate the ambiance of European country estates. The plants, in particular—English ivy, sweet William, arborvitae, juniper, pyracantha, privet, Kentucky bluegrass, and golden spirea—are not native to the bioregion or have been transformed into ornamental varieties of indigenous plants. Still, Slouka's argument underestimates the ubiquity of original nature and its power to make its presence known.

Sitting in my backyard a little more than an hour after this year's autumnal equinox, I imagine myself careening around the Sun. At first, the page on which I am taking notes is almost too bright to look at, but a cloud soon casts a shadow, and the temperature cools a few degrees, hinting at what's to come now that the Sun, from my perspective, has crossed the celestial equator, heading south. A gentle breeze stirs the overlong grass in my yard, particularly in the clumps where it has gone to seed. I can hear dead leaves scuttling along the road beyond my hedge.

Others go about their business. Insects seem to be everywhere, chirping constantly. Sparrows rustle in an overgrown yew and wheel overhead. A completely black squirrel who lives in a neighbor's tree appears suddenly between two shrubs that line my driveway, sits up as if to acknowledge me, then disappears just as quickly when I turn my head. No one orchestrates all of this activity, but the world is capacious, and we rush together past the cusp of autumn, acting and acted upon in a network of relations, some as fine and intimate as the embrace of lovers, some as vast and indiscriminate as the pull of gravity.

A great deal about familiar suburban settings distracts us from traces of original landscapes by focusing attention on virtual landscapes of our own conceptual and material construction. Even the street names in my neighborhood—I live on College Hill Drive, which is intersected by Vassar Place, Mount Holyoke, and Wellesley—look back to the eastern landscapes from which Euro-American settlement of the Midwest began, forming just one layer of a palimpsest of representation. My notes and this essay are, of course, focusing technologies that constitute another layer of representation. Such disturbed landscapes are so much a part of our experience that we need strategies for reading them critically if we are to undertake the work of restoration. One such strategy involves tracing the similarities between disturbed material landscapes such as my backyard and the virtual landscapes that seem so threatening to critics of technoculture.

One source of that threat is surely our recognition that the virtual is not always digital and the material is always, for us, invested with meaning. As Margaret Morse observes, "the forms of cyberspace are not solely virtual: material objects and environments that have been invested with computer-supported agency . . . or that have been given the skins of other times or places are also cyberspace" (200). Although I would reverse her terms, reserving "cyberspace" for digital environments and "virtual space" for any material or symbolic environments that model other spaces, Morse's argument points to a broader notion of the virtual that can inform our search for its breaks and edges. As Kevin Kelly asserts in *Out of Control: The New Biology of Machines, Social Systems, and the Economic World,* "Simulacra have become the terrain we live in. In most ways we care to measure, the hyperreal is real for us. We enter and leave hyperreality with ease" (240). Of course, critics of technoculture argue that we now find it far more difficult to leave hyperreality than to enter it, but perhaps the notion that the virtual and the real are separate places is no more true to our situation than the notion that nature and culture are mutually exclusive. Rather, the virtual is always embodied in the real, just as the real is always mediated for us by the virtual.

Alexander Wilson reminds us that "Our experience of the natural world— whether touring the Canadian Rockies, watching an animal show on TV, or working in our own gardens—is always mediated. It is always shaped by rhetorical constructs like photography, industry, advertising, and aesthetics, as well as by institutions like religion, tourism, and education" (12). And of constructed landscapes he asks perhaps the most pertinent question about digital VR: "[W]hat do these constructed environments have to do with what is now everywhere called the environment—the non-human world of rocks and water, plants and animals, that seems to both precede and envelop our many cultures? Do they help us understand that world? What do they promote, conceal, or exclude?" (11). Once I recognize my own backyard as a virtual landscape, I can see at its breaks and edges other landscapes that it mimics (the country estate) and masks (the indigenous ecology of central Ohio) as well as the unbounded, encompassing universe, full beyond all our artifacts.

If we think of our representations of landscapes as encompassed by and embodied in the world to which they refer, we have to modify my earlier characterization of representations as approximations that bring us more or less into proximity, but never unmediated contact, with real landscapes. Rather, representations of real or imagined landscapes are models—approximations of other landscapes through which we move bodily or in our imaginations—and they are bounded by our limited capacity to experience those landscapes. Wilson's questions about constructed environments—What do they "have to do with what is now everywhere called the environment. . . . Do they help us understand that world?" (11)—suggest an alternative to evaluating virtual landscapes in terms of how closely they correspond to some ideal but always absent real world. Instead, virtual landscapes can be judged by how they help us anticipate and understand our experiences of the landscapes they model and of landscapes in general. The test is not verisimilitude or allegiance but ethical engagement and critical understanding.

Let us look at another example. Reviewers who hyperventilate about the illusion of reality in *Riven* engage in a bit of hyperbole. For all its stunning multimedia effects, *Riven* cannot even begin to duplicate the complex, unbounded world I sensed in my backyard while contemplating the autumnal equinox. Still, *Riven*'s imagined landscape can clearly be captivating. Are players simply engaged in something akin to Samuel Coleridge's notion of the willing suspension of disbelief? In *Hamlet on the Holodeck: The Future of Narrative in Cyberspace*, Janet Murray offers another explanation: "When we enter a fictional world, we do not merely 'suspend' a critical faculty; we also exercise a creative faculty. We do not suspend disbelief so much as we actively *create belief*. Because of our desire to experience immersion, we focus our attention on the enveloping world and we use our intelligence to reinforce rather than to question the reality of the experience" (110). Because they are so new, digital VR environments such as Riven may help us understand how we create belief in other kinds of virtual environments, whether textual, digital, material—or hybrids of all three.

After exploring the archipelago of Riven for some time, I come to a high, rocky promontory overlooking the ocean. In the distance lie three islands connected by a suspended tramline. The hue of the virtual sky and the pattern of the clouds look remarkably real, except that the clouds are not moving (nor are the ocean waves, even though I can hear surf crashing on the rocks below). Birds wheel and call over the ocean, their movements and sounds, along with the chirping, buzzing, and clicking of as yet unseen insects, conferring a sense of life to the otherwise motionless tableau.

To my right, a log-and-rope bridge leads across a chasm and ends, I suppose, at another promontory, for I can't see anything but ocean beyond the bridge. What appear to be a huge blade and handle stick out above the rocks. The bridge creaks under my weight, and the sound of the surf grows louder, suggesting that I am standing over a chasm, but I can't look up or down to orient myself. Looking out over the ocean, I can see that the tramline approaches this island just below me. To my right, the huge handle (which now towers over my head) ends in an equally huge, round blade that looks like a pizza-cutter embedded in solid rock. Stepping off the bridge, I find myself at the top of a steep flight of stone stairs descending toward the ocean through a cleft in the rocks.

Descending the stairs, I soon pass into the shade of the rocky defile, but I feel no corresponding change in temperature. A bit further along, I catch sight of the shoreline and some offshore rocks upon which a pair of animals—a fantastic cross between a porpoise and a pelican—are basking. As I move closer, they raise their heads and grunt but then settle back to sleep on the rock, fins waving occasionally. When I first visited Riven, they would swim away when I approached the beach, but now they inevitably wait until my back is turned.

For all its exotic representations and media, part of what sustains my immersion in *Riven* is the utter familiarity of moving through a disturbed landscape that includes the presence of unthreatening animals, structures and artifacts, paths, and vistas that reflect a human sense of the picturesque. I find it easy to create belief in Riven not because it deposes or resembles an original, natural world but because it so closely models a few familiar experiences of landscapes. From these correspondences, I can sustain an illusion of moving through the otherwise strange world of Riven, and instead of alienating me from the real world, playing *Riven* reveals a great deal about my relationship to material landscapes and the elements of virtuality in those landscapes. At the very least, *Riven* represents these familiar human relationships to nature: (1) the world as created or transformed by human writing—for example, deeds, treaties, laws, contracts, and literature (in the story, an evil genius, Gehn, literally creates Riven by writing magical books); (2) the world as a resource (to create a linking book with which to escape Riven, Gehn harvests trees and indigenous fauna); and (3) the world as a weapon (the indigenous people of Riven are finally at risk because of Gehn's control of the land). With all due respect to Slouka, approximations and reenactments tell a kind of truth.

According to Murray, digital VR environments operate as "liminal objects, located on the threshold between external reality and our own minds" (99).

Drawing on the child psychologist D. W. Winnicott's work, Murray compares VR and "all sustained make-believe experiences, from children's play to Shakespearean theater" to a child's teddy bear, which "embodies . . . strong subjective elements [but] is also a real object with a physical presence outside of anything the child imagines about it" (99–100). The trick to sustaining immersion in such spaces, to living at the edge of a virtual world without falling through its breaks, is "to keep the virtual world 'real' by keeping it 'not there.' We have to keep it balanced squarely on the enchanted threshold without letting it collapse onto either side" (100). Drawing on memory and imagination, we supply the "fullness" that such liminal objects lack, overlooking the boundedness of their material embodiment.

Perhaps that is why books are such satisfying virtual environments. Text is a familiar medium whose material embodiment—paper and ink—has become all but transparent to highly literate readers. Yet as Edward Abbey writes of his attempt to represent the landscape in *Desert Solitaire: A Season in the Wilderness,* "Language makes a mighty loose net with which to go fishing for simple facts, when facts are infinite. . . . Since you cannot get the desert into a book any more than a fisherman can haul up the sea with his nets, I have tried to create a world of words in which the desert figures more as medium than as material. Not imitation but evocation has been the goal" (xii). In other words, readers must re-create a desert from the text.

Opening David Rains Wallace's *Idle Weeds: The Life of an Ohio Sandstone Ridge* in search of the telltale breaks and edges that separate the virtual text from its material subject, I come upon the following passage:

> The short-tailed shrew did not even remember the thrills of her courting period. She had been moving about with increasing hunger and discomfort as the fetuses in her uterus grew, and her three-week pregnancy was made even more arduous by a need to clean out and enlarge her nest. She had no idea why she was performing all this labor, and the precision of her response to a completely unknown situation remains one of the everyday mysteries that make such questions as the origin of the solar system seem almost simple by comparison.
> Late one night the shrew crawled panting back to her nest and unloaded her

burden. She licked each infant as it emerged from her vagina, removing the amniotic sac, which she immediately ate. Three of the blind, naked, and tooth-less infant shrews struggled and gasped as they felt the roughness of her tongue and the chill of the air. She allowed these to crawl to her six teats, now full of milk. The other two didn't move, they were defective and stillborn—a condition perhaps related to the poisons still bound up in the ridge's soil from former orchard operations. The shrew ate the dead infants along with the afterbirths. (50)

At least two aspects of this anecdote constitute liminal objects that enable us to immerse ourselves in a virtual landscape—the presumably human narrator's ability to read the shrew's thoughts and emotions as well as the narrator's intimate view of the shrew's nest. But other features of the text reveal breaks and edges that limit our ability to construct a real experience from the virtual model. The third-person omniscient narrator's point of view juxtaposes the shrew's perspective on the birth of her pups and a human awareness of agricultural pollution and "the origin of the solar system." These two perspectives blur in the anthropomorphic reference to the "thrills of her courting period." Further, in the deft pacing of the narrative—from the compressed reference to the shrew's "three-week pregnancy" to the more expansive and detailed account of the infants' birth—one catches yet another hint of the constructed nature of the narrative. As Wallace confesses in the acknowledgments to *Idle Weeds,* "There are many Blackhand sandstone ridges along the western escarpment of the Appalachian Plateau, and this book is not a literal portrait of any particular one. It is a composite of several places I have known, held together with some degree of poetic license" (iii)—in other words, an approximation. Wallace's compositional strategy resonates with Abbey's and with Morse's description of "the ultimate [VR] display": "the realism of the ultimate display does not depend on appearing like reality or verisimilitude or *referential illusion* (that is, referring convincingly to another world elsewhere), but on the power of language or the display to make reality itself, or *enunciative illusion* (that is, appears to call a symbol forth into existence by speaking or drawing it . . .)" (207–8). This is not imitation but evocation. Such power is dangerous only to the extent that we lack the critical ability to limn the breaks and edges of such virtual worlds, to understand their effects on our interactions with the material worlds we inhabit.

Yet even our attempts to preserve and protect material, nonhuman nature from the worst effects of human encroachment necessarily entail the virtual. Designating a species as endangered or a landscape as wilderness inevitably evokes our conceptions of evolution, biological diversity, and the wild. And in even the remotest places, if we are to negotiate more sustainable and ethical relationships to the land, we must deal with the legacy of human presence as we attempt to transcend it.

During a guided winter hike through a hilly, 4,500-acre park in southeastern Ohio, as our group enters the woods along the park road and begins to climb a side valley, we are surprised by two eighteenth-century fur trappers and a Shawnee brave in period costume. One of the trappers greets us while the other tends a fire and the brave squats silently off to one side. The trapper expresses surprise at meeting such a large group of men, women, and children so far from the nearest white settlement, particularly given the recent trouble with the Shawnee. He explains that he and his partner, based in Fort Pitt, generally aren't bothered by the Indians as they check their trap lines, even though the Treaty of Fort Stanwix designated this territory off-limits to white settlers, and the Shawnee have at times violently resisted white encroachment. We are warned to be careful and asked not to mention to anyone that we have met the trappers.

After reentering the twentieth century and climbing to a ridge trail, we learn from the naturalist leading the hike that these ridges and valleys formed when rivers and streams eroded an ancient seabed, and we learn to recognize pitch pine and chestnut oak bark by their scales and distinctive V-shaped ridges, respectively. Who can fathom such expanses of time or the intricate evolutionary processes that produce myriad variations of tree bark?

The period actors' reenactment was not very successful at sustaining a sense of immersion in an earlier landscape, but it had the perhaps unintended effect of exposing the breaks and edges of the woodland park. While the forests of eighteenth-century Ohio had been lived in continuously for thousands of years by Native Americans and were being explored and exploited by white settlers living on (and off) the land, the contemporary park is an island of managed forest defined in part by the absence of human settlement. In some sense, the closer it approaches the condition of an undisturbed, native Ohio forest, the more it becomes an artifact of human management. At the same time, however, the forest contains threshold objects such as its topography and its trees that allow us to see beyond the virtual. As Abbey notes, "A weird, lovely, fantastic object out of nature like Delicate Arch [in Arches National Monument] has the curious ability to remind us—like rock and sunlight and wind and wilderness—that *out there* is a different world, older and greater and deeper by far than ours, a world which surrounds and sustains the little world of men as sea and sky surround and sustain a ship. *The shock of the real*" (37; emphasis added).

The Boundaries of the Liminal World

I have argued that virtual landscapes of various sorts have the potential to serve as liminal objects, reminding us of our relation to a world that encompasses our representations of it. The narrative theorist Janet Murray would seem to agree. Despite current concerns over the seductive representational power of cyberspace, she remains unruffled:

> Part of the early work in any medium is the exploration of the border between the representational world and the actual world. It is commonplace in the twentieth century to point to elaborate simulations of reality (electronic and otherwise) as a new and dangerous thing, a distancing of human beings from direct experience. But part of our dismay at televised events, wax museums, and immersive theme parks . . . derives simply from the fact that we need time to get used to any increase in representational power. During this time one of our main activities, as creators and audience, involves testing for the boundaries of the liminal world. (103)

Murray is primarily concerned with establishing conventions that will allow audiences to sustain imaginative immersion in liminal worlds without falling over the edge (prematurely?) into the real world.[2] She draws comparisons to other media primarily to show how conventions have emerged in those media. But ecocritics should consider how new modes of representation provide opportunities to reconsider older representations of landscape that convention has made transparent. Because cyberspace often presents traditional representational strategies to us in new contexts, it can help us see the virtual at work in texts and physical landscapes alike and reveal the breaks and edges beyond which we can sense the real.

Conversely, ecocriticism has much to offer studies of cyberspace. First, while digital theorists such as Murray are interested in how to sustain immersion in cybernarratives and critics of technoculture worry that we will not want to return from virtual environments, ecocritics' allegiance to the real and knowledge of how people experience "the shock of the real" make their input invaluable if the architects of cyberspace are to construct digital landscapes that foster healthy relationships with real ecosystems. For instance, simulations of real ecosystems might help train backcountry travelers to protect and learn from those environments, and simulations of wilderness preserves might help maintain support for policies that restrict access to especially delicate ecosystems, much as a recreation of the cave paintings at Lascaux has helped preserve that prehistoric art.

On a more theoretical plane, ecocriticism can shed light on some of the central issues of cyberculture. For instance, ecocritics' attempts to avoid categorical distinctions between nature and culture might profitably complicate similar distinctions between the virtual and the real. After all, whether in the neural states of individuals or the genetic codes of species, all living things on Earth create virtual models of the ever-changing material structures and processes in which they are embedded and in which they have only limited, mediated abilities to perceive and predict. Adaptation, whether in the context of individual learning and behavior or the evolution of species, involves testing virtual models of one's environment. If our mental model of global warming turns out to be wrong, we will be less well prepared for what is to come. If our genetic makeup cannot adapt to environmental change (whether our environment is "natural" or of our own construction), then we are doomed as a species. But faced with an idea that does not pan out, we do not give up on thinking. Faced with mass extinctions in the past, life did not give up on evolution. If our virtual models of whatever sort are leading us into unhealthy relationships with our environment, then we need to change those models, not fantasize about abandoning virtuality. For all living things on Earth, at least, it would seem that the virtual and the real (or material) are inseparably bound.

Beyond nature writing lies a vast world of other representations that inform our relationship to nonhuman nature and, thereby, to a fuller conception of ourselves and our place in the world, including the unique qualities of our representations. Critical attention to all of our representations can help us locate their breaks and edges, the ecotones where our imagination engages the material world, and our symbolic representations, if we get them just right, light our way to the threshold of the real.

Notes

1. I italicize *Riven* when referring to the game, and I use roman type to refer to Riven, the virtual landscape.

2. Although Murray distinguishes perhaps too glibly for postmodern sensibilities between "the representational world and the actual world," her distinction is helpful for reflecting on the differences between our current experiences of virtual reality in digital and material landscapes.

Works Cited

Abbey, Edward. *Desert Solitaire: A Season in the Wilderness.* New York: Simon & Schuster-Touchstone, 1968.

Holmes, Joseph O. "*Riven:* The Sequel to *Myst.*" Rev. of *Riven,* from Red Orb Entertainment. *MacADDICT* Feb. 1998: 52–53.

Kelly, Kevin. *Out of Control: The New Biology of Machines, Social Systems, and the Economic World.* New York: Addison Wesley Longman, 1995.

Morse, Margaret. "*Nature Morte:* Landscape and Narrative in Virtual Environments." *Immersed in Technology: Art and Virtual Environments.* Ed. Mary Anne Moser. Cambridge: MIT P, 1996. 195–232.

Murray, Janet H. *Hamlet on the Holodeck: The Future of Narrative in Cyberspace.* New York: Free, 1997.

Slouka, Mark. *War of the Worlds: Cyberspace and the High-Tech Assault on Reality.* New York: Basic, 1995.

Wilson, Alexander. *The Culture of Nature: North American Landscape from Disney to the Exxon Valdez.* Cambridge: Blackwell, 1992.

Wallace, David Rains. *Idle Weeds: The Life of an Ohio Sandstone Ridge.* Columbus: Ohio State UP, 1986.

Contributors

Stacy Alaimo is Associate Professor of English at the University of Texas at Arlington. She is the author of *Undomesticated Ground: Recasting Nature as Feminist Space* and has published in journals such as *Feminist Studies, Camera Obscura, MELUS,* and *Studies in American Fiction.*

Karla Armbruster is Assistant Professor of English at Webster University in St. Louis, where she teaches American literature, interdisciplinary humanities, and professional writing. Her recent publications include a chapter entitled "Speaking for Nature" in *Literature of Nature* (Murphy, ed.) and essays on television nature documentaries, Josephine Johnson's *Inland Island,* and Ursula K. Le Guin's "Buffalo Gals Won't You Come Out Tonight?"

Michael Bennett is Associate Professor of English at Long Island University, Brooklyn. He is coeditor, with David Teague, of *The Nature of Cities: Ecocriticism and Urban Environments* and, with Vanessa Dickerson, of *Recovering the Black Female Body: Self-Representations by African American Women.* His book *Democratic Discourses: Antebellum American Literature and the Abolition Movement* is forthcoming.

Michael P. Branch is Associate Professor of Literature and Environment at the University of Nevada, Reno. He is a cofounder and past president of the Association for the Study of Literature and Environment (ASLE). He coedited *The Height of Our Mountains: Nature Writing from Virginia's Blue Ridge Mountains and Shenandoah Valley* and *Reading the Earth: New Directions in the Study of Literature and Environment,* and his books *John Muir's Last Journey: South to the Amazon and East to Africa* and *Reading the Roots: American Nature Writing before Walden* are forthcoming.

Thomas C. Crochunis is an independent scholar currently working as a publications research and development specialist for the U.S. Department of Education research laboratory at Brown University. He has written on British women playwrights in the years around 1800, edited a special issue of *Romanticism on the Net* on this topic, and is cofounder of a Web site that publishes the plays of and supports collaborative scholarly work on these women.

Terrell F. Dixon teaches environmental literature and ecocomposition at the University of Houston. He has served as Graduate Director and as English Department Chair, and he is currently Graduate Replacement Officer. His research interests include the literature of toxicity, environmental justice, and urban nature writing.

Elizabeth Dodd is Professor of English at Kansas State University, where she directs the Creative Writing Program. The author of two previous books, she has two books forthcoming: *Archetypal Light*, a collection of poems, and *Asylum and Other Essays*.

John Elder is Professor of English at Middlebury College. He is the author of *Imagining the Earth: Poetry and the Vision of Nature*, *Following the Brush*, and *Reading the Mountains of Home*; editor of *American Nature Writers*; and coeditor of *The Norton Book of Nature Writing*, *Family of Earth and Sky: Indigenous Stories of Nature from around the World*, and *Spirit and Nature*.

Cheryll Glotfelty is Associate Professor of Literature and the Environment at the University of Nevada, Reno. She is coeditor, with Harold Fromm, of *The Ecocriticism Reader: Landmarks in Literary Ecology*; cofounder of *ISLE: Interdisciplinary Studies in Literature and Environment*; and cofounder and past president of the Association for the Study of Literature and Environment (ASLE). Her essays on ecocriticism, on western American literature, and on women and nature have appeared in numerous publications.

Betsy S. Hilbert is Professor of English at Miami-Dade Community College's Kendall campus. Past president of the College English Association and an early member of ASLE, she is widely published in the field of environmental literature.

William C. Horne is Professor of English at Salisbury State University. His publications are mainly in Restoration and eighteenth-century literature, including *Making a Heaven of Hell: The Problem of the Companionate Ideal in English Marriage Poetry, 1650–1800*. He has also edited a collection of marriage poems and satires and is currently at work on a study of literature of the Arctic.

Mark T. Hoyer is Lecturer in the School of Extended Education at Saint Mary's College of California. He is the author of *Dancing Ghosts: Native American and*

Christian Syncretism in Mary Austin's Work and of numerous articles and chapters on Austin.

Richard Kerridge is Senior Lecturer in English and Course Director for the M.A. in Creative Writing at Bath Spa University College. He has published numerous articles on literature and environmentalism and on nineteenth- and twentieth-century novels and poetry. He is coeditor of *Writing the Environment,* the first collection of ecocritical essays to be published in Britain, and coauthor of *Nearly Too Much: The Poetry of J. H. Prynne.* He received the BBC Wildlife Award for nature writing in 1990 and 1991.

Lisa J. Kiser is Professor of English at The Ohio State University. She has written two books on Chaucer—*Telling Classical Tales: Chaucer and the Legend of Good Women* and *Truth and Textuality in Chaucer's Poetry*—and many articles and reviews about medieval literature and culture. She also served as editor for *Studies in the Age of Chaucer* from 1992–98.

Diane Kelsey McColley is Professor of early modern British literature at Rutgers University, Camden. Her books are *Milton's Eve, A Gust for Paradise: Milton's Eden and the Visual Arts,* and *Poetry and Music in Seventeenth-Century England.* She has also authored articles and chapters concerned with environmental readings of Milton and his contemporaries, and she was named Honored Scholar of the Milton Society of America in 1999.

Patrick D. Murphy is Professor of English at Indiana University of Pennsylvania. He is the author, editor, or coeditor of several books, including *Literature, Nature, and Other: Ecofeminist Critiques; Understanding Gary Snyder; Farther Afield in the Study of Nature-Oriented Literature; A Place for Wayfaring: The Poetry and Prose of Gary Snyder;* and *Literature of Nature: An International Sourcebook.*

Rebecca Raglon teaches in the English department at the University of British Columbia. Her most recent essays have appeared in *Environmental Ethics, Women's Studies, Weber Studies, Coyote in the Maze,* and *Natural Eloquence,* and one of her short stories appears in a collection of British Columbia stories, *West by Northwest.*

Kent C. Ryden is Associate Professor of American and New England Studies at the University of Southern Maine. A recipient of the American Studies Association's Ralph Henry Gabriel Prize, he is the author of *Mapping the Invisible Landscape:*

Folklore, Writing, and the Sense of Place and the forthcoming *Landscape with Figures: Nature as Artifact in the American Landscape.*

Marian Scholtmeijer teaches at the University of Northern British Columbia and Wilp Wilxo'oskwhl Nisga'a, a First Nations (Native Canadian) college. She is the author of *Animal Victims in Modern Fiction* and of articles on spirituality and animals, human and animal identity, feminism and animals, and animals and modern horror stories.

Adam Sweeting is Assistant Professor of Humanities at Boston University's College of General Studies. He is the author of *Reading Houses and Building Books: Andrew Jackson Downing and the Architecture of Popular Antebellum Literature.*

H. Lewis Ulman is Associate Professor of English at The Ohio State University. He is the author of *The Minutes of the Aberdeen Philosophical Society, 1758–1773* and *Things, Thoughts, Words, and Actions: The Problem of Language in Late-Eighteenth-Century British Rhetorical Theory,* and his essays have appeared in numerous publications.

Charlotte Zoë Walker is Professor of English and Women's Studies at the State University of New York, College at Oneonta. She has received an NEA Creative Writing Fellowship, and her publications include a story in the O. Henry Awards collection (1991) and the novel *Condor and Hummingbird.* She is the editor of the forthcoming collections *Sharp Eyes: John Burroughs and American Nature Writing* and *The Art of Seeing Things: Essays by John Burroughs.*

Kathleen R. Wallace is an independent scholar and writer currently working with the Ohio League of Conservation Voters in Columbus, Ohio. Formerly the Assistant Director of the First Year Writing Program at The Ohio State University, Wallace also has been a visiting fellow in English and American Studies at L. Kossuth University in Debrecen, Hungary. Her publications in ecocriticism include essays on Audre Lorde and urban nature in *The Nature of Cities* and women writing about Minnesota in *Mapping American Culture.*

Index

Abbey, Edward, 12, 19n. 3, 233, 244, 312, 346, 351–52, 354
Abram, David, 335
Adler, Ruth, 31
African American literature, 2, 6, 14–15; anti-pastoralism, 195–209; and ecocriticism, 177–78, 190, 205, 208, 213–14, 225; as environmental literature, 313; and environmentalism, 211–15, 225–26; land ownership, 225–26; and nature writing, 177; and pastoral tradition, 14–15, 196–99; representation of nature, 20n. 4, 226, 228n. 15; and sense of place, 177–78; urban environments, 198–205; wilderness, 196, 211–12, 215
African Americans: and ecocriticism, 195–97, 208; and environmentalism, 208, 227n. 3; in monster movies, 294n. 2; and nature, 213, 228n. 15; and rivers, 197; and urban environments, 205–7; and wilderness, 179, 196–197, 208–209, 214, 227n. 11. *See also* slavery
agriculture, artifacts of, 297, 303–308
Alaimo, Stacy, 16–17, 294n. 1, 3
Allport, Susan, 304
American environmentalism, 211, 213, 225, 227n. 2, 3, 265
American studies, 20n. 8
Anaya, Rudolfo, 313
Anderson, Chris, 333
Anglicus, Bartholomaeus, 52n. 8

animals: in Douglass's *Narrative*, 205; in film, 279–94; in Freeman's *Understudies*, 167–69; in Kafka's stories, 259–60; in Milton's *Paradise Lost*, 59–61; monstrous, 279–94; in Morrison's *Beloved*, 215, 219–20, 226–27, 227n. 10, 227–28n. 12; slaveowners as, 205
Anne of Bohemia, 52n. 11
Anthony, Carl, 227n. 9
anthropomorphism in Chaucer's *Parliament of Fowls*, 44, 48, 50
anti-pastoral, 15, 195–209
Applegate, Jesse, 245n. 3
Arctic exploration, 77
arctic literature, 11, 75–89
argument from design, 101, 102–106
Armbruster, Karla, 15, 174n. 11
Arrested Development, 207
Arrowsmith, William, 324n. 1
artifacts, cultural, 291–311
artifacts, material, 291–311
Austin, Mary, 12, 233

Bachelard, Gaston, 334, 339n. 5
Bacon, Francis, 9, 11, 70
Baillie, Joanna, 338n. 1
Bakhtin, Mikhail, 277, 337
Banks, Joseph, 77
Barhyte, Jacobus, 186
Bartram, William, 94

Bass, Rick, 93, 174n. 9
Bate, Jonathon, 19n. 3
Bate, Walter Jackson, 89n. 1
Bathurst, Richard, 77, 89n. 1
Baudrillard, Jean, 344
Baxter, Ron, 51n. 1
Beale, John, 68
Beast, The, 280–82
Benchley, Peter: *Jaws,* 279, 281; *The Beast,*
    280–82
Bennett, J. A. W., 52n. 7, 10
Bennett, Michael, 14–15, 20n. 5, 7
Benson, Larry D., 52nn. 5, 8, 11
Berman, Morris, 20nn. 11, 13
Berry, Wendell, 93
Bewell, Alan, 124n. 3
Bible, 9, 10; Deuteronomy, 10, 29–39;
    Genesis, 62
Birch, Thomas, 327, 330; *History of the*
    Royal Society of London, 77
Bird, Jon, 51n. 3
birds: in Chaucer's *Parliament of Fowls,*
    43–49; in Frost's poetry, 322–23
Birkerts, Sven, 2–3
black literature. *See* African American
    literature
Bodsworth, Fred, 251
"Book of Nature, The," 144, 160n. 1
Boswell, James, *Life of Samuel Johnson,* 77,
    84
botanical discourse in Stowe's *The Minis-*
    ter's Wooing, 111–24, 124nn. 5, 6
botany, 111, 113–15
Bradford, Curtis B., 81
Bradford, William, 98
Branch, Michael P., 11, 19n. 1
Bremer, Sidney H., 20n. 5
Brewer, D. S., 52n. 7
British romantics, 9, 12, 19n. 3
Brooks, Paul, 19n. 3

Browne, J. Ross, 238
Browne, Sir Thomas, 68, 151
Brunner, John: *Bedlam Planet,* 264, 266,
    277; *The Sheep Look Up,* 265
Bryant, William Cullen, 94
Bryson, Bill, 239–41
Buell, Lawrence, 19n. 3, 135, 141, 208,
    227n. 2
Buffon, Georges Louis Leclerc, Comte de,
    94
Bullard, Robert D., 227n. 3
Burroughs, John, 94

Callicott, J. Baird, 20n. 15, 227n. 8
Campbell, SueEllen, 20n. 6
Canonicus, 179–80
capitalism, in Harper's poetry, 182–86
Carlyle, Thomas, 94
Carnosaur 2, 284
Carson, Rachel, vii, 12, 19n. 3, 94
Cather, Willa, 12, 19n. 3
Chapman, General Samuel, 185
Chaucer, Geoffrey, 10; *Nun's Priest's Tale,*
    44, 49; *Parliament of Fowls,* 10, 41–51
Chaudhuri, Una, 331, 338n. 3
Cheney, Jim, 20n. 6
Cheng-Levine, Jia-Yi, 19n. 4
Chenu, M. D., 51n. 1
Christian, Barbara, 211, 226–27n. 1, 227n. 4
Christianity: and the environment, 9, 30–
    31; and slavery, 196
cities, 6; and African Americans, 206–207;
    in Douglass's *Narrative,* 198–205
Clare, John, 250
Clark, Walter Van Tilburg, 234
Clark, Willene B., 51n. 1
Clark, William, 94
class: in Chaucer's *Parliament of Fowls,* 44–
    46; in Hardy's novels, 127–28, 132, 138
Clemens, Samuel, 238–39, 243

ecocriticism (*continued*)
98, 313, 333–34, 338; and African Americans, 195–97, 208; and African American literature, 177–78, 190, 205, 208, 213–14, 225; and colonial American natural history, 91–93, 100, 106; critiques of, 195, 208–209; and cyberculture, 354–55; in England, 138; and environmental literature, 313; and Hardy's novels, 126, 138; and monster movies, 279–80; and Morrison's novels, 211, 213; and naming, 60; and outdoor experience, 312–24; and pedagogy, 313–14, 320; and theater, 325, 332–34; and urban environments, 6; and Virginia Woolf, 156

ecofeminism, 20n. 6; and Mary Wilkins Freeman, 164, 166, 173; and Virginia Woolf, 144, 152–59

ecofiction, 162–173, 174n. 9

ecology, 58, 130, 131; of forests, 333–34; of New England, 319, 322–23

Economou, George, 51n. 1

ecotones, vii

Eden, 58–72, 198, 208; in Douglass's *Narrative*, 200. *See also* Paradise

Edgarton, Sarah Carter, 124n. 5

Egede, Hans, 77, 81–84, 86, 89n. 2

eighteenth-century literature, 75–76

Elder, John, 2–3, 17, 19nn. 1, 3, 298

Eliot, T. S., 190

Elizabeth I, 77

Ellison, Ralph, 206

Elmer, Jonathan, 293

Emerson, Ralph Waldo, 94, 173, 173n. 1, 181

emigrant narratives, Nevada, 235–38

Emrich, Duncan, 245n. 4

Emslie, Macdonald, 52n. 9

Endecott, John, 95

Enlightenment, 100; and the environment, 8–9, 11

environment: of colonial America, 192n. 3; concept of, 3–4; historical attitudes toward, 8–9; medieval perspectives on, 9–11, 41–42; of New England, 297–311; and poststructuralist theory, 20n. 6

environmental crises in science fiction, 264–65

environmental ethics and science fiction, 269–76. *See also* moral ecology

environmental history, 20n. 8

environmental justice, 208; 227n. 3

environmental literature, 313

environmental theater, 330–31, 338n. 3

environmentalism, 134, 138, 280, 282; and African American literature, 211–15, 225–26; and African Americans, 208, 227n. 3; American 211–15, 225–26, 227nn. 2, 3, 265; discourse of, 57, 211, 213; and Morrison's novels, 211–16, 225–26; philosophy, 292–93

Evelyn, John, 57, 68

Evernden, Neil, 20n. 11, 51n. 2, 177

exploration narratives: Nevada, 234–38

Faulkner, William, 12, 19n. 3, 165, 181

Feder, Helena, 20n. 10

feminism: standpoint theory, 213; and Virginia Woolf, 152, 159

feminist criticism and Mary Wilkins Freeman, 164–65

Ferrell, Robyn, 20n. 6

Ferry, Anne, 321

fiction, representation of nature, 253–61

Fielding, Henry, 89n. 4

film, nature in, 17, 253, 279–96

Fitter, Chris, 72n. 2

Fitzgerald, F. Scott, 313

Flaherty, Robert, *Nanook of the North*, 80

Foster, Ruth, 226

Fowles, John, "green woman" concept, 162–63

Fox, Warwick, 20n. 6
Francis (Saint) of Assisi, 31
Frank, Pat, *Alas, Babylon*, 264
Franklin, Benjamin, 94
Franklin, H. Bruce, 198
Franklin, Sir John, 78
Franklin, Wayne, 20n. 8
Freeman, Mary Wilkins, 12, 14, 162–76; "Christmas Jenny" (in *A New England Nun and Other Stories*), 162–65; *Six Trees*, 169–73; *Understudies*, 165–68
Fremont, John Charles, 235
Fritzell, Peter, 227n. 2
Frobisher, Martin, 77
Frost, Robert, 17, 181, 297–311, 314–24; "The Ax Helve," 303, 308–10; "Mending Wall," 303, 304–308; "Mowing," 315–24; "The Need of Being Versed in Country Things," 322

Gaard, Greta, 20n. 6, 173n. 3
Gally, James W., 238
Ganim, John M., 52n. 13
Garrison, William Lloyd, 201
gender: in Chaucer's *Parliament of Fowls*, 44, 46–47; and Freeman, 14, 166–69; in monster movies, 281–83, 288; in Stowe's *The Minister's Wooing*, 112, 116, 118–20
Genesis, 62
genetic engineering, 283
geography, cultural and political, 20n. 8
georgic tradition, 57
Gilman, Charlotte Perkins, 12
Glacken, Clarence J., 20n. 11, 51n. 2
Glasser, Leah Blatt, 174n. 7
Glotfelty, Cheryll, 2, 12, 15, 20n. 9
Goethe, Johann Wolfgang von, 94
Golding, Arthyr, 71
Goldsmith, Oliver, 76
Goonan, Kathleen Ann, *The Bones of Time*, 268–69, 277

Gordimer, Nadine, 16; "The Termitary," 254–56, 260–61
Gottlieb, Robert, 227n. 2
Gould, Peter, 20n. 8
Gray, Asa, 111–12, 114
Great Chain of Being, 9
Great Migration (of African Americans), 206
Grosz, Elizabeth, 294

Habitat, 280, 288–89
Hampton Institute, 185, 191
Hansen, Elaine Tuttle, 52n. 12
Haraway, Donna J., 131–34, 213, 280, 285, 293–94
Hardy, Thomas, 12–13, 126–41; *Far From the Madding Crowd*, 130, 133; *Jude the Obscure*, 128–29, 135–36; *The Mayor of Casterbridge*, 129; *The Return of the Native*, 126, 134, 139; *Tess of the D'urbervilles*, 128, 130–34; *Under the Greenwood Tree*, 127, 130; *The Woodlanders*, 127, 135–37
Harlem Renaissance, 206
Harlow, Elizabeth M., 51n. 3
Harper, Michael S., 12, 14, 177–92
Harris, Susan K., 112
Hart, Fred, 238
Harte, Bret, 238
Hartsock, Nancy, 227n. 5
Hassig, Debra, 51n. 1
Hawkes, John: *The Frog*, 253–54
Hawthorne, Nathaniel, 2, 245n. 5
Hayden, Delores, 20n. 8
Hayden, Robert, 191
Hayles, N. Katherine, 53n. 16
Haynes, Todd, 290, 294n. 4
Heaney, Seamus, 249–50, 316
Hearne, Samuel, 78
Hegarty, Emily, 20n. 4

Hemingway, Ernest, 19n. 3
Herman, Bernard L., 301
Hesiod, 198
Hilbert, Betsy S., 10
history: environmental, 20n. 8; and land-
  scape, 177–92
Hoban, Russell, 16; *Turtle Diary,* 256–58,
  260–61
Hochman, Jhan, 20n. 7, 211, 227n. 1
Hofrichter, Richard, 227n. 3
Holiday, Billie, 207
Holmes, Joseph O., 341–42
Hopkins, Gerard Manley, 12
Horne, William C., 11
Houston, Pam, 174n. 9
Howarth, William, 7
Hoyer, Mark T., 13
Hudson, W. H., 152, 154
Hughes, Langston, 313
Hughes, Ted, 12
Hurston, Zora Neale, 2, 313
Huston, Hollis, 332, 333
hybrid animals, 279–94
hyperreality, 344–45

Ibsen, Henrik, 325, 329
imperialism: British, 155–56; European, 79,
  86, 88
indigenous people, 33; of the Arctic, 78–79,
  88–89; in colonial America, 96; as "culture of habitat," 137; cultures, 137–39;
  Native Americans, 35, 179–81, 183, 185,
  245n. 2; in science fiction, 264, 268–69
interdisciplinarity: between literature and
  science, 312–13; of ecocriticism, 15,
  20n. 14
intertextuality of nature and literature: in
  Woolf's writing, 143–61
Irving, Washington, 245n. 5
Isidore, 52n. 8

Island of Dr. Moreau, The, 280–82, 293

Jackson, J. B., 20n. 8
James, Henry, 2–3, 7–8, 20n. 10, 245n. 5;
  Portrait of a Lady, 20n. 9
James, William, 339n. 8
Jans, Nick, 79, 88
Jaws, 279, 281
Jeffers, Robinson, 12, 177
Jefferson, Thomas, 94
Jeffries, Richard, 141
Jewett, Sarah Orne, 165, 174n. 10
Judaism: and the environment, 29–39
Johnson, Rochelle, 19n. 1
Johnson, Samuel, 11, 75–89, 89n. 1; *Father
  Lobo's Voyage to Abyssinia* (translation
  of), 76; *Greenland Tale,* 11, 77–89; *The
  History of Rasselas,* 75–76, 80; *A Journey
  to the Western Islands of Scotland,* 76;
  Life of Drake, 84; periodical essays in
  The Rambler, The Adventurer, and *The
  Idler,* 75, 81, 83, 88
Johnson, Tetty, 89n. 1
Josselyn, John, 96
Justice, Steven, 52n. 13

Kafka, Franz, 16; "A Report to an
  Academy," 259–61
Kane, Elisha Kent, 78
Katz, Eric, 339n. 8
Katz, William Loren, 192n. 2
Keats, John, 146
Keeney, Elizabeth, 124n. 3
Kelly, Kevin, 348
Kemp, John C., 299
Kendrick, Brent L., 174n. 8
Kenner, Hugh, 321
Kerridge, Richard, 13, 19n. 1
Kiser, Lisa J., 10, 52n. 6
Kolodny, Annette, 20n. 12, 182

Kroeber, Karl, 19n. 3
Krutch, Joseph Wood, 233

labor, in Frost's "Mowing," 316–18
Lahar, Stephanie, 51n. 3
land ownership: in African American literature, 225–26; in Deuteronomy, 38
land: biblical attitudes toward, 38–39
landscape architecture, 20n. 8
landscape, 283, 310; of colonial America, 97–98; and history, 177–92; material, 345, 349; New England, 297–311; symbolic, 345; virtual, 18, 341–56
language: as constructing reality, 248–51, 261; of flowers, 111–24, 124nn. 5, 6; human, 49; natural, 65–70; nonhuman, 49
Las Vegas (Nevada), 239–41, 245–46n. 6
Lawrence, D. H., 12
Laxalt, Robert, 234
Lease, Gary, 53n. 16
Lee, Robert E., 189
Lefebvre, Henri, 334, 339n. 6
LeGuin, Ursula K.: *The Dispossessed*, 265; *The Word for World Is Forest*, 264–66, 277
Leiss, William, 20n. 11
Leopold, Aldo, 12, 19n. 3, 94, 197; "The Land Ethic," viii, 14, 189–90
Leslie, Michael, 68
Lewis, Meriwether, 94
Light, Andrew, 339n. 8
Lillard, Richard G., 234
Limerick, Patricia Nelson, 20n. 8, 245n. 1
liminal objects, 351–52, 354
Linnaeus, Carl, 12, 94, 319
literary place bashing, 234–43, 245n. 5
local color. *See* regionalism
Locke, Alain, 206
Lopez, Barry, 12, 20n. 12, 79, 93, 312
Lord, Nancy, 174n. 9

Love, Glen A., 177, 195, 198, 202
Luscher, Robert M., 173n. 1, 175n. 17
Lutwack, Leonard, 177
Lyon, Thomas J., 227n. 2

MacCormack, Carol P., 51n. 3
MacDonald, Bonney, 20n. 10
MacLean, Norman, 178
Macnaughten, Phil, 51n. 2
MacPherson, James, 86
Malcolm X, 207
maps, in Hardy's novels, 126–27
Marranca, Bonnie, 330–31
marriage: in Chaucer's *Parliament of Fowls*, 43, 45–46; in Stowe's *The Minister's Wooing*, 112–13
Marshall, Ian, 298
Marshall, Robert, 79, 336
Marx, Leo, 20n. 12
Mash, Melinda, 51n. 3
Massingham, H. J., 138
material culture studies, 17, 301–303
Mather, Cotton, 11, 100–101; *The Christian Philosopher*, 93, 102–106; *Curiosa Americana*, 101
McClintock, James, 19n. 3
McColley, Diane Kelsey, 10–11, 72n. 4
McGurl, Mark, 19n. 2
McMunn, Meredith T., 51n. 1
McNamee, Gregory, 19n. 2
medieval culture, 41–51; and the environment, 9–11, 41–42
Meigs, General Montgomery, 189
Meinig, Donald, 20n. 8
Mellor, Mary, 20n. 6
Meloy, Ellen, 240–41, 244–45
Melville, Herman, 12, 94, 185, 313
Merchant, Carolyn, 9, 20nn. 11, 13, 51n. 2, 192n. 3, 280, 293
Miantonomi, 180

Miller, Arthur, 325
Miller, Perry, 180
Millgate, Michael, 127
Milton, John, 313; *Paradise Lost*, 10–11, 57–72
Milton, Kay, 50, 53n. 16
Mimic, 280, 286–88, 292
Minnis, A. J., 52n. 4
Mondobo, Lord, 89n. 3
monster movies, 17, 279–96; and environmentalism, 280
monsters, 279–94
moral ecology, 178–82. *See also* environmental ethics
Morgan, Ross, 314
Morrison, Toni, 211–26; *Beloved*, 187, 214–15, 218–19, 220–21, 224–25; *The Bluest Eye*, 217; *Jazz*, 219–20; *Paradise*, 218, 222, 223, 226; *Song of Solomon*, 216–17, 223–24, 225–26; *Sula*, 221, 222, 226; *Tar Baby*, 211–13, 217–18, 221, 222
Morse, Margaret, 342, 348, 352
Morton, H. V., 138
Muhammad, Elijah, 207
Muir, John, 12, 19n. 3, 94, 238–39, 245n. 5
Murphy, Patrick D., 19n. 1, 20n. 4, 263
Murray, Janet H., 344, 354, 356n. 2

Nabhan, Gary Paul, 137–39
Naess, Arne, 20n. 6
Nanook of the North, 80
narrative, 13, 16; form in Hardy's novels, 126–41; representation of nature, 248–61
Nash, Roderick, 20n. 12, 227n. 7
Native Americans, 35, 179–81, 183, 185, 245n. 2
natural history: in colonial America, 11, 91–106; and Virginia Woolf, 152–55
natural sciences and Cotton Mather, 101–106

natural theology, 101, 102–106
naturalism, 325–29, 338n. 1
naturalist theater, 325–29, 338n. 1
nature: and African Americans, 213–15, 228n. 15; boundaries between humans and, 280–94; in fiction, 253–61; in Hardy's novels, 134–38; and human culture, 4, 7, 12–14, 297–98; human dominion over, 57, 58, 59–60, 70–72; human relationship to, 62–65, 169, 345–46; as independent of human culture, 212, 253; Lady Nature in Chaucer's *Parliament of Fowls*, 42–50; love of, 134–38; ownership of, 174n. 13; resistance to human narratives, 251–61; scale of, 62–65; social construction of, 44–51, 213, 215, 248; as unmediated, 49; and urban environments, 20n. 5; in virtual reality, 341–56
nature-culture dualism, 4, 7, 42, 50–51, 51n. 3, 280, 292
nature-oriented literature, 263–64
nature writing, vii–viii, 2–3, 7, 13, 15–16, 91–93, 95–100, 105, 126, 135, 138, 250, 254, 312–13; American, 212, 227n. 2; characterization of, 312–13; and deserts, 233; environmental impact of, 243–45; and white writers, 313; and writers of color, 313.
Nelson, Kent, 174n. 9
Nelson, Michael P., 20n. 15, 227n. 8
Nevada, 16, 233–45
New England: ecology, 319, 322–23; in Frost's poetry, 297–311, 319, 322–23; and Harper's poetry, 177–94; landscape, 297–311; slavery in, 179–80; and Native Americans, 179–81
New World. *See* colonial America
Newton, Isaac, 104
noble savage: eighteenth-century debate on, 84–85, 89n. 3; motif in Johnson's

Under the Sign of Nature: Explorations in Ecocriticism

Rachel Stein
Shifting the Ground: American Women Writers' Revisions of Nature, Gender, and Race

Ian Marshall
Story Line: Exploring the Literature of the Appalachian Trail

Patrick D. Murphy
Farther Afield in the Study of Nature-Oriented Literature

Bernard W. Quetchenbach
Back from the Far Field: American Nature Poetry in the Late Twentieth Century

Karla Armbruster and Kathleen R. Wallace, editors
Beyond Nature Writing: Expanding the Boundaries of Ecocriticism

Stephen Adams
The Best and Worst Country in the World: Perspectives on the Early Virginia Landscape

Mark Allister
Refiguring the Map of Sorrow: Nature Writing and Autobiography